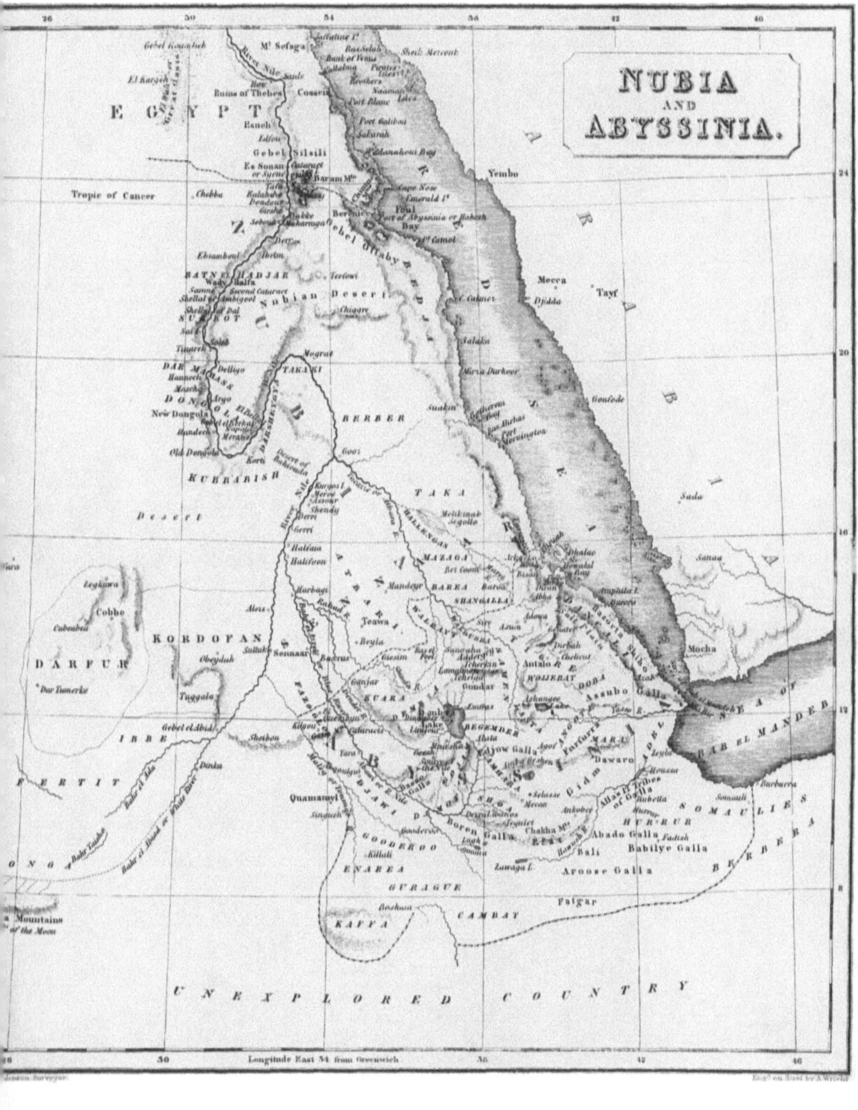
NUBIA
AND
ABYSSINIA.
EGYPT
Tropic of Cancer
Nubian Desert
KORDOFAN
DARFUR
KUBBABISH
BERBER
TAKA
MAZAGA
BARRA
SHANGALLA
KUARA
BEGEMDER
ENAREA
GURAGUE
KAFFA
CAMBAT
SOMAULIES
BERBERA
UNEXPLORED COUNTRY
BAB EL MANDEB
Mecca
Djidda
Tayf
Yembo
Sanaa
Mocha
Sada
Gonfode
Suakin
Sennaar
New Dongola
Old Dongola
Esneh
Edfou
Gebel Silsili
Chebba
Obeydah
Halfaia
Teawa
Gondar
Dahlac
Aroose Galla
Babilye Galla
Abado Galla
Bali
Falgar
Assubo Galla
Antalo
Dawaro
Barbarra
Quamamyl
Longitude East 34 from Greenwich

NUBIA AND ABYSSINIA.

OLIVER & BOYD, EDINBURGH.

NUBIA

AND

ABYSSINIA:

COMPREHENDING THEIR

CIVIL HISTORY, ANTIQUITIES, ARTS, RELIGION,
LITERATURE, AND NATURAL HISTORY.

BY THE REV. MICHAEL RUSSELL, LL.D.,
Author of "View of Ancient and Modern Egypt,"
"Palestine, or the Holy Land," &c.

ILLUSTRATED BY A MAP, AND TWELVE ENGRAVINGS, CHIEFLY
BY JACKSON.

LONDON
DARF PUBLISHERS LIMITED
1985

First Published 1833
New Impression 1985

ISBN 978 1 85077 052 7

PREFACE.

THERE is no country in the world more interesting to the antiquary and scholar than that which was known to the ancients as "Ethiopia above Egypt," the Nubia and Abyssinia of the present day. It was universally regarded by the poets and philosophers of Greece as the cradle of those arts, which at a later period covered the kingdom of the Pharaohs with so many wonderful monuments, as also of those religious rites which, after being slightly modified by the priests of Thebes, were adopted by the ancestors of Homer and Virgil as the basis of their mythology. A description of this remarkable nation, therefore, became a necessary supplement to the View of Ancient and Modern Egypt, which has been some time before the public.

In tracing the connexion of the primitive people who dwelt on the Upper Nile with the inhabitants of Arabia and of the remoter East, I have availed myself of the latest information that could be derived from Continental authors as well as from the volumes of such of our own travellers as have ascended above the Second Cataract. The work of Heeren on the Politics, Intercourse, and Trade of the Carthaginians, Ethiopians, and Egyptians, possesses considerable value, not less on account of the ingenious views which it unfolds, than for the happy application of ancient literature to the illustration and embellishment of the main hypothesis.

The reader will be surprised at the extent and magnificence of the architectural remains of Nubia, which, in some instances, have been found to rival, and, in others, even to surpass the more celebrated buildings of Egypt. It will no longer be denied by any one who has seen the splendid work of Gau, that the pattern or type of those stupendous erections, which continue to excite the admiration of the tourist at Karnac, Luxor, and Ghizeh, may be detected in the numerous monuments still visible between the site of the famed Meroë and the Falls of Es Souan. The more learned among professional artists are now nearly unanimous in the opinion that the principles of architecture as well as of religious belief have descended from Ethiopia to Egypt; receiving improvement in their progress downward, till at length their triumph was completed at Diospolis, in the palace of Osymandias and the temple of Jupiter Ammon.

The late expedition of Ishmael Pasha into Sennaar and the other countries bounded by the two great branches of the Nile, has added materially to our topographical knowledge of that portion of Africa,—one of the least frequented by Europeans. Cailliaud, English, and Linant have supplied to the geographer some important notices relative to the position of certain towns and mountains, of which only the names had formerly been conveyed to our ears. The Publishers have taken the utmost pains to embody in the map, prefixed to this volume, the results of the latest discoveries accomplished by British, French, and American travellers, under the protection of the Turkish army.

But no consideration associated with the history of Ethiopia is more interesting than the fact that the Christian religion, received about fifteen hundred years ago, continues to be professed by the great majority of the people. In regard to the mixture of Jewish rites with the institutions of the Gospel, still observable among the Abyssinians, I have suggested some reflections which seem calculated to throw a new light on that obscure subject. Of the literature of the same nation, so far as the relics could be collected from their chronicles and books of devotion, a suitable account has been given; connected in some degree with the brighter prospects which may yet be entertained by the friends of theological learning as arising from the well-directed efforts of certain benevolent associations in this country.

For some valuable information not hitherto published, I am indebted to William Erskine, Esq. of Blackburn, late of Bombay, who kindly placed in my hands two large manuscript volumes, containing Travels and Letters written in the East. Among these is a number of communications from Mr Nathanael Pearce, during his residence in Abyssinia, addressed to several British Residents at Mocha and Bombay, and embracing the more prominent events of his history between the years 1810 and 1818.

In like manner I have to express my obligations to Captain Armstrong of the Royal Artillery, who, in the course of his travels in Nubia, made drawings and measurements of the principal temples as far south as Wady Halfa. By means of these I have been enabled to ascertain the exact dimensions of several of those structures, the views of which have been given by some recent tourists with more attention to elegance than to professional accuracy in the details.

In order to render this little volume as complete as possible, the Publishers obtained the assistance of two eminent naturalists, Mr WILSON and Dr GREVILLE; to the former of whom the reader owes the instructive chapter on Zoology, while to the latter he is under a similar obligation for the Botanical outline, in which are ably described the vegetable productions of the Abyssinian provinces.

To complete the plan entertained with respect to Africa, there remains yet one volume, which will appear in due time, on the History, Antiquities, and Present Condition of the BARBARY STATES.

EDINBURGH, *March* 1833.

CONTENTS.

CHAPTER I.

INTRODUCTION.

Difficulties to be encountered by the Historian of Ethiopia—Record of Monuments; their Uncertainty—Obstacles which opposed the Knowledge of the Ancients—Supposition that Civilisation descended the Nile—Progress of Oriental Emigration—Resemblance of Nubian Temples to those of India—Fame of Ancient Ethiopians—Ambiguity of the Term—Two great Classes of Africans—Mixture of Arabians—Opinion of Heeren as to Language—Discoveries of Hornemann and Lyon—Tuaricks and Tibboos—Nubians—Abyssinians—Hypothesis of Heeren—Connexion of Commerce and Religion—Chain of Temples—Similar Connexion among Jews and Christians—Early Improvement of Ethiopians; mentioned in Scripture—Defence of the Opinion that Egypt derived Learning and Science from the Upper Nile, Page 17

CHAPTER II.

GEOGRAPHICAL OUTLINES OF NUBIA AND ABYSSINIA.

Plan to be followed in this Chapter—Nubian Valley—Sterility—Former Cultivation—Dondour—Derr—Ibrîm—Wady Halfa—Second Cataract—Beauty of Country in Dongola—Benefits of the Nile—Temple of Soleb—Elegance of the Building—Kingdom of Merawe—Gebel el Berkal—El Bellal—Hypothesis in regard to Meroë—Opinions of Ptolemy, Herodotus, Strabo—Sheygyans—Ishmael Pasha—Third Cataract—Berber—Shendy

el Garb—Shendy—Junction of the White and Blue Rivers—
Sennaar—Climate—Inhabitants—Manufactures—Expeditions
by the Troops under the Pasha—Bravery of the Natives—Description of the City of Sennaar—Advance of Egyptian Army
into Fazoglo—El Queribyn—Kilgou—Singueh—Conflicts with
the Natives at Tâby and Gassi—Reception at Fazoglo—Return to Sennaar—Aquaro—River Toumat—Quamamyl—Ishmael
disappointed as to Gold and Slaves—Poncet's Account of Sennaar—Abyssinia—Its Extent—Political Geography—Kingdoms and Provinces—Amhara—Tigré—Shoa, and the Eastern
Coast,..Page 39

CHAPTER III.

CIVIL HISTORY OF NUBIA AND ABYSSINIA.

Variety of opinion in regard to Ethiopians—Aboriginal and mixed
with Arabians—Queen of Sheba—Book of Axum—Abyssinians
converted to Christianity—Extent of their Dominions—Wars in
Arabia—Arrival of Portuguese—History of Nubia—Cambyses—
Macrobians—Table of the Sun—Explanation by Heeren—Ptolemy Euergetes—War with Candace—Success of Petronius—
Period of Darkness respecting Ethiopia—Prester John—Mission
of Covilham—Of Matthew—Alvarez—Camp of the Abyssinian
Monarch—Interview with David III.—Ordination of Clergy—
Stephen de Gama—Bermudez the Abuna—Oviedo—Peter Paez—
Jerome Lobo—Hatred towards Catholics—Poncet—Bruce—State
of Abyssinia—Ras Michael—Ozoro Esther—Manuscripts collected by Bruce—History of Abyssinia—Revolt of Judith—Restoration of the Line of Solomon—List of Kings—Galla—War
among Chiefs—Bruce goes to the Sources of the Nile—Fasil—The
Jumper—The Lamb—Kefla Yasous—Mr Salt—Outline of History—Pearce—His Adventures under Welled Selassé—Death of
Ras—Demise of the King—Rise of Subegadis—Invasion of Nubia
by Ishmael Pasha—Battles with Sheygyans—Act of Generosity—
Cruelty of Egyptian Army—Character of Sheygyans—Expedition
of Ibrahim—Death of Ishmael—Spirit of insurrection in con-
quered Provinces,..106

CHAPTER IV.

ARCHITECTURAL MONUMENTS OF NUBIA AND ABYSSINIA.

Rule for determining the Antiquity and Filiation of ancient States—Connexion between Egypt, Ethiopia, and India—Excavated Temples—Girshé, Seboua, and Derr—Different Orders of Architecture—Temple of Osiris at Ebsamboul—Labours of Belzoni, Irby, and Mangles—Magnificence of Interior, and Description of the various Halls—Discoveries of Mr Bankes—Visit of Defturdar Bey—Sir F. Henniker—Temple of Isis—Cave of Elephanta—Temples of Salsette and Ellora—Comparison with those of Ethiopia—Temples of Soleb, of Kalabshé, and Dondour—Opinion of Gau—Mixed Greek and Egyptian Forms—Gebel el Berkal—Principal Temple there—Pyramids—El Bellal—Progress in the Arts—Succession of Buildings—Meroë—Bruce, Strabo, Cailliaud—Assour—Pyramids—M. Rüppel—Naga and Messoura—Large Temple—Opinion of M. Heeren—Of Cailliaud—Ruins at Mandeyr and Kely—Constitution of Government at Meroë—Its Termination—Remains at Axum—Obelisk—Errors of Bruce—Corrections by Salt—Axum-Inscription—Adulis—Inscription—Cosmas—Reference to Dr Vincent—Luxor and Karnac—Sacred Ship—Bond of Religion—Lineage of the Gods—Hebrew Tribes—Decline of Learning in Ethiopia,...Page 183

CHAPTER V.

RELIGION AND LITERATURE OF ETHIOPIA.

Abyssinia received Christianity at an early Period—Influence of Religion on its Political State and Civil History—Story of Frumentius—Jewish Ceremonies mixed with the Gospel—Arian Heresy—Constantius—Invasion of Arabia—Heresy of Eutyches—Conversion of Nubians—Justinian and Theodora—Zara Jacob—His Letter to the Monks of Jerusalem—Council of Florence—Pagans of Samen—Arrival of Paez—Dispute with Clergy—The King Za Denghel becomes Roman Catholic—His Letter to the Pope—Accession of Susneus—His Adherence to the Roman Form—Rebellion—Formal Declaration in favour of Popery—Death of Paez—Arrival of Mendez—His Proceedings as Patriarch—

Encroachments and Tyranny—The King alarmed insists on Moderation—Rebellion—Basilides, or Facilidas, the Prince—Hopes of the People—Letter from the Pope—Additional Concessions—Popery abolished—Jesuits banished—Capuchins—Franciscan Friars—Attempt by Louis XIV.—Poncet and Brevedent—Massacre of Catholic Priests—Arrival of Abuna—His Proceedings—The Psalter—Doctrines of Abyssinians—Zaga Zaba, Ludolf, and Lobo—Mode of Worship—Form of Churches—Circumcision, Baptism, and Communion—Prayers for the Dead—Fixedness of Manners and Habits—Sabbath—Chronology—Last Attempt of Catholics—Literature—Resemblance to Jews—Books—Philosophy—Law—Medicine—Modern Translations,...Page 262

CHAPTER VI.

MANNERS AND CUSTOMS OF ETHIOPIA.

Present State of Abyssinia—Weakness of the Monarch—Nature of Succession—Court of Justice—Modes of Punishment—Similarity to the Persians—Humane Maxims—Aversion to eat with Strangers—Complexion and Features—Marriage Ceremonies—Manner of Christening—Whimsical Practice to preserve the Life of Children—Superstitions—Buda—Singular Anecdotes—The Zackary—Strange Delusion of *Tigré-ter*—Mode of Cure—Example witnessed by Mr Pearce—Case of his own Wife—Trembling Picture—The Crying Cross—Delusion by a Dofter—Opinion of Welled Selassé—Chastisement of the Dofter—Astonishing Mimic—Diseases and Death ascribed to Demons—Fevers—Small-pox—Inoculation—Practice of Galla—Scrofula—Tapeworm—Customs at Funerals—Criers—Lawyers—Practice in regard to Punishment of Murderers—Agriculture—Cookery—Usages at the Table—Cutting of the *Shulada*—Narrative of Bruce—Disbelieved in Europe—Questioned by Mr Salt—Description of a Feast—Mode of Feeding at Table—Attempt to reconcile Bruce and Salt—Change of Manners in the Interval—Character of the Nobility and Higher Classes—Rigid Fasts—Disorderly Conduct of the Clergy—Extract from Purchas' Pilgrims—Conclusion,..328

CHAPTER VII.

EXHIBITING THE MORE REMARKABLE FEATURES IN THE
GEOLOGY OF NUBIA AND ABYSSINIA.

Want of attention to this subject on the part of Travellers—Primitive Rocks—Granite, Gneiss, Porphyry, Quartz, and Serpentine—Similar Structure towards the Eastern Frontier—Mountains of Cosseir—Marble—Emerald Mountains—Batn-el-Hadjar—Dar Mahass—Primary Rocks—Secondary Formation at Berber—Primitive Strata re-appear—El Queribyn—Fazoglo—Singueh—Mountains of Abyssinia—Taranta—Lamalmon—Ganza—Singular Shapes—Occasioned by Periodical Rains—Theory of the Earth—Reflections,..........................Page 377

CHAPTER VIII.

NOTICES REGARDING SOME OF THE PRINCIPAL FEATURES
IN THE ZOOLOGY OF THE COUNTRIES DESCRIBED IN THE
PRECEDING CHAPTERS.

Peculiarity in the Physical Structure of the Inhabitants of Upper Egypt—Animals numerous in Abyssinia—Monkeys—Bats—Canine Animals—Fennec—Hyenas—Lynxes—Feline Animals—Supposed Origin of our Domestic Cat—Jerboa—Different Kinds of Wild Hog—Hippopotamus—Rhinoceros—Equine Animals—Giraffe—Antelopes—Birds of Prey—Lammergeyer—Vulture—Owls—Pigeons—Hornbills—Parrots—Bustard—Storks—Water Fowl—Reptiles—Crocodile—Cerastes—Fishes—Shells—Pearl Muscles—Insects—Tsaltsalya Fly—Locusts,............385

CHAPTER IX.

GENERAL DESCRIPTION OF THE VEGETATION AS FAR AS IT
IS KNOWN—BRIEF ACCOUNT OF THE MOST REMARKABLE
AND USEFUL PLANTS.

Vegetation of the Country—The Baobab—Acacia vera—Tamarind—Kantuffa—Kuara—True Sycomore—Kolquall—Cusso—Balsam of Mecca—Wooginoos—Coffee-tree—Wansey—Ensete—Doum-tree—Dhourra—Teff—Papyrus,........................424

ENGRAVINGS.

Map of Nubia and Abyssinia. Engraved by Wright. *To face the Vignette.*
Vignette—Great Pyramid at El Bellal. Engraved by Branston.
View of the Temple of Soleb from the North-east. Engraved by Jackson, ...*Page* 52
View of El Queribyn. Engraved by Jackson, ... 81
Ozoro Esther. Engraved by Jackson, ...144
Kefla Yasous. Engraved by Jackson, ...158
View of the Temple of Samné. Engraved by Jackson, ...211
Mountains between Lasta and Samen. Engraved by Branston, ...289
Tecla Mariam. Engraved by Jackson, ...337
Ethiopian Hog—Addax—Fennec. Engraved by Jackson, ...394
Vultur Kolbii. Engraved by Jackson, ...412
Arabian Bustard. Engraved by Jackson, ...414
Saddle-billed Stork. Engraved by Jackson, ...415

NUBIA AND ABYSSINIA.

CHAPTER I.

Introduction.

Difficulties to be encountered by the Historian of Ethiopia—Record of Monuments; their Uncertainty—Obstacles which opposed the Knowledge of the Ancients—Supposition that Civilisation descended the Nile—Progress of Oriental Emigration—Resemblance of Nubian Temples to those of India—Fame of Ancient Ethiopians—Ambiguity of the Term—Two great Classes of Africans—Mixture of Arabians—Opinion of Heeren as to Language—Discoveries of Hornemann and Lyon—Tuaricks and Tibboos—Nubians—Abyssinians—Hypothesis of Heeren—Connexion of Commerce and Religion—Chain of Temples—Similar Connexion among Jews and Christians—Early Improvement of Ethiopians; mentioned in Scripture—Defence of the Opinion that Egypt derived Learning and Science from the Upper Nile.

IN attempting to trace the history of the countries known to the ancients by the name of Ethiopia, we have to encounter the numerous obstacles which arise from the absence of a national literature, as well as from a succession of conquests made by a variety of barbarous tribes. Here indeed, as in Egypt, we possess the record of monuments which indicate the genius and religion of the people by whom the land was occupied at a very distant period; but it is manifest that, in reading the language supplied by the arts, it must be extremely difficult to avoid the ambiguity inseparable from their expression in regard to the precise date at which they flourished. The ruins of cities, of temples, and of obelisks, may no doubt bear evidence to the wisdom of former ages, to the power of conquerors, and to the spirit of magnificence which threw a transient splendour even over the path of destructive armies; still, we cannot discover in them the genealogy of the nations to whom they were indebted for their origin, nor the earliest rudiments of that mechanical skill of which they illustrate so strikingly the progress and the perfection. A cloud hangs over the horizon of that remote antiquity with which we are desirous to become acquainted; and as the current of time carries us still farther away from the point whither our researches are directed, we can hardly be said to enjoy the encouragement which arises from the hope of a successful result.

Egypt, from its vicinity to the Mediterranean, as also to the great thoroughfare which connected Asia with Europe, was comparatively well known to the historians of Greece. An intercourse was long maintained between the philosophers of that country and the priesthood of the Nile, which has proved the medium of much valuable information respecting the early kingdoms of Thebes and Memphis. But the difficulty of penetrating into Western Ethiopia checked at once the ardour of ambition and the enterprise of science. Neither the arms of Cambyses nor the curiosity of Pythagoras could find a path into the regions of the Bahr el Abiad, so as to lay open the wonders of Meroë, or reveal to Europe the mysteries of its learning, its science, and its religious faith.

There is little doubt, however, that the treasures of knowledge, like the fertilizing current of the Nile, have descended the valley, which, beginning at Sennaar, terminates at Alexandria; and moreover, that the progress of civilisation must originally have taken the same direction, moving from the south towards the north. The ancient historians are unanimous in the opinion, that the City of a Hundred Gates owed its foundation to a people who dwelt above the Cataracts; and that at a more recent period, when Lower Egypt began to possess a rich soil fitted for all the purposes of agriculture, and prove itself equal to the maintenance of a large population, the principal seat of government was removed to Memphis. A similar cause perhaps, at a still later date, gave rise to the removal of the capital to its present position, as well as to the erection of the several towns which from time to time have occupied the productive plains of the Delta.

To account for the facts just stated, we must suppose that the stream of emigration which, issuing from the mouths of the Euphrates, pursued its course both eastward and westward along the coast of Asia, had at an early age reached the Straits of Bab el Mandeb. The adventurers, instead of proceeding up the Red Sea, which is remarkable for its dangerous navigation, appear to have made their way into Abyssinia by some of those mountain-passes that still connect the Arabian Gulf with the higher valleys of the Nile. There is indeed the best reason to believe that those lateral defiles which form the line of communication between the sea and the great rivers of Ethiopia, witnessed the earliest expeditions from the East; consisting of those daring spirits who, in the pursuits of commerce, or in search of more fertile lands, or of hills enriched with gold, pushed their discoveries into Habesh, Nubia, and Sennaar.

The most obvious confirmation of the opinion now stated, may be drawn from the striking resemblance which is known to subsist between the usages, the superstitions, the arts, and the mythology, of the ancient inhabitants of Western India and those of the first settlers on the Upper Nile. The sanctuaries of Nubia, for example, exhibit the same features, whether as to the style of architecture or the forms of worship which must have been practised in them, with the similar temples that have been recently examined in the neighbourhood of Bombay. In both cases they consist of vast excavations hewn out in the solid body of a hill or mountain, and are decorated with huge figures, which shadow forth the same powers of nature, or serve as emblems to denote the same qualities in the subordinate divinities which were imagined to preside over the material universe.

We have elsewhere mentioned as a proof of this hypothesis, the very remarkable fact, that the sepoys, who joined the British army in Egypt, imagined that they found their own temples in the ruins of Dendera, and were greatly incensed at the natives for neglecting the ancient deities, whose statues are still preserved. So strongly, indeed, were they themselves impressed with this identity, that they proceeded to perform their devotions with all the ceremonies practised in their native land. There is a resemblance too in the minor instruments of their superstition,—the lotus, the lingam, and the serpent,—which can hardly be regarded as accidental. But it is, no doubt, in the immense extent, the gigantic plan, the vast conception, which appear in all their sacred buildings, that we most readily discover the influence of the same lofty genius, and the endeavour to accomplish the same mighty object. The excavated temple of Guerfeh Hassan, for example, reminds every traveller of the cave of Elephanta. The resemblance, indeed, is singularly striking, as are in fact all the leading principles of Nubian architecture to that of the Hindoos. They differ only in those details of the decorative parts, which trifling points of variation in their religious creeds seem to have suggested; but many even of the rites and emblems are precisely the same, especially those of the temples dedicated to Iswara, the Indian Bacchus. In either country, the hardest granite mountains have been cut down into the resemblance of splendid buildings, the fronts of which are adorned with sculpture. In both, also, large masses of rock have been excavated into hollow chambers, whose sides are decorated with columns and statues carved out of the same stone, or lifted up into the air in the form of obelisks and pillars. By whom and by what means these wonderful efforts have been accomplished, is a mystery sunk too deep in the abyss of time ever to be clearly revealed. But we need only compare the monolithic temples of Nubia with those of Mahabalipoor, the excavations of Guerfeh Hassan with those of

Elephanta, and the grottos of Hadjur Silsili with the caverns of Ellora, to be convinced that these sacred monuments of ancient days derived their origin from the same source.*

It is universally admitted that, if we except the ancient inhabitants of Egypt, there is no aboriginal people of Africa who have so many claims to our attention as the Ethiopians, a nation which, from the remotest times to the present, has been regarded as one of the most celebrated and the most mysterious. In the earliest traditions of nearly all the civilized tribes of the East, the name of this remarkable section of mankind is to be found; and when the faint glimmering of fable gives way to the clearer light of history, the lustre of their character is still undiminished. They continue the object of curiosity and admiration; and we discover that the most cautious and intelligent writers of Greece hesitated not to place them in the first ranks of knowledge and refinement. The praise bestowed upon them by Homer is familiar to the youngest reader. He describes them not only as the most distant of the human race, but also as the most righteous and best beloved by the gods. The inhabitants of Olympus condescended to journey into their happy land, and partake of their feasts; while their sacrifices were declared to be the most agreeable that could be offered to them by the hands of mortals. In the Iliad, Thetis informs her son, that

> "The sire of gods and all th' ethereal train,
> On the warm limits of the farthest main,
> Now mix with mortals, nor disdain to grace
> The feasts of Ethiopia's blameless race.

---

* View of Ancient and Modern Egypt, 2d edit. p. 23.

Twelve days the powers indulge the genial rite,
Returning with the twelfth revolving light."*—POPE.

To what, it has been asked, shall we attribute this early renown of one of the most sequestered nations of the earth? How did its fame penetrate the formidable desert with which it is surrounded, and which even now presents an almost insuperable bar to every one who attempts to reach its ancient capital? To suppose the allusions contained in the foregoing passage to be the mere offspring of the poet's fancy, will not be allowed by any reader who is at all acquainted with the nature of early tradition. But if they are more than fiction,—if the reports concerning this wonderful people are founded in truth,—then they become of the greatest importance to ancient history, and possess the strongest claims to our notice.†

But it must not be concealed that considerable ambiguity attaches to the term Ethiopian; because it was applied by all classes of writers among the Greeks, not so much to denote a country bounded by certain geographical limits, as to describe the complexion of the inhabitants, whatever might be their position with respect to other nations. It will not seem strange, therefore, that we find Ethiopians scattered over a considerable part of the ancient world. Africa, no doubt, contained the greater portion of them; but it is equally true that a large tract of Asia was occupied by a race who bore the same designation; and as India was often made to comprise the southern division of the former continent, so, in like manner, Ethiopia was frequently

---

* Ζεὺς γαρ ἐπ' ὠκεανον μετ' ἀμυμονας Αἰθιοπηας.—Lib. i. v. 123.
†. Heeren's Historical Researches, vol. i. p. 294.

described as including Southern India. Homer, who seems to have collected all the fragments of historical and geographical knowledge which were scattered among the learned of his age, recognises the distinction now explained, and speaks of the Ethiopians as extending from the rising to the setting of the sun.

> " But now the god, remote a heavenly guest
> In Ethiopia, graced the genial feast,
> (A race divided, whom, with sloping rays,
> The rising and descending sun surveys);
> There on the world's extremest verge revered
> With hecatombs and prayer, in pomp preferr'd,
> Distant he lay."*

The ancient historians were wont to divide the Africans into two great classes, the Libyans and the Ethiopians; to whom Herodotus adds the Greeks and Phenicians, who as settlers occupied the northern coasts. This division was generally followed by succeeding writers, although with little accuracy in the use of names; and while we admit that there might be no real difference in the lineage of the two principal families now pointed out, it is at least manifest that they presented to the eye of the Grecian geographers such peculiarities, especially in the colour of the skin, as seemed to justify the discrimination which we find established in their works. But it is obvious, at the same time, that there was a greater affinity between the Ethiopians on the eastern shores of the Arabian Gulf and those on the African side, than between these last and the other swarthy tribes in the interior of Libya. Herodotus, indeed, observes that the Asiatics have

---

* Αἰθίοπας, τοὶ διχθὰ δεδαίαται, ἔσχατοι ἀνδρῶν
'Οἱ μὲν δυσομένου ὑπερίονος, οἱ δ' ἀνιόντος.—*Odyss.*, lib. v. 23.

straight hair, while such as dwell above Egypt have it very much curled. It is certain, however, that all the black inhabitants of Africa do not display this quality; for many of the natives of the Upper Nile, though their skins are of a very dark hue, have hair resembling that of Europeans, being neither curled nor woolly.

The father of history mentions a circumstance, which is not less true at the present time than it was at the remote period in which he lived. He relates that, in the extensive district which stretches from the first cataract to Sennaar, there were two different classes of inhabitants, very easily distinguished from each other. The one, described by him as aboriginal, he includes under the general appellation of Ethiopians; while the other, which appeared to have sprung from an Arabian race, must have removed into the country at an early epoch, where they continued, even in his day, to follow a wandering mode of life. That such was the case under the Persian government, is evident from what we are told respecting the army of Xerxes, whom they must have attended in his expedition into Greece. The Arabians and Ethiopians are associated by the historian under one leader. "Arsanes, son of Darius by Artystone a daughter of Cyrus, commanded the Arabians and the Ethiopians who came from beyond Egypt."* In later times the Arabs seem to have possessed a still larger portion of Nubia, and to have occupied the banks of the Nile from Philæ to the neighbourhood of Meroë; a fact which is confirmed by Pliny, on the

---

* Herodotus, book vii. c. 69.

authority of Juba, the Numidian king, who wrote a work on the geography of Africa.*

It would now be extremely difficult to draw a precise line of distinction between the original tribes and those whose lineage might perhaps be traced to the Arabian immigrants. The latter have not only dwelt in the land more than two thousand years and mingled freely with the older stock, but their language also has been so generally adopted by the natives, that it can no longer be employed as a decisive characteristic. Heeren is, however, of opinion that all who do not speak Arabic must be aboriginal, as he considers it very improbable that the Asiatic settlers would exchange their more improved tongue for the rude dialect of barbarous hordes, to whom, in all respects, they would naturally consider themselves superior. But no one, who views all the difficulties of the case, will maintain that, after the lapse of twenty-three centuries, the line of descent can be otherwise marked than by those physiological qualities in feature and form, which neither length of time nor the most intimate mixture can altogether obliterate.

From the discoveries made by recent travellers in the western parts of Africa, it is no longer doubtful that there has existed in it, from very ancient times, a numerous people who are neither Moors nor negroes. Hornemann and Lyon have made us acquainted with two nations in that quarter, who appear to have possessed all the vast range of country which stretches from the shores of the Mediterranean to the banks of the Joliba. They are

---

* Heeren, vol. i. p. 306.

indeed divided into many tribes; but all speak the same language, which is entirely different from the Arabic, and is found in fact to be no other than that which is used by the Berbers in the Atlas mountains. With regard to their colour, though it certainly is not uniform, the difference seems to depend in a great measure on the place of abode and the manner of living; and, properly speaking, it amounts to nothing more than a mere variation of tint, which is lighter or darker according to circumstances. The western portion of this race are white, as far as the climate and their habits will allow it. Others are of a yellow cast, like the Arabs; some are swarthy; and in the neighbourhood of Soudan there is a tribe which is said to be completely black. Their lineaments, however, do not at all resemble those of the negro. They are slimly made, and rather tall. Commerce is their principal occupation, which they carry on between the interior and the countries bordering on the northern coast. Their moral character has been favourably estimated; and it is thought that, if their talents were duly cultivated, they would probably become one of the first nations in the world.[*]

The account of Hornemann is confirmed by Captain Lyon, who asserts that the Tuaricks, one of the tribes here alluded to, are the finest race of men he ever saw; tall, straight, and handsome, with a certain air of independence which is very imposing. They are generally white; the dark-brown of their complexion being only occasioned by the heat of the climate. Their weapons are a long sword and a

---

[*] Hornemann, p. 129.

dagger, without which no one is ever seen abroad, and an elegant spear highly ornamented and sometimes made entirely of iron. Their language has been already described as the Berber, which they maintain to be very ancient, and is still spoken extensively in Western Africa.

The Tibboos are a different people from that now described, in appearance, manner of living, and even in language. Their colour is a bright black; but their features partake not in the smallest degree of the negro character. They have aquiline noses, fine teeth, and lips formed like those of Europeans. In the language of Herodotus, however, they would be included among Ethiops; having the dark skin, which, in his estimation, formed the distinguishing mark of all the nations to whom he applied that term.

It is probable that the Nubians, those at least who do not boast an Oriental extraction, are of the same race with the ancient Berbers the progenitors of the Tuaricks, and perhaps of the Tibboos. They are not known by their present name till the era of the Grecian kings of Egypt. It is first mentioned by Eratosthenes; and soon afterwards came into common use, both as a general denomination for all the tribes dwelling on the banks of the Nile from Es Souan to Meroë, and also in a more limited sense for the inhabitants of the modern Dongola. Their language, of which Burckhardt has given us some specimens, is quite different from the Arabic; and in this, as well as in their external appearance, they present an affinity to the natives of the Arabian peninsula. They are of a dark-brown colour, with hair somewhat curled, either by nature or art, but not at all woolly. Their visage has no resemblance to the negro physiognomy. The men are well formed, strong and muscular, with fine countenances. They are very thinly clad; but are all armed with a spear five feet long, a dagger, and a large shield made of the skin of the hippopotamus.*

In ascending the Nile we meet with several other tribes who, it is very probable, either belong to the Nubian race, or derive their descent from a common origin. They possess good forms and features, manifest a warlike disposition, and carry into the field of battle the same kind of weapons which were used by their remote ancestors. They commonly fight on horseback, and are armed with a double-pointed spear, a sword, and a large buckler. Hence the fine passage in the book of Jeremiah : " Come up, ye horses; and rage, ye chariots; and let the mighty men come forth; the Ethiopians and the Libyans, that handle the shield."†

When the traveller who has reached the junction of the two great branches of the Nile turns his face eastward in the direction of the Arabian Gulf, he finds his notice attracted to a variety of tribes whose genealogy it is extremely difficult to determine. The Abyssinians properly so called, are, we may presume, the descendants of a people who at various times have migrated from the opposite shores of the Red Sea, and who in pursuit of commerce, or of a safe retreat from powerful enemies, disputed with the natives the possession of their singular country. But we refrain from entering into details on this

---

* Burckhardt's Travels in Nubia, p. 144. Waddington and Hanbury, Travels in Ethiopia, p. 59.
† Chap. xlvi. 9.

subject, as we shall have a better opportunity in the next chapter for considering the geographical relations of the several states which extend from Masuah to the borders of Sennaar. We shall therefore at present only bestow a few remarks on an hypothesis, illustrated with not less ingenuity than learning by Heeren, in regard to the early civilisation and commerce of the African nations, especially the inhabitants of Meroë, Thebes, and their dependent colonies at Ammonium, Adule, Azab, and Axum.

It is established by the clearest testimony of ancient history, that at a very remote period the Ethiopians carried on a considerable trade, in which the Arabians, long known as navigators and voyagers to India, bore a prominent part, as might indeed be inferred from the relative position of the several countries. Of this international traffic in the southern regions the strongest evidence still remains; and there is no doubt that the gold of Africa, the spices of India, and precious productions of Arabia, occupied the laborious carriers of the desert long before the date of our historical records. The prophet Isaiah notices the commerce of the Egyptians and Ethiopians, in a manner which renders it perfectly clear that these celebrated nations had already enriched themselves by their exertions in this branch of industry. " The labour of Egypt, and merchandise of Ethiopia, and of the Sabeans, men of stature, shall come over unto thee, and they shall be thine."*

Commerce and religion, we are reminded by the author, were always indissolubly connected in the

---

* Chap. xlv. 14.

East. The long journeys in the desert, and the marauding habits of the roving barbarians by whom the wilderness was infested, rendered some spiritual influence necessary for its protection; and hence it is presumed, that mercantile transactions were usually conducted in the vicinity of temples, and sometimes within their walls. " Mecca remains still, through its holy sanctuary, the chief mart for the commerce of Arabia." The situation of Nubia has always made it the grand route for caravans between Ethiopia and the countries on this side of the desert. At the present day a communication of that kind is maintained across the waste, from Upper Egypt to Sennaar and Atbar the ancient Meroë. This was indeed the natural emporium for the produce of Inner Africa; being the extreme point of the gold-countries towards the land of the Pharaohs, while, from its proximity to Arabia Felix, it constituted the most appropriate mart for goods conveyed from the remoter East.

Of the vast trade still carried on there modern travellers have given us ample accounts; observing at the same time, that the great salt-works, whence the surrounding country is supplied, are but at a short distance from Shendy. The commerce with Egypt being established, it is manifest that Meroë must have extended its traffic far into the south of Africa; and M. Heeren is even inclined to doubt whether the extensive ruins at Axum, Azab, Meroë, and Adule, really belonged to cities, supposing them rather to have been extensive places of trade, adorned with temples, and appropriated to caravans,—an hypothesis to which he is led by the nature of the country, and the wandering life pursued by its inhabitants. In a word, the conclusions which he draws from a minute examination of all the notices which history has preserved relative to those ancient states, are, that a commercial intercourse existed between Southern Asia and Africa, between India and Arabia, and thence between these countries and Ethiopia, Libya, and Egypt,—that its principal seat for Africa was Meroë, the chief route of which, he thinks, is still pointed out by a chain of ruins extending from the shores of the Indian Sea to the Mediterranean,—that Adule, Axum, and Azab, were links of it between Arabia and Meroë; and that Thebes and Ammonium united the Nile, Egypt, and Carthage,—and, finally, that its chief stations were sacerdotal establishments, the head of which was Meroë, whence all the colonies were sent out. Hence he draws an inference, which will not be hastily questioned by any competent judge, that the first seats of commerce were also the first seats of civilisation. Exchange of goods led to exchange of ideas; and by this collision of mind was first struck out the sacred flame of humanity.*

The connexion between merchandise and the usages of religion was not confined to the wandering tribes of Africa, but may be traced throughout the ancient world wherever men collected in great numbers to celebrate the rites of a national faith. As the adoration presented to the gods was not thought complete without the addition of more expensive offerings, the worshipper repaired not to the stated festival unless accompanied with beasts for sacrifice, or with frankincense and other spices to

---

* Historical Researches, vol. i. p. 475.

perfume the air. The vicinity of a temple was thus naturally converted into a market, more especially at the holy seasons of the year. In the Sacred Scriptures the reader will discover numerous facts which establish the view now given of the relation between commerce and piety. Even the consecrated fane at Jerusalem was contaminated by the presence of dealers, who sought their own advantage rather than the honour of the Great Being whom they professed to venerate. A similar abuse was long tolerated in the Christian church; and hence most of the periodical transactions of a commercial nature became associated with the names of the more popular saints. Every one knows that the *feriæ*, or holidays of the Roman communion, supplied the term for our *fairs* in all the counties of Great Britain.

There is accordingly no small appearance of truth in the observations of Heeren relative to the mutual influence of religion and traffic among barbarous tribes. The sight of a magnificent temple in the wilderness secured at once a demand and a protection for the commodities which the wandering merchantmen brought from afar. It may still remain a question, whether the sanctuary was erected for the assurance of the caravan; or, whether the Arab and Ethiopian bent their course through the desert in a line indicated by those religious establishments? But there can be no reasonable ground for doubt, that the dwellers on both shores of the Red Sea respected the worship of Jupiter Ammon as the means whereby they at once added to their wealth and secured their acquisitions.

We must not neglect to mention that the nomadic tribes, who continue to carry on the trade between Egypt and Abyssinia, appear in the same character in one of those triumphant pageants which Ptolemy Philadelphus exhibited on his accession to the throne. When the procession of the Nubian caravan appeared, " there came," says an ancient writer, " a train of camels, carrying three hundred pounds of frankincense, crocus, cassia, and cinnamon, together with two hundred pounds of other costly spices and drugs. These were followed by a host of Ethiopians armed with lances; one band of these bore six hundred elephants' teeth, another two thousand pieces of ebony, and another sixty vessels of gold, silver, and gold-dust."

But the appearance of Indian produce in the Western World was familiar to all classes of men long before the days of the Grecian kings of Egypt. The spices of the East, especially cinnamon, come as early before us as the Mosaical records; and in such quantities, too, as plainly show that they must already have formed an important article of commerce. The holy oil of the sanctuary required the following ingredients: " Moreover, the Lord spake unto Moses, saying, Take thou also unto thee principal spices, of pure myrrh five hundred shekels, and of sweet cinnamon half so much, even two hundred and fifty shekels, and of sweet calamus two hundred and fifty shekels, and of cassia five hundred shekels, after the shekel of the sanctuary, and of oil-olive an hin. And thou shalt make it an oil of holy ointment, an ointment compound after the art of the apothecary: it shall be an holy anointing oil."[*]

The reader will observe that most of the ingredients specified in this sacred order were derived

---

[*] Exodus, xxx. 22, 23, 24, 25.

from the shores of Indostan, and must have been objects of commerce among the traders of Arabia, who repaired thither in ships, year after year, to exchange for them the commodities of their own land, as well as of Ethiopia and the more southern parts of the African continent. In the history of the patriarch Joseph, mention is incidentally made of the same traffic carried on by the inhabitants of the desert, the progeny of Ishmael. The earlier annals of this intercourse, which connected in the bonds of mutual benefit and intelligence the most cultivated nations of the ancient world, are irrecoverably lost; and it is in vain that we attempt by conjecture, or investigation, to supply their absence. The facts of which we are in possession justify a retrospect of not less than four thousand years, if we follow the light of that scriptural chronology which has obtained the sanction of nearly all the learned; and our researches are thereby removed to a period when the nations of Europe had not even begun to assume a settled form, or to dispute with one another the territory on which the foundations of their power were afterwards to be laid.

In tracing the progress of civilisation in Egypt, we arrived at results which argued a very high antiquity. We found reason to ascribe to the Pharaohs of the eighteenth dynasty the gigantic labours of Thebes, and the magnificent palaces which adorned either side of the Nile in that stupendous capital. What an astonishing era of art, fully two thousand years before the Augustan age at Rome!

But the vast works at Karnac, Luxor, and Medinet Abou, are much less ancient than the buildings which have been discovered above the Cataracts.

The eye of science has recently been invited to countries which stretch southward along the Upper Nile, and to examine the memorials of kingdoms whose names have not yet been enrolled in the eternal tablets of history. In Nubia and Ethiopia, says a foreign writer, numerous and primeval monuments proclaim so loudly a cultivation contemporary, aye earlier than that of Egypt, that it may be conjectured with the greatest confidence, that the arts, sciences, and religion, proceeded from Nubia to the lower country of Mizraim; that civilisation descended the Nile, built Memphis, and, finally, somewhat later, wrested by colonization the Delta from the sea. From Meroë and Axum downwards to the Mediterranean, there arose, as is testified by Diodorus, improved and powerful states, which, though independent of each other, were connected by the same language, the same writing, and the same religion.*

Thus we find, that in proportion as we ascend into the early ages of human history the closer becomes the connexion between Egypt and Ethiopia. The Hebrew writers seldom mention the one without the other; and the inhabitants of both are usually described as a commercial people. When Isaiah celebrates the victories of Cyrus, their submission is spoken of as his most magnificent reward. When Jeremiah extols the great victory of Nebuchadnezzar over Pharaoh-Necho at Carchemish, the Ethiopians are allied to the Egyptians; and when Ezekiel threatens the downfal of Egypt, he unites it with the most distant Ethiopia. Whence this

---

* Lettres de Turin.

general and early spread of a name which glimmers in the oral history of so many nations, and which is renowned as well by Jewish poets as by Grecian bards? Whence this fame of the Ethiopians, while the deserts which surrounded their land seemed to form an eternal barrier between them and the inhabitants of the North? These questions cannot be satisfactorily answered, except by allowing the early civilisation which history and tradition unite in ascribing to the sacerdotal states that sprung from Meroë.

We are not ignorant that, in maintaining the obligations of Egypt to the more ancient Ethiopia for her learning, civilisation, and knowledge of the arts, we have to encounter the opposition of several learned writers, whose opinions on this subject have been determined by an inspection of the Nubian valley. It is obvious, no doubt, that the narrow limits of the latter country, hemmed in between a double range of barren mountains, which occasionally protrude their rocks to the very margin of the river, could not have supplied the means of luxurious refinement to a great nation. But it is equally certain, on the other hand, that beyond the confines of Nubia there are extensive and most fertile regions, which, aided by the periodical overflow of the Nile and the influence of a tropical sun, were capable of supporting in the utmost comfort a very large population. Besides, Ethiopia from her natural position, surrounded by deserts which no stranger could penetrate and by mountains almost inaccessible, enjoyed a degree of security highly favourable to her progress in the liberal arts; while the adventurous inhabitants of the contiguous wildernesses, who carried on her trade, connected her with Arabia and India on the one hand, and with the shores of the Mediterranean on the other. It was not perhaps till the days of Solomon that the Red Sea was used as the channel of trade for Syria and Palestine, when the mariners of Arabia had acquired sufficient confidence to navigate all the gulf, and to visit the shores of the ocean beyond the straits. Prior to that period the rich produce of the East was conveyed by the erratic hordes of the desert, who, preferring the short passage at Azab or Masuah, pushed forward with their loads to the upper regions of the Nile.

The possession of wealth lays the best foundation for learning and the arts; and the perusal of ancient history will convince every reader, that in the early stages of society these are devoted to the decoration and advancement of religion. The stately temple is seen to rise long before any attention is paid to the comforts of private life; and the precious metals, as well as the richest spices and perfumes, are lavished on the instruments of worship, while as yet the blessings of civilisation are very sparingly enjoyed by the mass of the people. On this subject, instead of entering into details unsuited to the nature of our undertaking, we refer to the Essay by Heeren on the Trade of the African Nations.

CHAPTER II.

Geographical Outlines of Nubia and Abyssinia.

Plan to be followed in this Chapter—Nubian Valley—Sterility—Former Cultivation—Dondour—Derr—Ibrîm—Wady Halfa—Second Cataract—Beauty of Country in Dongola—Benefits of the Nile—Temple of Soleb—Elegance of the Building—Kingdom of Merawe—Gebel el Berkal—El Bellal—Hypothesis in regard to Meroë—Opinions of Ptolemy, Herodotus, Strabo—Sheygyans—Ishmael Pasha—Third Cataract—Berber—Shendy el Garb—Shendy—Junction of the White and Blue Rivers—Sennaar—Climate—Inhabitants—Manufactures—Expeditions by the Troops under the Pasha—Bravery of the Natives—Description of the City of Sennaar—Advance of Egyptian Army into Fazoglo—El Queribyn—Kilgou—Singueh—Conflicts with the Natives at Tâby and Gassi—Reception at Fazoglo—Return to Sennaar—Aquaro—River Toumat—Quamamyl—Ishmael disappointed as to Gold and Slaves—Poncet's Account of Sennaar—Abyssinia—Its Extent—Political Geography—Kingdoms and Provinces—Amhara—Tigré—Shoa, and the Eastern Coast.

It is our intention to consider as one country the extensive space which is bounded by the Nile on the west, and the Red Sea on the east; and which, when measured from south to north, has for its limits the tenth and twenty-fourth degrees of latitude. In this compass we necessarily include Nubia, Dongola, Sennaar, and Abyssinia, the states of the Shangalla, as well as the wild districts inhabited by the ancient Troglodytes and Fish-eaters. There is, it must be acknowledged, a considerable diversity in the lineage of the people, their history, speech, and religious usages; but at the same time they possess so many things in common, that it appears much more convenient to place them under one point of view than to interrupt the narrative by a detail of minute distinctions. We shall, therefore, in delineating the geographical distributions of this large portion of Eastern Africa, ascend the Nile in the footsteps of the best-informed travellers, until we reach the boundaries of recent discovery in the southern provinces of the kingdom of Sennaar; and, after returning to the bank of the Blue River, make our progress eastward through Abyssinia to the shores of the ocean and the Arabian Gulf.

No sooner does the traveller pass the cataract of Es Souan, than he finds himself in Nubia, a country of which it is now impossible to fix the precise extent. Indeed, we cannot otherwise define it than by saying, that it occupies the valley of the Nile from Philæ to Dongola, and is bounded on either side by formidable deserts, which can only be crossed by large bodies of men assisted by that useful animal the camel. The first section, which terminates at Ibrîm, has been so long subject to Egypt that it is usually known as Turkish Nubia; but we are told that the natives of the upper country, who roam in comparative independence as far as the second cataract, restrict the proud name to their own land, which, till lately, spurned the dominion of every foreign sword.

For a considerable distance above Syené, the mountains press so closely on the banks of the river, that there is very little ground on either side for the purposes of agriculture; and the small portion that is suitable for raising a crop is continually threatened by the approach of the sand which the winds of the desert carry towards the stream. From the structure of the valley, through which the Nile here forces a passage, it is obvious that there could not at any time have been an extensive population. The labour of man would have exerted its powers in vain against the sterility of nature, which, amidst rocks and shingle, occupies, by an everlasting tenure, a wide domain in the Lower Nubia. But beyond the parallel of Wady Halfa, as we have already remarked, there is ample space for the great nations which are said to have flourished in Ethiopia. At the southern termination of the second cataract immense plains stretch out from the margin of the river, manifesting even in their present neglected state the most unequivocal symptoms of a prolific soil.

Nor can there be any doubt that, in former ages, the annual inundation carried its riches much beyond the limits of modern cultivation. The rocky barriers, which now scarcely oppose an obstacle to navigation, must at one period have checked the current so materially as to throw back the water on all the level land on both sides of the contiguous valley. The voice of tradition in this case is not to be altogether despised. On the contrary, we must believe that there was some ground for the descriptions of the ancient historians, who represent the falls of the Nile as accompanied with a great rush and a deafening noise; indicating that the rocky shelves, which have been broken and washed down by the weight of the yearly flood, extended from bank to bank at a considerable elevation. Even in the northern district of Nubia, where the dominion of the desert is now indisputably established, the sources of fertility would be much greater than in our days; and, indeed, without assuming the means of supporting an affluent people, we shall find no small difficulty in accounting for the costly temples and other edifices, the remains of which may be traced from Elephantiné to Sennaar.

The first five miles after leaving Philæ, the course of the navigator is south by east, then it turns towards the west, and finally resumes the former direction. The first object that attracts his attention is Debode, a village situated on the left bank of the river, where are the ruins of a small temple. Here the Nile flows in a regular deep stream, for the most part washing the base of the eastern and western mountains; but wherever the inundation has covered the rocks with soil, or has even thrown up mounds of sand and mud, such spots are cultivated and planted with date-trees. A succession of hamlets meet the eye on both sides as the traveller proceeds into the Nubian valley; but few of them are of so much consequence as to deserve our notice. Dondour is remarkable for a small temple, still in considerable preservation, of which a distinct idea may be formed by examining the drawing inserted in Mr Legh's amusing narrative. The greater part of the enclosure is quite perfect, and the propylon also is very little injured; but the inside, it would appear, has never been completed. There are two columns which must have formed the entrance into the building, and which are ornamented with serpents. The inner shrine, or sekos, consists as usual of three apartments; the first measures eighteen feet in length and twenty in breadth; the columns are three feet in diameter, and the height, ascending to the top of the cornice, is nearly seventeen feet. The winged globes on the architraves of the temple and propylon are supported in the wonted manner by two serpents. The hieroglyphics are relieved and sculptured in a good style, showing the common objects—priests with jugs offering to Isis, and Osiris who is represented with the hawk's head, and carrying a crosier in his hand. Behind the structure is a small grotto, which has the appearance of a later date, and is most probably to be attributed to the early Christians; there being an inscription with the characters $A + \Omega$ among the fragments which are found in the area.*

These ruins, however, are surpassed in magnificence and interest by those of Guerfeh Hassan and Sibhoi, of which the relics are yet sufficiently entire to enable a scientific eye to delineate their plan and determine their object. It is justly observed, that the period when these edifices were constructed is a matter of pure conjecture; but it has been remarked, at the same time, that the most striking difference between the temples above and below the Cataracts is the high state of preservation of the stones and outward walls of the former, which have scarcely suffered from the effects of age. From this circumstance, it might at first sight be supposed that these remains of antiquity were more recent than the temples in Egypt; but that opinion is not warranted by any other evidence. It would be difficult, indeed, by any reasonable allowance in dates, to account for the fact now stated; and the real

---

* Legh's Narrative of a Journey in Egypt and the Countries beyond the Cataracts, p. 142.

cause, it is probable, must be sought in the mild unchanging climate which prevails between the tropics. The corroding hand of time works very slowly in the absence of frost and rain and of those extreme variations of the atmosphere which, in the zones called temperate, wage an incessant war with all the works of human art.*

Derr, which is at present considered the capital of Lower Nubia, is the residence of a chief who, while he acknowledges a nominal subjection to the Pasha of Egypt, seizes every opportunity of setting his authority at nought. The name just used, however, seems to apply to a district rather than a town or any particular collection of houses; and the abode of the governor himself can only be distinguished by having in its vicinity a few mud cottages, and a somewhat denser population. But his power, in the absence of law and supported by three thousand barbarian troops, is extremely formidable. Plundered himself from time to time by the agents of the supreme government, he extorts a revenue from his miserable subjects at the point of the spear. He is constantly surrounded by more than three hundred armed slaves, ready to execute any order of capricious cruelty which he may be pleased to issue; for as his soldiers are his own property, purchased from the dealers of Dongola or Sennaar, they are in his hands the most passive instruments whether for good or for evil. Jealous of interference or inspection, he dreads the approach of strangers. When Mr Legh and his friend Mr Smelt made their journey into his district, it was

---

* Legh, p. 150.

with the utmost reluctance that he allowed them to proceed beyond Derr. He began by asking in a very boisterous manner what they wanted, and why they had come. It was in vain they replied, that they were desirous to pay their respects to him, and to see the remains of antiquity with which his country abounded. He answered that there was nothing curious to see; but " I suppose," he added, " you are come to visit the tombs of your ancestors?" They then solicited permission to go to Ibrîm, which he flatly refused; alleging first there was no object there worthy of their attention, and next that he had no horses to convey them. In short, it was not until his obstinacy had been subdued by the present of a handsome sword, that he yielded his consent to their farther progress.

The town which the travellers were so desirous to visit is situated on the right bank of the Nile, at the southern extremity of a ridge of mountains, rising in some parts perpendicularly from the river so as scarcely to leave room for a road. It stands on the eastern slope of the hill, having a citadel which, being built on the summit, must have formerly been a strong position. Its height has been estimated at about two hundred feet above the current, which washes the foot of the rock whereon it is placed, and is at this point about a quarter of a mile broad. The walls that enclosed the fortress and the governor's house can still be traced with ease. But no inhabitant now remains; not a vestige of life is to be seen within its boundaries. The destruction of Ibrîm by the Mamlouks, when they passed into Dongola, had been so complete that not even one solitary native was to be found wandering among its ruins, nor so much as a date-tree to indicate that it was once the abode of human beings. Burckhardt informs us that those savage horsemen carried away about twelve hundred cows, all the sheep and goats, and imprisoned the most respectable of the people, for whose ransoms they received upwards of a hundred thousand Spanish dollars. On their departure they put the aga to death, after having devoured or destroyed all the provisions they could find. This scene of pillage, as might have been expected, was followed by a dreadful famine.

Ibrîm is said to be the ancient Primmis, and the account of it given by Strabo, as fortified by nature, is confirmed by the actual appearance of the place. But when this geographer states that the Romans, in marching from Pselcha or Kalabshe, passed over the mounds of sand under which the army of Cambyses was buried, he is imagined to be at variance with Herodotus, who relates that the host of the Persian monarch, when surprised by the clouds of moving dust, was proceeding to chastise the Ammonians. Hence it is inferred, that their route must have lain in a direction quite contrary to that of the Romans under Petronius, who was sent to punish the Ethiopians for an irruption into the Thebaid. These remarks, however, are founded on the assumption that the Ammonians must necessarily be the inhabitants of the particular district in Libya where the celebrated temple of Jupiter was erected; whereas there is reason to believe that a sanctuary, dedicated to the same god under the character of Ammon, stood in the peninsula of Meroë near Shendy, the principal seat of the Ethiopians. It is therefore not at all improbable, that the troops of Persia and of Rome followed the same line of march. Near the town of Moscho there is still a position known by the name of *Cambysis Ærarium*,—the Treasury of Cambyses,—while it is admitted that the legions advanced as far as Napata, a station considerably further to the south.

The space between Ibrîm and the second cataract presents no interest but such as may be attached to its ancient buildings, more especially the temple of Ebsamboul, which we shall hereafter describe with some degree of minuteness. The obstruction in the river, occasioned by numerous rocks and small islands, which begins at Wady Halfa, continues about a hundred miles, and in the low state of the flood puts a stop to all such vessels as cannot be partly carried overland on men's shoulders. The falls vary according to the period of the inundation; a fact which may to a certain extent explain the discrepancy between the several authors whose works have been recently given to the world, and who received very different impressions in the vicinity of the principal cataract. One tells us, that the declivity was so trifling that the descent of the stream, so far from creating a rushing noise, could hardly be perceived by the eye; while another assures us that it was heard in the night at the distance of about half an hour, or nearly two miles. Burckhardt, whose statement we have just copied, adds, that the valley is very romantic; that when the inundation subsides many small lakes are left among the rocks; and that the banks of these, overgrown with large tamarisks, have a picturesque appearance among the black and green stones. The tract is called the Dar el Hadjar or Batn el Hadjar, the district of cliffs or bed of shelves.

An American, who engaged in the service of Ishmael Pasha during the expedition to Dongola and Sennaar, and who has published an interesting narrative of his voyage up the Nile, begs his readers to remember that what is called the second cataract is properly a succession of swift rapids, which, as we have already observed, extend fully a hundred miles from Wady Halfa to Sukkot. He counted nine of these; some of which, particularly the second, fifth, seventh, and ninth, were very dangerous to pass, although the river had subsided but a few feet. Before his party arrived at the fifth, called the Shellal of Ambigool, two boats were wrecked against the rocks which crowd the channel; and before they could pass the ninth, the Shellal of Dal, several accidents of the same kind took place. To clear these two falls it was necessary to employ about a hundred men to drag the boats one after another against the current. At the former the stream is interrupted by a ledge of rocks reaching nearly across, over which it precipitates itself. Between this shelve, indeed, and the western shore, there is a practicable passage, wide enough to allow a boat to be hauled up the current, which here runs very furiously.*

Near the upper part of the second cataract the country becomes extremely beautiful and fertile; verifying all the reports respecting the excellence of the soil in the provinces beyond Nubia. In some places the river is not less than five or six miles broad, enclosing numerous islands on which agricultural produce might be increased to almost any amount. The scenes of verdure on the left bank

---

* Narrative of Expedition, p. 5.

far surpass the finest views of rural magnificence in the Saïd, while the mode of culture is not inferior to that pursued in the most improved districts of the Lower Nile. The author of the Narrative asserts that some of the grounds watered by the stream might, by the hands of enlightened industry, be made capable of producing every thing which the art of man operating upon a fine soil under a soft climate could possibly effect. Many parts of Dongola exhibit the same rich qualities, and present the same hopes to the farmer; and, in short, it is manifest that nothing besides a good government is required to render those extensive districts the abode of plenty, contentment, and civilisation.

The Nile has with justice been represented as one of the wonders of the globe. Its course has been compared to the path of a good man amidst a wicked generation. It passes through a desert, dry, barren, and hideous; on the portions of which, contiguous to its banks, it deposites the richest soil, which it continually waters and nourishes. This gift has been the source of subsistence to several powerful nations, who have established and overthrown mighty kingdoms, and have originated the arts, the learning, and the refinement, of the greater part of the ancient world. Those nations,—instructors and pupils,—have perished; but the remains of their stupendous labours, the pyramids and the temples of Egypt, Nubia, Dongola, and Meroë, are more than sufficient to excite respect for the great people who founded them.

Under this impression a voyage up the Nile may be considered as presenting an epitome of the life of man. We meet at almost every stage with the monuments of his tyranny, his superstition, or his luxury, but with few memorials of his talents directed to the improvement and protection of his fellow-creatures. We also every where perceive the traces of Almighty justice on his crimes. On the banks of this ancient river we behold cities, once famous for power and wealth, reduced to a heap of sand like the wilderness; and temples, once renowned, and colossal idols, at one time feared, now prostrate and confounded with the dust of the worshippers. The flocks lie down in the midst thereof; the cormorant and bittern lodge in the towers and palaces: their voice sings in the windows, and desolation is in the thresholds. The Nile, meantime, which has seen so many generations rise and disappear, still moves onward to distribute its fertilizing fluid to the countries on its borders; like the good Providence, which seems unwearied in trying to overcome the ingratitude of man by the many favours it bestows upon him.

At a considerable distance above the second Cataract the traveller encounters the rapids of Doulga, where the river again becomes embarrassed with rocks and small islands. Navigation is so much impeded by these obstructions, that hardly any attempt is made to render it the medium of commerce on the confines of Shendy, or in that extensive reach which terminates at the borders of Sennaar. But between these two cataracts there are many objects that demand attention; among which, in order to diversify our narrative, we shall submit to the reader a brief account of the temple of Soleb, as also of the remarkable peninsula inclosed by a bend of the Nile, and known as the modern Merawe.

View of the Temple of Soleb from the North-east.

Near the parallel of the twenty-first degree of latitude, and about four hundred paces from the western bank, stand the ruins of the magnificent fane just mentioned. In advancing towards it the eye is first attracted by an elevated stone-foundation thirty feet in thickness, extending in front of the temple, and of equal length with the portal.

The remains of two sphinxes are seen at either side of the approach, where there was a staircase which led to the main building, now in a state of complete dilapidation. The front of the portal, of which only a part is left, is about a hundred and seventy-five feet long; and the width of the steps is not less than fifty-seven feet. The wall, which is twenty-four feet thick, is not solid, but contains a variety of cells, set apart, it may be presumed, for a variety of uses no longer obvious to the uninitiated.

The first chamber is more than a hundred feet in breadth, and eighty-nine in depth; round three sides of which runs a single row of pillars, while on the fourth there are indications of a double row; making in the whole thirty columns, of which seven are still standing and perfect. They seem all to have been executed from the same model; the diameter of the base being sixty-seven inches, and the height about forty feet. They are inscribed with hieroglyphics only, and exhibit no figures which can properly be referred to the hand of the sculptor.

There is a second chamber, in which it is still possible to trace a row of twenty-four pillars resembling those in the first; but their fragments are scattered about in every direction. The very bases of some of them are rooted up, and the mud-foundation on which they stood is completely exposed. So entire yet so partial a ruin, it is remarked, can only be attributed to the sudden yielding of the ground; for an earthquake would not have spared the columns which remain in other parts of the edifice.

It is difficult to ascertain the dimensions of the adytum, as no trace of the side-walls can be detected, and only a few feet of the one which had formed the remote end of that splendid sanctuary. It is manifest, however, that it must have contained twelve pillars and not more, and of these there are three still entire. The rest have fallen chiefly towards the Nile, under the assault of their powerful enemy the desert; and even one of those which stand is already so much inclined in the same direction, that it must shortly take a place beside the others. The lower parts of all the columns bear representations of figures about three feet high, of which the inferior half is concealed by a tablet inscribed with hieroglyphics. They are executed in the very best style, as are all the sculptures remaining in the temple, though in some places they have not been finished. Among these Jupiter Ammon appears twice; and to him it is more than probable that the whole structure was originally dedicated.

Mr Waddington observes, that the temple of Soleb affords the lightest specimen he had any where seen of Egyptian or Ethiopian architecture. The sandstone, of which most of the columns are composed, is beautifully streaked with red, giving them from a distance a rich and glowing tint. As the walls have almost entirely disappeared, and the roof fallen in, there remains no ponderous heap of masonry to destroy the effect of these beautiful pillars, backed by the mountains of the desert or the clear blue horizon.

Here the man of taste does not contemplate a gloomy edifice, where heaviness is substituted for dignity, height for sublimity, and size for grandeur, nor measures a pyramidal mass of stone-work, climbing up to heaven in defiance of nature and propriety. " We seemed," says the traveller just named, " to be at Segesta, at Phigalea, or at Sunium, where lightness, and colour, and elegance of proportion, contrasted with the gigantic scenery about them, make the beauty of the buildings more lovely, and their durability more wonderful. There is no attempt to imitate or rival the sublimity that surrounds them; they are content to be the masterpieces of art, and therefore they and nature live on good terms together, and set off each other's beauty. Those works that aim at more than this, after exhausting treasuries, and costing the life and happiness of millions, must be satisfied at last to be called hillocks."[*]

Upon inspecting the map of Nubia it will be observed, that at a point near Old Dongola the river turns towards the north-east, and gives an insular form to a large extent of land distinguished as the province or kingdom of Merawe. In this tract there are some magnificent monuments near the spot which is supposed to have contained the ancient capital. For example, there are the remains of seven temples, of which the largest is 450 feet long (almost equal to St Paul's) by 159 broad. The principal apartment is 147 feet by 111, and the next is 123 by 102. This edifice is generally speaking in a very ruined state; and some of the materials are in so

---

[*] Journal of a Visit to some Parts of Ethiopia, p. 290.

confused and shattered a position, as to indicate that they had been broken down and unskilfully replaced. The other temples are of much smaller dimensions, but several of them more perfectly preserved; and in two, most of the chambers are excavated in the solid rock. This is part of a lofty eminence, called Gebel el Berkal or the Holy Mountain, along the foot of which all the monuments are erected. Here are also seventeen pyramids, while at El Bellal, seven miles farther up the river, there is a more numerous and lofty range of these structures, none of which, however, rival those of Memphis. A general character of ruin pervades the whole, and some, indeed, are reduced to masses of mere rubbish; a state which seems at least partly owing to the friable nature of the sandstone used by their architects. The sculptures and ornaments, which can still be traced, bear marks of very different periods of art; some being extremely rude, and others nearly as perfect as any in the palaces of Egypt.

The examination of these monuments, whether temples or pyramids, has led to an ingenious hypothesis relative to the site of the ancient Meroë, which is maintained with a considerable show of argument and learning in a popular journal. It is well known, that all the ancient authorities describe the geographical position of the Ethiopian capital as an island formed by the junction of the Nile with the Astapus or river of Abyssinia, and with the Astaboras, which is undoubtedly the modern Tacazze, still called Atbara. The city of Meroë, then, if it stood in the country bounded by the two latter rivers, must necessarily have been above the point at which they unite; a conclusion fully confirmed by the direct statement of Eratosthenes. Near Shendy, accordingly, forty miles above that junction, there has been discovered a range of buildings and pyramids of very considerable extent and magnificence. Bruce in his journey observed some of them, and threw out a conjecture that they marked the site of Meroë, and thereby led to the natural inference, that the kingdom recorded in history under the same name must have had its territory between the Tacazze and the Blue River. The judgment of the Greek geographer and of the Scottish traveller have hitherto prevailed against every other supposition. It is insinuated, indeed, that M. Cailliaud and Mr Waddington were not perfectly satisfied with the arguments of their predecessors; but farther consideration, or an unwillingness to oppose an impression almost universal, has induced them to acquiesce in the more common conclusion.

But, says the author to whom we have alluded, " notwithstanding so great a concurrence of authorities, we cannot but think it pretty clear that the city of Meroë was not at Shendy but at Merawe, and that the kingdoms of the same name coincide ; though Meroë in its glory probably extended to Dongola on the one side and Shendy on the other."*

The first coincidence, it is remarked, is that of name, which is complete; for both Burckhardt and Waddington observe, that the modern term, though written Merawe, has the precise sound of Meroë. Resemblance of name, it is admitted, is often accidental, though strict identity is very seldom so ; and amid the general change it is still common, es-

---

* Edinburgh Review, vol. xli. p. 190.

pecially in those unfrequented tracts of Africa, that great capitals, as Axum, Augila, and Es Souan, for example, should continue to enjoy their old appellations. At all events, the author concludes, resemblance, and still more sameness, becomes almost decisive when there is a coincidence also of circumstance and situation. Now here we have, bearing the name of Meroë, a capital presenting in its vicinity monuments that correspond exactly in character, magnitude, and antiquity, to those which ought to mark the site of that celebrated metropolis of Ethiopia. There are no other ruins in that country which can be compared to these; for, according to the measurements of Cailliaud, those of Shendy are decidedly inferior. The length of the greatest temple there is not quite 280 feet; of that at Merawe it is 450. The elevation of the highest pyramid at the former place is 81 feet; of that at the latter it is 103. Now all the ancient accounts unite in representing Meroë as without a rival among the cities of Ethiopia; but if Shendy be Meroë, says the reviewer, there must have been a much more splendid capital nearer to Egypt and yet unknown in Egypt. We have then, he concludes, a combination of circumstances in favour of the position of Merawe, which only the most decided proof would be sufficient to negative.

Such proof, it is conceded, is with some apparent reason supposed to exist in those ancient writings which appear absolutely to require that Meroë must be above the junction of the Nile and the Tacazze. But it is imagined that a closer examination will probably alter our views as to the decisive nature of these statements. It has never been observed, says the reviewer, that by far the highest ancient authority is in direct contradiction to them. To this preeminence Ptolemy seems fully entitled, from the advanced era at which he lived, the great extension of communication in his time, and in fact the more accurate and detailed manner in which he lays down his positions. His residence, too, at Alexandria, then the centre of the commerce carried on between Africa and the East, gives peculiar weight to his opinions respecting Egypt and the surrounding countries. His observations respecting Meroë are as follows:

" Meroë is rendered an island by the river Nile coming from the west, and by the river Astapus flowing from the east. It contains these towns:

	Long.	Lat.
" Meroë,	61·30*	16·26
Sacolche,	61·40	15·15
Eser,	61·40	13·30
Village of the Dari,	62	12·30
Then the junction of the Nile and the Astapus,	61	12
Then the junction of the Astaboras and Astapus,	62·30	11·30"

In this table it is clear that Ptolemy places Meroë far below the junction of the Nile with the Astapus, the Astaboras, or any great stream whatsoever. He makes the difference of latitude indeed much too great; but into this error he appears to have been betrayed by extending his itineraries nearly in a direct line up the river, without allowing for the circuitous course which it pursues above Dongola. Beyond Meroë the knowledge of Ptolemy, it is granted, becomes obscure; though from Egypt to that point he gives a continued chain of geographical positions, at a time when there is every reason to believe that the intercourse between the two countries was frequent. It seems then scarcely possible

---

* Longitude from *Ferro* Island, where the first meridian used to be placed.

that he should have made a mistake as to this particular; or that so grand a feature should have escaped his notice, as that the Nile, which for more than three hundred leagues had not been augmented even by a rivulet, receives below Meroë so mighty a tributary as the Tacazze.

The author of the hypothesis, whose arguments we are endeavouring to abridge, maintains also that the narrative of Herodotus, though less detailed than the other, appears to point to the same spot. According to that ancient writer, travellers ascending the Nile above Elephantiné journeyed first forty days to avoid the cataracts, then embarked, and were conveyed in twelve days to Meroë. The place where they took shipping was, he thinks, probably on the borders of Dongola, where the long line of rapids is found to terminate. From thence to Merawe twelve days would correspond with the same rate of advancing; whereas to Shendy, the supposed site of the proper Meroë, that space of time would be much too small. Again, Meroë is stated by this historian to be midway between Egypt and the Land of the Exiles, described by other writers as an island formed by the Nile, and which the reviewer thinks can be no other than Sennaar, where the Blue and White rivers give to the intervening country something of an insular aspect. Now, Merawe, he remarks, is exactly at an equal distance between Egypt and the kingdom just named, whereas Shendy would violate altogether the relation of equality between the two divisions.

Farther, Strabo, following the authority of Eratosthenes, supplies a statement which seems to have a reference to Shendy, and is, says the reviewer, the only one that can cause a doubt. But elsewhere he describes Meroë as " bounded upwards on the south by the junction of the rivers Astapus, Astaboras, and Astasobus." This, he adds, agrees very closely with our idea on the subject, and is quite contrary to that which would represent the Astaboras as the *northern* limit of Meroë. His statement also, that this is the last kingdom of the Ethiopians, after which the Noubæ commence and occupy the Nile downwards to Egypt, is still true only in regard to Merawe.

But, returning to the main objection, the author is aware it will be asked, How was the idea so prevalent among ancient geographers, that Meroë was formed by the junction of the great rivers,—and why does Ptolemy himself, in the title of his chapter, admit the same notion, though his statement is rather in contradiction to it? The following remarks, he thinks, will afford a sufficient explanation of the manner in which the mistake originated.

All who are conversant with the early history of geography must be aware of the many errors with which it abounds. Among these none are more frequent than such as respect the continuous course of great rivers, and the distinction between islands and large peninsulas. The latter terms, indeed, are often used as synonymous, though perhaps only through the influence of this original blunder. Now, the reader need only look at the map of the country here considered as Meroë, under its modern name of Merawe, intersected by what might almost be called three parallel branches of the Nile, in order to perceive how probable it is that the first imperfect account should represent it as an island enclosed by three separate rivers. The original opinion, indeed, which is still to be found in Mela and Pliny, was, that the Astapus and Astaboras were branches of the Nile itself, first separating and forming Meroë into a species of delta, and then reuniting; an idea which seems to have a peculiar reference to the parallel streams of the modern Merawe. Then, after it was found that the Nile in this neighbourhood received some large tributaries, it was very natural to consider them as the river-branches employed in the formation of Meroë. The original idea of it, as of an island enclosed by these streams, appears to have become rooted in the minds of geographers, even after they had obtained a knowledge of the facts by which their opinion was directly confuted.*

" Such are the considerations," say the reviewers, " which, in our apprehension, establish the identity of the ancient with the modern Meroë. If the discussion has been tedious, it should be remembered that it involves not merely a curious problem in geography, but the site of monuments calculated to throw light on the arts and history of one of the most celebrated nations of antiquity."†

In describing the local peculiarities of Nubia, we could not omit all notice of so able an attempt to oppose the settled opinions on this interesting point, although we do not concur in the conclusions to which the author has permitted himself to be carried. We can hardly imagine it possible that any geographer, who had examined the country, could be so far deceived by the winding course of the Nile as to regard the several sections of the stream which

---

* Pom. Mela. lib. ix. c. 10. Plin. Hist. Nat. lib. ix.
† Edinburgh Review, vol. xli. p. 193.

run north by west, south-west, and north, as three separate and distinct rivers bearing different names. Besides, the ancient writers uniformly mention a junction of the currents; for even Pliny and Pomponius Mela, to whose statement some importance is attached by the reviewer, while they countenance the supposition that the Astapus and Astaboras might be branches of the Nile, relate most unambiguously, that they reunited with their parent waters,—a view of the case which necessarily implies a point of meeting. It is obvious, in the next place, that no one who had observed the direction of the current in the two portions of the Nile which wash the eastern and western shores of Merawe, could ever hold the opinion that they any where unite and become one river; for while on the left hand it flows towards the south-west, on the right hand it runs nearly due north. We may also remark, that the Land of the Exiles is not usually restricted to Sennaar, but is rather imagined to have been situated near the sources of the Abyssinian river, where the curvature of the channel produces the appearance of an island. On this supposition, the estimate of Herodotus, who places Meroë at an equal distance between Egypt and the province occupied by the military refugees, will apply with sufficient accuracy to Shendy, the region enclosed by the Tacazze and the Bahr el Azrek.

Between Dongola and Merawe, the country, many parts of which are rich and beautiful, is occupied by a race of men called Sheygyans, remarkable for valour in the field as well as for a roaming manner of life, and in some respects more allied to the freebooter than to the agriculturist or soldier. After being forced from their lands by Ishmael they took refuge near Shendy, from which position, as they found him still advancing southwards, they sent messengers demanding terms of peace. The pasha replied, that the only conditions on which they could obtain their request were, the surrender of their horses and arms, and a return to their own territory, where they were to bind themselves to live tranquilly and without disturbing their neighbours. The ambassadors answered that they would not give up their horses and arms. The Egyptian commander rejoined, that he would go to Shendy and take them ; they said " Come !"

It is reported that, previous to the advance of the Turkish force from Wady Halfa, deputies from the chiefs of Sheygya arrived at the camp to ask for what reason the pasha menaced them with war. He replied, " Because you are robbers who live by disturbing and pillaging the countries around your own." They observed " That they had no other means to live." Ishmael said, " Cultivate your land and live honestly." They answered with great simplicity, " We have been bred up to live and prosper by what you call robbery ; we will not work, and cannot change our manner of living." The invader thundered in their ears, " I will make you change it !" We shall hereafter have occasion to revert to the history of these undaunted barbarians ; meantime we trace the progress of discovery upwards along the course of the Nile, which from Dongola to Sennaar is yet almost entirely unknown to the European reader.

In passing Merawe the river flows from the northeast, and accordingly, although the traveller is ascending the stream, he has, in fact, turned his back upon the country to which his inquiries are directed. As this remarkable curve in the Nile was not fully ascertained till the period when the son of the Egyptian pasha made his famous expedition into Sennaar, we have endeavoured to assist the comprehension of the reader by adjusting our map.

Ishmael attempted to force his boats through the obstructions of the cataract; but every effort failed, except in regard to those which did not draw more than three feet of water. By the assistance of all the male population on the banks, nine of the class now described were dragged as far as Berber, after an incessant toil of fifty-seven days. Mr English, who accompanied the Turkish armament, observes that the river is spotted with an infinity of islands and rocks. In some of the passages where it was deep, the current was as swift as a mill-sluice, which made it necessary to employ the crews of perhaps twenty boats to drag up one at a time. In other places where the water was shallow, they were sometimes compelled to pull them by main force over the stones at the bottom. He is decidedly of opinion, that when the river is full and the flood strong this cataract must be almost impassable upwards; as, on account of the strange direction of its course, little or no aid can be derived from the wind. Besides the rush in some parts, from the straitness of the passages between the rocks and islands, must in the time of the inundation be very furious; while, from the natural obstacles which cover the shore, the cordel used for dragging could hardly overcome the difficulties which would be incessantly presented.

The canja belonging to Ishmael,—probably the

first boat that ever passed the third cataract of the Nile,—accomplished the voyage to Berber, after having been lifted three times over impracticable shallows. The natives had never before seen a vessel impelled by sails. They called it a "watermare;" comparing it by this appellation to the swiftest animal with which they are acquainted. They ran in crowds to the bank of the river to see it mount the current without the aid of oars.

The Melek of Berber, whose name is Nousreddin, appears to occupy a moveable capital, or rather to select for that purpose any one of the numerous villages which skirt the eastern side of the Nile. The houses are built of clay, and roofed with unhewn timber; that of the king is like the rest, only somewhat larger. The country is fertile and well cultivated; abounding in dhoura, cotton, barley, fine horses, camels, dromedaries, kine, sheep, goats, and fowls. The natives, though resembling the Fellahs of Upper Egypt, are not, generally speaking, either so handsome or so well formed; and many of them have defective teeth, occasioned, it is thought, by the habit of chewing tobacco, which is of a very inferior quality in that district. In their deportment they are extremely mild and polite. Every man you meet gives the greeting of peace, and shows a disposition to accommodate the stranger in all things reasonable; an effect which is ascribed to the circumstance, that they are in a great degree a commercial people, as Berber is every year visited by numerous caravans from Abyssinia, Sennaar, Darfûr, and Kordofan.*

---

* Narrative of Expedition, p. 112. We are told by Mr English, that the ordinary price of a virgin wife in Berber is a *horse*, which

The territory of Berber does not appear to be very extensive, only stretching along the banks of the river from the third cataract for about eight days' journey upwards. On the eastern side it is separated from Shendy by the Bahr el Uswood or Black River. The cultivable land reaches generally to the distance of one or two miles from the margin of the stream, by which it is regularly overflowed at the season of the inundation, and rendered very fruitful. The country contains abundance of salt, which the natives find in the hilly ground along the borders of the desert. It is mixed with calcareous earth, which is separated by washing and the usual process of evaporization. The metropolis which Nousreddin honours with his court appears to have houses sufficient for a population of five or six thousand; but the actual inhabitants, it is probable, seldom amount to that number. The language is Arabic, perfectly intelligible to the natives of Egypt, but containing some words at present disused in that kingdom. There is a mixture of Hebrew terms in the ordinary speech of the people, common we may presume to both those ancient dialects; and it is a remarkable circumstance, that the chiefs of Dongola, Sheygya, Berber, Shendy, and Halfaia, should bear the same title which is employed in the Jewish scriptures to designate the petty sovereigns of Canaan.

On the western side of the Nile, opposite to the island or peninsula of Meroë, there is a large vil-

---

the bridegroom is obliged to present to the father of the girl he demands in marriage. "I remember asking a young peasant of whom I bought provisions one day, why he did not marry? He pointed to a colt in the yard, and told me that when the colt became big enough, he should take a wife."—*Narrative*, p. 122.

lage called Shendy el Garb,—that is, Shendy on the west bank. The road to it from Berber leads through a country consisting of immense plains of fertile soil, extending many miles from the river, and for the most part covered with herbage. There are numerous hamlets, situated at a considerable distance from the stream, in order to be secure from the inundation. The houses are generally built with straw-roofs neatly thatched, and having a decided slope; a proof that this country is within the reach of the annual rains. When visited by the Egyptian army, the current at El Garb was much contracted, although its bed was frequently found to extend more than a mile and a half in breadth. The town, which is respectable in its appearance, contains about six thousand inhabitants, and has three market-places, where the people of the country exchange their dollars and dhoura for a variety of useful commodities.

Shendy, on the east bank, is also the capital of the country which surrounds it, and can boast of a population not less numerous than its rival on the other shore. Large areas, walled round for the reception of the merchandise brought by the caravans, are to be seen in various parts of the town; the streets are wide and airy; and regular markets are established, where, besides meat, butter, grain, and vegetables, are also to be purchased spices imported from Jidda, gum-arabic, beads, and other ornaments for the women. It stands about half a mile from the river, surrounded by land rather indifferent in its qualities; so that the place derives its sole importance from being the staple of the traffic, including slaves, which continues to be carried on between Sennaar, Mecca, and Egypt.

This portion of ancient Ethiopia possesses a great interest, as connected with the junction of the two principal branches of the Nile, the White and the Blue Rivers,—a distinction, as will soon appear, that arises from the very different colour of their waters. The latter, or Abyssinian stream, is not half as broad as the other at the point where they meet; the Bahr el Abiad being about a mile and a quarter from bank to bank. It is also troubled and whitish, and has a peculiar taste bordering on positive sweetness. The Turkish soldiers said that " the water of the Abiad does not quench thirst;" a notion probably originating in the circumstance that they were never tired of drinking it, so light and pleasant was it to the palate. The Bahr el Azrek, or Nile of Mr Bruce, was perfectly pure and transparent, but by no means so agreeable as a beverage; a fact which the author of the Narrative ascertained by drinking first of the one, and then walking about two hundred yards across the point and drinking of the other.

The Abyssinian branch enters the Bahr el Abiad nearly at right angles; but such is the mass of the latter that the former cannot mingle its waters with it for many miles below their junction; and as the one is light-coloured and the other dark, the eastern part of the united river is black and the western side white for more than a league after their meeting. The latter colour is occasioned by a very fine clay held in a state of suspension, and to which the singular flavour that distinguishes the Abiad is undoubtedly to be ascribed. Below the point of union the Nile presents a truly magnificent spectacle. Between Halfaia and Shendy it traverses a deep gloomy defile formed by rocky hills, and runs with considerable force about twelve or fifteen miles. On emerging from this strait, it again spreads itself out majestically amidst immense plains bounded only by the horizon; and after receiving the Bahr el Uswood, it displays a current not less than two miles broad even before the inundation.

During his stay in Sennaar, the American officer endeavoured to obtain information from the people of the country, as well as from the caravan-merchants whom he happened to meet, in regard to the two great rivers which compose the Egyptian Nile. He was told that the source of the eastern or Abyssinian branch is in the Gebel el Gumara, or Mountains of the Moon, about sixty days' march of a camel, in a direction nearly south. It receives, at various distances above their city, several streams which come from the south and east, taking their rise in an Alpine range that stretches into the dominions of the Galla. The course of the Bahr el Abiad, they assured him, is nearly parallel to that of the Azrek, but that its source is much more remote, although, like the other, among the eminences of the Gebel el Gumara. It is also augmented by the accession of a number of tributaries, which issue from mountains southward of Sennaar. On his asking whether the White River were open and free from shellals or rapids, they answered, that at a place called Sulluk, about fifteen days' march above Shendy, there was one which they believed boats could not pass. When he inquired whether, by following the banks of the said river, or of the one which empties itself into it from the west, it were possible to reach a city called Tombat or Timbuctoo, they replied that they knew nothing of such a place, having never been farther west than Kordofan and Darfûr.

This was all he could learn; but he himself is disposed to believe that the main stream of the Abiad cannot have its source in the same latitude with the Azrek, because it commences its rise twenty days sooner than the other; while the colour of its water proves that it flows through a tract of country differing in quality of soil from the regions pervaded by the eastern current. He is farther inclined to think, that the Nile of Bruce has not its principal fountain in Abyssinia, but rather in the lofty range assigned for its origin by the people of Sennaar. On viewing the mass of water that passed downward while he was in the kingdom now mentioned, even before the flood had attained two-thirds of the usual magnitude it acquires during the rainy season, he thought it very improbable that the main source of such a river was not distant more than three hundred miles.

The territory included between the Abiad and the Azrek is usually called El Gezira, or the Island; because, in the season of the rains, the numerous rivers which run into them from the mountains in the south encompass the district with their spreading waters.

Mr English is satisfied that the representations made of the climate of Sennaar are much exaggerated. Except during the rainy part of the year, the country presents an elevated plain, not only dry but well ventilated by the breezes from the south and east, which are generally cool, because they come either from the mountains of Abyssinia or from the huge ridges that compose the Gebel el Gumara. He was there at midsummer, and at no time did he find the heat very uncomfortable, provided he was in the open air and under a shade. Within doors, he allows, the temperature was much raised; and, in the absence of the proper means to secure comfort, its effects were extremely disagreeable. The houses, he adds, were full of lizards, which, if you lie on the floor, you may feel crawling over you all night. He saw a singular species of snake or serpent. It was about two feet long, and not thicker than a man's thumb, striped on the back, with a copper-coloured belly and a flat head. It had four legs, which did not appear to be of any use, as they were short, and seemed to hang from the lower part of its sides. All its motions, which were quick and rapid, were made on the belly, after the usual manner of serpents.*

As to domestic customs and habits, there is a general resemblance among all the nations who occupy the borders of the Nile from Es Souan to Sennaar, though the inhabitants differ somewhat in complexion and character. Those in the province of Sukkot, for example, are not so black as the Nubians and the Dongolese. They are also frank and prepossessing in their deportment. The last-mentioned class are dirty, idle, and ferocious; a description which might likewise be applied to the Sheygyan, were it not that, so far from being indolent, he is either an industrious peasant or a daring freebooter. The natives who dwell near the third cataract have the reputation of being honest and obliging; although it

---

* Narrative of Expedition, p. 185.

must be admitted, that in point of civilisation they are much inferior to the people of Berber, the most improved of all the tribes on the Upper Nile. The inhabitants of those extensive tracts, of which Shendy and Halfaia are the capitals, are a sullen, crafty, and rather bloodthirsty race; while the peasants of Sennaar, those especially who were found at a distance from the principal town, were comparatively mild and virtuous. Throughout the whole of these countries there is one general characteristic in which they resemble the Indians of America,—courage and self-respect. The chiefs, we are told, after coming to salute Ishmael Pasha, made no scruple of sitting down opposite to him, and entering into conversation without the slightest embarrassment, in the same manner as they are accustomed to do with their own meleks, with whom they are very familiar. With the greatest apparent simplicity, they were wont to propose very troublesome questions to the invader; such as, "O great sheik, what have we done to you or your country that you should come so far to make war upon us? Is it for want of food in your own land that you come to seek it in ours?"

The manufactures of the several clans beyond Wady Halfa are limited to the following articles: Earthen-ware for domestic use, and bowls for pipes; cotton cloth for garments; knives, mattocks, hoes, ploughs, and water-wheels for agriculture; horse-furniture, including most excellent saddles very neatly fabricated; stirrups in the European form, and not like those of the Turks, such as are made for the chiefs being usually of silver; large iron spurs; bits with small chains for bridles, to prevent them from being severed by the stroke of an enemy's sabre; long and double-edged broadswords, with the guard frequently made of a precious metal; iron heads for lances, and shields made of elephants' skin; to which may be added, very beautiful straw-mats worked by the women.

When the Sultan of Sennaar surrendered his country to the disposal of the Grand Seignior, the pasha sent notices to all the chiefs of the kingdom, making known to them this act of submission, and demanding their allegiance and homage. But the leader of the mountaineers in the south-western district not only refused to acknowledge Ishmael as his lord-paramount; he even scorned to look on his letter. Similar replies were made by the governors on the eastern side of the Nile, who, while they declined to recognise the act of their sovereign, called him a coward and a traitor for giving up his dominions to a stranger. This resolute conduct on their part led to two expeditions, from which some valuable information has been gained in respect to the distant provinces that they were sent to subdue.

The Divan Effendi at the head of three hundred men crossed the Nile, and soon crushed every attempt made by the spirited barbarians to oppose the new government. "We marched," says he, "without resistance for eight days in the direction of the rising sun, through a country, fine, fertile, and crowded with villages, till we came to some larger ones near a mountain called Catla, where we found four or five hundred men posted in front of them to resist our march. They were armed with lances, and presented themselves to the combat with great resolution. But on experiencing the effect of our fire-arms they took to flight towards the mountain; two hundred of them were hemmed in and cut to pieces, and three of their chiefs were taken prisoners, as well as all the inhabitants we could find; after which we returned."

On being asked with regard to water at a distance from the river, the Effendi replied, that "there were wells in abundance in all the numerous villages with which the country abounds, and also many rivulets and streams, which at this season descend from the mountains." The troops, he added, had forded two small rivers, probably the Rahad and the Dender, the scenery all around being very fine, and presenting many beautiful birds and insects. He brought one of these last with him, which proved to be a scarabæus, covered with a close crimson down, exactly resembling scarlet velvet. The people of the country he described as very harmless, and exceedingly anxious to know what had brought the Egyptian army to Sennaar to trouble them.*

But the other expedition under Hagi Achmet was attended with still more important results. This officer, one of the roughest under the command of Ishmael, was intrusted with four hundred cavalry and three able lawyers, a force which was deemed sufficient either to persuade or compel the reluctant mountaineers to submission. He marched rapidly during ten days in a direction almost southwest of Sennaar, through a well-peopled country, without encountering any resistance till he came to the lofty ridge of Bokki inhabited by pagans, the followers of the chief who had rejected the pasha's letter. They were drawn up on high ground not

---

* Narrative of Expedition, p. 176.

easy to be approached; but their position was soon stormed, and after a desperate struggle they found that spears and swords, though wielded by vigorous hands, were not a match for fire-arms. They fled to another mountain in the rear of that in which they had first taken post; and being again attacked with cannon and musketry, they were obliged to retreat to a third stronghold, still deeper in the recesses of their hills, and inaccessible to cavalry. On this occasion, however, part of them were surrounded by the horsemen of Achmet, and fifteen hundred put to the sword. Believing that he had given them ample proof that resistance on their part was unavailing, and finding that his troops were suffering much from the continual rains, Hagi, after sweeping the villages of all the people who remained, resumed his march to the camp of his master. In the course of their journey his men had to ford several deep rivers, already rushing in full stream from the mountains; and before they reached Sennaar both they and their horses were much exhausted.[*]

The natives of Bokki are described as a hardy race, tall, stout, and handsome. They are said to be pagans, worshippers of the sun, which, however, they consider it profane to look at. The prisoners resembled in their dress the savages of America; being nearly covered with beads, bracelets, and trinkets, made of pebbles, bones, and ivory. Their complexion is almost black. Their manners and deportment are prepossessing, bearing the stamp of simplicity and confidence, together with that air of self-esteem which is never offensive in the mere

---

[*] Narrative, p. 193.

child of nature. The arms of these people excited great surprise; they consisted of well-formed and rather elegant iron helmets, coats of mail made of leather and overlaid with plates of iron, long lances, extremely well fabricated, and a hand weapon exactly resembling the bills anciently used in England by the yeomanry. With such instruments of assault they were very formidable in personal combat. They had never seen fire-arms, but, nevertheless, withstood them with great intrepidity. They said that a fusee was a coward's weapon, who stands at a safe distance from his enemy and kills him with an invisible stroke.

We have been more minute than usual in our details respecting the state of society among the people above the junction of the rivers, because, till the famous expedition of Ishmael Pasha, no European in modern times had visited that remote country. Of the city of Sennaar itself, which in the days of Poncet was remarkable for its population, little now remains besides a heap of ruins. There are indeed in some of its quarters several hundred habitable but almost deserted houses; and at every step the traveller treads upon portions of burnt bricks, among which are often found fragments of porcelain and even of marble. The most conspicuous buildings now are a mosque and a large palace adjoining to it. The former is in good preservation; its windows are covered with bronze gratings skilfully manufactured, and the doors are handsomely and curiously carved. The interior, when viewed by the American officer, was desecrated by uncouth figures of animals portrayed upon the walls with charcoal. This profanation had been perpetrated by the infidels who dwell in the mountains, a march of thirteen days southward of the capital; and who at some period not very long past had taken the town, and left upon the walls these tokens of their disrespect for the religion of the Prophet.

The palace is large but in ruins, except a single pile of building in the centre, which is six stories high, and has five rows of windows. When stationed on the roof, the visiter obtains the best view that is any where to be had of this barbarian metropolis; which appears to be about three miles in circumference, of an oblong form, and stretched along the western bank of the Abyssinian Nile. In examining the structure of the older description of houses, the most remarkable thing in the eye of a European is the workmanship of the doors. These are composed of planks carefully planed and jointed, frequently adorned with carving, and strengthened or studded with very broad-headed nails; the whole inimitable by the present population of Sennaar. The houses themselves are rarely of more than one story in height, having roofs terraced with fine clay spread over mats laid upon rafters. Such is the present appearance of a town that has evidently been once rich and flourishing, but which, during eighteen years prior to the date of the Egyptian expedition, had been the victim of repeated wars and rebellion.

The country in the neighbourhood of Sennaar consists of wide plains, in which are numerous and spacious villages. A long rugged mountain, the only one in sight, stands about fifteen miles to the westward of the town. Below it is a small but pretty island, whose inhabitants earn a livelihood by raising vegetables for the market; and the opposite bank of the river presents several verdant patches devoted to the same object. At a greater distance the ground appeared to be chiefly covered with trees and brushwood, among which were seen a number of elephants in search of food.

We have hitherto followed the progress of the invading army under the command of Ishmael, the son of Mohammed Ali, guided by the narrative of the American officer in the service of that prince. Cailliaud and his friend M. Letorzec were likewise attached to the camp, and enjoyed the countenance of the military chief, who appears to have shaped his conduct towards them under the impression that the knowledge of his exploits in Upper Nubia would be communicated to Europe through the medium of their writings. From Sennaar to the remote Singueh we accompany the French author, whose work is not only the most recent, but also the most satisfactory on this branch of our geographical survey. In truth there is no other publication in the languages of the West to which we can have recourse; and we may add, that no Frank traveller in the memory of man has ever penetrated into those distant provinces on the Blue River, which about ten years ago were traversed by the Egyptian troops in their celebrated expedition against the meleks of the south. It may be noticed, that before the army commenced their march, the Pasha Ibrahim, afterwards so well known in Greece, had joined his brother with a reinforcement, and was prepared to share with him the perils of a new campaign.

It was on the fifth of December 1821 that these chiefs left Sennaar at the head of their respective divisions, and proceeded along the western bank of the Abyssinian Nile. After a few days they separated; Ishmael keeping near that stream, and the other holding more to the westward in the direction of the Bahr el Abiad. Ibrahim had twelve hundred men under his command; his colleague had fifteen hundred; while an equal number was left to guard the camp and secure the new conquests.

The march through a country impeded with wood was necessarily tedious, and seldom relieved by the occurrence of any interesting events. The invaders, who were supplied with a few pieces of cannon, required the aid of camels and other beasts of burden, which on some occasions increased the difficulties of their passage. It was not, therefore, till the 17th day of the month, that, after having seen a number of inferior villages, they arrived at El Queribyn, a small town built on the declivity of a hill, and flanked on either side by a rocky eminence.

After a number of observations, M. Cailliaud ascertained the position of this place to be in 12 degrees and about 7 minutes of north latitude, and in 31 degrees 30 minutes of east longitude, reckoning from Paris, or 33° 50′ east from London. El Queribyn is dependent on Sennaar; and the inhabitants being assured that no injury would be inflicted on them, remained in their huts, of which the annexed drawing, says the author, exhibits a correct representation.

Proceeding still towards the south, though verging occasionally in an eastern direction, the troops under Ishmael pursued their march into Fazoglo Envoys had previously arrived from the melek of that country, expressing his readiness to submit to

View of El Queribyn.

the Pasha of Egypt; suggesting at the same time that his arms might be successfully employed against the unbelieving pagans who inhabit the neighbouring mountains. This hint coincided but too closely with the main object of the general, which was to capture the natives and send them to the lower provinces as slaves, or to find employment for them in the gold mines, said to abound in their rocky frontier. An attack on the defenceless Caffres soon followed, attended with very revolting circumstances. About seventy prisoners, chiefly women, crowned the first attempt of the Turks against that simple race, who were entirely ignorant of the use of fire-arms.

Advancing to Kilgou, a village situated on a hill, Ishmael gave orders to attack it with such impetuosity as would preclude either escape or defence. His instructions were executed with the utmost promptitude; the rocks were scaled, and a great number of the inhabitants found themselves in the grasp of an enemy whom they had not only not provoked, but whose approach they had not anticipated. The resistance, however, did honour to their courage and ingenuity. They retreated to their fastnesses on the higher grounds; and the soldiers, when they attempted to follow them, saw their ranks thinned by huge masses of stone rolled down the sides of the mountains, or by spears which were handled with great dexterity. The pasha himself, who advanced at the head of a party of Mamlouks, made a very narrow escape from the darts of the mountaineers. A colonel of Albanians was pierced with many wounds and left on the field. Still the issue of the combat was unfavourable to the bold barbarians. Their missile weapons were exhausted, and the bravest of their number slain; in which circumstances they were compelled to place their whole confidence in flight toward precipices, where their assailants could not pursue them except by musket-shot. Ishmael sustained a loss of forty wounded and twelve killed; but he considered himself amply indemnified by the capture of five hundred and seventy-two prisoners, as also by the intelligence that a hundred and eighty of his opponents had fallen.

The inhabitants of this district, whom M. Cailliaud describes as negroes, have curled hair, thick lips, and projecting cheekbones; but few of them showed flat noses, while many had even fine features. Among all who were brought into the camp he did not discover one that could speak Arabic. We may add that Kilgou is in lat. 11° 33′ 35″ north, and long. 33° 56′ east.

The two great objects of gold and slaves, which had animated the zeal of Ishmael throughout the whole of this expedition, induced him to extend his march from the village just named towards the mountains of Tâby and Gassi, where he expected to make a large addition to his human booty. His disappointment may therefore be conceived, when he found that the inhabitants of the numerous hamlets which were scattered along its declivities, were prepared not only to meet his soldiers among the ravines and precipices, but also to attack his camp in the night. Unwilling to protract a war, where his loss would probably have exceeded any advantage he might gain, he gave orders to strike his camp and march upon Fazoglo, the ruler of which had already proffered his friendship and allegiance.

The Egyptian prince, on approaching this capital, was met by Hassan at the distance of five leagues, accompanied by his ministers riding on beautiful Abyssinian horses, and surrounded by a hundred guards armed with lances. When Ishmael came in sight, the melek and his attendants dismounted, and advancing on foot prostrated themselves before him. The king made him a present of two valuable steeds. Meanwhile the guards stepped forward, and after raising the wonted shout, formed into line, dropped down on one knee, and turned the point of their spears to the ground in token of submission. In return for this kind reception, the pasha gave orders that his troops should not pass through the villages, lest the inhabitants should receive any injury from the soldiers, whose license, he acknowledged, he could not always check.

For the reason just stated M. Cailliaud did not enter Fazoglo on that occasion; though he was soon afterwards permitted by the general to pay it a visit. He found it a small place, and altogether unworthy of the extensive province to which it gives a name. It stands about a quarter of a mile from the western bank of the Blue River, which is here about three hundred paces broad, and at the distance of a four hours' march northwards from Yara. The position of the latter, as determined by sundry astronomical observations, was found to be lat. 11° 14' 47" north.

Before proceeding towards Sennaar, the pasha, who had not obtained the number of slaves which he thought necessary to complete his triumph, renewed the scenes of Kilgou and Tâby at a hill named Aquaro. The natives, full of courage, and confident in their numbers and position, had sent notice to Ishmael when at Fazoglo, that if he came to their mountains they would break his legs. After a fruitless treaty, meant to deceive the simple Ethiopians, an attack was made on their villages, which were situated on the highest ground. The use of cannon and other fire-arms enabled the Turks to succeed so far as to carry off, at the expense of thirty-five killed and wounded, about a hundred women and children.

Aquaro does not exceed a thousand feet in height, and is not more than a quarter of a league from east to west. It belongs to a district called Dar el Keyl, under the government of a chief, Abou Zinguir. The son of Mohammed Ali was very desirous to make an impression here, satisfied that the result of any decided success would soon realize itself in the submission of the neighbouring tribes. But happily for these poor people his first attempt was far from answering to his expectation.

The army next directed its march towards the south-west with the view of reaching the Toumat, a river, which in our English maps is denominated the Maleg. It flows from the remoter parts of Abyssinia, and after following some time a north-western direction turns to the east, and falls into the Bahr el Azrek about the eleventh degree of latitude. At the point where it was reached by the pasha its breadth was fully six hundred feet; the banks were covered with herbaceous plants and beautiful shrubs, and it meanders through a vast plain finely studded with trees of various kinds. To the north-west were seen in the distance the mountains of Guincho and Soudeh, while in the south-east arose those of

Khachenkaro, inhabited in part by pagan negroes. M. Cailliaud was able to ascertain that the camp on the Toumat was situated in lat. 11° 2' 30" north, and in long. 34° 33' east from Greenwich.

On the 16th of January 1822, the pasha led his troops across the river and kept his face still towards the south and west. After a march of three days he arrived at a small town called Abqoulgui in the province of Quamamyl, whither he was drawn by the report of productive gold mines. The village now mentioned is in lat. 10° 38' 45" north, and in long. 34° 53' 10" east from London. On the south is seen blending with the horizon the mountain of Mafis, and in the west the long chain which bears the name of Obeh. The territory is washed by the Toumat, running here nearly from south to north, and by a number of torrents more or less deep which fall into it. This district is reputed the richest of any in auriferous substances, and that in which the natives have devoted themselves with the greatest activity and success to the acquisition of the precious metals.

But the hopes of Ishmael were completely blasted in regard to the immense treasures which he expected to find in the mountains of Quamamyl. After spending seventeen days in gathering sand, washing it, and collecting the minute particles of gold which it appeared to contain, he resolved to push his researches still farther into the south, and examine the mines reported to have been worked in the lofty range of Singueh or Quebeych, under the tenth degree of latitude. After a toilsome march of two days he was doomed to experience a renewal of his disappointment. The natives, more vigilant and politic than those at Kilgou, attacked his lines day and night, stole his horses, interrupted his supplies, and exhausted the remaining strength of his weary troops. At length he found it necessary to yield to circumstances, and on the 11th of February he struck his tent and began his retreat to Fazoglo.

M. Cailliaud, who had approached nearer to the equator than any other European on the course of the Nile, endeavoured to collect, from the guides attached to the army, some information respecting the White River and the countries contiguous to their own. Of the Bahr el Abiad, they could tell nothing more than that it comes from the distant west, where a savage people dwell, who use poisoned arrows and eat the bodies of their enemies. He learned that the territory of Singueh is dependent on Dar Fôq, and constitutes the most southern province of Bertât. It extends a march of two days southward as far as Fadassy, a place which comprehends several villages and borders on the lands of the Galla. They gave him the names of many torrents and streams which at various points fall into the Nile; but the account is so extremely vague, and the nomenclature so inaccurately expressed, that we despair of being able to communicate to our readers any portion of the knowledge which the laborious Frenchman took so much pains to acquire.

At Fazoglo the two travellers, Cailliaud and Letorzec, left the pasha with the view of returning to Egypt, and on the 18th of February they embarked on the Nile to proceed by water to Sennaar. They passed through a very desolate tract of country, seeing hardly a single human habitation on either side of the river. The stream was very much encumbered with rocks and small islands, which were not passed without considerable danger; and at the cataract of El Querr, where the water rushes downward with considerable force, they had nearly experienced the fate of Mungo Park in his attempt to explore the Niger. It was not till the 26th of the same month that they found themselves in safety under the walls of Sennaar, and in front of the house which they had formerly occupied.

Most readers are aware that this town, the capital of an extensive kingdom, which, according to our maps, occupies so large a portion of Eastern Africa between the White River and the Red Sea, was visited by Doctor Poncet in the year 1699, and by the celebrated Bruce in 1772. The descriptions given in their several works are extremely interesting, more especially when compared with those of Cailliaud, the last traveller who has ascended above the junction of the two great branches of the Nile. The pious author of the " Voyage to Ethiopia" tells us that " this city, which contains near a league and a half in compass, is very populous, but has nothing of neatness, and besides is ill governed. They number in it near a hundred thousand souls. The houses are only one story high, and are ill built; but the flat roof which covers them is very convenient. As to the suburbs they are only wretched cottages covered with reeds. The king's palace is surrounded with high walls of brick baked in the sun, but has nothing regular in it: you see nothing but a confused heap of buildings without symmetry or beauty. The apartments are furnished richly enough with large carpets after the manner of the Levant.

" We were presented to the king the day after

our arrival. The first thing was to make us put off our shoes : this is a point of ceremony which all strangers must observe ; for as to the native subjects of that prince, they never appear before him but barefooted. We entered immediately after into a large court paved with little square tiles of different colours, after the manner of Fayence. Round it stood the guards armed with lances. When we had almost passed over the court they obliged us to stop short before a stone, which is near to an open hall where the king usually gives audience to ambassadors. There we saluted the king according to the custom of the country, falling upon our knees and thrice kissing the ground. That prince is nineteen years of age, black, but well shaped and of a majestic presence, not having thick lips nor flat nose like the most of the people. He was seated upon a rich bed under a canopy, with his legs across after the Oriental fashion ; and round him twenty old men seated after the same manner, but somewhat lower. He was clothed in a long vest embroidered with gold, and girt with a kind of scarf made of fine calico. He had a white turban on his head ; and the old men were clad much after the same manner. At the entrance of the hall, the prime minister standing complimented the king in our names, and delivered back his answer to us. Then we saluted the prince a second time, as we had done in the court, and we presented him with some crystals and other curiosities of Europe, which he graciously accepted. He ordered his guards to attend us to our lodgings, and afterwards sent us great vessels filled with butter, honey, and other refreshments ; and moreover two oxen and sheep.

"This prince dines twice a-week at one of his country-houses, which is at a league's distance from the town. The order he observes in his march is this: Between three and four hundred horsemen, mounted on fine horses, make the first appearance. After these comes the king attended by a great number of footmen and armed soldiers, who with a loud voice sing forth his praises, and play upon the tabor, which makes no unpleasant harmony. Seven or eight hundred young maids and women march together with these soldiers, and carry upon their heads great round baskets of straw, of different colours and finely made. These baskets, which represent all sorts of flowers, and the covers whereof are pyramidwise, are filled with copper dishes tinned over, and full of fruits and several meats ready dressed. These dishes are served first before the king, and are afterwards distributed among those who have the honour to attend upon him. Two or three hundred horsemen follow in the same order as those that went foremost, and close the whole march. The king, who never appears in public but with his face covered with a silk-gauze of various colours, sits down to table as soon as he is arrived. His usual diversion is to propose prizes to the lords of his court, and to shoot with them at a mark with a gun, at which they are not yet very expert. After they have spent the best part of the day in this exercise, they return in the evening to the town, observing the same order as at their setting out in the morning. This entertainment is regularly taken on Wednesday and Saturday every week."[*]

---

[*] Voyage to Ethiopia by M. Poncet, M.D. p. 20, &c.

In regard to the character of the people, their mode of living, dress, commerce, diseases, superstitions, and general habits, the details supplied by Poncet are not at variance with those given by Bruce more than seventy years afterwards. The merchants still retained a considerable share of the trade with Arabia, and even the western parts of India.

The latter does not mention the number of inhabitants in Sennaar at the time he paid his visit; simply remarking that it was very populous, and contained many good houses after the fashion of the country.* He adds that the dwellings of the great officers consisted of two stories; an improvement since the period of the French traveller, who found them generally restricted to one floor. But its present condition,—a mass of ruins interspersed with a few paltry huts,—indicates the melancholy events which have recently filled up its history, and deprived it at once of its wealth and power. It is not consistent, however, with our plan to enter more minutely into the annals of that declining state; we therefore proceed to the eastern bank of the Nile, with the view of exhibiting a brief outline of the provinces which constitute Abyssinia, the proper Ethiopia of early authors.

The kingdom which bears this name was, in the estimation of the writers who flourished in the middle ages, the region now called Abyssinia; a country concerning which, even at the present day, we have not much certain or authentic information. The accounts given by the Arabian geographers, Bakoi, Edrisi, and more particularly by Macrizi, show nothing so clearly as that the Mohammedans have

---

* Travels, vol. vi. p. 382.

had little intercourse with this Christian empire. The only knowledge which till lately was possessed by the learned of Europe was almost entirely derived from the Portuguese travellers, Alvarez, Bermudez, Paez, Almeida, and Lobo, whose works were abridged by Tellez, and illustrated with some ability by Ludolf, the Strabo of Eastern Africa. To these we may add the few notices furnished by Thevenot and Poncet. An important narrative by Petit-la-Croix, dated in 1700, partly drawn up from information furnished by Abyssinians whom the author had known in Egypt, exists in manuscript in the library at Leyden. The volumes of Bruce and Salt are well known to every reader; to which a species of supplement has very recently been provided by the publication of the Life and Adventures of Nathaniel Pearce.

Confined to such materials, the geographical outlines of that ancient kingdom have not been exhibited with unimpeachable precision. The limits which separate the Abyssinians from the Nubians, from the Galla on the south-west and south, and from the territory of Adel on the south-east, have hitherto depended on the uncertain issue of frequent appeals to arms. But if we include the coasts of the Red Sea, and the provinces occupied by the savages just named, we may assign to this empire a length of 560 miles and a breadth of 640; measuring from the 15th to the 7th degree of latitude, and from the 34th to the 44th degree of east longitude.

Although we are certain that the term Ethiopian is of Greek origin, and was applied to every people of a deep complexion, the Abyssinians nevertheless still call themselves Itiopawian, and their country

Itiopia. But they undoubtedly prefer the denomination of Agazi or Ghez for the kingdom, and Agazian for the inhabitants. The name of Habesh, given to them by the Mohammedans, and from which is derived the European appellation, is an Arabic word signifying a " mixed race," on which account the natives scornfully disclaim it.*

Regarded in a general point of view, Abyssinia forms an extensive table-land gently inclining to the north-west, and having two great steeps on the east and south; the first looking towards the Arabian Gulf, the second to the interior of Africa. It is doubtful whether these vast declivities consist of regular chains, or are only crowned with isolated mountains like Lamalmon and Amba Gedion, the configuration of which appears to be very extraordinary. They shoot up almost every where in sharp peaks, which are ascended by means of ropes and ladders, bearing no slight resemblance to the ramparts and turrets of deserted towns. Father Tellez imagines that the loftiest of these summits are higher than the Alps; but we find none of them capped with snow, except perhaps those of Samen in the province of Tigré, and of Namera in the district of Gojam.†

As to the political geography of Abyssinia, there prevails a great degree of doubt even among the writers of best reputation. Ludolf speaks of nine kingdoms and five provinces. Thevenot, from the information of an Ethiopian ambassador, says there are seven kingdoms and twenty-four provinces.

---

* Ludolf, Hist. Æthiop. lib. i. c. i.
† Lobo, Hist. B. 1. p. 141. Ludolf, lib. vi. Malte Brun, vo. iv. p. 125.

Bruce mentions nineteen provinces; and, lastly, Petit-la-Croix enumerates thirty-five kingdoms and ten provinces once belonging to the Abyssinian monarch, of which he retains only six kingdoms and a half, with the ten provinces. We cannot enter into such details as might seem necessary to explain these topographical distributions, or to trace the line which divides one section of the country from another. An inspection of the map, and a due attention to the itineraries which we shall have occasion to introduce, will afford much more valuable assistance to the comprehension of the reader, than the most laboured delineations of obscure and ever-changing boundaries.

When we cross the Blue River, about the twelfth degree of latitude, we find ourselves in the province or kingdom of Dembea, consisting of fertile plains surrounding the Lake Tzana, and containing Gondar, the modern capital. This city, according to the report of a native communicated to Sir William Jones, almost equals Cairo in extent and population. Bruce, however, reduces the number of inhabitants to about fifty thousand, if we may proceed on the usual principle of assigning five individuals to a family; a statement which we shall afterwards find does not fall short of the truth. The same province contains the town of Emfras, comprehending about three hundred houses.

To the south of Dembea the Nile winds round the kingdom of Gojam, which it thereby reduces to the form of a peninsula. This part of the river has a most magnificent cascade, the whole body of its water falling down from a height of forty feet, with tremendous force and noise, into a basin where it wheels round in numerous eddies. This province, although abounding in all sorts of productions, derives its principal riches from numerous herds of cattle.

Eastward of Gojam are seen the countries of Begemder and of the Edjow Galla. The former is remarkable for its fine flocks of sheep. Its inhabitants are very warlike, and send into the field a formidable contingent of horsemen.

Amhara, a little farther to the south, has always been esteemed one of the principal provinces of Abyssinia, and contains a numerous as well as brave race of men. Here is the famous state-prison of Amba Geshen, which is now succeeded by another in the district of Begemder. It seems to be composed of steep mountains, having a cavern, either natural or excavated by the hands of man, into which the prisoners are made to descend by means of a rope. Here the monarch causes to be kept under his own eye all those princes of his family from whom he thinks that he has any thing to apprehend; and it is often to this tomb of living beings that the grandees of the kingdom repair to select the ruler whom they are about to call to the throne.

Lasta is a mountainous country, inhabited by tribes who are pleased to pronounce themselves independent, and who possess a considerable source of wealth in their mines of iron. Shoa consists of a large valley very difficult of access, and which has given occasion to one of the most beautiful fictions in the English language, the romance of Rasselas. The province of Damot, situated beyond the Lake of Tzana, is celebrated for gold mines and cattle with monstrous horns. Lobo, who dwelt some time there, extols it as the most delightful country he had ever seen. The air is temperate and healthy, the mountains beautifully shaded with trees, without having the appearance of wild or irregular forests. Vegetation never falls asleep in that rich soil and happy climate. The operations of sowing and reaping are common to all the seasons of the year; and the whole scene has the aspect of a pleasure-garden, which never fails to reward with a most plentiful return the labour bestowed upon it.

We may remark in passing, that all the provinces now described, if we except Shoa, are usually at the present day comprehended under the grand division of the empire which takes the name of Amhara. This is the region, as we are told, which gives customs and manners to the modern Abyssinians; while the Amharic, being the dialect used at court, has obtained the distinction of the royal language, and is spoken through at least one-half of the kingdom. It appears to be compounded of the Ethiopic and a variety of terms derived from the tongues of Africa, influenced deeply by those modifications which are sooner or later extended to all unwritten forms of speech.

In recent times the most important section of the empire is that which embraces the province of Tigré, bounded, as Mr Salt informs us, on the north by the Bekla, Boja, Takué, and several wild tribes of Shangalla; on the west by the mountains of Samen; and by the Denakil, Doba, and Galla territories, on the east and south; including not less than four degrees of latitude, and nearly an equal extent in a longitudinal direction. The high range of the Samen hills, stretching from Waldubba to the south of Lasta, together with the line of the Tacazze, which flows in a north-easterly course along its base, sufficiently point out the natural boundary between Tigré and Amhara.

This large and very populous district contains a number of cities which make a considerable figure in the history of Ethiopia, more especially Axum, Dixan, Chelicut, and Antalo. The first of these was the ancient residence of the Abyssinian monarchs, who still go thither for the purpose of being crowned. It is true that the learned are not agreed respecting the antiquity of this place, which appears not to have been known either to Herodotus or Strabo, and is first mentioned by Arrian in the Periplus of the Erythræan sea. We shall have occasion in a future chapter to describe some of its architectural remains; meantime it will be sufficient to observe, that the modern town reckons about six hundred houses, but displays no remarkable buildings. On the eastern frontier stands Antalo, which during the visit of Mr Salt was the seat of government, being the residence of the viceroy Ras Welled Selassé. It consists of about a thousand hovels constructed of mud and straw, in the midst of which rises the palace, distinguished for magnitude rather than by the elegance of its plan or workmanship. In this province is the monastery of Fremona, which has always been the chief establishment of the Jesuits. It is about a mile in circumference, surrounded by walls flanked with towers and pierced for small arms. In Mr Bruce's eyes it had more the air of a castle than of a convent, and appeared to him to be the most defensible place that he had seen in Abyssinia. Generally speaking, Tigré is fertile and well peopled; but the inhabitants are described as a very ferocious, bloodthirsty, corrupt, and perfidious race.

On the western side of the provinces now described are Siré, Samen, Wogara which is sometimes called Wojjerat, Walkayt, and Waldubba. This last is occasionally extolled as one of the granaries of Abyssinia. The humid vales of Siré produce numerous palms and a variety of fruit-trees; enjoying, besides, all the beauty which arises from the vicinity of the Tacazze, whose banks are covered with the most luxuriant verdure. Nor is Samen, which when viewed from a distance appears only as a series of mountain-chains, in any degree destitute of agricultural wealth. On the contrary, the table-land of Amba Gedion, which has so steep an ascent as to render it almost inaccessible, is said to be sufficient both in extent and fertility to support many thousands. It was the fortress of the Abyssinian Jews, who were once masters of the province.

The more remote districts in the south are chiefly under the yoke of the ferocious Galla and other savage tribes hostile to the government of Gondar. To the eastward are the countries of Angote and Bali; and we are told of those of Gooderoo, Fatgar, of Efat, of Cambat, and particularly of the kingdom of Enarea, which, from Bruce's account, seems to be an elevated plain, watered by several rivers which have no visible outlet, and deriving from its lofty position the comfort of a temperate climate. The natives are said to trade with the people of Melinda on the Indian Ocean, and with the inhabitants of Angola on the Ethiopic. The hilly district of Kaffa, it is presumed, must be conterminous with Enarea on the south. But we have already alluded to the obscurity which still prevails respecting the interior of the empire, and more especially those regions on its distant boundaries towards the south and south-east.

The high grounds which divide Abyssinia from the coast of the Red Sea are known among geographers as constituting the country of the Troglodytes or cave-dwellers. The nature of the soil and climate has in all ages kept the inhabitants in a uniform state of savage wretchedness. Separated into tribes, and subject to hereditary chiefs, they lived formerly, and in many parts still continue to live, on the produce of their flocks, consisting principally of goats, aided by a little skill in the art of fishing. The hollows of the rocks are their ordinary dwellings; a kind of lodging which was anciently adopted in many other countries of the world. We find traces of such a usage at the foot of Caucasus and of Mount Atlas, in Mœsia, in Italy, also in France and Spain, and even in some parts of our native land. In Sicily there is an example of a whole town formed by excavation in the body of a hill. But of all the races who have dwelt in caverns, the Troglodytes of the Arabian Gulf have longest preserved the habits and the name.*

Mr Belzoni, who in his excursion to the Red Sea came near the countries now under consideration, met with a fisherman who was probably a fair specimen of that class of the inhabitants. He lived in a tent only five feet broad, with his wife, daughter, and son-in-law. He had no boat, but went forth

* Malte Brun, vol. iv. p. 145. Narrative of Discovery and Adventure in Africa, 2d edit., pp. 404, 405.

on his vocation seated on the trunk of a doomt-tree, and accompanied by the youth who made part of his family. This very simple raft was ten or twelve feet long, at each end of which was a piece of wood attached in a horizontal direction, so as to prevent the log from turning round. At one of the points a small pole was stuck upright to serve as a mast, on the top of which there was a slight spar secured horizontally like that below. A woollen shawl thrown over it, and fastened at each end as well as to the slip of wood, formed a kind of sail; while the two fishermen, mounted on the trunk as if on horseback, by means of a cord attached to their substitute for canvass, took more or less wind as was required. But, as the traveller remarks, " it is only when the wind blows either from north or south that such a contrivance can serve; for if it blows from the east they cannot set off their boat from the shore; or if it blows from the west it will carry them too far out to sea. When the fishermen are thus at some distance from the shore, I know not by what means the rest of the operation is executed; but from what I could see they darted their long thin spear at the fish when they happened to see any, and by these means they procured their subsistence."[*]

Beginning at the confines of Egypt and proceeding southward, the reader will observe that the coast makes a great concave sweep, forming what is called both by ancient and modern geographers Foul Bay. At the bottom of this gulf is the port of the Abyssinians, and behind is the country known by the name of Baza or Bedja. According to the Ara-

---

[*] Narrative of Operations, &c. vol. ii. p. 69.

bian authors it is a kingdom separated from Nubia by a chain of mountains, rich in gold, silver, and emeralds. The accounts supplied from antiquity, respecting the name and boundaries of this province, are very discordant. The term Baza, it is thought, may be found in that of the promontory called Bazium by the ancients, and now Ras el Comol. The inhabitants, who are denominated Bugeha by Leo Africanus, Boguites in the inscription at Axum, and Bedjah by the greater number of Arabian historians, lead a nomadic and savage life. They derive an abundant subsistence from the milk and flesh of their camels, cattle, and sheep. As every father exercises a patriarchal rule in his own family they have no other government. Full of loyalty to one another, and hospitable to strangers, they at the same time continually rob the neighbouring agriculturists and the trading caravans. Bruce asserts that they speak a dialect of the Abyssinian language; but Abdallah maintains that they belong to the race of Berbers or Barabras. M. Quatremère has endeavoured to demonstrate the identity of the Bedjahs with the Blemmyes of the ancients; though the descriptions of these writers apply perhaps with greater precision to the Ababdehs, the inhabitants of the desert which expands between the Nile and the Arabian Gulf.*

Suakin is chiefly entitled to notice as being one of the principal ports which now connect Abyssinia with the opposite coast; having in this respect superseded the more ancient harbour of Aedad, the Gidid of Portuguese authors. It is in fact a Turkish town, and is garrisoned by troops under the com-

---

* Quatremère, Hist. Géog. sur l'Egypte, ii. p. 135—139. Strab. Geograph. lib. xvii. c. 1.

mand of the governor of Mecca. Passing the promontory of Ras-Ahehas the traveller comes to a desert shore lined with islets and rocks. It was in this wild region that the Ptolemys procured the elephants which they required for the use of their armies; and here Lord Valentia found a large harbour, to which he gave the name of Port Mornington. About the sixteenth degree of latitude is the island of Dhalac, the largest in the Red Sea, being more than sixty miles in circumference. It produces goats with long silky hair, and furnishes a sort of gum-lac, which exudes from a particular shrub. The celebrity it once enjoyed for pearls has long since passed away; the specimens which are now procured being of a yellow colour and little esteemed.

In a gulf formed on the coast stands Masuah, which, though situated on an arid rock, possesses a safe harbour, and may now be regarded as the main approach to Abyssinia from the east. Near it is Arkeeko, which has also the advantage of a good anchorage, rendered however of small value by its exposure to the prevailing winds. This low, sandy, and burning coast is occupied by some nomadic tribes, the Shiho, who are very black, and the Hazorto, who have a copper-coloured complexion. These people, like the ancient Troglodytes, inhabit holes in the rocks, or hovels made of rushes and seaweed. Leading a pastoral life they change their dwelling as soon as the rains have produced a little verdure on their parched soil ; for, as is well known, when the wet season ends on the coast it begins among the mountains. They are said to have abjured their allegiance to the sultan, and acknowledged the supremacy of the native monarch.

The portion of the shore now delineated, used to

be called the Midre Baharnagash, or the Land of the Sea-king, whose government formerly extended from Suakin to the Straits of Bab el Mandeb. Baroa, its ancient capital, situated on the Mareb, was in Bruce's time in the hands of the Naib of Masuah; and it is still considered as the key of Abyssinia towards the gulf. Farther to the south the coast takes the name of Dancali, or, according to Niebuhr, Denakil, consisting of a desert plain, and supplying no valuable production except salt. Beyond the straits, terminating the Arabian Gulf, succeeds the kingdom or province of Adel, a country concerning which our information is so imperfect, that we presume not to tantalize the reader with an appearance of facts having no better foundation than ingenious conjecture. On the shores of the ocean are the Somaulies, a people who are supposed to possess the lands which in ancient times belonged to the Macrobian Ethiopians mentioned by Herodotus, and celebrated for an unusual length of life. Of these we shall have occasion to take some notice in the sequel; meantime we proceed to give a tabular view of the Abyssinian provinces, which will serve much better than the most minute description to illustrate the distribution, the extent, and the relative position, of the several parts of that great empire.

I. AMHARA.

1. Amhara Proper.
2. Dembea.
3. Damot.
4. Gojam.
5. Begemder.
6. Angote.
7. Walaka.
8. Marrabet.

II. TIGRE.

1. Tigré Proper.
2. Agamé.
3. Enderta.
4. Wojjerat or Wogara.
5. Wofila.
6. Lasta.
7. Avergalé.
8. Samen.
9. Temben.
10. Siré or Shiré.
11. Walkayt.
12. Waldubba.

III. MIDRE BAHARNAGASH, OR DISTRICT OF THE PRINCE OF THE SEA.

1. Masuah.
2. Arkeeko.
3. Weah.
4. Zullo.
5. Tubbo.
6. Amphila.
7. Madir.
8. Arena.
9. Duroro.
10. Jarvela.

IV. INDEPENDENT STATES IN THE SOUTH.

1. Shoa.
2. Efat.
3. Gooderoo.
4. Enarea.
5. Guragué.
6. Kaffa.
7. Cambat.
8. Hurrur.
9. Gidm.
10. Adel.
11. Bali.
12. Dawaro.

We do not think it expedient to encumber our pages with the more minute geographical distinctions, which are not only expressed in language extremely uncouth, but are moreover applied to districts whose limits are still undetermined. The curious reader will find numerous details in the works of Bruce, Salt, Lord Valentia, Niebuhr, and Malte Brun, darkened however by an unnecessary variation in the nomenclature, and sometimes, we are sorry to add, by the cloud of ignorance and of controversy.

CHAPTER III.

Civil History of Nubia and Abyssinia.

Variety of opinion in regard to Ethiopians—Aboriginal and mixed with Arabians—Queen of Sheba—Book of Axum—Abyssinians converted to Christianity—Extent of their Dominions—Wars in Arabia—Arrival of Portuguese—History of Nubia—Cambyses—Macrobians—Table of the Sun—Explanation by Heeren—Ptolemy Euergetes—War with Candace—Success of Petronius—Period of Darkness respecting Ethiopia—Prester John—Mission of Covilham—Of Matthew—Alvarez—Camp of the Abyssinian Monarch—Interview with David III.—Ordination of Clergy—Stephen de Gama—Bermudez the Abuna—Oviedo—Peter Paez—Jerome Lobo—Hatred towards Catholics—Poncet—Bruce—State of Abyssinia—Ras Michael—Ozoro Esther—Manuscripts collected by Bruce—History of Abyssinia—Revolt of Judith—Restoration of the Line of Solomon—List of Kings—Galla—War among Chiefs—Bruce goes to the sources of the Nile—Fasil—The Jumper—The Lamb—Kefla Yasous—Mr Salt—Outline of History—Pearce—His Adventures under Welled Selassé—Death of Ras—Demise of the King—Rise of Subegadis—Invasion of Nubia by Ishmael Pasha—Battles with Sheygyans—Act of Generosity—Cruelty of Egyptian Army—Character of Sheygyans—Expedition of Ibrahim—Death of Ishmael—Spirit of insurrection in conquered Provinces.

In regard to all ancient nations which had no immediate intercourse with the Hebrews, the Greeks, or the Romans, the historical notices are extremely obscure or altogether fabulous. On this account we remain in comparative ignorance of every thing which respects the origin of the two interesting countries whose annals we are now about to trace. Ethiopia, it is true, is repeatedly mentioned in the Sacred

Volume; but all the allusions to it are conveyed in language so general, that we are not supplied with a satisfactory light relative to the lineage of the people, their first form of government, their religion, or their laws. Hence there prevails among modern writers a great variety of opinion on all the heads now specified; and more particularly in reference to the extraction and language of the early colonists who occupied the country which stretches from the Red Sea to the Nile, and from Sennaar to the borders of Egypt. The remarks of Herodotus, the first European historian whose attention was drawn to Nubia, apply to a period which will be deemed comparatively recent, if the date be measured by the antiquity claimed for the surrounding nations, being confined to the enterprise of Cambyses, who, stimulated by the fame of certain golden mines, wished to carry his arms beyond the sources of the Bahr el Azrek.

It is not our intention to exhaust the patience of the reader on merely hypothetical views respecting the origin of the various tribes which now dwell on the banks of the Upper Nile and the western side of the Red Sea. The more probable opinion, as we have already suggested, is that they are descended from a race of aboriginal Africans, who in the course of time mixed with the primitive inhabitants, and among the Sabæans and Hamyrites, with whom they established an early connexion. This opinion is farther confirmed by the fact that, in the history of Arabia Felix, collected from several indigenous authors by Schultens, the Abyssinians are described as a different people from the natives of the eastern shore of the gulf. It is admitted, that in the intercourse carried on with the opposite coast vast numbers of Arabians must have mingled with the Axumites; but still it appears that in feature, colour, habit, and manners, they form a distinct order of men.*

The Abyssinians themselves, although perfectly ignorant of the time and circumstances which marked the settlement of their ancestors on the western shores of the Arabian Gulf, have insisted upon connecting their original faith, their civil polity, as well as the pedigree of their royal house, with the visit of the Queen of Sheba to King Solomon at Jerusalem. The events now alluded to are incorporated in a treatise called the Chronicle of the Kings of Abyssinia; the author of which says, "We write the law and custom of the government of Ibn Hakim (or Menilec), the son of Solomon. With him came the twelve doctors of the law that form the right-hand bench in judgment." He next mentions the other officers of eminence who came along with this prince; such as "the master of the horse, high chamberlain, and he who carried the Ten Commandments and holy water." This work, of which the authority does not stand high, is sometimes entitled Kebir Zaneguste,

---

* The learned editor of Bruce's Travels founded, on the radical distinction between the languages of Egypt and Arabia, an argument that the former country could not have been peopled from the latter; and, by the same process of reasoning, arrived at the conclusion that the Egyptians and Ethiopians were of the same lineage, and probably descended from a Libyan tribe quite unconnected with the Oriental Cushites. In the Appendix to the seventh volume, however, of the last edition of that work, Dr Murray inserted a "Chronological Table of the Kings of Abyssinia," in which he remarks, "that the Abyssinians, being undoubtedly a colony of Arabs from Hamyar or Yemen, can have no just pretensions to any affinity with the Jews." In maintaining the Arabic origin of the Abyssinians, Dr Murray contradicts the general current of tradition, and is hardly consistent with himself.—See *Appendix to volume* ii. *No.* 2. entitled, "Additional Proofs that Egypt was peopled from the South and the Confines of Ethiopia."

or Glory of the Kings. It is regarded indeed by the natives as a faithful repository of their ancient history; though the slightest attention to it will convince the reader that it is the production of an ignorant monk, who used the Septuagint translation of the Bible as the groundwork of a ridiculous fable, with the sole view of ministering to the vanity of his countrymen.*

The chronicle begins with a list of the emperors, from Arwe, or the Serpent, to Menilec, some of whom are said to have reigned several centuries. From this son of Solomon downwards the succession has an aspect somewhat more probable, though no dependence can be placed upon its accuracy.

	Y.	M.		Y.	M.
Menilec reigned	29	0	Haduna reigned	9	0
Za Hendadyn,	1	0	Za Wasih,	1	0
Awda,	11	0	Zah-Dir,	2	0
Za Awsyn,	3	0	Za Awzena,	1	0
Za Tsawe,	3	10	Za Berwas,	29	0
Zagesyn,	half a day		Za Mahazi,	1	0
Za Maute,	8	4	Zabaesi Bazen,	16	0
Za Bahse,	9	0	And in the 8th year of his reign Christ was born.		
Kawude,	2	0			
Kanazi,	10	0			

In a subsequent part of this catalogue is found Zahekale; which is without doubt the name of the sovereign who reigned in Abyssinia at the time when the Periplus of the Erythræan Sea was written. The author of that work, adopting the slight modification required by the Greek language, calls him Zoskales; and, according to the native document just quoted, he is represented as having ruled between the years 76 and 99 of the Christian era. It is, as Mr Salt remarks, an extraordinary circumstance that this date should agree very nearly with

---

* Bruce's Travels, vol. iii. p. 1.

the period to which Dr Vincent has attributed the appearance of the celebrated treatise by Arrian, namely to the tenth year of Nero, or A. D. 64, making a difference of not more than twelve years, —a singular coincidence, which necessarily adds a very important confirmation to both accounts.*

In the same list, extracted from the Chronicle, are the names of the princes who swayed the sceptre when the Axumites were converted to the Christian religion. From the narrative of Rufinus and other ecclesiastical writers, it is manifest that the person named Frumentius was the Abba Salama, or Fremonatos, as he is elsewhere denominated, who, after having resided some time in Abyssinia, was raised to the rank of a bishop by Athanasius, the patriarch of Alexandria. It subsequently appears, that during the following reign, when the Arians gained the ascendancy, the Emperor Constantius sent an embassy through Theophilus an Indian, with a letter addressed to the ruling sovereigns Aizana and Saizana, for the purpose of persuading Frumentius to relinquish the doctrines of his patron, and to adopt those of his successor Georgius. That such monarchs governed Abyssinia is clearly proved by the inscription which Mr Salt discovered at Axum; and though there may be some slight chronological difficulties to overcome, there is little doubt that the names of the two princes who swayed the joint sceptre in the year 356,—the date of the imperial mandate,—have been satisfactorily ascertained.†

At this period, the middle of the fourth century, the power of the Abyssinian kings seems to have been fully established, and their conquests to have ex-

---

* Salt's Abyssinia, p. 463. † Ibid., 464.

tended over part of Arabia, and from Zeyla up to the junction of the Tacazze with the Nile. Such at least are the limits of the jurisdiction implied in one of the Adulitic inscriptions, published by the author whose name we have just recited, and which is understood to commemorate the transactions of a native sovereign, and in all probability the same prince who erected the monument at Axum.

About two hundred years elapse before the Abyssinians, or Axumites as they were then denominated, assume again a prominent place in the page of history. But at the termination of this interval, owing to the complete command which they had already gained in the Red Sea, they began to take the lead in the politics of Eastern Africa. Hence they are frequently mentioned both in the Greek and Arabian authors; whose accounts in general are extremely consistent; though, from the variation in names and other sources of obscurity, no small trouble has been experienced in reconciling them to each other.

In the sixth century the arms of Abyssinia appear to have been attended with considerable success against the Persians in Arabia, who about this period laid claim to a large portion of that peninsula. But it is admitted that the conquest of Yemen was not attended with advantages equivalent to the hazard and glory of the war by which it had been gained; for the troops sent over became so enamoured of the country that they permanently settled there, and soon lost every tie, except a nominal allegiance, which had bound them to the parent state. In the year 592, as nearly as can be calculated from the dates given by the native writers, the Persians, whose power seems to have kept pace with the decline of the Roman empire, sent a great force against the Abyssinians, possessed themselves once more of Arabia, acquired a naval superiority in the Gulf, and secured the principal ports on either side of it.

It is uncertain how long those conquerors retained their acquisition; but, in all probability, their ascendancy again gave way to the rising greatness of the Mohammedan power; which soon afterwards overwhelmed all the nations contiguous to Arabia, spread to the remotest parts of the East, and even penetrated the African deserts from Egypt to the Congo. Meanwhile Abyssinia, though within two hundred miles of the walls of Mecca, remained unconquered and true to the Christian faith; presenting a mortifying and galling object to the more zealous followers of the Prophet. On this account implacable and incessant wars ravaged her territories, as the native princes on the eastern borders were supplied with money and arms by the Sheriffes, whose attention never ceased to be directed to the conquest of that country. She lost her commerce, saw her consequence annihilated, her capital threatened, and the richest of her provinces laid waste; but her constancy to the true religion remained unshaken, and her belief afforded throughout the protracted struggle the most vigorous motives to her patriotism. Yet there is reason to apprehend that she must shortly have sunk under the pressure of repeated invasions, had not the Portuguese arrived at a seasonable moment to aid her endeavours against the Moslem chiefs.

The event now mentioned took place about the middle of the sixteenth century, when Claudius sat on the throne, who, as well as his father David, to whom he had just succeeded, had been for some years engaged in a defensive war against Mohammed Gragné, king of Adel, one of the most bloodthirsty barbarians whose names history has recorded. The appearance of European troops, as might be expected, soon changed the aspect of affairs; and after many desperate battles, in which the Portuguese were chiefly engaged under their brave commander Diego de Gama, the Moors were driven back, their leader killed, and their armies nearly destroyed. The fleet, meantime, riding triumphant in the Red Sea, cut off from the invaders all hope of succour, and prevented the approach of those reinforcements which would have been sent by the Arabian governors.

But, before we enter into any details relative to the intercourse of Abyssinia with the nations of the West, we must return for a short space to the consideration of certain notices contained in the works of Greek and Roman writers, respecting the more ancient condition of the country on the Upper Nile.

We have already alluded to the expedition undertaken by Cambyses, the Persian monarch and conqueror of Egypt, against the Macrobian Ethiopians, whose country was said to possess vast quantities of gold. With this view he selected an embassy from among the Ichthyophagi, or fish-eaters of Elephantiné, who understood their language, and sent them to the sovereign of the distant nation with presents, consisting of a purple robe, a golden necklace, bracelets, perfumes, and a cask of palm-wine. The Macrobian monarch soon discovered that these ambassadors were spies. He looked at the gifts of which they were the bearers, and immediately returned the robe, the perfumes, the bracelets, and the necklace, taking these last for a species of fetter. The wine, which he found very agreeable, he was pleased to retain. He asked how long the Persians lived, and what their king was accustomed to eat. They informed him that he subsisted chiefly on bread, describing at the same time the nature of corn; and added, that the greatest age to which his subjects attained was eighty years. He answered, that he was not surprised at their living no longer, considering the rubbish on which they fed; and that probably they would not live even so long were it not for their good drink, in which he allowed they certainly excelled the Macrobians. Upon being asked in his turn to what age his people arrived and upon what they subsisted, he replied a hundred years and sometimes longer, and that their food was boiled flesh and milk. He sent to Cambyses, as an acknowledgment of his gift, a great bow, and told the ambassadors to inform their master, that when he could bend it as easily as one of his own country he might undertake an expedition against the Macrobians.

When the spies expressed astonishment at the length of life in Ethiopia, they were conducted, says Herodotus, to a certain fountain, in which having bathed they became shining as if anointed with oil, and emitted from their bodies the perfume of violets. But they asserted that the water was of so unsubstantial a nature, that neither wood nor any thing still lighter than wood would float on its surface, but every thing instantly sank to the bottom. If their representation in this respect was true, the constant use of it, concludes the historian, may probably explain the extreme length of life which the Ethiopians attain.*

There was shown to the envoys, as one of the most remarkable things in that strange land, what was called the Table of the Sun. This was a meadow in the skirts of the city, in which much boiled flesh was laid; placed there by the magistrates every night, and free to all who might choose to eat it during the following day. The inhabitants, whose inquiries were not allowed to be very profound, were taught to say that the earth brought it forth. The ambassadors were next led to the prison, where the captives were bound in golden fetters; brass among the Ethiopians being one of the greatest rarities. Finally, they were conducted to see the sepulchres or tombs, which are represented as being made of glass in the following manner: The corpse, after being prepared as in Egypt, is covered over with plaster, upon which is painted the portrait of the deceased as like as possible. It is then placed in a case of glass or native crystal, which they dig up in great abundance. The dead body remains in this frame, without any disgusting appearance or smell, a whole year; the nearest relation keeping it in his house and offering it sacrifices; after which it is taken into the city and deposited with the others.

After executing their commission the envoys re-

---

* Thalia, chap. 23. "Cada Mosto, who made a voyage to Senegal in the year 1455, affirms that the natives made use of a certain oil in the preparation of their food, which possessed a threefold property; that of smelling like violets, tasting like oil of olives, and of tinging the victuals with a colour more beautiful than saffron."— *Beloe's Herodotus.*

It is not improbable that the fountain of the Macrobians was supplied with an essence similar to the one now described, extracted from the pulp or kernels of certain fruits.

turned; and Cambyses, we are told by the Greek historian, was so incensed at their recital, that he determined to proceed instantly against the Ethiopians, without even providing for the necessary sustenance of his army, or reflecting that he was about to visit the utmost boundaries of the earth. The moment that he heard the report of the Ichthyophagi, like one deprived of all the powers of reason, he commenced his march with the whole body of his infantry, leaving no forces behind but such Greeks as had accompanied him to Egypt. On his arrival at Thebes he selected from his host about fifty thousand men, whom he ordered to make an incursion against the Ammonians, and to burn the place from which the oracles of Jupiter were delivered; he himself with the remainder of his troops marched against the Macrobians. Before he had performed a fifth part of his intended expedition, the provisions which he had carried with him were totally consumed. The soldiers proceeded to eat the beasts which carried the baggage; but these also soon failed. If, observes Herodotus, after these incidents Cambyses had permitted his passions to cool, and had led his army back again, he might, notwithstanding his indiscretion, still have deserved praise. But instead of this his infatuation continued, and he persevered in his march. His men, as long as the earth afforded them any sustenance, were content to feed on roots and plants; but no sooner had they arrived among the sands of the desert, than some of them were prompted by famine to proceed to the most horrid extremities. They drew lots, and every tenth man was destined to satisfy the hunger of the rest. When the king received intelligence of this fact, he became alarmed at the idea of his troops devouring one another, and resolved to abandon his design. After losing a great part of his army, he arrived in due time at Thebes, from whence he proceeded to Memphis, where he permitted the Greeks to embark for their own country.*

It is generally agreed that the Macrobians, or long-lived Ethiopians, occupied the country which stretches eastward from the Straits of Bab el Mandeb along the African coast. The following extract from Cosmas, usually called Indicopleustes, relates, it is probable, to the same people, and perhaps affords an explanation of the least credible part of the narrative given by the spies of Cambyses,—their notice in regard to the Altar or Table of the Sun: " The land of frankincense," says he, " lies at the farthest end of Ethiopia, fifty days' journey from Axum, at no great distance from the ocean, though it does not touch it. The inhabitants of the neighbouring Barbaria, or the country of Sasu, fetch from thence frankincense and other costly spices, which they transport by water to Arabia Felix and India. This country of Sasu is very rich in gold mines. Every year the King of Axum sends some of his people to this place for gold. These are joined by many other merchants, so that altogether they form a caravan of about five hundred persons. They carry with them oxen, salt, and iron. When they arrive upon the frontiers of the country they take up their quarters, and make a large barrier of thorns. In the mean time, having slain and cut up their oxen, they lay the pieces of flesh, as well as the

---

* Herodotus, Thalia, chap. 25.

iron and salt, upon the thorns. Then come the inhabitants, and place one or more parcels of gold upon the wares, and wait outside the enclosure. The owners of the flesh and other goods then examine whether this be equal to the price or not. If so, they take the gold, and the others take the wares; if not, the latter still add more gold, or take back what they had already put down. The trade is carried on in this manner because the languages are different, and they have no interpreter: it takes about five days to dispose of the goods which they bring with them."*

From this statement M. Heeren concludes, with much show of reason, that the Altar of the Sun is the market-place in which the trade with the strangers is transacted. When we consider that even now almost all the commerce of Africa is carried on under the protection of sanctuaries and temples, we can scarcely wonder that religious notions should be connected with this mercantile establishment, upon which perhaps the subsistence of the inhabitants depended.

This kind of dumb trade will not appear strange to those who are acquainted with the usages of barbarous nations in other parts of Africa, where the practice is still continued. When it is said that the chiefs of the people laid the flesh down at night, and that in the day any one who chose might eat of it, while the inhabitants at large reported that it sprang from the earth, we are only to infer, that this important trade was conducted under the inspection of the public magistrates; that every one took what he thought proper on leaving an equivalent; and that

---

* Cosmas, pp. 138, 139. This author wrote about the year 535.

as the merchants who supplied it came from a distant land, and were not themselves seen in the transaction, a vulgar error, like the one mentioned, might very naturally arise. By the boiled flesh noticed by Herodotus must probably be understood dried flesh, as this is the usual way it is preserved in those regions, where, as Mr Bruce informs us, it is still considered a great dainty.*

The views now stated derive a strong confirmation from the fact, that a trade in similar commodities continues to be carried on at the present day. Lord Valentia, who crossed over from Mocha, has given us some interesting information on this head upon which we may rely, and which besides has the merit of being as new and accurate as it is authentic. "The coast from Bab el Mandeb to Guardafui is inhabited by the Somaulies, a very dark race with woolly hair, neither completely negroes nor Arabians. They are not savages, as Bruce has depicted them, but a friendly well-disposed people. Their country is the natural staple for the commerce between Africa and Arabia, and in it the greatest marts are found. Gums, myrrh and frankincense, cattle and slaves, are the commodities exported; in exchange for which, as well as for gold and ivory, they receive the productions of the East, including those from the remoter parts of India."†

After the attempt of Cambyses on the Upper Nile, some centuries elapsed before the ambition or covetousness of Europeans again carried their arms beyond the first cataract. There remains, indeed, some evidence that Ptolemy Euergetes, one of the

---

* Heeren's Historical Researches, vol. i. p. 333.
† Valentia's Travels, vol. ii. p. 370.

successors of Alexander, made an attempt to add Ethiopia to his Egyptian dominions; but as he appears to have advanced by the way of the Red Sea, and to have aided his troops by means of a naval armament, his invasion was not attended with any such results as to secure a place among the monuments of history. It was not till the reign of Augustus, about twenty years before the beginning of the Christian era, that the Romans, who had already rendered themselves masters of the kingdom of the Pharaohs, came into collision with the independent states which still flourished near the ancient Meroë.

Strabo and the historian Dio agree in tracing the origin of the war with Candace, queen of the Ethiopians, to the effort made by Ælius Gallus, who appears to have commanded in Upper Egypt, to subdue Arabia. This expedition is at the same time remarkable for being the only one which that warlike people ever attempted against the inhabitants of the Desert. The burning sands and pestilential winds of the Arabian plains taught the subjects of Cæsar, that courage, even when seconded by the most perfect discipline, cannot overcome the obstacles opposed by the laws of nature.*

---

* The conquest of Arabia, indeed, seems to have been viewed as one of those events which, if realized, would celebrate the good fortune rather than the wisdom of him who accomplished it. Horace, in allusion to the fatal enterprise of Gallus, indulges in pleasantry at the expense of his friend Iccius, who appears to have been seized with a military rage.

" Icci, beatis nunc Arabum invides
Gazas, et acrem militiam paras
Non ante devictis Sabææ
Regibus."—*Ode* xxix. lib. i.

Iccius, the blest Arabia's gold
Can you with envious eye behold;
Or will you boldly take the field,
And teach Sabæa's kings to yield?

As the neighbouring provinces of the Thebaïd were left destitute of troops, the soldiers of Candace, after forcing the garrisons of Philæ, Syené, and Elephantiné, committed great ravages on the low country, demolished the emperor's statues whereever they appeared, and finally collected a very considerable booty. Petronius, who was at that time Prefect of Egypt, feeling that it was inconsistent with the dignity of the Roman name to allow this insult to remain unpunished, hastily assembled about ten thousand men, and proceeded against the Ethiopians.

The invaders were not qualified to resist in the open field an attack by the legions; for their armour consisted chiefly of a huge buckler of raw hide, hatchets, and spears headed with iron. Only a few could boast of swords, a weapon to which they were not accustomed. The issue of a battle in such circumstances could not remain long doubtful, however unequal the numbers opposed. The warriors of Candace accordingly, after a brief conflict, fled, and were pursued by Petronius into the farthest recesses of their difficult country. The queen, unable to defend her capital, had retired to a stronghold, whence she sent messengers to make proposals for peace; but the Roman general would not listen to conditions until he had reduced and plundered the royal city Napata, the true position of which it is now not easy to determine.

His success, however, did not secure to him the advantages of a permanent conquest. Finding himself about 900 miles above Syené, and being assured that if he advanced he should have to encounter all the horrors of a sandy desert, without provisions or water, he resolved to return; leaving in Primmis, a town situated on the Nile below the great cataract, a garrison of four hundred men, with supplies for two years. Candace made an attempt to surprise this fort and expel the Roman soldiers; but the vigilance of Petronius was not to be deceived in a matter of such importance. Still he could not fail to perceive that no object worthy of the expense and exertions which must be incurred would be obtained by the prosecution of the war. He was therefore the more easily induced to enter into a negotiation with the queen, who, finding that she was unequal to her enemies in the field, had renewed her solicitations for peace. It is related, that when she was told she must send ambassadors to Cæsar, she asked who he was, and where he lived. Guides were supplied to conduct her envoys to Augustus, who happened to be at Samos. He received them favourably; and not only acceded to the request of their mistress, but relieved her from the tribute which Petronius had thought proper to impose.

We have already remarked that the situation of Napata cannot be satisfactorily determined; and we may now add, that the obscurity which prevails in regard to this point arises from the indistinct statements left by the ancient geographers. Pliny, with a view to describe the expedition of Petronius, mentions a variety of towns which he reduced on his march; and adds, that the greatest distance to which he attained was eight hundred and seventy miles southward from Syené. But he likewise gives the substance of a report made by certain spies, or *exploratores*, sent by Nero to ascertain the distance from the borders of Egypt to Meroë; and agreeably to this authority he places Napata five hundred and twenty-four miles above Es Souan. If, indeed, we suppose that the longer measurement refers to the course of the river or the route pursued by the army, and that the shorter denotes the distance in a straight line, the result will nearly coincide with the estimated space between Philæ and Merawe, or even the position of the modern Shendy. Hence Napata may be placed either in the kingdom of Dongola near the Gebel el Berkal, where there are the remains of magnificent buildings, or beyond the Tacazze, on the site of the renowned Meroë.

As the historians have simply recorded that the Primmis or Premnis, where the Roman prefect established his garrison, was below the great cataract, geographers, misled by this ambiguous description, have given the name in question both to the town of Old Dongola and to Ibrîm. The allusion, it is obvious, will apply to either; for while the one is only a little removed from the Falls of Wady Halfa, the other is at no great distance from similar rapids, usually designated the third cataract. Perhaps, in the modern Ibrîm, we may allow ourselves to discover a contraction of the more ancient appellation Primmis; for if the Latin termination be removed, and one labial consonant substituted for another, we obtain a very similar sound. It is therefore probable, that the fortress which Petronius selected for the soldiers whom he deemed it expedient to leave in Nubia as a check on the Ethiopian queen, was that situated on the strong rock which overhangs the Nile in the province of Wady Seboua.

The name of the female sovereign to whom reference has just been made, will naturally associate itself in the mind with the narrative contained in the eighth chapter of the Acts, where we read of " a man of Ethiopia, an eunuch of great authority under Candace queen of the Ethiopians, who had the charge of all her treasure, and had come to Jerusalem for to worship." As more than fifty years elapsed between the expedition of Petronius and the mission of Philip the Deacon into the Desert of Gaza, it is not probable that the ruler mentioned in the sacred narrative is the same individual who had to solicit peace from Augustus Cæsar. It is more likely that the appellation was hereditary in the royal house, and was conferred on the reigning monarch in the manner observed by the Pharaohs, the Greek princes in Egypt, and the Roman emperors. There is indeed a tradition, that the people of the Upper Nile were long governed by queens; and the practice, still followed in some parts of Dongola, of placing a young woman at the head of their armies, may have originated in that usage.

From the facts brought to light by the invasion of Petronius it is manifest, that about the commencement of the Christian era there was in Ethiopia an independent kingdom apparently unconnected with Abyssinia. The dominions of Candace appear to have extended over the valleys watered by the river, and perhaps over part of the neighbouring deserts with which these fertile plains are encompassed. There is no allusion made by Strabo or Dio to the territories which stretch towards the Red Sea; and it is remarkable that, among the various catalogues of sovereigns obtained by Bruce and Mr Salt during their residence in the former country, the name of this celebrated queen has not been found.

The subsequent history of this particular section of Ethiopia is shrouded in utter darkness. We know not when the successors of Candace ceased to enjoy power, or by what series of events their throne was cast down; whether by the regular assault of Abyssinian armies led by an ambitious prince, or by the inroads of the savage tribes who occupied the mountains of the south and the wilds of the Libyan Desert. More than a thousand years passed away, during which no European acquired any knowledge of Nubia, or set a foot within its borders: on which account we can only conjecture that the zeal of the Moslem, soon after the triumph of their khalifs over Egypt, might induce them to carry their conquests along the banks of the Nile; or that the Galla and those other barbarous hordes, who have so often alarmed the emperor at Gondar, may have extinguished the lights of civilisation which once illumined the remote regions of Meroë.

A similar obscurity prevails for seven or eight centuries in regard to Abyssinia, which is only occasionally brightened by the uncertain information afforded by the ecclesiastical writers, who laboured to connect its affairs with those of the patriarchate of Alexandria. It is not till the epoch when the Portuguese, attracted at once by their zeal for religion and their love of gold, penetrated into Eastern Africa, that our inquiries respecting its history and condition begin to be rewarded with any degree of success. In relating the progress of discovery made by this people along the western coast, we had occasion to observe,* that, among the splendid objects by which their exertions were animated, by far the

---

* Narrative of Discovery and Adventure in Africa, 2d edit. p. 67.

most prominent was that of reaching the territory of the prince whom they denominated Prester John.* Vain were all the inquiries made on that shore for this mysterious monarch; but intelligence was received of a Christian prince ruling over Abyssinia, whom at length they thought they might conclude to be the royal priest. As soon, too, as the Portuguese sovereign had conceived the idea of penetrating, by a voyage round the Cape, into the Indian Seas, a knowledge of the neighbouring kingdoms became very important. To meet this double object, Covilham and De Payva were, in 1487, despatched, the one to enter Abyssinia, the other to penetrate to the shores of India. The former died in the vicinity of the Red Sea; but the latter was fortunate enough to reach Calicut and Goa on the coast of Malabar; whence he crossed to Sofala in Eastern Africa, and even obtained some information respecting the southern boundary of that continent. Having made the circuit of the Indian Ocean, he

---

* " Rex Habessinorum vix alio quam *Presbyteri Johannis* titulo notus hucusque fuit Europæis, quem illi Lusitani imposuere. Occasio fuit talis. *Petrus* Petri filius Lusitaniæ princeps, *M. Pauli Veneti* librum (qui de Indorum rebus multa, speciatim vero de Presbytero Johanne aliqua magnifice scripsit), Venetiis secum in patriam detulerat; qui (Chronologicis Lusitanorum testantibus), præcipuam *Johanni* Regi ansam dedit Indicæ navigationis, quam Henricus Johannis I. filius, patruus ejus, tentaverat, prosequendæ.

" Cæterum inter præstantissimos historicorum constat, regem quendam Christianum olim in extremâ Asiâ, haud procul regno *Tenduc*, Catayam versus, regnasse, magna potentia et fama, qui a Persis vicinioribus, ad significanda illius sacra, *Prester Chan*, h. e. *Chanus* seu *Princeps adoratorum*, i. e. Christianorum, ut quidam putant; vel, ut Scaliger vult, *Fristeyeani*, i. e. *Apostolicus*, dictus fuit. Utcunque demum id nominis pronunciaveris, ab Italis, tunc temporis commercia Orientis tractantibus, auditum, et per Europam vulgatum, imperitum vulgus pro Italico *Preste* vel *Prete* Gianni sive Giovanni accepit; et sic Presbyteri Johannis nomen apud omnes Europæ populos inolevit."—*Ludolphi Hist. Æthiop.* lib. ii. c. 1.

was enabled, on his return to the Arabian Gulf, to transmit the most flattering accounts as to the practicability and advantage of the projected voyage. Both in going out and returning, he collected many particulars as to the empire of Abyssinia, and determined to crown his discoveries by visiting the court of that interesting monarchy. Iscander or Alexander, then the reigning king, received him in the most cordial manner, and conducted him to the royal residence at Shoa. Treated with the highest honours, he was either persuaded or compelled to take up his residence in the country, whence he never returned to Europe.

About 1510, Helena, then queen of Abyssinia, anxious to obtain the alliance of Portugal against the Turks, sent Matthew, an Armenian merchant, ambassador to Lisbon. He went by the circuitous route of India, where his dignity not being at first recognised, he was somewhat roughly treated, and detained several years. When at last, in 1513, he reached Lisbon, the court received him with all that delight which might be expected on seeing realized the flattering vision of Prester John, which had so long glittered before their eyes. After the most favourable reception, he was sent back with a fleet, which, in 1515, proceeded to India under Lope Soarez, who was appointed to succeed Albuquerque. There went out also as ambassador to Prester John, Duarte Galvam, a statesman of capacity and experience, but already arrived at the advanced age of eighty-six. The governor, soon after his arrival in India, sailed for the Red Sea; but the other, whose years indeed rendered him very unfit for such an expedition, sunk under the climate, and died at the island of Camaran. The ships, meanwhile, met with so many disasters, that they never reached the port of Masuah. Soarez quitted the gulf, and the enterprise was not resumed till he was succeeded by a more able commander, named Lope Sequeira. This officer sailed from Goa on the 13th February 1520, and arrived at Masuah on the 24th April. At the neighbouring port of Arkeeko he had an interview with the Baharnagash, who, as vassal to the monarch of Abyssinia, held sway over a wide extent of maritime territory. He gave the Portuguese a cordial welcome, and undertook to convey to court both Matthew and a European embassy. At the head of this mission Sequeira placed Rodrigo de Lima, with eight or ten subordinate members, among whom was a friar, Francisco Alvarez, who afterwards wrote a narrative of the expedition.

The embassy left Arkeeko on the 30th April, and on the 4th May arrived at the monastery of St Michael, which was dependent on a more extensive establishment called Bisan, or that of the Vision. Here they were attacked by an epidemic malady, which proved fatal to the merchant and to one of his countrymen. To escape its malignant influence they hastened forward, first to Bisan and then to Dobarwa, the residence of the Baharnagash, to which he had now returned. On this occasion he received them rather coldly, and not without reluctance afforded them the means of proceeding. The passage, too, of the high and rugged mountains of Tigré was found rather formidable. Violent storms of wind and rain often compelled them to seek shelter under the rocks; while the fury of the torrents and the roaring of the gale through the immense woods could not be heard without alarm. Numerous wild animals stalked around, showing no fear at the presence of man; apes were sometimes seen in bands of several hundreds. On descending into the plain, they found it desolated by the more dreadful scourge of locusts. When the inhabitants saw the air darkened by those destructive insects, they became, it is said, "as dead men," crying out, "We are undone, for the locusts come!" Great numbers of both sexes were observed flying to other districts in search of food, their own lands having been entirely consumed by this dreadful visitation.

Amidst these difficulties and annoyances, the mission slowly reached the southern province of Angote, which they found a delightful region, watered by numerous streams, and having seedtime and harvest continued throughout the year. The viceroy invited them to a feast, where they found neither chair, tablecloth, nor towel. Mats were spread on the floor, and a wooden board was covered with round cakes; over which was placed the delicate dish, which Alvarez scarcely dares to mention, —" pieces of raw flesh, with warm blood,"—which the governor and his ladies devoured with delight. But the Portuguese could not allow these dainties to enter their lips. The wine also, or rather hydromel, " walked about with great fury;" the mistress of the house, though concealed behind a curtain, taking an ample share.

In proceeding to the court or camp of the Abyssinian monarch, Alvarez saw the lofty hill on which, by a singular and jealous policy, the princes of the blood-royal are constantly confined. It was of great extent, begirt by a circuit of lofty and perpendicular cliffs appearing to reach almost to the sky. On its summit was a large plain, whence other hills arose interspersed with valleys, of which the most beautiful was chosen as the retreat of the august prisoners. The strangers having approached too near it, were advertised of their error by a sudden shower of stones.

After passing through the provinces of Amhara and Shoa, the embassy, on the 16th October, came in view of an almost endless range of tents and pavilions overspreading an immense plain. This was the grand array or regal camp of the King of Abyssinia, who, engaged in continual war, had at this time no other capital. They forthwith advanced between two rows of about 40,000 persons, among whom a hundred were constantly employed with whips in their hands to maintain order. On this occasion they saw only the *cabeata*, or chief priest and minister, who conveyed several courteous messages between them and the monarch, whom, however, they neither saw nor heard. But on the 20th they were again sent for, when they observed an elevated seat, which they call a bed, with rich curtains of silk and gold concealing the king from their view, but not preventing their holding some conversation with him. His first address was not altogether cordial; he even showed some jealousy of their motives in coming to Abyssinia; but he listened to their explanations, and at length showed on the whole a more friendly disposition.

Finally, on the 1st November, they were admitted to a more formal audience, when a series of curtains were raised, each richer than the other, till at last one, the richest of all, was lifted, behind which appeared Prester John seated, in a splendid dress of silk and gold, and holding in his hand a silver cross. This prince, who was David III., is described as a young man of about twenty-three, of low stature, and "of the colour of ruddy apples." The discourse soon turned upon the authority of the Pope and the communion of Rome, which the ambassador represented to be the only true church, and to which Abyssinia was bound to submit. The emperor resisted this claim, and seems to have maintained the theological argument with considerable acuteness. Respecting the marriage of priests, he quoted the decrees of councils, of which the envoy was obliged to confess his own ignorance. He asked also whether, supposing the Pope were to order any thing contrary to Scripture it would be obeyed; and the Portuguese not venturing an absolute negative, the king declared that his people had no idea of such a servile submission.

The ambassador afterwards accompanied the king, with the Abuna or ecclesiastical primate, to the great monastery of Machan Celacen, where he witnessed the high ceremonies of baptism and of the ordination of priests and clerks; but the practical details connected with these offices afforded much room for animadversion. The number of priests ordained was 2356; and the examination,—a very short and superficial one,—had no other object than to ascertain whether they were able to read. The qualifications of the clerks were necessarily still lower, as they were admitted of all classes and ages, a great proportion being mere infants. Among these ecclesiastical functionaries there was a continued crying, " as of so many young kids," on account of being kept so long from suck; and Alvarez was seriously alarmed at the administration of the host, lest these tender throats should have choked on the coarse dough of which it was formed. He assures his readers, that he remonstrated strongly with the Abuna on this premature elevation to the dignities of the church, as well as other practices, the irregularity of which was candidly admitted by that prelate.

The embassy, after remaining five years in Abyssinia, sailed from Masuah on the 28th April 1526, with presents and a letter to the King of Portugal. Thus the communication between the two courts was continued, and the reluctance which the emperor at first showed to embrace the Catholic religion was overcome in a surprising degree. In 1535, the place of Abuna, or head of the church, was conferred upon Bermudez, a Romish priest then resident in the country. This nomination was accompanied with a request which throws some light upon its motive. The country being hard pressed by the Moors of Adel, the government of Lisbon was urged to send a body of troops to defend it against those enemies of the faith. Bermudez himself repaired to Goa to hasten the sailing of the desired expedition. The ardour of the Portuguese youth for this species of crusade drew forth a much greater number of volunteers than were desired by the viceroy, who despatched only 450 under Don Stephen de Gama; and though that officer fell early, his followers, by their superior arms and discipline, rendered essential services. The Moors were defeated, and obliged to sue for peace; after which the Catholic zeal of the monarch remarkably cooled, to the infinite rage of the Abuna, who made remonstrances so violent, that open hostilities ensued between the two nations. The Portuguese, notwithstanding their small numbers, were able to maintain a defensive position, till at length the king, by a stratagem, got the chief priest into his power, and sent him into an honourable exile, as governor of Efat, an extensive province. It is described by him as consisting of a valley so deep, and enclosed by such high and craggy mountains, that the entrance appeared to resemble the descent into hell. After taking possession, however, he found it an agreeable and fertile district; the inhabitants even made cotton cloths, and practised other arts, better than the rest of the Abyssinians; yet they were pagans, " barbarous and evil." It contained gold, which abounded still more in the neighbouring countries; one of which paid in tribute two full-grown lions, three whelps, and several hens and chickens, all framed of this precious metal. Bermudez seems to have exercised his sway in a very tyrannical manner. He and his people amused themselves with firing muskets over the heads of the natives, enjoying their terror at the effect of these unknown weapons; and this, on some occasions, was done so recklessly, that several persons were killed. The king, incensed at these pastimes of the governor, confined him on the top of a high mountain; but, being rescued by the valour of his countrymen, a compromise was at length effected, in virtue of which he received lands, ample possessions, and a new title; however, he soon afterwards left the country.

The King of Portugal and the Pope were for some time discouraged by the unfavourable result of this mission. But a convert who came to Rome assured them, that the failure was entirely owing to the brutal conduct of Bermudez, and that a judicious agent might yet add Abyssinia to the domain of the Catholic church. Nugnez Barretto was accordingly invested with this office; but when, upon reaching the Red Sea, he learned that it was infested by Turkish ships his courage failed. Oviedo, however, the second in rank, with some priests of an inferior order, boldly pushed forward, and arrived in safety. On reaching the royal camp, he was received in the most friendly manner, and immediately admitted to an audience. But instead of tempering his zeal with any measure of discretion, he seems to have studiously overacted the part of Bermudez. Representing to the king the enormous errors into which he had fallen, the missionary called upon him immediately to bring his subjects into a state of spiritual allegiance to the Roman See. His majesty replied, that he was exceedingly well inclined to the Portuguese, and would grant them ample possessions, with liberty to convert the whole nation if they could; but that to compel the people to change their religion would create great discontent, particularly as they were at present quite satisfied with their Abuna. He promised, however, to consult his friends on the subject. Oviedo, though most indignant that a third party should be addressed on such an occasion, agreed to pause, and meantime challenged the Abyssinian doctors to a conference. This was readily accepted. Being supernaturally aided, as he conceived, he gained the most complete victory over his opponents; but unhappily they considered their own triumph as equally decisive, and hence affairs stood exactly as they were before. The Catholic, indignant at such blindness, and seeing no hope of effecting any thing by persuasion, determined to have recourse to the most violent measures. Assuming the full papal authority, he issued a rescript, devoting the whole nation to the judgment of the church, and even to be spoiled by the faithful in every possible manner, " in person and goods, in public and private." Such a decree, without any means of enforcing it, occasioned, of course, a violent persecution against the mission. Oviedo was banished to a remote and desolate mountain, where he nearly perished with famine. He transmitted the most earnest entreaties to the King of Portugal to despatch fifteen hundred men, with which he undertook to conquer all Abyssinia; but this proposal, though seriously pondered, was never reduced to practice.

The next missionary was Peter Paez, sent out in 1589,—a man of superior talents and address, who, instead of attempting to carry his objects by threats and violence, successfully applied himself to conciliate at once the sovereign and the nation. It is to be regretted that his narrative, which is supposed still to exist, and would probably supply the fullest account of the country yet written, has never been given to the public; only some detached extracts from it being found in the General History of Ethiopia by Tellez. He derides the pompous descriptions which former travellers had given of this empire, the palace of which, instead of containing, as had been pretended, spacious halls and superb domes, resembled more the humble cottage in which Æneas was received by Evander. The imperial table presented none of those conveniences which in Europe are by the humblest citizen considered indispensable; neither plate, nor knife, nor fork, nor spoon, nor chair to sit upon. Women entered bearing baskets of junk resembling broad-brimmed hats, whence they drew numerous cakes, with which they entirely covered the board. Above these they placed the chief delicacy, pieces of raw and warm flesh, which were wrapped in the cakes, in portions so enormous that it appeared quite impossible for any mouth to admit them. The attendants, however, forced these pellets between the jaws of their masters, and continued to stuff the guests, one after another, " as if they were stuffing a goose for a feast." All this while deep silence reigned, and eating engrossed the universal attention; but as soon as the table was cleared, the cups were introduced, and began to circulate with the utmost freedom.

As there was nothing in Abyssinia which could be called a house, Paez undertook to erect one for the monarch, such as in Europe might be considered a handsome villa. It was exceedingly difficult to instruct the native architects in the use of the hammer and chisel, in the operation of cutting, rounding, and hewing the stones, as well as in the various processes of carpentry; but when this had been in some degree effected, and the people saw high walls of hewn stone ascending, and one story rising above another, they considered it little less than a miracle. By these and other personal services, the priest so ingratiated himself at court, that he prevailed upon the king, not only to embrace the Catholic faith himself, but to make it the established religion of his dominions. This missionary, moreover, is generally supposed to have visited the sources of the Nile; his description of them, indeed, quoted by Kircher, closely corresponds with that afterwards given by Bruce.

The Romish religion continued to maintain its ground, and about the year 1620 was professed with ardour by the king, Socinios or Segued, who applied for a fresh supply of clergymen. In compliance with this request Jerome Lobo set sail from Goa in January 1624. The approach to Abyssinia was then very difficult, as the Turks were masters of the Red Sea; and an attempt to reach it from the mouth of the Arabian Gulf, by the southern country of Cambat, had been frustrated by the ruggedness of the territory and the barbarous character of the people. Lobo, much at a loss, sought to open up a new path by Melinda, which, however, could only have been suggested by deep ignorance of African geography. On landing at Paté, or Patta, he was warned of the dangers attending this route, which would soon bring him among the Galla, one of the most savage races in existence. His zeal however still urged him onwards, till he reached the kingdom of Jubo, the natives of which were barbarians indeed; eating raw flesh, adorning themselves with the entrails of cows, and killing such of their children as happened to be born on plundering excursions. He found the king in a tolerably large straw-hut, surrounded by courtiers bearing each a long staff, which, whenever the stranger entered, they employed in driving him back to the door. Lobo, who had attended by permission, having inquired the cause of such an ungracious salutation, was assured that it was the regular mode of reception at this court; and they swore on the head of a sheep besmeared with butter, that they would do him no injury. It was rather annoying to be attended by men whose kindness was thus expressed; and when the traveller heard that nine nations equally savage, and engaged in continual war, intervened between Jubo and Abyssinia, he thought it high time to seek an entrance by another channel. He therefore returned to Patta, whence he sailed, and, having passed the Straits of Bab el Mandeb, landed at Baylur in Dancali; the sovereign of which country, being dependent on Abyssinia, had been instructed to provide for his safety and comfort. Having waited on the monarch at his capital, which consisted of twenty mud-cabins and six tents, he was ushered into the palace, where one apartment sufficed for the prince and his horse. The good priest had no reason to complain of his reception, though extraordinary efforts were made to extort presents from him; but by using the name of the King of Abyssinia, he escaped all violent exaction. To reach his destination, however, it was necessary to pass extensive deserts, including the great plain whence salt is supplied to the whole empire; and here hunger, thirst, the bites of serpents, and the attacks of plunderers, created much suffering and alarm. At length he arrived at Fremona, the missionary head-quarters, and began to enter upon his functions; but he soon found that, though supported by royal authority, his doctrine was viewed by the great body of the people with the utmost aversion. On entering a village, he was surprised to hear all the inhabitants joining in one chorus of shrieks and lamentations; and on inquiring what dreadful calamity had befallen them, was informed that it was nothing but his own arrival, and that they were deploring the fate of such of their countrymen as they feared would be entrapped by his fatal tenets. Wherever he went he found a similar impression prevail; and on attempting to address them, and especially on presenting the host, which they believed to be strained from the juices of the animals held most odious in Abyssinia, they uniformly fled at full speed. It had also been imagined that the landing of missionaries coincided with the appearance of locusts; and in this instance that absurd prejudice was unfortunately strengthened. Lobo had the pain of witnessing the distress occasioned by that plague, and saw the monastery besieged by crowds of starving creatures who unjustly imputed to him their miseries.

He afterwards visited the southern province of Damot, which, as we have already stated, appeared in his eyes the most delightful country he ever beheld, shaded with noble trees, having seedtime and harvest at all seasons. He describes also the sources of the Nile, as if he had visited them; but whether he actually did so, or merely wrote from information communicated by others, has never been clearly ascertained.

For some years the Catholics, generally odious to the nation, were supported and protected by the ruling power. The king, however, having sunk into a state of dotage, the administration fell into the hands of his son, who himself had long entertained a secret antipathy to this body, and under whose sanction the great men found themselves at liberty to give vent to their long-cherished animosity.

They proceeded to the most violent extremities; and the missionaries learned that a plan was actually matured for delivering them all into the hands of the Turks. In their distress they sought refuge with a chief in Tigré, who had raised the standard of rebellion; but by this step they exposed themselves to the very calamity which they had hoped to escape. He sold them to the Pasha of Suakin, a furious Mussulman, who had repeatedly expressed the delight with which he would kill every one of them with his own hand. From this dreadful situation, however, they were rescued by a high ransom, and conveyed to Goa. The persecution continued till 1638, when all the monks remaining in the country were barbarously put to death, and the Roman religion finally rooted out of Abyssinia.

About twenty years after, Signor Baratti, an Italian gentleman, made his way into that country, where he found the enmity against the Catholic church still unabated. The native clergy had even drawn up a special creed to guard against its errors. They declared that the Virgin, the apostles, and martyrs, ought indeed to be reverenced, but not to be worshipped, or to have prayers addressed to them; that the Bishop of Rome has no authority over the church in general; that the cross is a mere badge of the Christian profession, having no virtue in itself; and that the marriage of priests to one wife is lawful. It would thus appear that they were much more rational in their doctrines than those who had made such efforts for their conversion.

In 1698 Poncet, whose name we have already mentioned, and who had practised as a physician at Cairo, received an invitation from the King of

Abyssinia, who stood in need of his medical skill. He followed a different route from any former traveller, taking his departure from Upper Egypt with the Sennaar caravan. During four days they passed through a desert of moving sand, where the gentlest breeze raised a cloud that darkened the air. They then reached the great oasis of Elwah, which they found a delightful spot, filled with palm-trees and gardens, and the fields covered with senna. They next proceeded across a branch of the Great African Desert, and he was the first who gave to Europeans an idea of its excessive dreariness. He describes it as destitute of every species of shrub or plant, and presenting only the dead bodies and scattered bones of men and camels. Even when he reached the Nile at Moscho, cultivation, which extended only a league in breadth, was sustained by artificial means, water being raised from the river in machines worked by oxen. Dongola appeared a poorly-built town, almost choked by the sand which blew in from the surrounding wastes. From Korti he crossed the desert of Bahiouda, less desolate than the former; whence, passing by Derri and Gerri, he arrived at Sennaar. Having spent three months in that city, as we have elsewhere observed, he proceeded on his journey eastward, crossing several ranges of mountains, amid vast forests of trees unknown in Europe. Abyssinia now possessed a capital called Gondar, instead of the moveable camp in which the kings formerly travelled from place to place. It was an extensive town, with 100 churches, yet consisting in fact of a vast cluster of cottages; and there being no shops, the goods were exposed in mats in a large open space. Poncet having succeeded in curing the emperor, was sent home by way of Tigré and Masuah, without meeting any of those perils which are usually encountered by unprotected adventurers.

A long period now elapsed, during which Abyssinia was almost forgotten, when it was brought again into notice, and more fully described than ever, by one of the most enterprising of modern travellers. This was James Bruce, a writer who has been much accused of exaggeration and even of inaccuracy in his statements; yet it seems now generally admitted that, with the exception of a few incidents somewhat highly coloured, his narrative is substantially correct.

Fortified with a firman from the Porte, and with a letter from the Sheriffe of Mecca, he landed on the 19th September 1769 at Masuah, where, notwithstanding all these securities, he narrowly escaped being robbed and murdered by the Naib of Arkeeko, a brutal and unprincipled chief. He sailed to Arkeeko, which he left on the 15th November, and proceeded over Taranta, a high mountain-range which separates the coast from the interior. This eminence was covered to the top with noble trees, often so close together as to resemble arbours; the chief species being the cedar and the kol-quall, the latter peculiar to that country. There were many beautiful birds without song; while others, destitute of beauty, had pleasing notes, but quite different from those of England. In the caves of these mountains, or in little conical wooden cabins, dwell the Hazorta and the Shiho, pastoral tribes, who possess numerous herds, especially of goats, which, according to the season, they drive to the top of the mountains or to the lower valleys. They hold at defiance the powers of the plain, but have themselves so little reputation for hospitality that their treatment of travellers gave rise to the Abyssinian proverb, " Beware of the men who drink two waters."

At the foot of Taranta, Bruce passed through Dixan, lately belonging to the Baharnagash, or Lord of the Sea, who, we have already observed, had been one of the most powerful princes in this part of Africa. His territory was now very much narrowed, and he was reduced to a complete dependence upon the governor of Tigré. Bruce found him in a village near Dixan, a good-humoured simple person, with a very beggarly train. A general poverty indeed pervaded this district, which the inhabitants sought to relieve by stealing.

The traveller came next to Adowa, which ranked as capital of Tigré, though it is only a large village. Near it was Fremona, the great convent at which the Portuguese missionaries had fixed their headquarters. After passing through the province of Siré, a wide and fertile plain bounded by the broad and luxuriantly-wooded course of the Tacazze, Mr Bruce entered Samen, a country containing the loftiest mountains in Abyssinia, which the companions of Alvarez represented as even far surpassing in height the Alps and the Pyrenees. He and Salt, however, have ascertained them to be much inferior, though the occasional appearance of snow on their summits indicates in this climate a very high elevation. Their forms are often peculiarly rugged and precipitous, being compared by Bruce, though with some exaggeration, to pyramids pitched on their apex. He was obliged to pass Lamalmon, a lofty ridge, which lay on his way to Gondar. He had a

Ozoro Esther.

difficult and rather dangerous clamber along a narrow rugged path on the edge of a precipice, but found on the top a broad plain well cultivated, where the cool air restored his vigour, which had suffered under the suffocating atmosphere of the lower valleys. He then descended, and at length descried, in the midst of a thick grove, Gondar, the capital of Abyssinia.

The most dreadful commotions agitated at that moment the interior of the country. He relates that Ras Michael, the governor of Tigré, had murdered Joas the king, and set up in his room Tecla Haimanout, a youth of fifteen, in whose name he exercised the real sovereignty. Michael had married

Ozoro Esther, daughter to the queen-dowager, whose beauty and rank made her the most distinguished female in Abyssinia. Another political interest distracted the kingdom. On its southern border were numerous tribes of the Galla, a race regarded even by the Abyssinians, who themselves have to boast of so little refinement, as uncouth, savage, and horrible. They have numerous cattle, which supply them with food, and whose entrails, worn round the waist or plaited in the hair, though often in a putrid state, are used as the favourite ornaments of their persons. They were wont in former times to ride upon cows; but recently they have obtained a breed of small active horses, and the irregular cavalry thus mounted constitutes their chief military force. They can endure severe privations, perform the most rapid marches, and cross broad rivers holding by the horses' tails. In battle they make a sudden and rapid onset with shrill and barbarous howls, which few troops can withstand. By their numbers and ferocity they had overrun many of the finest provinces of Abyssinia, and had even formed an alliance with the royal family, which, however, was held in horror by the people in general. Their chiefs, Gusho, Powussen, and Fasil, temporized with Ras Michael in the hope of speedily destroying him.

Mr Bruce found himself for some time an object of considerable neglect. The violent passions which agitated the contending parties left little room for curiosity; and his character of Frank, combined in their eyes with that of Catholic, excited a mingled feeling of aversion and contempt. He was first drawn into notice by his medical skill. Ayto Confu, son to Ozoro Esther, had been seized with the small-pox, and as he was treated in the usual manner of the country, by being wrapped in enormous loads of clothes, and having the external air wholly excluded, the disease seemed approaching to a fatal termination. A great Abyssinian saint, who had not eaten or drunk for twenty years, having failed in his attempts to cure the prince, the stranger was called in as a last resource, and by improved treatment soon produced a most favourable change. His attentions on this occasion, with the general attractions of his person and manner, rendered him a decided favourite with the princess, through whom he was introduced to the first circles at the imperial court.

One principal cause of the importance attached to the travels of Bruce is the acquisition of many valuable manuscripts made by him while resident in Abyssinia. His work contains a history of that country, translated chiefly from records supplied to him in the native language; and though there may be some slight discrepancy, as to dates and the order of events, the narrative is amply confirmed by all the information which it has been possible to procure from other sources. The Chronicle of Axum, already mentioned, proved the depository of a great variety of facts in regard to the regal successions; its object being to " show forth the glory of Rome and Ethiopia," two nations which were imagined to divide between them the sovereignty of the world, in direct inheritance from Adam. Of this treatise Mr Bruce brought two copies from Gondar; the one written in an older hand, divided into chapters, containing an appendix on Abyssinian history and customs; the other beautifully but more incorrectly written, without sections, and supposed to have been a transcript made for him while living in that city. He arranged the several manuscripts on the modern annals of Abyssinia into five volumes, the first of which is the newest copy of the Book of Axum. The second volume, however, is esteemed far more authentic. It is, says Dr Murray, written in a very neat but small hand on thin parchment, and appears to be about a hundred years old. It contains ninety-three leaves, of which eleven are on the Adeline war of Amda Sion, seven on the history of Zera Jacob, eight on that of Beda Mariam, interspersed with some chapters relating to his father.*

In this volume, we are assured, there are many curious particulars relating to the monarchy, both in its prosperous and declining state; though the monkish annalists often give abundance of minute facts without assigning any cause. Many pages are filled with wild declamatory speeches full of Scripture quotations; in which the reader, expecting to find historical notices, is miserably disappointed. But there are not wanting passages replete with natural feeling, bold enough to surprise, and sufficiently tender to melt the heart. The construction of an Oriental language, it is true, gives a somewhat turgid air to these performances; which, however, with all their defects, are fully entitled to a place among the chronicles of our own Gothic ages.†

The third volume of the collection begins with the history of Susneus, in seventy-five leaves and ninety-nine chapters. It is the best written of the

---

* Bruce's Travels, vol. iii. p. 409.   † Ibid.

whole, and being at the same time minute, accurate, and interesting, supplied Mr Bruce with nearly all the incidents mentioned in that reign. The character is small and neat; great attention has been bestowed in correcting the errors of the transcriber, and in removing statements of facts which were either doubtful or offensive. The Roman faith is reprobated wherever it is mentioned; but the edifices with which the Franks ornamented the kingdom are described with much admiration though with little art. It contains an epitome of the history of Facilidas, together with some diffuse observations on the reign of Hannes the First.

The fourth volume is occupied with the annals of Yasous Tallak, of Tecla Haimanout the First, of Tiflis, and of David the Fourth. The fifth presents an account of the government under Bacuffa, his son Yasous the Second, and Joas his grandson, who was murdered in the year Mr Bruce entered Abyssinia. The history of Ras Michael forms an interesting episode in the latter portion of the narrative, and fully authenticates the character given of him by that celebrated traveller.*

---

* Bruce, vol. iii. p. 413. The following is a list of the Ethiopic MSS. brought from Gondar by Mr Bruce:—

I. The Old Testament, in five large quarto volumes, each about a foot in length and breadth. These contain all the books in our canon, except the Psalms and several of the Apocrypha.

II. Two copies of the Gospels in four volumes, two of which are in small quarto, answering in size to the two volumes which contain the writings of the Apostles and the rest of the New Testament, mentioned in No. IV.

III. The Synodos or Constitution of the Apostles, beautifully written, and containing about 300 folia. An analysis of this large volume is given by Ludolf in his Commentarius ad Historiam Abyssiniæ. It forms what is called a kanoun, or positive law of the church, beyond the letter of which the clergy have no judicial powers.

The annals of Abyssinia may be divided into three great portions. The first comprehends the period which elapsed before the interruption of the ancient royal race by the successful rebellion of Judith, or Goudit as she is sometimes called; the second embraces the interval during which the usurping dynasty exercised the supreme power; and the last extends from the restoration of the line of Solomon in the person of Icon Amlac down to the present day.

In regard to the most ancient division, the light of history does not direct our researches much farther than to ascertain the names and order of the several monarchs who mounted the throne. We have already given the list from Menilec to Bazen, who swayed the sceptre at the beginning of the Christian

---

IV. The Acts of the Apostles and all the Epistles in our canon, with the Revelation of St John, in two small quarto volumes, uniform with the Gospels before mentioned.

V. A Chronicle of the Kings of Abyssinia, from Arwè to Bacuffa, with a very curious preface on the law and customs brought from Jerusalem by Ibn Hakim the son of Solomon. From this preface is extracted the information respecting the great officers of the Negus, given in the introduction to the history of Abyssinia. As the MS. contains a perpetual chronicle of all the princes, from Icon Amlac to Bacuffa inclusively, it has been of great use in preserving entire the chain of history, which is broken in the larger annals. It consists of about 120 folia of the quarto size.

VI. The Kebir Zaneguste or Glory of the Kings, the celebrated Book of Axum, described at length in the text.

VII. The Annals of Abyssinia in five volumes quarto; the principal source of the history given in the third volume of Bruce's work. Of these we have already specified the contents.

VIII. The Synaxar ($\Sigma υναξαρια$) or lives of the Ethiopic Saints, arranged according to their order in the national calendar, in four volumes quarto. Most of the idle legends contained in this book are translations from the Greek and Coptic. The saints are nothing inferior to their western brethren in strength and faith. They perform greater miracles, live more ascetic lives, and suffer more dreadful martyrdoms, than these holy men; all which is nothing surprising in the native country of credulity, superstition, and religious zeal.

era. From him to Dalnaad, under whom the government was overthrown, there were about sixty sovereigns, whose united reigns amount to nearly nine hundred and fifty years. For their titles, which could not in any respect prove interesting to the general reader, we willingly refer to the volumes of Bruce and Salt, where they are given at full length, and with as much precision as could be derived from records not every where free from obscurity.

Judith is said to have been of a Hebrew family, the descendant of one of those men of rank in the Jewish tribes, who, upon the conversion of the Abyssinians to the Christian faith, withdrew into the strong mountains of Samen, where they exercised during several generations a separate and independent authority. She is described as a woman of great beauty and talents, who, inflamed with zeal for the religion of her fathers, resolved with the aid of her countrymen to subvert the doctrine of Christ and destroy the apostate race of Solomon. To accomplish these views, she began by attacking the young princes, confined according to national usage on the high hill of Damo, and massacred them all, with the exception of an infant, who was conveyed into the loyal province of Shoa. The conqueror immediately took possession of the throne, and removed the seat of government to Lasta; where, after enjoying supreme power in her own person not less than forty years, she transmitted it to her descendants, who continued to rule over the greater part of Abyssinia about the space of three centuries.

During all this period, and indeed down to the year 1255, very little is known respecting the affairs of the country. The Arabian authors mention from time to time that the clergy sent to Egypt to have an Abuna consecrated,—that the sceptre had again fallen into the hands of a Christian king, though not of the race of Solomon,—and occasionally indicate the name and title of the actual monarch.

About the middle of the thirteenth century the kingdom was restored to the representative of the ancient house, whose family continued to flourish in Shoa, where indeed their hereditary right had never been called in question. This event was accomplished by the interposition of Tecla Haimanout, a native monk of Abyssinia, who had been raised to the episcopate, and is known as the founder of the famous monastery of Devra Libanos. He prevailed upon the reigning sovereign to abdicate the throne in favour of Icon Amlac, in virtue of a treaty by which it was provided that a portion of land should be given to the retiring prince,—that one-third of the kingdom should be ceded for the maintenance of the church,—and that no Abyssinian should thereafter be elected Abuna, but that the head of the ecclesiastical body should always be named by the patriarch of Egypt. The following catalogue is collected from various chronicles, and presents at least an approximation to the truth of history.

Icon Amlac,	1255	Andreas,	1417
Woodem Arad,	1269	Hesbinaan,	1424
Kudma Asgud, Asfa Asgud, Senfa Asgud,	1284	Amda Yasous, Bed el Nain, Isba Nain,	1429
Bar Asgud,	1287	Zara Jacob,	1434
Egba Sion,	1292	Beda Mariam,	1468
Amda Sion,	1301	Secunder, his son Amda Sion,	1478
Sef Arad,	1331		
Grim'asfaré,	1359	Naod,	1494
David,	1369	Levana Denghel, David,	1507
Theodorus,	1401		
Isaac,	1402	Claudius,	1539

Menas Adamas }	...1558	Yohannis,	1665
Segued, }		Yasous Tallak,	1680
Sertza Denghel, or		Tecla Haimanout,	1699
Malac Segued, and	...1562	Theophilus,	1706
his son Yacob,		Oustas,	1709
Zâ Denghel,		David,	1714
Yacob restored,	1604	Bacuffa,	1719
Socinios,	1607	Yasous,	1729
Facilidas,	1632	Ayto Yoas,	1753

The fate of the last of these kings has been already mentioned. From Mr Salt's volume we have derived this supplementary list:

Tecla Haimanout reigned	8 years	Adimo,	2 years
Solomon,	2 —	Ayto Gualoo, or Egwala Sion, who according to the latest accounts was succeeded by Itsa Yoas in 1818.	17 —
Tecla Georgis,	5 —		
Yasous,	4 —		
Haimanout,	1 —		
Iskias,	6 —		
Beda Mariam,	2 —		
Yunus,	two months		

The modern history of Abyssinia is confined to a narrative of insurrections and petty wars, either against the general government or among the subordinate chiefs themselves. When Mr Bruce resided there, the main power was in the hands of Ras Michael the governor of Tigré, who, while he acknowledged a nominal subjection to the king, directed all the weighty affairs of state. The most formidable enemies of the crown were the princes of the Galla, who not only claimed a right to be heard in all public matters, but occasionally asserted a degree of independence quite inconsistent with monarchical rule. The Ras attempted to gain Powussen, the chieftain of Begemder, by giving to him his grand-daughter in marriage. Festivities of the most unrestrained description followed this event, which it was expected would secure peace to the kingdom, and gratify the more powerful of the Galla tribes.

But the gay scenes at Gondar were soon succeeded by a furious intestine war among the persons by whom they were celebrated. Several of the Galla leaders, among whom was Michael's new relative, united in a conspiracy to destroy him. He escaped only by a precipitate retreat into the province of Tigré, across the swollen stream of the Tacazze. The triumphant confederates entered Gondar, and set up as king a worthless youth called Socinios, in whose name they administered all the affairs of state. Mr Bruce, the adherent of Michael, lost all his honours, but was allowed to live unmolested with Ozoro Esther and her mother in their palace of Koscam. This uneasy situation he sought to vary by an attempt to fulfil the grand object of his ambition; namely, to reach the sources of the Nile, which he was assured were situated in a high pastoral region eastward of the Lake of Dembea.

The country now to be visited was under the sway of Fasil, a rude but powerful Galla chieftain, who had promised to protect the traveller, and from whom accordingly a favourable reception was expected. He was found in a little tent, wrapt in a lion's skin, and sitting upon a handful of straw spread on the floor. After the first salutation had passed he seemed disposed to take no farther notice of him, when Bruce, receiving from his guide a hint to speak, reminded the governor of his promises, and solicited his permission and aid to visit the source of the Abay, the name here given to the Abyssinian Nile. Fasil without any ceremony started various objections, in the course of which he allowed it to transpire that he considered Franks, as he reproachfully termed them, as little better than boys and women, and unfit to travel in a land of warriors. The visiter then burst into a furious passion, loaded him with reproaches, boasting that with a handful of Europeans he would trample all his bands of naked savages in the dust. In the midst of this tirade the blood burst from his nose, and his attendants hurried him out of the tent. No sooner had he cooled, than he bitterly repented of the unseasonable intemperance which had apparently cut him off for ever from the fondest object of his heart, and on which he meant to establish his fame with future ages. It soon appeared, however, that this high and fierce bearing had been suited to the personage to whom it was addressed; for he learned that Fasil was giving directions for his proceeding early next morning. By daybreak horses were ready; but the servants mounted him on a steed so unruly, that, but for his equestrian skill, his life would have been in danger. The Galla leader declared himself wholly ignorant of this trick, and gave Mr Bruce full liberty to cut the groom in pieces. He sent forward with him Woldo, a huge half-naked savage, holding a stick, which he continually brandished; also a horse, intended not to be ridden but led before him, and which, serving as the credentials of his coming from Fasil, would secure him against all violence. The animal accordingly met every where the profoundest homage, and was only pitied for being employed in so mean a service as that of escorting a Frank. After passing through Dingleber, which commanded a fine view of the Lake Dembea, he saw a band on the opposite side of the river, which, Woldo stated, belonged to the Jumper, under whose auspices they must now place themselves; whispering, that he was the greatest thief and murderer in all the country; and on Bruce remonstrating as to this choice of a protector, he added, "So much the better." With two whistles and a yell he brought fifty men to assist in conveying over the baggage, and they found the Jumper busy at his toilet, rubbing his naked body with melted tallow, and embellishing his locks with the entrails of a cow. He was tall, lean, sharp-faced, with small eyes, and resembling somewhat a lank greyhound. He showed no signs of curiosity or judgment, but prodigious bodily activity, and was accounted the greatest spoiler of all the Galla. He recommended them to his brother the Lamb, whom they found encamped in the dry bed of a river, watching the proceedings of a neighbouring market, whence, however, all had absented themselves on his account. He appeared equally stupid and indifferent, though he bestowed much courtesy on Fasil's horse. The gentleness of his character, which had procured him this appellative, was shown by his murdering men and children only, and usually sparing the female sex. When the party, after taking leave, had proceeded a considerable distance, they were alarmed by a confusion of wild and barbarous cries, and on looking round saw a band of savage horsemen brandishing their lances in the air. They put themselves in the best possible attitude of defence, till they heard the cry "Fasilali!" This company was under the direction of their friend the Lamb, who, having heard of their being in danger from a party of Agow horse, had galloped up to defend them. Mr Bruce was so much pleased with this attention, that he presented the barbarian with a huge piece of raw beef, in the course of eating which he expressed severe disappointment at not having met the Agows, and being thereby supplied with an opportunity of showing how dexterously he would have cut them all in pieces.

The traveller lost no time in following out his main object, and was conducted to the village of Geesh, where the Nile, as it was termed, was only a scanty rivulet; and he stepped across it fifty or sixty times in triumph. He then viewed, with still higher rapture, the two fountains which unite in forming this celebrated stream. In fact, however, he laboured under an error; the main source of the Egyptian river, as we have already stated, not being here, but in a remote part of Africa, south of Darfûr, and called in its upper course the Bahr el Abiad. But that the Abyssinian branch is the Nile had been the belief of most geographers in latter times, and nothing could ever induce him to relinquish it. He stoutly denies also, though seemingly on slender grounds, the claim of Paez to be considered the first discoverer even of these interesting springs.

Mr Bruce now returned to Gondar; on his way to which he was hospitably entertained by Shalaka Welled Amlac, a friendly chief, in his palace, which consisted of one large apartment sufficient to accommodate his wives, family, horses, and mules, and was hung round with trunks of elephants killed by his own hand. In the capital our countryman was at first ill received; but the fortune of war soon enabled Ras Michael to enter that city and expel from it the Galla chiefs. A time of agreeable relaxation was then expected; but that leader, now triumphant, and enraged at the treachery of many of the citizens, gave full scope to the vindictive propensity which stains his memory. The streets streamed with blood, and Mr Bruce could not stir out without seeing dead bodies lying even in the court of the palace. Shuddering with horror, he began anxiously to negotiate for permission to return to Europe; but he was, in the mean time, obliged to accompany the army to the battle of Serbraxos, where he distinguished himself, and was rewarded with a gold chain and a splendid suit of apparel. In that action the Ras's forces kept possession of the field; but his loss was so great, while the Galla constantly received new reinforcements, that he was compelled to fall back upon Gondar, where he was soon enclosed, and reduced almost to the state of a prisoner.

Amid these agitations, the traveller gladly embraced the permission which he at last obtained to return home. He passed first through the woods and marshes of Ras-el-Feel, of which he had been made the nominal governor. At Tcherkin he was vastly surprised to meet his great friend Ozoro Esther, who had with her Tecla Mariam, the greatest beauty in Abyssinia; and they were soon joined by her son Ayto Confu. This party, like himself, had retired from the disturbed vicinity of the court, and he spent a fortnight with them in festivity, as well as in hunting the elephant and rhinoceros, which abound in those vast forests.

Among the principal characters who figured at court, in the camp, and in the field, none was entitled to higher respect than Kefla Yasous. His conduct at the battle of Limjour, where the royal troops were thrown into consternation by the arrival of Fasil, saved the king, and prevented the dis-

158 CIVIL HISTORY OF

Kefla Yasous.

astrous effects of a hasty retreat. The above portrait is understood to be a faithful likeness of that brave warrior, while it represents the head-dress of an Abyssinian chief after a successful contest either with a personal or a public enemy. The horn displayed on the forehead will illustrate the allusions made in Sacred Scripture to the horn of the righteous, and to the lifting up of the horn on high while the proud man speaketh with a stiff neck.

It was in the year 1771 that Mr Bruce left Abyssinia, uncertain as to the effect of recent events on the fortunes of his most intimate acquaintances. There could be no doubt that the Galla had obtain ed the ascendancy in the capital, and were now in a condition to dictate to the monarch, who held his throne at their pleasure. Nor was it till 1805 that Mr Salt, who accompanied Lord Valentia in his voyage from India, made an excursion into that country, and thereby found the means of adding somewhat to our knowledge of its actual situation.

Five years afterwards he was intrusted with a mission to the court of Gondar; but it deserves to be noticed, that on neither occasion was he able to penetrate farther than to the northern division of Tigré. He found, however, that all Bruce's great friends and enemies, Ras Michael, Ozoro Esther, Ayto Confu, and Guebra Mascal, were dead. Welled Selassé, whom that traveller had known as a promising young man of twenty-four, had, on the death of the Old Lion, as Michael was called, raised himself to the dignity of Ras, and to the government of all the provinces which the other had ruled. Meantime Gusho, the Galla chief, was master of Gondar, and contended with Selassé for the supreme sway, with the right of nominating a person who should bear the empty title of king.

The enmity between these two potentates was so great as to render it impossible to proceed from the one to the other, and thus baffled all Mr Salt's attempts to reach the capital. There remained, indeed, a third division of Abyssinia, consisting of the southern provinces of Shoa and Efat, which appeared still to be governed by a prince descended from the ancient royal family. But these districts have not been visited by any recent traveller, though they unquestionably form one of the finest parts of the kingdom, and contain a greater proportion, perhaps, than any other of the ancient Ethiopian learning. It is enough to mention, however, that they cannot be approached without passing through the lands of those barbarous tribes who at present enjoy the supreme power in the neighbouring regions.

During Mr Salt's first visit he was supplied by Ligantur Metcha, a priest of some rank, with a sketch of the political changes which had taken place subsequently to the departure of Bruce. The character of Joas, the events of his reign, and his assassination by Ras Michael, as related by that author, were all fully confirmed. He was succeeded by Hannes, who after holding the sceptre only five months died of disease, and not by poison as it is recorded in the Travels. Tecla Haimanout, the son of that prince, a remarkably fair and handsome man, next mounted the throne. He was greatly attached to the Ras, who, during his reign, was often in a state of open hostility with Fasil of Gojam, whom he beat at the battle of Fagitta, a short time, as Metcha remembered, before Bruce came into the country. A powerful party was afterwards formed against Michael, and Gusho was made Ras; upon which the old warrior retired to his province of Tigré. After governing eight years, Tecla Haimanout was driven from his throne by Wordo Wussan (Powussen), and soon after died in retirement at Waldubba, leaving one son, Welled Solomon.

Upon this vacancy Ayto Solomon, though in no respect related to his predecessor, succeeded to the throne, supported by the forces of Begemder and Gojam. The reign of this prince continued only two years, and at his death, Tecla Georgis, brother of Tecla Haimanout, was raised to the sovereign authority by Confu Adam and Ras Ayto, who then commanded the provinces of Gojam, the Agows, and Damot. Soon after his accession (1801) died Ras Michael in the eighty-eighth year of his age, and was succeeded in the government of Tigré by Welled Gabriel his son. Tecla Georgis, having reigned only five years, was dethroned, and after wandering long through various parts of the country, finally retired to the mountains of Waldubba. To him succeeded Yasous the Third, who was raised to the supreme power by Ras Ayto. The new king died of the small-pox after reigning four years, and through the united interest of Ayto and Welled Gabriel was replaced by Beda Mariam: the latter of these chiefs, a short time afterwards, was slain in battle by Ras Ally of Begemder.

After sitting two years on the throne, Mariam was deposed by the Ras just named assisted by the Edjow Galla; upon which he went to Samen, where he lived under the protection of Ras Gabriel. His successor was Ayto Ischias, son of the late Sultan Yasous, who, after having enjoyed the sovereignty six years, was dethroned by Ras Merrid son of Ayto of Gojam, and obliged to flee from his capital. In conjunction with this commander, Ras Welled Selassé raised Ayto Solomon son of Tecla Haimanout to the head of affairs; but he was not able to maintain himself in his royal estate though supported by the powerful interest of Tigré, for after two years he was obliged to seek protection in the house of his friend the governor of that province.

It was now the turn of Begemder to assume the superiority, and Ras Iserat accordingly thought himself entitled to place Ayto Yunus on the throne.

This sovereign, however, had not ruled more than three months, when Guxo chief of the Edjow Galla removed him, and elevated Ayto Edimo brother of Tecla Georgis, who, having lived but two years, was succeeded by Ayto Gualoo, the monarch whom Mr Salt found in possession of power.

This narrative, communicated to the traveller, is, as he himself remarks, very probably true, because it agrees with the circumstances of the country; and the period of the several reigns taken together exactly coincides with the time which had elapsed since the days of Joas the First.

It is worthy of remark that the royal family were no longer confined to the mountains of Wechné, this custom having been some years abolished. They now lived in a state of dependence on the chiefs of the several provinces.

Welled Gabriel the son of Michael commanded in Tigré eight years, after which Guebra Mascal was appointed by Tecla Georgis; but the latter had scarcely taken possession of his province when he was attacked by Welled Selassé, then at the head of an army in Enderta, who seized his person, and after keeping him some time in confinement gave him a village, where he spent the remainder of his life. Selassé was master of Tigré at the period under our consideration, and, as we shall afterwards find, he continued to enjoy it many years.

At the departure of Mr Salt from Abyssinia in 1805, he left behind him a sailor belonging to the Antelope whose name was Pearce, and who, having deserted from one of his Majesty's ships, and wounded a soldier on duty at Bombay, preferred the choice of a new country to the hazard of punishment and disgrace at home. He had spent five years among the half-civilized natives of Tigré, sometimes under the protection of the Ras, who had promised to befriend him, and occasionally trusting to his own resources, when his patron, in the character of British envoy to the Abyssinian emperor, appeared again in the Red Sea. The adventurous mariner, who had not neglected to acquire a competent knowledge of the language and manners of the people, proved extremely useful to Mr Salt in his attempt to penetrate through the rebellious provinces in order to deliver to his imperial highness the letter and presents with which he was charged. He communicated at the same time a short account of the occurrences which had taken place during his residence in that strange land. He does not conceal that his turbulent and restless disposition frequently made him forfeit the countenance of his superiors, and even reduced him to great distress; but his zeal, courage, and ability, whenever an opportunity occurred for their exercise, never failed to restore him to the approbation of the prince as well as to the full enjoyment of all his privileges.

An occasion of this nature presented itself in March 1807, when a powerful league was formed by several of the most formidable chiefs in the interest of Ras Michael's family for the destruction of Welled Selassé. The latter, indeed, raising a powerful army, quickly reduced the insurgents to unqualified submission; but while the negotiations for peace were going on a plot was formed by some of the confederates to burn the Ras in his quarters at Adowa, where in the full confidence of victory he lay at some distance from his troops, and very slenderly attended. The scheme had nearly succeeded, and part of the building was already in a blaze, when Pearce, who was encamped with the army outside of the town, being awakened by the glare of light, seized his musket, and hastening to the spot, rushed undauntedly through the flames to the assistance of the old man. The fire was soon extinguished and the conspirators punished. The Englishman was immediately replaced in the good graces of the governor, who increased his pay, gave him a white mule as a mark of distinction, and appointed him to a situation of trust and honour.

But the jealousy of his enemies and his own impetuous temper quickly occasioned an absolute rupture between him and the Ras; upon which he threatened to go over to his great rival Gojee; a menace which so incensed the aged ruler that he told Pearce, though he would prevent his putting that plan in execution, he might go any where else he thought proper provided he never appeared in his presence again. In consequence of this dispute he left Antalo, and for some time led a wandering life in different districts of Abyssinia, till he heard that Welled was on the point of being once more attacked by the Galla, under the furious leader whose name has just been specified. This intelligence made him forget his quarrel; and, accordingly, collecting what forces he was able to muster, he directed his march towards the capital of Tigré.

On his arrival, we are told, many of the chiefs expressed their astonishment at seeing him, and strongly urged him not to venture into the presence of Selassé; but Pearce, proudly conscious of the motives that had prompted him to return, felt no apprehension, and requested an audience, to which he was instantly admitted. As he approached the old Ras, he thought he saw, as he himself expresses it, something pleasant in his countenance, as he turned to one of his officers and said, pointing to the English sailor, "Look at that man! he came to me a stranger about five years ago, and not being satisfied with my treatment left me in great anger; but now that I am deserted by some of my friends, and pressed upon by my enemies, he is come to fight by my side." He then with tears in his eyes desired Pearce to sit down, ordered a cloth of the best quality to be thrown over his shoulders, and gave him a mule and a handsome allowance for his support.

Nor did this enthusiastic volunteer belie the expectations that were entertained of him. Soon afterwards the Ras, having assembled his army, marched against the barbarian foes who had attempted to take him at disadvantage. After some skirmishing, mixed with a show of negotiation, Gojee shifted his ground to the plains of Marzella, which he had determined should be the scene of battle, while the other took his station near the sources of the Tacazze. A last effort was tried by the Ras for an accommodation, which was haughtily rejected by the Galla chieftain, and both parties prepared for a decisive engagement. In the action which ensued Selassé appears to have arranged his forces with considerable skill; but an impetuous charge on his centre made by the savage followers of Gojee compelled it to give way. Enraged at the sight Welled called for his favourite horse; which being held back by his officers, who felt anxious for his personal safety, he urged his mule forward and galloped into the front; where, by his conspicuous appearance and gallant demeanour, he quickly infused fresh energy into his troops, and retrieved the fortune of the field. On this critical occasion Pearce was among the first to advance; and the Ras, seeing him in the thick of the fight, cried out, "Stop, stop that madman!" But he called in vain; for the other dashed on, killed at one blow a Galla chief who was pressing forward at the head of his men, and by his courage throughout the day gained the admiration of all around him. Gojee himself escaped with difficulty, and his whole army was totally routed. In the course of many desperate enterprises in which the Ras was engaged subsequently to this celebrated victory, Pearce, who always accompanied him, had several opportunities of distinguishing himself, and of establishing a high character for intrepidity and conduct.

The facts now stated are the substance of the communication made by this singular man to Mr Salt, during his residence in Abyssinia as envoy from the British crown. Mr Pearce, who had resolved still to remain in the country, was joined by Mr Coffin, supercargo of the ship in which the ambassador went out. The former was earnestly requested by his learned friend to keep a regular journal of passing occurrences, and more especially of the adventures in which he himself might be engaged,—a request with which he complied to the utmost of his power. That diary is now in the hands of the public, and affords to the European reader the only means of knowing what took place in Abyssinia subsequently to the year 1810.

The political incidents which diversify the narrative of the seaman are not of sufficient interest to engage the attention of the general reader. Welled Selassé found it necessary to be almost constantly in the field, to check the ravages or defeat the pretensions of some ambitious chief. It would seem, indeed, that at one period the Abyssinian monarchy was on the very point of dissolution, and about to be parcelled out among a number of princes or local governors, according to the amount of the forces which they could muster under their respective banners. The Galla in particular, to whom war is pastime and plunder one of the legitimate means of subsistence, never ceased their incursions into the territory of the more civilized inhabitants; for although they were frequently beaten by the troops of Tigré, their ranks were never permanently thinned nor their spirits broken. Pearce relates, that the kings living at one time during his stay in the country were as follows:—Tecla Georgis, in Waldubba; Itsa Ischias, in Gondar; Ayto Gualoo, then on the throne in that city; Itsa Yoas, likewise in the capital; Itsa Yonas, in Gojam; and Beda Mariam, in Samen. They are all, he adds, related to each other, and, as they boast, descended from the true race of Menilec; "but the kings of Abyssinia have so many wives from far and near that it makes it difficult to determine to whom the crown should descend, and this point is generally decided more by might than by right."*

In the month of May 1816 Ras Welled Selassé breathed his last, leaving the province in a very distracted condition. His death was kept secret from the

---

* Life and Adventures of Nathaniel Pearce, vol. i. pp. 111, 112.

people, every one being sensible of the calamities which would follow. " Welleta Tisral began to scream and lament, which would have given the alarm had not one of the slaves knocked her down senseless, and threatened her life if she even sobbed. Every thing was carried away by stealth to the *giddam* of Temben; and on the second night after his death his body was wrapped up in a clean cloth, and, as if stolen, was taken by the slaves, Mr Coffin, and Buggerunde Tusfu, over the wall of his garden to the church where they had already opened the grave of his brother Manassé. Allicar Barhé and the Abuna were informed of the event; but before they arrived the others had taken up the bones of Manassé, which were in a great coffin made out of the door of his house when he died in December 1809. The Ras's body was put beneath, and Manassé's bones then laid on the top."*

The two following years were spent in sanguinary struggles for the government of Tigré, which appears to have been more highly valued than the jurisdiction of the king. This great object was at length obtained by Subegadis, a brave intelligent young man, whose elevation had been predicted by Mr Salt, to whom he was intimately known. He is in stature about five feet ten inches, broad shouldered, and his whole frame partaking of that iron-like and sinewy character which denotes the true child of the hills, and enables him to endure without inconvenience the most arduous exertions and the severest privations. His countenance is handsome, a little inclining to the Roman; his teeth are

---

* Pearce, vol. ii. p. 84.

white and regular; his hair is jet black and in profusion, and, which is very remarkable in that country, his large expressive penetrating eye is of a dark gray. His complexion, as well as that of his family, is fair for an Abyssinian, and indeed he sometimes makes it his boast that he is descended from white people,—a circumstance which the great antiquity of his race renders by no means improbable.

From the nature of his pursuits, it was not to be expected that his habits should have been distinguished by a very rigid morality. But the Ras, a little time before Mr Coffin left the country, when he had become settled in his government, began to devote his thoughts seriously to religious subjects. He dismissed all his wives with a handsome provision, except the daughter of Hilier Mariam whom he had recently married, and to confirm his promise of remaining faithful to her received the sacrament at the church of Axum. The last accounts obtained from Abyssinia left Subegadis preparing for a march to Gondar to establish his power in that quarter of the country; and, as nearly all the principal chiefs in that neighbourhood were dead and their armies dispersed, it is more than probable that he accomplished his purpose, and perhaps placed himself on the imperial throne.*

Ayto Gualoo, the nominal sovereign of the empire, died in May 1818, a short time before Pearce sailed for Egypt. He was suceeded by his brother Itsa Yoas, who was anointed and crowned on the 14th of June under the protection of the Ras Guxo, who thought fit to prefer him to all his ne-

---

* Pearce, vol. ii. p. 291. Note by Editor.

phews, the sons of the late monarch, who, says Pearce, "are a wild and wretched set." But as Subegadis rose to power through a different interest, it is very probable, as we have already suggested, that he may have deposed King Yoas, and seized the sceptre either for his own hand or for that of some dependent prince whom he has been pleased to honour.

Leaving the history of Abyssinia we return to the Valley of the Upper Nile, the annals of which acquire a peculiar interest at the very moment when all channels of information respecting the other are obstructed. We have elsewhere mentioned the expedition into Nubia and Sennaar under the command of Ishmael Pasha, whose steps we followed with the view of extending our geographical knowledge of those remote countries. It was, we are told, the ambition of Mohammed Ali to possess all the banks and islands of the Egyptian river, and to be master of all who drink of its waters from its sources to the Mediterranean. His plans of conquest are said to have even comprehended Abyssinia; but it is understood he relinquished his designs against that kingdom in consequence of a formal assurance that an attack on a Christian state so situated would probably involve him with the British government. He therefore determined to limit his conquests to Dongola, Dar-Sheygya, Berber, Shendy, Kordofan, Darfûr, and Sennaar.

The army, which amounted to about ten thousand men, included the natives of various countries,—Turks, both European and Asiatic, Arabs, Bedouins, and Moggrebins. Departing from Cairo in the summer of 1820, Ishmael pursued his march without opposition to New Dongola, which he found evacuated by the Mamlouks, who had some months before retired to Shendy. He next advanced into the territory of the Sheygyans, a people famed for their love of liberty, and celebrated among the surrounding tribes as most vigilant and successful warriors. They acknowledged the authority of two chiefs or meleks, whose names were Shoous and Zibarra; the former of whom ruled the kingdom of Merawe, while the latter exercised the sovereignty of the lower district, the capital of which is Hannech.

After a vain attempt at negotiation the pasha resolved on an appeal to arms. The first skirmish appears to have taken place near Old Dongola, where Ishmael, some of his officers, and a few soldiers, were suddenly attacked by those brave horsemen of the desert. The assailants were soon repulsed; but a more serious action followed in the course of a few days in the vicinity of Korti, whither the Sheygyans had retreated. On this occasion the Egyptian commander had with him only six hundred cavalry, some mounted Bedouins, but no cannon. The enemy advanced to the charge with great fury and uttering loud screams. The Arabs, who rode on dromedaries, and were indifferently armed, could not withstand the impetuosity of the onset. They were driven back on the main body in great disorder; but at this critical moment the son of Mohammed Ali ordered his more regular troops to check the conquerors by a volley of carbines and pistols. The conflict was no longer doubtful. The barbarians fled in dismay, while such of them as fought on foot fell on their faces, holding their shields over their heads, and imploring mercy.

Mr Waddington relates, that the Sheygyans are singularly fearless in attack, and ride up to the very faces of their enemy with levity and gayety of heart as to a festival, or with joy as if to meet friends from whom they had been long separated. They then give the *salam* "peace be with you,"—the peace of death which is to attend the lance that instantly follows the salutation : mortal thrusts are given and received with the words of love upon the lips. This contempt of life, this mockery of what is most fearful, is peculiar to themselves,—the only people to whom arms are playthings, and war a sport,— who among their enemies seek nothing but amusement, and in death fear nothing but repose.*

But the result of the affair at Korti appeared in the submission of several of the inferior chiefs, and in the surrender of their strongholds. The pasha continued his march into the province of Sheygya, where Melek Shoous had collected the whole force of the republic with the determination of risking another battle. The position selected by the barbarian was extremely advantageous, and which, had there been no difference in the arms used by the contending hosts, would probably have secured to him a decisive victory. But the mass of peasantry whom he had dragged or induced into the field had no other weapons than lances, shields, and two-edged swords ; and they were placed in the front, rather to receive and exhaust the shot of the Egyptians, than to maintain any effectual resistance in the moment of attack. The pasha posted his troops parallel to the enemy, placing the greater part of his horse-

---

* Travels, p. 98.

men opposite to the open ground between the mountain and the river, and pushing the artillery a little in advance. The natives, uttering loud cries and brandishing their lances, rushed forward; and many of the infantry, with no other arms than those already described, threw themselves upon the cannon, and were blown to atoms.

The desperate courage of these wretched peasants, says the American officer, was astonishing; they advanced more than once to the muzzles of the pieces, and wounded some of the artillerymen in the very act of loading them. But after feeling the effects of a few rounds, which dashed horse and man to pieces, they fled in dismay, leaving their foot-soldiers " to be rode over and shot down by our cavalry, who destroyed many hundreds of them in the pursuit. I say ' shot down,' for the sabre was found an unavailing weapon, as these people are so adroit in the management of their shields that they parried every stroke. I have seen upon the field where this battle was fought several shields that had not less than ten or fifteen sabre-cuts, each lying upon the dead body of the man who carried it, and who had evidently died by two or three balls shot into him. The soldiers have told me that they had frequently to empty their carabine and pistols upon one man before he would fall."*

This unusual valour or military fanaticism has been ascribed to an assurance given by the magicians, that the armies of Sheygya should prove invulnerable in the presence of the invaders. These wizards supplied the men with heaps of consecrated

---

* Narrative of Expedition, p. 84.

dust, the sprinkling of which on their persons was to produce the desired effect; and hence they advanced against the Egyptian line rather in the attitude of dancing than of fighting, with countenances expressive of the utmost confidence and derision.* But being so miserably deceived by the charms in which they had been taught to put their trust, they inflicted a dreadful vengeance on the authors of them; for their first act after the battle was to put to death the whole race of necromancers, and even to destroy the village where they dwelt.

It is a singular fact that the pasha had not one man killed in this action, and only one officer and sixteen men wounded; and these, with scarcely any exception, in the back, the natural consequence of their manner of fighting. They discharge all their fire-arms, and then retire into the rear to reload, while the second and succeeding ranks are firing; when loaded they advance again, and therefore, after the first round, the whole is a scene of confusion. The Sheygya left six hundred men on the field of battle, and they were allowed to remain unburied where they fell. Nor did Melek Shoous and his cavalry discontinue their flight till they reached the territory of Shendy, leaving their numerous castles, dependent villages, and a rich beautiful country, in the hands of the conqueror.

Ishmael, it is said, exerted himself to save the flying enemy, and succeeded in preserving some of the infantry, chiefly Nubians; being inhabitants of that part of Dongola which was tributary to the Sheygyans, and attached to their army, perhaps more

---

* Life and Adventures of Giovanni Finati, vol. ii. p. 374.

by force than from inclination. Whatever truth there may be in this statement, it is admitted by every historian of his campaign, that he conducted himself with great generosity towards the daughter of the Melek Zibarra, who fell into his hands either in the field or while attempting to escape from her father's residence after the defeat. At all events, his treatment of this barbarian princess was very noble; for when presented to him, though said to be young and beautiful, instead of availing himself of the rights of conquest, he ordered her to be richly dressed, and a camel provided for her, and that she should be conducted back immediately to her parent. The latter, upon the first sight of her Egyptian ornaments, turned away his face, and asked if she had submitted to be dishonoured; but when she told him the truth, he embraced her and seemed disposed to make no farther resistance to the young victor, who had so wisely respected the domestic virtues.*

Resistance was soon subdued by the superior arms and discipline of the Turkish army. The cannon-shot, and more especially the destructive effects of the shells, taught the brave Sheygyans that courage alone could not save them from the bondage with which they were threatened. Yet even in this case, as Mr Waddington remarks, their terrors were derived from their superstition. A shell was thrown into one of the castles, where it rolled and bounded from side to side, as if endowed with the faculty of

---

* "When our troops approached the castle of Melek Zibarra, his daughter, a girl of about fifteen, fled in such haste that she dropped one of her sandals, which I have seen. It was a piece of workmanship as well wrought as any thing of the kind could be even in Europe."—*Narrative*, p. 85.

self-motion; and the natives collecting around it, were much amused with its appearance until it burst and wounded several of them. Then they fled, exclaiming that the "spirits of hell were come against them and were too strong for them." To the last they had no fear of man or his inventions; but, astounded by the power and novelty of the means employed to destroy them, they came to the hopeless conclusion, that a supernatural agency of the most malignant kind had conspired with their mortal foes to complete their subjection.

Cailliaud, in describing the conflict to which we now allude, maintains that the barbarians were drunk. Some of them, says he, threw themselves on the weapons of the enemy, holding in their hand a vessel full of an intoxicating liquor, and appeared as joyful as if employed at a feast. Others cast dust at the heads of the Turks as a mark of their contempt; while a third party saluted them as brethren and friends.* Perhaps the dust mentioned by the French traveller might be the charmed earth which the wizards had prepared, as the means of securing to their countrymen a cheap and certain victory over their invaders.

The fury and avarice of the conquerors occasioned many atrocities which, it is maintained, their commander could not altogether prevent; though the great number of ears and even of heads sent to Cairo indicate that his consent had accompanied some of the worst scenes which disgraced his triumph. Usage alone, says Cailliaud, could excuse the pasha for having encouraged so many frightful mutilations.

---

* Voyage à Meroë, tome ii. p. 58.

Those shameful trophies were despatched by him to his father as a testimony of his brilliant success.

Giovanni Finati, who with the artist Linant employed by Mr Bankes followed the path of the Egyptian army, confirms beyond all question the remarks of Cailliaud. The exasperation of the soldiers at having been so gallantly opposed, and their greediness of plunder or reward, drove them to horrible excesses and outrages; so that it was no wonder that a single victory did not suffice, and that a high-spirited people continued to do all they could against their oppressors. The signs of this, he adds, were but too visible; "for half the natives whom we met, many even of the women, were deprived of one or both of their ears, others mutilated in their limbs; while bones and carcasses, and hovels that had been burnt, were every where to be seen by the way." The persecution seemed, in fact, to have been carried almost to extermination. The whole district was laid waste, and thereby reduced, at least for the time, to a sullen obedience.

Before we leave the people of Sheygya we may repeat the tribute which has usually been bestowed on their hospitality and literature; qualities hardly to be expected among tribes whose doom it was to live by their swords. Burckhardt assures us that they are renowned for their kindness to strangers, and that the person of their guest or companion is held sacred. If a traveller possesses a friend among them, and has been plundered on the road, his property will be recovered even if it has been taken by the king himself. They all speak Arabic exclusively, and many of them write and read it. Their learned men are held in great respect by them; they have schools wherein all the sciences are taught which form the course of Mohammedan study, mathematics and astronomy excepted. " I have," says he, " seen books copied at Merawe, written in as fine a hand as that of the scribes of Cairo." They are also famous for various kinds of manufactures, especially for a superior description of mat, in which they surpass all the natives of Mahass and Dongola.*

We have elsewhere delineated the march of the pasha from Shendy to the tenth degree of latitude; describing his reception at Sennaar, and the various success which attended his exertions against the natives of the hill-country beyond El Querebyn and Fazoglo. After passing Dar-Sheygya he met no enemy who could oppose him in regular combat, although his progress was occasionally checked by the mountaineers in the east and south, whose rocks he invaded in search of gold.

In regard to Ibrahim his brother, who commanded the army whose object it was to explore the unknown regions on the banks of the Bahr el Abiad, we are not in possession of any more minute details than were communicated to Cailliaud by M. Asphar, a Coptic surgeon who had accompanied the expedition. We learn generally that, after a march of fourteen days from the Bahr el Azrek or Nile of Abyssinia, the troops under Toussoun Bey arrived at Dinka, a town situated on the White River, about the eleventh degree of latitude, or nearly in the parallel of Fazoglo. As to the manners and usages of the inhabitants, we find not that they differ materially from those of the tribes farther to the

---

* Burckhardt's Travels, p. 65.

north. The stream is described as being very broad at that point; but its precise dimensions are not stated by the physician, whose curiosity did not extend to such matters. Upon inquiry, the natives assured the Turks that the negroes who possess the countries beyond them are cannibals, and employ poisoned arrows in battle; and that on the western side of the river there are other negroes, called Shillooks, not less barbarous. Having spent eight days at the town already mentioned, the troops returned by the way of El Querebyn to Sennaar, which they reached some time before the division under Ishmael had concluded their campaign in the neighbourhood of Singueh.

The long absence of the army, added to a succession of unfavourable rumours that were circulated by the disaffected, had disposed some of the chiefs near the junction of the rivers to make an attempt to throw off the yoke which had been so violently imposed. Certain examples of severity, deemed necessary by the pasha, contributed also not a little to inflame their minds. But the following occurrence accelerated the rupture, and paved the way for the melancholy fate which terminated the career of Ishmael. With the view of raising a supply of provisions or money, he insisted on Nimir, the tributary melek of Shendy, to meet his cousin who ruled on the opposite bank, with whom he had been some time at variance, and into whose company he had made a vow never to enter. This excuse however, was treated with disdain, and he was commanded to attend. The melek reluctantly complied; but when a large demand was made on his territory, he boldly observed that the whole country was ruined, and could not possibly meet such a claim. The pasha checked him with great haughtiness, and even struck him across the face with his pipe. A common interest and offended pride now reconciled the cousins, and made them act in concert with equal promptitude and secrecy. Ishmael's quarters were at Shendy, though this fatal conference had taken place on the opposite bank, where his retinue and guard were very small, occupying merely a few huts and tents. There was indeed a detachment of troops at no great distance; but it was agreed between the confederates that, while Nimir should attack the pasha and his personal attendants, the other should fall upon the soldiers, or at least keep them in check. That very night, accordingly, each of them contrived to collect a considerable force; and no sooner did the melek hear the firing begin at Mettamat, where the advanced guard was stationed, than he slew the sentinels who surrounded the cottage where their commander slept, and immediately heaped up a pile of straw and brushwood which he set on fire. Alarmed by the dreadful situation in which he found himself placed, Ishmael sprung to his feet, and seizing a sabre endeavoured to force his way through the flames; but Nimir, who longed for the opportunity of wiping away the stain which had been inflicted on his honour, was ready to strike the blow, and slew him with his own hand. Surprise on the one part, and ferocity on the other, afforded little time for resistance; and in a brief space, accordingly, not a single Egyptian soldier was left alive in Shendy or the neighbouring districts.

Cailliaud, who had already left the country, was

supplied with some details relative to this tragical event. He tells us that the pasha's medical officer, a native of Greece, was spared at the first, but only that he might afterwards be subjected to a more cruel death. The barbarians began by extracting all his teeth, which they divided among the several chiefs of the province, who sewed them carefully in little leather bags to wear on their persons as a species of amulet; for, in the opinion of these superstitious people, the possessor of a physician's tooth has no malady to fear. Having completed this cruel operation, they deprived their victim of life.

The ruler of Egypt, informed of the unhappy destiny which had befallen his favourite Ishmael, gave orders to Mohammed Bey, his daughter's husband, who was then serving in Kordofan, to inflict on the people of Shendy a suitable punishment for their treachery. Nimir and his accomplices had indeed taken flight, and sought refuge in Darfûr; but the great body of his subjects, who were necessarily ignorant of the plot, could not remove themselves from the fury of the avenger. Nor did the son-in-law of Ali, who was noted for cruelty of disposition, fail to discharge with the utmost punctuality the office which was intrusted to him. Passing the White River, he marched by Sennaar into Shendy, where he found innumerable victims to sacrifice to the manes of the murdered general. His excessive rigour, however, produced the effect which always arises from a similar policy. An insurrection took place in all the conquered districts, from Singueh to the Lower Nubia, which not only weakened the influence of Egypt among the native rulers, but has created additional obstacles either to a successful negotiation or to a permanent conquest.*

Mohammed Ali has not since made any farther attempt on the countries beyond the Cataracts. His expectations as to gold and precious stones were entirely disappointed; while in regard to slaves, whether for domestic purposes or for recruits to his black regiments, he finds that there is greater economy in dealing with the traders from Kordofan and Darfûr, than in sending an expedition of ten thousand soldiers into their perilous deserts. The affairs of Greece and of Syria have now more importance in his eyes; and Ibrahim, whose health gave way under the parching sun and pestilential exhalations of Sennaar, has since distinguished his military talents in the fields of the Morea, under the walls of the celebrated Ptolemais, and on the plains of Damascus.

---

* Cailliaud, tome iii. p. 337. Giovanni Finati, vol. ii. p. 418.

CHAPTER IV.

Architectural Monuments of Nubia and Abyssinia.

Rule for determining the Antiquity and Filiation of ancient States—Connexion between Egypt, Ethiopia, and India—Excavated Temples—Girshé, Seboua, and Derr—Different Orders of Architecture—Temple of Osiris at Ebsamboul—Labours of Belzoni, Irby, and Mangles—Magnificence of Interior, and Description of the various Halls—Discoveries of Mr Bankes—Visit of Defturdar Bey—Sir F. Henniker—Temple of Isis—Cave of Elephanta—Temples of Salsette and Ellora—Comparison with those of Ethiopia—Temples of Soleb, of Kalabshé, and Dondour—Opinion of Gau—Mixed Greek and Egyptian Forms—Gebel el Berkal—Principal Temple there—Pyramids—El Bellal—Progress in the Arts—Succession of Buildings—Meroë—Bruce, Strabo, Cailliaud—Assour—Pyramids—M. Rüppel—Naga and Messoura—Large Temple—Opinion of M. Heeren—Of Cailliaud—Ruins at Mandeyr and Kely—Constitution of Government at Meroë—Its Termination—Remains at Axum—Obelisk—Errors of Bruce—Corrections by Salt—Axum-Inscription—Adulis—Inscription—Cosmas—Reference to Dr Vincent—Luxor and Karnac—Sacred Ship—Bond of Religion—Lineage of the Gods—Hebrew Tribes—Decline of Learning in Ethiopia.

In the absence of written records there can be no doubt that the arts, more especially those which are connected with religion, are our best guide in tracing the affiliation and relative antiquity of early nations. Various circumstances, it is acknowledged, constantly interfere to diminish the accuracy of all such calculations as have no other basis, and to weaken our confidence in the most cautious inferences to which we are led by the researches of the mere archæologist. This ambiguity applies in a particular manner to the deductions of authors respecting the period during which any class of monuments may be supposed to have been erected. But it will not be denied, at the same time, that wherever we find a striking similarity in the works, the habits, the opinions, and the taste of ancient communities, we may safely admit the conclusion that there must have been some intercourse between them.

Proceeding on this broad principle, every one who has examined the remains of Eastern kingdoms has been struck with the conviction that the people of Egypt, of Nubia, and of India, have derived their notions of religious architecture from the same source. In all the three countries are beheld similar excavations in the living rock, carried to an immense extent, and decorated with colossal figures; huge masses of building raised above ground, and displaying a profusion of statuary and carving; and also those monolithic shrines, or chambers cut out in a single stone, which seem to defy all the mechanical powers that modern invention has supplied to the arts. That the land of the Pharaohs was indebted to Ethiopia for the rudiments, and perhaps even for the finished patterns, of architectural skill, is no longer questioned by any writer whose studies have qualified him to form a judgment. Gau, whose splendid work on Nubia has accomplished every thing which the antiquary could desire, hesitates not to maintain as one of his first principles, that the country just named was the cradle of Egyptian architecture, and that its monuments embrace the whole period during which this art flourished in the latter. In other words, he states that all the architecture of Egypt has its types in the buildings of Nubia, from the first rude effort to cut a temple in the rock to the construction of those detached edifices which were afterwards erected under the government of the Greeks and Romans.*

When we consider the troglodyte habits of the natives in all hot climates, the eagerness with which, by retiring into caverns, they shun the alternate plagues of the solar beams and the drenching rain, we shall not be surprised to learn that they prepared, in similar recesses, a dwelling for their gods and a convenient asylum for the rites of their religion. At a later period, when they began to enjoy the blessings of security and wealth, and had opened their minds to the sentiments of taste, they appear to have added to their excavated temples the ornament of a portico, a propylon, and sometimes even to have hewn down the face of the mountain itself into the form of a splendid building. The progress of a corresponding refinement has been traced both in India and Nubia. We may distinguish, says Gau, in the architectural history of this period three great epochs : the first comprehends the temples cut in the sides of hills; the second those which are detached from the rock-cut chambers, but retain the colossal masses of the primitive type ; and the third embraces the small edifices of Maharraga, Gartaas, Dondour, and several structures in Egypt.

In laying before our readers some account of the monuments, which continue to perpetuate the genius and power of the ancient inhabitants of the Upper

---

* Gau's Nubia, Preface. British Museum, p. 130.

Nile, we shall follow the line of research suggested by the distinguished author to whom we have just referred, and describe them according to the simplicity of their formation, which, under the light they are now contemplated, is equivalent to their comparative age.

We may however remark in the outset, that although Gau, as a professional writer, has the merit of reducing to scientific principles the distinguishing features of the several orders of building, the notion of measuring their relative antiquity by a reference to the simplicity of their structure had suggested itself to other authors on more general grounds. Waddington, for example, discovered at Gebel el Berkal two temples, which, from being excavated in the solid rock and having only their exterior chambers formed of masonry, resemble those of Girshé, Seboua, and Derr. The smaller of the two has six halls or apartments, five of which are cut in the body of the mountain; while the other, which constitutes the entrance and is thirty-six feet square, stands on an artificial stone foundation, by means of which it is elevated to the height of the rock wherein the former are hollowed out. For the dimensions of the temple and of its subordinate parts we refer to the original work, where they appear to be given with much accuracy. It is necessary however to observe, that near the adytum, or sacred shrine, there are figures of Jupiter Ammon and of Horus. There are vestiges of hieroglyphics, too, in all the chambers. On the whole, the learned author concludes, from the plainness of the masonry, from the rudeness and decay of the remaining sculptures, and from the raggedness and decomposition of the walls, though they had been sheltered probably for ages by the solid rock from the sun and wind, that this is older than any of the temples of Egypt or even of Nubia.*

Burckhardt visited the ruined structure at Seboua; before which, he tells us, is a propylon similar to that of Gorne at Thebes. The pronaos has five columns without capitals on each of its longest sides: in front of each, and joined to it, is a colossal figure (like those at Gorne) sixteen feet in height, having the arms crossed upon the breast, with the flail in one hand and the crosier in the other. Opposite to the entrance there lies on the ground a huge statue, the head and bust of which are buried in the sand: it probably stood on the side of the gate, like the colossi at Luxor; it is a male figure, and in the same attitude as those on the façade of the temple of Isis at Ebsamboul. In front of the propylon, and about thirty yards distant from it, are two statues ten feet in height, and seven paces from each other; their faces are towards the river, and they are attached by the back to a stone pillar of equal elevation; they are rudely executed, proportion being so little observed that the ears are half the length of the head; they both wear the high bonnet, and represent unbearded males. An avenue of sphinxes leads from the bank to the temple; but the greater part of them are now buried. Four remain by the side of the two last-mentioned statues, differing from each other in shape and size, but all having the bodies of lions with the heads of young men, and the usual narrow beard under the chin. "The whole fabric appears to be of the

---

* Journal of a Visit to some Parts of Ethiopia, p. 169.

remotest antiquity, and to have been imitated by
the more modern architects of Egypt; for the propylon and the pronaos, with its colossal figures, are
found at Gorne on a larger scale; the two statues
in advance of the propylon are the miniatures of
those in front of the Memnonium; and the sphinxes
are seen at Karnac."*

The sculptures, as well from the friable nature
of the stone as from their great age, are much obliterated; but a Briareus with two bodies may still
be distinguished on the outside wall of the propylon. A similar remark applies to the rock-cut temple of Derr, on which the same representation is
seen; the pattern, as it would appear, for those more
magnificent labours of the statuary which adorn
the ruins at Luxor and Edfou. It is deserving of notice, however, that the excavated fane at
Derr has no construction in front like that of Gebel el Berkal; no outer chambers, or pronaos, or
propylon, formed of stone and mortar. It shows,
says Gau, in its marks of age, and in the imperfection of its execution, traces of the highest antiquity, and of the infancy of the art. This infant
state is easily recognised in all parts of the architecture, and in the remnants of the primitive sculpture; as, for example, the statues with their backs
to the pillars of the pronaos, and that in the niche
of the sanctuary, which is a portion of the solid rock.
The bas-reliefs of the interior walls show, on the
contrary, the progress which the arts made in the
interval between the commencement and the completion of this excavation. In fact, it appears that
this, which is certainly one of the oldest monu-

---

* Travels, p. 90.

ments in Lower Nubia, contains in itself a history of the gradual improvement of architecture and sculpture as applied to sacred places. Here, as elsewhere, the procession of the ship is exhibited on the walls of the adytum; an emblem to which we shall hereafter call the attention of the reader, as being connected at once with the ancient current of population, and with the origin of many of the religious opinions that were common to Egypt and Ethiopia.

The temple of Girshé evidently belongs to the more simple order of structures, and indicates a very imperfect condition of all the arts connected with architecture. There is a portico, consisting of five square columns on each side, cut out of the rock, with a row of circular ones in front, constructed of several blocks, and which originally supported an entablature. Of these only two remain. Before each of the square-sided columns stands a colossal statue of sandstone about eighteen feet high, holding a flail in one hand, the other hanging down. They all represent male figures, with the narrow beard under the chin, and the high sphinx-cap on the head; the shoulders being covered with hieroglyphical inscriptions. On both sides of the portico is an open alley hewn in the rock, from whence, perhaps, the materials of the first colonnade were taken. The pronaos, which is entered from the portico by a large gate, is eighteen paces square, and contains two rows, three in each, of immense columns or rather props, for they are without capitals, measuring five feet by seven in the plan. In front of each of these is a colossal figure more than twenty feet in height, representing the usual juvenile character, with the corn measure or bonnet on his head, the hands crossed upon the breast, and holding the flail and crosier. All those statues are rudely executed; the outlines of their bodies being very incorrect, and their legs mere round blocks; yet they had a striking effect in this comparatively small apartment. "Indeed," says Burckhardt, "accustomed as I had been to the grandeur of Egyptian temples, of which I had examined so many incomparable specimens, I was nevertheless struck with admiration on entering this gloomy pronaos, and beholding these immense figures standing in silence before me. They immediately recalled to my memory the drawings I had seen of the caves near Surat and other Indian excavated temples, which in many respects bear a strong resemblance to those of Nubia. On the side-walls of the pronaos are four recesses or niches, in each of which are three statues of the natural size, representing the different symbolical male and female figures which are seen on the walls of the temples of Egypt. The centre figures are generally clothed in a long dress, while the others are naked. All these as well as the colossi are covered with a thick coat of stucco, and had once been painted; they must then have had a splendid appearance. A door leads from the pronaos into the cella, in the middle of which are two massy pillars, and on either side a small apartment which was probably a place of sepulture; in the floor of each are high stone benches which may have served for supporting mummies, or perhaps as tables for embalming the bodies deposited in the temple. Of the sculpture and hieroglyphics with which the walls of this temple were covered very little is now discernible, the sandstone being of a very friable nature and soon falling to decay. Added to this the walls are quite black with smoke from the fires kindled by the neighbouring shepherds, who often pass the night in the temple with their cattle; enough, however, still remains to show that the sculptures are rudely executed. The colossal figures are in good preservation, particularly those of the pronaos."*

We need hardly observe that this is the same place which by other travellers is called Guerfeh Hassan or Gwersh Hassan, and is described with much minuteness in several of their works. Sir F. Henniker says of it,—" Here is an excavation in the mountain, on entering into which the astonishment and delight that seizes your mind is equal to that which would be felt on entering a room twice as high as rooms generally are, and in which stand six giants three times as tall as a tall man. They are drawn up in line, three on either side, but do not improve upon examination; for they are so ill proportioned, that they appear to have been made by a stone-cutter's journeyman rather than by a sculptor; the ankle is thirty-three inches in circumference, but the foot is only a yard long, and from the sole to the knee it is scarcely more."†

But of all the temples belonging to the class of excavations that of Ebsamboul is by far the most striking. The desert in the course of centuries had so completely overwhelmed it with sand, that nothing more appeared to the eye of the traveller through Nubia than the bust of one of the colossal

---

* Burckhardt's Travels, pp. 99, 100.
† Notes during a Visit, p. 154.

figures which were placed in front of the entrance. The dimensions of this statue were, however, so great as to excite a deep feeling of curiosity among all who examined it. Finati, who was in the service of Mr Bankes, relates, that when he stood upon a level with the necklace he could hardly reach the beard, while one of the sailors climbed and sat across upon the ear; yet the countenance, he adds, seen at its proper distance, appeared very beautiful.

At a later date a party, consisting of Mr Belzoni, Captains Irby and Mangles, Giovanni himself, who attended in character of janizary, and two servants, undertook to remove the sand so far at least as to ascertain whether there were a door or any other access to the interior. They at first relied upon the assistance of the natives, who willingly entered into terms; but the increasing fatigue, the hopeless nature of the undertaking, and perhaps other motives which were never very distinctly understood, induced them to break their engagement. If our travellers neglected the means of attracting and conciliating the people, they proved at least that they knew admirably well how to make shift without them; for no sooner was all external aid withdrawn, than with a zeal and spirit, and a perseverance not to be exceeded, they undertook at a very hot season of the year, and with a scanty supply of necessaries, to complete the labour in their own persons. They continued working day after day in the sand, from sunrise till after dark, relieving each other in turn every four hours, and stripping to the skin for the exertion. Some of the number, says Finati, and especially the two captains, did each with his own hands the work of ten Nubians.*

Alluding to the scanty supply of food amidst their unremitting toil, he remarks, that "one of the expedients resorted to for driving us to desist or forcing us to terms was to starve us out of the place, and in consequence little or nothing was brought thither for sale; it was very rare that we had any meat during all our stay, and no milk or butter latterly, so that we were frequently reduced to a meal or two of dhoura corn boiled in water, with occasionally a glass of date-brandy after it."

After a continuance of these exertions and privations upwards of three weeks, a corner of the doorway at length became visible. At that very moment, when fresh clamours and new disputes were going on with the natives, Finati, being the slenderest of the party, crept through into the interior, and was thus perhaps, as he himself remarks, the first that entered it for a thousand years. Unlike all the other grottos in Egypt and Nubia, its atmosphere, instead of presenting a refreshing coolness, was a hot and damp vapour, resembling that of a Turkish bath, and so penetrating, that paper soon became as much saturated with moisture as if it had been dropped into the river. It was, however, a consoling as well as an unexpected circumstance, that the run of sand extended but a very little inside the door, while the remainder of the chambers were all clear and unencumbered.

The first impression convinced them that it was evidently a very large place; but their astonishment increased when they found it to be one of the most

* Life and Adventures, vol. ii. p. 201.

magnificent of temples, enriched with beautiful intaglios, paintings, and colossal figures. The pronaos is fifty-seven feet long and fifty-two wide, supported by two rows of square pillars in a straight line from the front to the door of the sekos. Each pillar has a figure not unlike those of Medinet Abou, finely executed, and very little injured by time. The tops of their turbans reach the ceiling, which is about thirty feet high; the pillars are five feet and a half square. Both these and the walls are covered with splendid carvings, the style of which is somewhat superior, or at least bolder than that of any in Egypt, not only in the workmanship, but also in the subjects. They exhibit battles, storming of castles, triumphs over enemies, and numerous sacrifices. Some of the colours are much injured by the close and heated atmosphere, the temperature of which was so great, that the thermometer must have risen to a hundred and thirty degrees.

The second hall is about twenty-two feet high, thirty-seven wide, and twenty-five and a half long. It contains four pillars more than three feet square; and the walls are also covered with fine hieroglyphics in pretty good preservation. Beyond this is a shorter chamber, but of the same width, in which is the entrance into the sanctuary. At each end of it is a door leading into smaller apartments in the same direction with the adytum, each eight feet by seven. The sanctuary itself is twenty-three feet long and twelve feet broad. It presents a pedestal in the centre, and at the end four colossal figures in a sitting posture; all in good order, not having been mutilated by any violent means.

On the right side of the great hall, entering into

the temple, are two doors at a short distance from each other, which lead into two separate rooms; the first thirty-nine feet in length and eleven and a half wide; the other forty-eight feet and a half by thirteen feet three inches. At the end of the former are several unfinished hieroglyphics, of which some, though merely sketched, give fine ideas of their manner of drawing. At the lateral corners of the entrance from the first into the second chamber are doors, each of which conducts into an apartment twenty-two feet and a half long and ten feet broad. These rooms open into others, forty-three feet in length and eleven feet wide.

But the most remarkable subjects in this temple are a group of captive Ethiopians in the western corner; the hero killing a man with his spear; another lying slain under his feet; and the storming of a castle in the vicinity. The outside or external front is truly magnificent. It is a hundred and seventeen feet wide and eighty-six feet high; the space from the top of the cornice to the top of the door being sixty-six feet six inches, and the dimensions of the door itself twenty feet. There are four enormous colossal figures in the attitude of sitting; the largest indeed in Nubia or Egypt, except the great sphynx at the Pyramids, to which they approach in the proportion of nearly two-thirds. From the shoulder to the elbow they measure fifteen feet six inches; the ears three feet six inches; the face seven feet; the beard five feet six inches; across the shoulders twenty-five feet four inches: their height is about fifty-one feet not including the caps, which are about fourteen. On the top of the door is a statue of Osiris twenty feet in length, with two colossal hieroglyphic figures, one on each side, looking towards the god. The temple has, besides a cornice with hieroglyphics, a torus and a frieze under it; the first is six feet broad, the last four feet. Above the cornice is a row of sitting monkeys, twenty-one in number, which are eight feet high and six across the shoulders. Belzoni remarks that it must have had a fine landing-place now buried under the sand; adding, that it is the best and largest temple excavated in the solid rock in Nubia between the first and second cataracts, or even in Egypt.*

Finati states that the floors of all the apartments were covered over with a very black and fine dust, which, observing its resemblance to the remains of decayed lintels in most of the doorways, he conjectured to be pulverized wood. He observes also, that in the great hall there were eight colossal statues standing, four on a side, which seemed to bear the ceiling on their heads. There were found in it two detached figures of lions with faces of birds, which were dragged out for the purpose of being transmitted to Mr Salt, with some other loose pieces of statuary collected in the several chambers; some of these to the right and left being less finely painted than the principal one, and appearing to have been devoted to sepulchral uses. The labour of taking plans and measurements, and some views as well as sketches from historical subjects delineated on the walls, occupied Mr Beechey a few days; after which the party, who still found the utmost difficulty in obtaining provisions, descended the Nile.†

---

* Belzoni's Narrative, vol. i. p. 330.
† Life and Adventures, vol. ii. p. 208.

At a subsequent period Mr Bankes visited Ebsamboul; on which occasion, says his faithful janizary, was achieved a still greater labour, being no less than the uncovering of one of the four colossal sitting figures down to the very feet; for in the excavation which took place under the auspices of Belzoni, the disinterring of the statues was not accomplished lower than the waist, the doorway in the centre being then the sole aim and object. For this new purpose, therefore, the number of men employed was very great, and almost three weeks were devoted to it. When the work was finished the effect was unusually striking, from the complete preservation in which every part of this enormous statue was found; and attendant figures, also larger than life, were brought into view, one between the feet, and one at each extremity of the chair. A few letters scratched on the surface of the legs had, from the antiquity which he was disposed to ascribe to their form, excited Mr Bankes' curiosity so much that, judging it likely that the limbs of the colossus which was nearest to the door would furnish the best examples, he undertook to pursue the inquiry farther.

But to accomplish this object it was necessary so far to undo what had been done, that the sand was rolled down again on much of that statue which had been uncovered, in order to lay bare what was wanting of the adjoining figure; the distance from the river being too great to get rid of the dust altogether without a greater expenditure of time and labour than he could afford. Within three or four days, notwithstanding, a large and long inscription began to make its appearance, and to show itself above the surface by degrees; yet it lay so deep, and the position was so awkward for opening it, that it was a work of difficulty and contrivance to obtain the last line, which was only at length brought about by consolidating the sand with immense quantities of water poured upon it. The discovery, however, which delighted all who were concerned in making it, was considered an ample recompense for the toil.*

But as soon as the writing was copied, the inferior part of the statue was again covered by the sand, which became dry and ran down. The next task was to clear the fourth colossal head,—which had never before emerged above the surface,—for the sake of making a general drawing of the whole; and the exterior was thus left greatly disencumbered for travellers who might come after, as the level of the drift was lowered many feet throughout its whole extent, especially where it encroaches with the greatest weight upon the front. The inside of the temple, meanwhile, was lighted up every day, and almost all day long, with from twenty to fifty small wax candles fixed upon clusters of palm-branches, which being attached to upright poles spread like the arms of a chandelier more than half way to the ceiling. This enabled Mr Bankes and the other draughtsmen to copy all the paintings in detail as they stood, almost naked, upon their ladders.†

While the party were so busied within and without, it happened that the Defturdar Bey, son-in-law

---

* The inscription, Mr Bankes informs us, relates to the king Psammeticus, and is certainly among the very earliest extant in the Greek language.

† Life and Adventures of Giovanni Finati, vol. ii. p. 314.

of Mohammed Ali, and governor of the upper country, came to investigate on the spot how far the second cataract was practicable for boats, preparatory to the expedition against Dongola and Sennaar, then secretly in contemplation. He stopped in passing, to pay his compliments to Mr Bankes, when he was induced to creep into the temple. He was much astonished to find so many lights burning, and so many hands employed in such an atmosphere, for purposes which he could not comprehend, and which it was in vain to endeavour to explain to him, for he always returned to the question, "What treasures have they found?"*

It is rather unpleasant to reflect, that the labour bestowed at Ebsamboul was not attended with any permanent effects; for the winds of the desert, and the natural lubricity of sand, soon rendered the approach to the temple nearly as difficult as before. When Sir F. Henniker visited that country, about two years afterwards, the doorway was covered up, and the natives informed him that it would require the services of thirty men for twelve days to effect an entrance. "To prove that they are not to be believed," says he, "I forced in a pole; round this I wound a sheet, and having spread another on the surface of the sand to prevent it from flowing down upon us, we succeeded after seven hours' exertion in constructing a kind of wind-sail or chimney. By means of this I entered, and immediately beheld eight majestic statues, whose size when compared with that of man, and still more magnified by the dimness that surrounds them, calls upon me

---

* Life and Adventures of Giovanni Finati, vol. ii. p. 317.

to corroborate the reports in favour of this temple above all others. Ebsamboul is the *ne plus ultra* of Egyptian labour, and is in itself an ample recompense for my journey. There is no temple of either Dendera, Thebes, or Philæ, that can be put in competition with it; and I am well contented to finish my travels in this part with having seen the noblest monument of antiquity that is to be found on the banks of the Nile."*

The fane now described is distinguished as the temple of Osiris; for it is well known that there are two at a very short distance from each other, the smaller of which is dedicated to Isis, whose name it usually bears. This, as well as the other, is entirely excavated in the sandstone rock, the front of which has been hewn down, and three statues cut out of it ornament either side of the door. These six gigantic figures are sculptured in relief, standing erect, with their arms hanging stiffly down. Beneath each hand is also an upright statue seven feet in height, which does not however reach above the knees of its principal. The part of the rock, which has been smoothed for the face of the temple, is a hundred and eleven feet long. The devices begin on the north side, with a human figure extending his right hand, armed with an instrument like a sickle, towards Osiris who is seated. Before him is a table of hieroglyphics well executed, probably expressing the object of his application to the divinity. The next ornament is a colossal statue of about thirty feet, wrought in a deep niche of the precipice; it is standing, and two tall feathers rise

---

* Notes during a Visit to Egypt, &c. p. 160.

up from the middle of the head-dress, with the globe or moon on each side. In a projection of the rock, shaped like a buttress and covered with hieroglyphics, is a colossal statue of Isis carved in high relief. The dress of the head is lofty, and enclosed as usual between two horns: the hair falls on each shoulder in a round mass; the left hand is brought across the breast and holds something like a mace. Then comes a similar projection in the cliff, covered also with hieroglyphics, followed by another niche in which is a statue more massy than either of the other two, and of large dimensions. The sides of the door are in like manner crowded with hieroglyphics, over which are seated Osiris and the hawk-headed deity. On each side of the passage in entering offerings are presented to Isis, who holds in her hand the lotus-headed sceptre surrounded with numerous inscriptions and emblems. Near to a priest of Ammon sits a most miserable palsied figure, the very victim of terror; he holds a feeble scourge in his hand, and is painted red; the other figures are yellow. Close to him there is a table loaded with sacred gifts, which are offered to a hero or a god, who has his hand extended towards the other in a most threatening attitude. The six columns in the middle of the chamber are also covered with hieroglyphics, and representations of the ram-headed, the hawk-headed, the ibis-headed deity, together with the lion-headed goddess or Isis, all with the globe or moon over them. The capitals of the columns are human heads, and are adorned with numerous hieroglyphics.

In the second chamber similar figures, inscriptions, and devices, present themselves. Much interesting sculpture also is lavished upon this as well as upon the third apartment, a great part of which is well executed; and in a niche at the upper end of the latter is seated a small statue of Nephthé the wife of Typhon.*

This temple, which is only a few yards from the brink of the river, and about twenty feet above the present level of its water, has been much more completely examined than the larger one, because its approach is at all times free from sand. The front is ninety-one feet long ; the depth of the excavation, measured from the door to the extremity of the adytum, is seventy-six feet. A number of ovals, or cartouches as they are called by Champollion, containing the name and prænomen of Ramesses the Great, are cut in several places of the square border that encloses the front of the temple like a frame, and on the buttresses between the colossal figures. Gau remarks, " that this façade, though cut in the mountain, displays very distinctly the general character of the great propyla, of which it presents the original form in bas-relief. We easily recognise the outline of each of the two parts of the propylon with the doorway between them, and the appendage of the statues, which are so cut out of the rock as to differ in no respect from the colossi, which at a later period were placed in front of the propyla. The interior is in good preservation, with the exception of the statue in the recess of the sanctuary, and it is richly adorned with painted bas-reliefs. The principal colour of the figures is yellow ; the ceiling is blue, a favourite tint for that purpose among

---

* Travels along the Mediterranean and Parts Adjacent. By Rob. Richardson, M. D. vol. i. p. 426.

the Egyptians; and a border of three colours runs all round."*

Every reader is aware that, between the order of religious houses now delineated and a similar class in India, the resemblance is so great as to have suggested to many eastern antiquaries the notion of a common origin, as well in regard to the mythology as the principles of architecture. Of all the excavated temples in Indostan, that in the island of Elephanta is the best known in this part of the world, having been frequently described by European travellers. " The entrance into it," says Mr Erskine, " is by a spacious front supported by two massy pillars and two pilasters, forming three openings under a thick and steep rock overhung by brushwood and wild shrubs. The long ranges of columns that appear closing in perspective on every side; the flat roof of solid rock that seems to be prevented from falling only by the massy pillars, whose capitals are pressed down and flattened, as if by the superincumbent weight; the darkness that obscures the interior of the temple, which is dimly lighted only by the entrances; and the gloomy appearance of the gigantic stone figures ranged along the wall, and hewn, like the whole temple, out of the living rock, joined to the strange uncertainty that hangs over the history of the place,—carry back the mind to distant periods, and impress it with that kind of religious awe with which the grander works of ages of darkness are generally contemplated."

" The whole excavation consists of three principal parts; the great temple itself, which is in the centre,

---

* Gau's Nubia, p. 8.

and two smaller chapels, one on each side of the great temple. These two chapels do not come forward into a straight line with the front of the chief temple, are not perceived on approaching the temple, and are considerably in recess, being approached by two narrow passes in the hill, one on each side of the grand entrance, but at some distance from it. After advancing to some distance up these confined passes, we find each of them conduct to another front of the grand excavation, exactly like the principal front which is first seen; all the three fronts being hollowed out of the solid rock, and each consisting of two huge pillars with two pilasters. The two side fronts are precisely opposite to each other on the east and west, the grand entrance facing the north. The two wings of the temple are at the upper end of these passages, and are close by the grand excavation, but have no covered passage to connect them with it.

"The great temple is about one hundred and thirty feet and a half long, measuring from the chief entrance to the farthest end of the cave, and one hundred and thirty-three feet broad from the eastern to the western entrance. It rests on twenty-six pillars (eight of them now broken) and sixteen pilasters; and, neither the floor nor the roof being in one plane, it varies in height from seventeen and a half to fifteen feet. The plan is regular, there being eight pillars and pilasters in a line from the northern entrance to the southern entrance of the temple, and the same number from the eastern to the western entrances. The pillars, which all appear to run in straight lines parallel to each other and at equal distances, are crossed by other ranges running at right angles in the opposite direction; they are strong and massy, of an order remarkably well adapted to their situation and the purpose which they are to serve, and have an appearance of very considerable elegance. They are not all of the same form, but differ both in their size and ornaments, though this difference also does not at first strike the eye.

"The figure that faces the principal entrance is the most remarkable in this excavation, and has given rise to numberless conjectures and theories. It is a gigantic bust representing some three-headed being, or three of the heads of some being to whom the temple may be supposed to be dedicated. One head faces the spectator, another looks to the right, the third to the left; a fourth may be imagined to be concealed behind. It may give some idea of its bulk to mention, that from the top of the cap of the middle figure to the bottom of the image is seventeen feet ten inches, while the horizontal curved line embracing the three heads at the height of the eyes is twenty-two feet nine inches in length.

"Travellers have entertained very different ideas of the degree of genius and art displayed in this temple, and the figures around it; some are disposed to rate them very high, and speak in rapturous terms of the execution and design of several of the compartments. To me it appears, that while the whole conception and plan of the temple is extremely grand and magnificent, and while the outline and disposition of the several figures indicate great talent and ingenuity, the execution and finishing of the figures in general (though some of them prove the sculptor to have great merit) fall below the original idea, and are often very defective. The figures have somewhat of rudeness and want of finish; the proportions are sometimes lost, the attitudes forced, and every thing indicates the infancy of the art, though a vigorous infancy.

" Nothing presents itself in these excavations which can lead to a satisfactory solution of the important and curious question, In what age or by what dynasty was this vast temple completed? One fact is worthy of notice, that a greater number of magnificent cave-temples present themselves in a small space on this coast than are to be met with in any other part of India. The caves of Elephanta, those of Kenneri, Amboli, and some others on the island of Salsette, the fine cave of Carli on the road by the Bor Ghaut to Poonah, the still more extensive and magnificent ranges at Ellora, not to mention some smaller cave-temples in the Concan and near the Adjanta pass, are all on Mahratta ground, and seem to show the existence of some great and powerful dynasty, which must have reigned many years to complete works of such labour and extent."*

We have indulged in this copious extract from an article which is in itself extremely interesting, to enable the reader to compare the excavated temple of Elephanta with those of Ebsamboul. The general plan is the same in both,—massy pillars, huge figures, emblematical devices, and mysterious ornaments. The serpent and the lotus tend still farther to identify the ancient superstitions to the uses of which those stupendous works were under-

---

* Account of the Cave-Temple of Elephanta, by W. Erskine, Esq.; in Transactions of the Literary Society of Bombay, vol. i. pp. 210, 249.

taken. But no tradition on which we can rely connects the spacious temples of the Upper Nile with those of Western India, although there can be little doubt that, in remote ages, there was an intercourse more or less regular between their inhabitants. Gau holds the opinion that the monuments of Indostan are later in their origin than those of Nubia; and we may remark, as in some degree confirmative of this notion, that one of the figures in the cave of Elephanta is described by Mr Erskine as having thick lips, and bearing in other respects a resemblance to an African countenance. Conjecture on this subject, however, cannot possibly lead to any satisfactory result, because we do not yet possess such knowledge relative to the architecture, the sculpture, and mythology of the East, as would justify a decided conclusion in regard to their precise objects.

But the works now mentioned, as well as those which have been found in the neighbouring island of Salsette, are greatly surpassed by the excavations of Ellora in the province of Hydrabad. Here we have a granite mountain in the form of an amphitheatre, completely chiselled out from top to bottom, and filled with innumerable temples. To describe the galleries and columns which support various chambers lying one above another, the stairs, porticos, and bridges over canals, also hewn out of the solid rock, would be impossible. Suffice it to state, that the chief temple, called Kailasa, is entered under a balcony, after which we come to an antechamber 138 feet wide and 88 long, with many rows of pillars, and adjoining rooms which may have been apartments for pilgrims or the dwellings of the priests. From this chamber we pass through a great portico and over a bridge into an immense hall, 247 feet long and 150 broad, in the middle of which is the shrine, consisting of one mass of rock. This monolith itself measures 103 feet long and 56 wide, while it rises to the most surprising height of 100 feet in a pyramidal form. It is hollowed out to the height of 17 feet, and supported by four rows of pillars, with colossal elephants which seem to bear the enormous mass and give life and animation to the whole. From the roof of this stupendous sanctuary, which has a gallery of rock round it, bridges lead to other side arches which have not yet been explored. The whole mass besides is covered with sculptures.*

A more minute comparison of the cave-temples of India with those excavated by the ancient Ethiopians, would lead us away from our proper subject. We may venture to remark, however, that there are many points of resemblance between the pagodas of the former country and the regular structures of Egypt, all the parts of which are above ground. For example, the pyramidal entrance to the one is analogous to the propylon of the other, while the large-pillared rooms which support a roof of stone are found frequently in the edifices of both regions. Among the numerous divisions of the cave at Ellora, there is an upper story of the *Dasavatara*, or the temple of Vishnu's incarnations, the roof of which is supported by sixty-four square-based pillars, eight in each row. This chamber is about a hundred feet wide, and somewhat deeper;

---

* British Museum, p. 182.

and as to general design may be compared with the excavated chambers of Egypt, which are supported by square columns. The massy materials, the dark rooms, and the walls covered with highly-wrought sculptures; and the tanks near the temple, with their enclosures of stone, and the steps for the pilgrims, are also equally characteristic of a pagoda and an Egyptian temple. To this we may add the high thick wall, of a rectangular form, carried all round the sacred spot. There is a farther resemblance worth noticing between some of the Hindoo temples and that of Phtha at Memphis. The latter had four chief entrances, or propyla, turned to the cardinal points of the compass; and this is also the case with the pagoda of Chillumbrum, and with another at Seringham. The first of these, according to Indian tradition, is one of the oldest in their country; which opinion is confirmed by the appearance of the principal temple contained within the walls; but other parts, such as the pyramidal gateways, the highly-finished sculptures, and the chain festoons, must be the work of a later date. It seems probable, then, that this vast religious edifice was the produce of many ages; each adding something to enlarge and perfect the magnificent undertaking of former times.*

It is rather hazardous, says the author on whose statements we now rely, to point out minor resemblances between Ethiopian and Hindoo buildings, when the latter are so imperfectly represented. But one of Daniel's views exhibits an example of the latter in the background, which has a very Egyptian appearance. It is near Mahabalipoor. There are

---

* British Museum, p. 186.

four pillars in front, the two extreme ones occupying the angles, and having behind them, in a right angle with the first row, three others, of which one indeed may be a pilaster. Thus the front row and the side rows form a portico, which is covered over with flat stones, exactly in the fashion of the Nile. In the centre of the wall, at the back part of the gateway, there appears to be a door.*

Leaving the rock-temples both in India and Nubia, over the history and design of which so dark a cloud is still suspended, we return to an examination of the more perfect class of structures; the intermediate stage, it is probable, between the excavations just mentioned and the magnificent buildings of Karnac and Luxor. We have already described the ruins of Soleb, which present to the eye of the artist so many things worthy of his admiration, and belong, it has been justly concluded, to an advanced era in the architectural history of the Ethiopian tribes.† We therefore select the temple of Samné, as an additional specimen of the style now alluded to, which we have also taken the further pains to illustrate by means of the annexed view from the west, supplied by a recent traveller.

It is built, we are told, of sandstone, and differs in its shape from other Egyptian edifices, though it somewhat resembles in its plan the small chapel at Elephantiné. It consists of a principal building about thirty-six feet in length and nine in width. On each side stood originally four small pillars, of which two remain on the one hand and three on the other; one of the former has a polygonal shaft, the

---

* British Museum, p. 187.   † See page 53 of this volume.

View of the Temple of Samné.

remainder being square; they are all covered with sculptures, and the pillars are joined to the main building by blocks of stone which serve as a roof to the vestibule. The inner walls of the apartment are adorned with hieroglyphics and mystic representations of the divine worship. On both sides a long ship is delineated, with Osiris in it; and the group of two figures resting their hands upon each other's shoulders is every where repeated. The roof is painted blue, and there are some remains of colour on several of the carvings.

Near the back-wall, opposite the main entrance, a statue about five feet in length lies on the floor, the head of which has been cut off; the arms are crossed upon the breast, while in one hand is the flail, and in the other the instrument usually called a crosier. On the outer wall Burckhardt distinguished some figures of Mendes, the Jupiter Ammon of the Greeks and later Egyptians. All the sculptures are rather coarsely executed; and the lines dividing the compartments wherein the hieroglyphics are cut are not straight, the effect either of intention or of great ignorance in the first principles of art. But it deserves notice, that the same remark applies to the architectural labours of the Hindoos, in which there are constant deviations from rectilinear position, even in the arrangement of the finest columns. Some of the hieroglyphics on the pillars have evidently been left unfinished, and those which are completed do not appear to have proceeded from the hand of a master. A part of the wall, too, seems to be of a date different from the rest, as it is constructed of stones, at once much larger and better hewn. There must, in fact, have been another similar building near this temple, for the capitals of many columns are scattered about on the ground, and there is a large block of granite covered with hieroglyphics, surrounded with heaps of rubbish. The structure itself is enclosed with ruined edifices formed of brick, unquestionably of great antiquity, and covering the hill which overhangs the shore. It is concluded that they were places of strength, and connected with certain fortifications, the remains of which can still be detected.*

In the volumes of Burckhardt, Captain Light, Legh, Richardson, Henniker, Cailliaud, and Waddington, there is to be found an ample description of the ruinous temples on either side of the Nile, from Es Souan to Meroë, occasionally accompanied with excellent drawings and plans. But there is so much sameness in the details, especially as to the measurements, the number of chambers, the statues, columns, inscriptions, and hieroglyphics, that we refrain even from an abridgment of their researches, which, in certain cases, could not be easily understood without the aid of engravings and other architectural delineations. We cannot however omit the temple of Kalabshe, which is distinguished for a beautiful propylon, represented in the work of Captain Light in the finest style of art. The remains of the building are an abutment of masonry, that rises above the bank of the river, at about a hundred and eighty feet from the front, to which there is a paved approach. On each side of this pavement there appears to have been a row of sphinxes, one of which is seen without the head. At the end of

---

* Burckhardt, Travels in Nubia, p. 75.

it there seems to have been steps leading to a terrace thirty-six feet in breadth, from which rise two pyramidal moles eighteen or twenty feet thick, with a gateway between them, forming a façade of not less than a hundred and ten feet. Inside there is a court of about forty feet, which appears to have had a colonnade joining the propylon with the portico. This last consists of four columns, attached for half their height to a wall, raised in the centre to form an entrance. The front of it is plain, with the exception of a winged globe over the gateway. A lateral wall divides it from a suit of four inner apartments, within the first of which there appears to have been a colonnade, as some fragments of shafts and capitals still remain. The three others are covered with the usual hieroglyphics and symbolical figures, the colouring in general being still fresh and bright.*

The temple of Dondour is likewise worthy of attention, owing to the peculiarities of its style. The greater part of the enclosure, according to Mr Legh, is quite perfect, and the propylon also has been but little injured. It is obvious, at the same time, that the interior has never been completed. There are two columns which form the entrance into the body of the building, and are ornamented with serpents. The sekos consists, as usual, of three apartments; the first measures eighteen feet in length and twenty in breadth; the columns are three feet in diameter, and about seventeen in height to the top of the cornice; the winged globes on the architraves of the temple itself, as well as of the propylon, are supported in the wonted manner by two snakes. The

---

* Light, p. 64.

hieroglyphics are sculptured in a good style, showing the common subjects,—priests, with vessels in their hands, making offerings to Isis and Osiris. Behind the ruin is a small grotto, which may perhaps be attributed to the early Christians, as there was found among the fragments an inscription with the characters A + Ω.

This temple has been classed by Gau among those Nubian structures that belong to the last of the three epochs of art, which he thinks he has discovered in the ancient buildings on this part of the river. It is a parallelogram, the front of which is $21\frac{3}{4}$ feet, and the length $43\frac{3}{4}$; a proportion which may be observed in some of the Grecian structures. Part of the wall that surrounded the whole is still standing, and an alley appears to have led from the gateway to the river, where there was probably a flight of steps, of which the traces may be distinctly seen in the remains of some temples. The sacred houses were of necessity placed near the bank in Nubia, for the purposes of ablution and those other religious ceremonies in which the use of water was essential; for there was no room for tanks or reservoirs at a distance from the stream. In Egypt, on the contrary, we often find them considerably removed from the Nile; but, in this case, a tank was necessary, and the traces of these artificial basins are still so numerous as to leave no ground for doubt that every holy edifice was provided with them. In India, where we see in institutions still existing so many curious points of resemblance to the ancient ritual of Egypt, there are often great flights of steps leading down to the rivers, forming a safe and convenient approach to the Ganges, where the pious

Bramin, while he makes his ablutions, at once discharges a religious duty and enjoys a healthful recreation.*

It is said, that it is impossible not to recognise in the pillars of Dondour the mixed Greek and Egyptian form ; and the study of it is the more important, as it will afford exact ideas of the kind of buildings erected in the valley of the Nile at different epochs in the history of the country. " Instead of taking every thing for genuine Egyptian because it is in Egypt or Nubia, we are now enabled, by a more accurate classification of the monuments and the aid of the inscriptions, to rectify former incorrect notions on the subject, and in fact to make a real and valuable addition to the history of civilized Egypt. Between the rock-cut temples, such as those of Derr and Ebsamboul, and the buildings of a later date, there was an intermediate step that ought to be noticed. The first architectural attempt in Nubia would probably be the improvement of some hole in the rock ; or, even if the country possessed no natural caves for imitation, the mountains themselves would afford facilities for constructing a durable habitation. A farther step would be, after having got possession of a hole, to extend the excavation, to form several chambers separated by the native rock, and when a room of larger dimensions was designed, to have square pillars for the support of the roof. In the course of time the outer front, with the inner walls and pillars, would receive decorations, derived both from the imitations of the natural form of the country and the historical remem-

---

* British Museum, p. 139.

brances of the nation. But what a prodigious period must have elapsed between the rudest rock-excavation, such as Derr was in its primitive state, and the highly-finished sculptures of the great temple of Ebsamboul!"*

We have already conducted the reader to Gebel el Berkal, where in ancient times there must have been an establishment of priests, and not improbably an extensive town. The name of Merawe, now bestowed on the district, has very naturally suggested the notion that this was the site of the celebrated Meroë; an opinion which, after considering it at some length, we have not hesitated to pronounce untenable. But there can be no doubt that it was a place of great importance in a religious point of view, as is fully manifested by the numerous remains of sacred architecture which still meet the eye of the traveller.

The principal temple is about four hundred and fifty feet long, and one hundred and fifty-nine in width; but it is, as we are assured by Mr Waddington, so much ruined as to retain nothing of its ancient grandeur and beauty, and even to have rendered the ground plan, in some places, extremely indistinct. The dimensions of the first chamber are 147 feet by 112. On the right hand are the fragments of four pillars, forming part of a row, to which, no doubt, there was one corresponding on the opposite side. There are a few hieroglyphics still visible on the wall, but those on the columns are entirely obliterated.

The second chamber, which is not so regular as the

---

* British Museum, p. 141.

one just described, seems to have measured 123 feet by 103. Parts of nine pillars composing a colonnade may be observed, though there is only one, 24 feet in height, remaining entire. The third apartment is much less, being only about 46 feet square. It contains a row of five pillars on each side, and between every two of those on the right is a sculptured pedestal where statues have formerly stood. The reader may remember, that there are pedestals similarly situated in the second chamber of the temple of Osiris at Ebsamboul, and confined to the same side.

The dimensions of the fourth chamber are $59\frac{1}{2}$ feet by 14 feet five inches. It contains a black granite pedestal, five feet square, beautifully sculptured; and here, no doubt, was raised the statue of the god to whom it was dedicated, or the king whose memory it was meant to perpetuate. On the left of this hall, and separated from it by two or three little cells, is a fifth chamber, measuring forty-eight feet three inches by twenty-four feet eight inches, and presenting a larger though similar pedestal, destined, of course, to the same purpose with the other. The holes by which the figure has been joined to it are still observable.

The sixth chamber is separated from the fourth by two walls, with a narrow passage between them. It is twenty-five feet eight inches in length and nine feet broad, communicating by means of a door with two little rooms on the right. A single apartment, 36 feet by 10, occupies the space between the former chamber and the exterior wall on its left.

In regard to the structure at large, Mr Waddington states, that of two facts he is positively certain; namely, that its present remains are the work of very different and probably distant periods; and that even in the composition of those parts which belonged indisputably to the original building, many stones were employed which had been taken from some more ancient edifice. The discovery of a sculptured stone among the mortar in the middle of the thick outer wall proves this point, while the extreme irregularity of the foundations, and the positions of some of the columns, leave no doubt, he thinks, as to the other. Whether these anomalous parts have been additions, or whether they were portions of some older temple left to stand, as chambers in the larger one erected on its site, must now remain uncertain. The propyla are much ruined, and even such sections of them as continue entire are rough and extremely decomposed, resembling more nearly the front of the temple of Seboua than any other in Nubia or Egypt.

Some lineaments of sculptured figures may still be traced on the inside of the second portal, though in most inexplicable confusion. The head of one appears in the place which ought necessarily to be occupied by the feet of the one above it; while legs and arms are every where distributed with an equal disregard to nature; but all are so extremely defaced that, says Mr Waddington, "I had rather believe my senses to have been deceived than that such absurdities have been allowed to disgrace one of the noblest buildings ever erected."*

The peculiar form of Gebel el Berkal, as Rüppel remarks, must have fixed attention in all ages. From the wide plain there rises up, perpendicularly

---

* Journal of a Visit to some Parts of Ethiopia, p. 164.

on all sides, a mass of sandstone nearly four hundred feet high, and about twenty-five minutes' walk in circuit. The unusual shape of this eminence must have become still farther an object of curiosity from the phenomena with which it is connected. The clouds, attracted from every point to this isolated mass, descend in fruitful showers; and hence we need hardly wonder if, in ancient times, it was believed that the gods paid visits to man, and held communion with him on this sacred mount. Temple rose after temple, and who can say how far many a devotee journeyed to ask advice of the oracle?*

The appearance of those architectural remains suggests the notion of a very remote antiquity. It has been remarked, in regard to the principal temple, that the traveller nowhere observes any sculptures which had been intentionally erased or disfigured; proving, it is imagined, that the ruins were in their present state when Christianity was introduced into the country. The idols were already broken, and the ravages of time or of war had been so effectual that they needed not the hand of fanaticism to complete them. But even in the walls of that ancient fane, which had sunk under the pressure of age so many centuries ago, there are found fragments of a building still older; which had decayed before the other was founded, and supplied by its fall materials for the more modern structure.

The vicinity of Gebel el Berkal is remarkable also for pyramids, which, though much inferior to those of Egypt, had probably the same object, and originated in the same views of vanity or superstition.

---

* Rüppel, p. 86, quoted in British Museum, p. 160.

They are seventeen in number, the largest of which has a base of about eighty feet square, but has suffered too much from years to enable the most practised eye to determine its other dimensions. Several of them have had spacious vestibules, or porticos, adorned with elegant sculptures and statues.

At El Bellal too, a village situated six or seven miles higher up the Nile and on the opposite bank, are many structures of the same description. There are the remains of nearly forty, eleven of which are larger than any of the perfect ones of Gebel el Berkal. That which possesses the greatest importance has a base of a hundred and fifty feet square, while its height is a hundred and four feet. It has been built in stories; but is most curious from its containing within itself another pyramid of a different age, stone, and architecture. This interior building, which the other has enclosed like a case, seems to form about two-thirds of the whole mass; it is of neat workmanship, and composed of a hard light-coloured sandstone, more durable than that which, after sheltering it for ages, has at last decayed and fallen off, and left it once more exposed to the eyes of men.*

We have in an earlier section of this chapter described the remains of the two temples at Gebel el Berkal, which are partly excavated in the rock and partly constructed, like those of Girshé and Seboua. The existence of such sacred buildings, it has been remarked, can only be explained on the supposition that they are still older than those in Nubia; for, when we take all the facts together, we can hardly

---

* Waddington, p. 176. A drawing of the pyramid of El Bellal forms the vignette to the present volume.

imagine that the Egyptian style of architecture originated in the country just named, and spread upwards towards Abyssinia and downwards to Thebes and Memphis. In the valley of the Nile, below Syené, a small temple to Typhon the evil deity is often found near a larger one consecrated to a more beneficent object of adoration. For example, there is a typhonium near the fane of Isis at Dendera, and one also close to the greater temple at Edfou. At Berkal, in like manner, we have the remains of a similar shrine in one of the two excavated mansions already specified, or rather, perhaps, of a chapel jointly belonging to Isis and Typhon. Eight of the pillars in the court of this temple, according to Cailliaud, have square capitals with the Isis head on two sides, resembling in this respect those at Dendera; but the upper member of the capital differs somewhat from that in the latter place, while it is exactly the same as the one on the square pillars at Ebsamboul. The sculptures in the adytum are executed in high relief, and painted yellow and blue. On one of the walls, among five figures of deities, Isis and Ammon are distinctly recognised.[*]

Proceeding upwards we arrive once more at that mysterious land which is enclosed at its lower extremity by the Tacazze and the Bahr el Azrek, and where, it is supposed, are still to be found the relics of the primitive faith of Ethiopia, as well as the tokens of her earliest civilisation. There can be no doubt that the most ancient traditions which have reached us through the medium of the Greek historians and philosophers, point with equal steadiness

---

[*] British Museum, p. 161.   Cailliaud, plate 67.   Rüppel, p. 87.

and uniformity to a remote country on the Nile, where the parents of learning and religion had their abode, and whence issued, at different epochs, those benevolent missionaries who carried the rudiments of knowledge to Egypt, Greece, the northern shores of Africa, and, finally, to the barbarous coasts of Europe. So far are we able to trace the vestiges of refinement and the progress of the arts ; which, attracting our attention in the kingdom of the Pharaohs, carry us gradually towards the south, till we reach a people whose origin is lost in the obscurity of distant time, and the names of whose teachers have utterly perished. We indeed find marks of their resemblance and affinity to nations beyond the Arabian Gulf, and even on the borders of Indostan ; but all our attempts to identify these fail to attain success, because we have neither historical records nor the aid of such other monuments as, on such a subject, are necessary to command belief.

In ascending from the boundaries of Egypt to those of Abyssinia and Sennaar, the traveller may remark such a difference in the style, as well as in the plan of the buildings, as indicates not only a certain progress in the arts, but also a peculiarity in the object contemplated by them. As we formerly observed, the valley of the Nile above the first cataract was once covered on both sides with towns or villages, of which Pliny has left us the names, amounting in all to about forty. In his time, it is true, they no longer existed ; and he informs us that they were not destroyed by the Romans, but by the earlier contentions between the Ethiopians themselves and their neighbours the Egyptians. As Heeren justly remarks, we have no right to suppose that these were flourishing cities. The great works of architecture here as well as below Syené were confined to public edifices; for the Nubian during the day lived almost entirely in the open air, and his cabin was little more than a resting-place for the night. Hence, it is not surprising that towns, consisting of a mere assemblage of huts, should have so entirely disappeared as to leave behind no trace of their existence.

But though the dwellings of man have vanished, those of the gods remain. The ruins of a series of temples on both sides of the river may be distinctly marked, from Elephantiné to the junction of the two great branches which compose its stream. The first is the fane of Debode, twelve miles above Philæ; which is followed at nearly the same distance by that of Kardassy, which again is succeeded by that of Teefa or Tafa, five miles farther south. Soon afterwards appear the two temples of Kalabshé; one built from the ground, the other hewn in the rocks. At about ten miles above this point are seen the relics of Dondour, and then at a like interval those of Girshé; both of which we have described at some length. Ten miles upwards is the temple of Dakke; after a similar space is that of Maharraga; and sixteen miles thence rise to the view the ruins of Seboua, half above ground and half subterranean. Thirty miles farther on stands the temple of Derr; and after proceeding about sixty miles the traveller beholds the magnificent excavations of Ebsamboul, with their sacred carvings and colossal sentinels. This is followed by Samné; but at the cataract of Wady Halfa the chain is broken, for it is not until after a journey of a hundred and fifty miles that, not far from the island of Sai, a large temple is seen; and then thirty miles farther in the same direction is discovered the edifice of Soleb, which Mr Burckhardt considers as the most southern of the Egyptian temples. The first series certainly ends here, but a new one begins on the frontiers of Meroë; for about two hundred miles farther along the bank, near the Gebel el Berkal, temples again appear accompanied with groups of pyramids. Two hundred and forty miles beyond these remarkable ruins we reach the point where the Tacazze or Astaboras falls into the Nile; forming the celebrated island, as the Greeks were pleased to describe it, to which our attention is now more immediately to be directed.*

The famous city of Meroë, according to the report of the most intelligent travellers, must have stood a little below the present Shendy, in lat. 17° N., and long. 34° 30′ E. Bruce saw its ruins at a distance, concerning which he speaks in the following terms:—" On the 20th of October, in the evening, we left Shendy, and rested two miles from the town and about a mile from the river; and next day, the 21st, we continued our journey. At nine we alighted to feed our camels under some trees, having gone about ten miles. At this place begins a large island in the Nile, several miles long, full of villages, trees, and corn: it is called Kurgos. Opposite to this is the mountain Gibbainy, where is the first scene of ruins I have met with since that of Axum in Abyssinia. We saw here heaps of broken pedestals, like those of Axum, plainly de-

---

* Heeren's Historical Researches, vol. i. p. 349. Plin. Hist. Nat. lib. vi. c. 35.

signed for the statues of the dog; and some pieces of obelisks, likewise with hieroglyphics, almost totally obliterated. The Arabs told us that these ruins were very extensive, and that many pieces of statues, both of men and animals, had been dug up there. The statues of the men were mostly of black stone. It is impossible to avoid risking a guess that this is the ancient city of Meroë."

The conjecture of our countryman has been established by the investigations of later travellers; and we find that those remains of antiquity, of which he obtained a hasty glance, are not confined to one place, but are scattered over a considerable extent of surface. The whole strip of land from Shendy to Gerri teems with them, and must therefore be regarded as a portion of the classic ground of Ethiopia. So far as our information extends at present, these ruins may be included in three principal groups, and associated with the names of Assour, Naga, and Messoura, or Meçaoura as it is written by Cailliaud. The first of these lies to the north of Shendy, about two miles from the river; the others are at the distance of several leagues from the Nile in a southerly direction, proceeding from the same point. The monuments found here consist both of temples and pyramids; all private dwellings having been long ago destroyed. According to Strabo these last were built of only split palm-trees and tiles: the sand, however, is in many places so covered with bricks that a town must formerly have stood there. In short, it is concluded that the site of the ancient Meroë can be no longer regarded as doubtful. It stood near the present Assour, or between that village and Tenetbey, where are still discovered the remains of a few temples, and of many other edifices constructed of sandstone; the whole extending, according to the measurement of Cailliaud, to a circumference of four thousand feet.

Eastward of Assour is what has been called the great churchyard of Pyramids, the existence of which likewise tends to prove that there was at one period a considerable city in the neighbourhood. It is impossible to behold the number of these monuments without astonishment: eighty are mentioned in the plan of Cailliaud; but the precise amount cannot be ascertained, as the ruins of many are indistinct. They are divided into three sections, one of which is due east from the assumed situation of Meroë, while the two others are a league from the river, one north and the other south. The northern group is at once the most extensive and best preserved. They certainly appear small compared with the structures of a similar kind in Middle Egypt, the height of the largest not being more than eighty feet; but viewed in reference to number they are much more wonderful.

Like those at Sakhara, these pyramids are formed of granite; and hence the decay into which they have fallen must suggest a very remote period as the time when the people, to whom they owe their foundation, enjoyed the power and wealth which such monuments imply. The larger class of them have usually attached a small building in the shape of a temple, finished in the Egyptian style, with a propylon and door which lead first to the portico and thence to the sanctuary. It is therefore manifest, if the real entrance is where it is thus indicated, that it was not the intention of the Ethiopian architects to conceal the approach to the repositories of mortality,—an object which was accomplished with so much labour by their successors on the Lower Nile. But as none of them have been examined, it is not known whether there be any mummies or sarcophagi in the interior; and, until such an investigation be completed, we must necessarily remain ignorant as well of the object contemplated by such piles of masonry, as of the many arts which might be employed in doing honour to the great. Indeed, according to Strabo, the Ethiopians did not embalm their dead, but buried them in earthen vessels near the sanctuary. The corners of the pyramids are partly ornamented, and the walls of the pylones are decorated with sculpture, in some of which the figures appear to be employed in making offerings for the departed; a representation which renders it extremely probable that they are the tombs of kings and other distinguished persons.*

M. Heeren is of opinion that pyramid-architecture was native in Ethiopia from the earliest ages; and also that, if we compare this style of building with the similar one adopted in Egypt, we shall have another proof of what we have elsewhere attempted to establish, that what had its rise in the former country was perfected in the latter.†

The statement of Cailliaud has been confirmed by the narrative of M. Rüppel of Frankfort, published in a continental journal, who also mentions the existence of similar groups of pyramids in Kurgos. On the other side of the Nile, as he relates, his

---

* Heeren's Historical Researches, vol. i. p. 394. Cailliaud, Voyage à Meroë, vol. iii. p. 104, &c.
† Historical Researches as above.

way lay for fifty-seven minutes across a plain of slime or mud. Traces were visible of an ancient canal running parallel to the bed of the river, a proof that this territory was once highly cultivated. Ten minutes after,—for in such circumstances distance is measured by time,—he came to a great mass of hewn and burnt stones. But age had destroyed every thing. With difficulty were some shafts of columns discovered, whose capitals were ornamented with the heads of animals; whence it may be inferred that they once belonged to a temple. Having walked twelve minutes farther on, he observed a number of pyramidical mausolea. There were thirteen, all of hewn stone, forty feet in height, but without an entrance. Near them was a lion's head in black granite, evidently a sitting sphinx.

After thirty minutes more, towards the east, a group of twenty-one tombs appeared; some of which were pyramids with indented borders, while others had pointed angles with edges of plainer workmanship. One of these monuments, the most southerly, differs from all the rest, being a prismatic steeple, standing upon a socle twenty feet square. It has an eastern entrance leading to the hall or gallery, as in the sepulchres at Assour. The walls are ornamented with beautiful sculpture; the reliefs being like those of Meroë, but in greater perfection, and representing in all cases the apotheosis of the dead. Here is also one of those pyramids which has a peculiarity in its approach. On both sides of it are two female figures holding lances in their hands, and in the act of piercing with them a band of prisoners. The drapery, grouping, and keeping, of this piece of sculpture, surpass every thing of the kind that M. Rüppel had seen in Nubia or Egypt, not excepting the magnificent temple of Dendera.

A little farther to the south-east, a third group was descried, consisting of nine pyramids, the inner walls of which are diversified with carving. The reliefs in this instance represent female figures only, while in all others they bear a reference to the divinity of heroes to whom offerings or sacrifices are made. There are none of these, however, so lofty as in the second assemblage; for some of the latter were at least ninety feet in height, whereas not one of the nine exceeded forty feet in elevation. They were all built of hewn stone without mortar.*

The antiquities of Naga and Messoura are of another kind, consisting chiefly of temples. Those of the former place lie about six leagues south-east of Shendy, and nearly the same distance from the Nile; presenting a larger one in the centre, and various smaller ones scattered about in every direction. The remains of the principal edifice clearly prove to what god it was dedicated. An avenue of statues, being rams couching on pedestals, leads into an open portico of ten columns, out of which, after passing through a similar gallery, we arrive at the pylone. Adjoining this is a colonnade consisting of eight pillars, beyond which there is a hall leading into the sanctuary. The doors, the columns, and the walls, are of hewn stone; the remainder of the structure is composed of bricks, with a coating upon which traces of painting are still visible. The gateways and pillars are sculptured in a style of

* See Writings by Edward Rüppel from the Camp near Kurgos, 29th Feb. 1824, in Europæische Blæter, Oct. 24, 1824; quoted by Heeren.

great beauty, exhibiting gods, kings, and queens, with attendants, sacrifices, and oblations. The building is of vast size, extending in length from the first pylone to the opposite extremity not less than eighty feet. There is also something peculiar in the portico. The duplicate gallery of rams, before entering and after passing it, is not common elsewhere; and the plan of the whole seems indeed to show that architecture had not yet attained to that perfection which it exhibits in the great works of Egypt.*

The western temple is smaller, but still more richly embellished. On the pylones or gateways the same scenes are represented as in the pyramids of Assour; a male warrior on the one side, and a female warrior on the other, destroying a number of captives whom they have bound together by the hair. They are king and queen, as they have both the emblem of dominion on the head-dress; over each is a spread eagle with a globe; and both are magnificently dressed. It is evident, then, as M. Heeren maintains, that these representations possess many peculiarities, and are not purely Egyptian. This remark does not indeed apply to religious rites; for there appears nothing here in the worship of Ammon and his kindred gods which is essentially different from the usages followed in the Thebaid. The real point of distinction applies to the human personages who are performing the duties of piety. The queens appear with the kings, and not merely as presenting offerings, but themselves as heroines and conquerors,—a circumstance which has not yet been discovered in any of the sculptures of Egypt or Nubia.

---

* Historical Researches, vol. i. p. 399.

They must therefore, it is presumed, relate to the rulers, male and female, of Meroë, and have been intended to commemorate their deeds. Speaking of this very kingdom, Strabo remarks that, among the Ethiopians, " the women are also armed ;" and we know from other sources, that ladies mounted the throne with the same authority as the other sex. Herodotus mentions Nitocris among the ancient queens of Ethiopia who governed Egypt; and in a carving already mentioned, representing the conquest of the former country by Sesostris, there is a female monarch with her sons who appears before him as a captive. A long succession of queens under the title of Candace must have reigned here; and even when at length the seat of the empire was removed from Meroë to Napata, near Gebel el Berkal, a sovereign of the same name exercised the supreme power. It is therefore quite agreeable to the usage of the Ethiopians to see a queen in a warlike habit near her consort, though it must be admitted to be peculiar to that celebrated people.

The perfection to which sculpture had been brought at Naga is very striking, there being nothing in the Egyptian statues superior to it, while in boldness of outline it seems even to surpass the finest specimens of the latter. These colossal figures, says Cailliaud, which are ten in number, are remarkable for the richness of their drapery and the character of the drawing; their feet and arms are stouter than those of Egypt, yet they are in the same style. A similar excellence in the reliefs at Kurgos is extolled by Rüppel. Are we to suppose, asks M. Heeren, that Ethiopian artists became thus accomplished? Or do these monuments rather belong to that brilliant period of the empire of Meroë,—the eighth century before our era,—when the dynasty of Tirhako and Sabaco ruled over Upper Egypt, and to whom it would be easy to send artists from below the Cataracts, to adorn their metropolis and perpetuate their fame?

The third station, called Messoura, is equally interesting. Cailliaud, to whom we are indebted both for a description and a drawing, relates, that in an extensive valley in the desert, eight hours' journey from Shendy towards the south-east, and six leagues from the Nile, are very considerable ruins. They consist of eight small temples, all connected by corridors and terraces. It is an immense edifice, formed by the junction of a number of chambers, courts, and temples, and is surrounded by a double enclosure. From the main structure in the centre the passage to the others is through galleries, or along terraces, varying from three hundred to one hundred and eighty-five feet in length. Each temple has its particular chambers; and all the buildings are placed in an exact order, consisting, as has been noticed, of eight temples or sanctuaries, forty-one chambers, twenty-four courts, three galleries, and fourteen staircases or flights of steps. These remains cover a plat of ground two thousand five hundred feet, or about half an English mile in circumference.

But in this immensity of ruins every thing is on a smaller scale,—the monuments as well as the materials employed. " The largest temple is only fifty-one feet long; upon the pillars are figures in the Egyptian style; others in the same portico are fluted like the Grecian; on the basis of one I thought I discovered the traces of a zodiac. Time and the elements, which have destroyed the ancient Saba, seem to have been willing to spare to us the observatory of Meroë; but until the rubbish be cleared away a complete plan of it cannot be expected. It excites our wonder to find so few hieroglyphics in all these ruins: the six pillars which form the portico of the central temple alone present a few examples, for all the other walls are without sculpture. Six hundred paces from the ruins are the remains of two other small temples, as also the outlines of a considerable tank surrounded by little hills, which must have protected it from the sand. But here there are not any traces of a city, no heaps of rubbish, no tombs. If Meroë had stood in this place, the pyramids would not have been built at the distance of two days' journey from it. I believe that a seminary of learning was established on this spot; the form of the building and the architecture seem to prove it; but the city itself was in the neighbourhood of the sepulchres where the pyramids are still found.*

The same author informs us, that at the distance of a hundred yards in a south-easterly direction from the great enclosure are some other ruins; among which are the relics of a small temple, resting on six columns, with a regular gateway. The interior is rather more than thirty-six feet in length. The pillars are covered with sculptured figures, including some of mounted elephants led by their guides,—a

---

* Là, étudiant mieux la distribution des différens corps de bâtimens en ruine que j'avais sous les yeux, je demeurai convaincu que ce lieu fut jadis consacré à l'enseignement,—un collège enfin.—*Cailliaud*, vol. iii. p. 142. The translation given in Heeren's work is extremely faulty and erroneous. See vol. i. p. 400—404.

species of picture which is never seen in Egypt. The nature of these representations, the form of the materials, and the very decayed condition of the whole building, induced the traveller to conclude that this little monument is much more ancient than the larger edifices to which our attention has just been drawn.

The details now given derive some interest from the conclusion which Heeren has founded upon them in regard to one point in the ancient religious establishment of Ethiopia. He thinks that the constructions at Messoura were the "Oracle of Jupiter Ammon." "A mere glance at the ground plan," says he, "leads to this idea. It is only thus that the singularity of the foundation can be accounted for; that labyrinth of passages and courts which must be wandered through before arriving at the entirely secret temple in the midst. Scarcely could there be a better introduction contrived for reaching the sanctuary."*

For the support of this opinion he relies chiefly on the authority of Diodorus, who relates that the temple of Jupiter did not stand in the city of Meroë but at some distance from it in the wilderness. When, again, the ruler of that kingdom resolved to free himself from the dominion of the priests, he went, says the same historian, with a company of soldiers to the retired or sequestered spot where the sanctuary with the golden temple stood, and taking the inmates by surprise, he put them all to death. Nor is the smallness of the edifice any objection to this view of the subject; for the same remark might

---

* Historical Researches, vol. i. p. 403.

be applied to the Ammonium in the Libyan desert. This was probably intended merely for the preservation of the sacred ship, which is understood to have been placed between the pillars of the holy shrine. Its situation, too, in the waste, also follows the example now adduced, and will appear still less extraordinary, when we reflect that it was constructed on one of the great trading routes between the Mediterranean and the Red Sea. "Thus we stand," says he, "on that remarkable spot which antiquity regarded as the cradle of the arts and sciences; where hieroglyphic writing was discovered; where temples and pyramids had already sprung up, while as yet Egypt remained entirely ignorant of their existence."[*]

It does not belong to us to weigh the probability which attaches to the opinion now stated. No one will question its ingenuity, or deny that the authorities quoted from ancient writers are suitably applied. But, at the same time, we must not forget the remarks made in regard to the institution at Messoura by M. Cailliaud, who informs his readers that the tradition of the country is that the name of the place is derived from the old fakirs who once inhabited those vast edifices. The figure of the elephants, too, caparisoned and mounted, rather strengthens the belief that the school of the desert, if it really was a place of education, was connected in its origin or tenets with the learning of the remoter East. There is, however, no irreconcilable discrepancy between the two conclusions now examined; for nothing was more common than to have a seminary of

---

[*] Historical Researches, vol. i. p. 406.

priests established near the temples of the gods, and to combine thereby in the mind of the student the practical parts of divine worship with the abstract tenets of the faith into which he was initiated.

Cailliaud was assured by certain Arabs, as well as by his own guides, that on the road from Naga, or Gibel-Ardan as it is sometimes called, there are several places distinguished for magnificent ruins covered with sculptures. The first station, they added, was at the distance of two days' journey, which corresponds perfectly to Mandeyr, the ancient capital of the Arabian shepherds. A day and a half farther on, at a village called Kely, according to the same authorities, there are other remains which occupy a great extent of surface. From thence, they add, there is a road that in the same space of time leads to Abou-Ahraz; and that near it are wells hewn out in the rock, which tradition carries back to a very remote antiquity. Agreeably to these statements, there can be no doubt that the line of march hereby indicated is the one which passed from the Nile, in the latitude of Naga, to Axum and the port of Adulis. But the ruins at Mandeyr and Kely have not yet been inspected by any modern traveller.

We now possess all the certainty which can be attained from the annals of ancient times, that the city of Meroë was situated a little northwards of the present Shendy; and also that a number of dependent establishments, founded on the basis of religion, were scattered over the adjoining desert.

Before we pass into Abyssinia, we shall quote from Diodorus an account of its constitution and government. The form of this celebrated state, then, was that which we often find in southern regions, more especially at remote periods: it was a hierarchy, where the power was in the hands of a race or caste of priests, who chose a king from among their own order. The laws of the Ethiopians, says the author now named, differ in many respects from those of other nations; but in none so much as in the nomination of their kings,—which is thus managed: The priests select some of the most distinguished of their brethren, and upon whomsoever of these the god fixes, he is carried in procession, and forthwith acknowledged sovereign by the people; who falling down adore him as a divinity, because he is placed over the government by the choice of Jupiter Ammon. The person thus appointed immediately enjoys all the prerogatives which are conceded to him by the laws, and is supplied with rules for the direction of his conduct; but he can neither reward nor punish any one beyond what the usages of ancestry and the royal statutes allow. It is a custom among them to inflict upon no subject the sentence of death, even though he should be legally found deserving of that punishment; but they send to the malefactor one of the servants of justice, who bears the symbol of mortality. When the criminal sees this he goes immediately to his house and deprives himself of life. The Greek custom of escaping punishment by fleeing into another country is not there permitted. It is said that the mother of one who would have attempted flight strangled him with her own girdle, in order to save her family from the greater disgrace of having one of its members denounced as a fugitive. But the most remarkable of all their institutions is that which relates to the death of their king. The priests at Meroë, who attend to the service of the gods and hold the highest rank, send a messenger to him with an order to die. They make known to his majesty, that Heaven requires this sacrifice at his hands, and that mortals should not oppose its decrees; and perhaps add such reasons as could not be controverted by weak understandings prejudiced by an ancient custom.*

We have already alluded to the catastrophe by which this mode of administration was brought to a close. In the reign of the second Grecian king who sat on the throne of Egypt, when the light of philosophy had already penetrated into Ethiopia, the sovereign of Meroë, whose name was Ergamenes, resolved to shake off the domination of the sacerdotal caste. At the head of an armed band he proceeded to their principal temple, and subjected the whole body to a general massacre; by which bold measure, subjoins the historian, he rendered himself a monarch in reality as well as in title.†

Heeren very judiciously observes, that in a state whose government so widely differed from any thing to which we have been accustomed, it is reasonable to suppose that a similar peculiarity would apply to the people, who could hardly bear any similitude to the civilized nations of modern Europe. Meroë, he thinks, rather resembled in appearance the larger states of interior Africa at the present day; a number of small nations of the most opposite habits and manners, some with and some without settled abodes, constituting what is called an empire, although the general political band which holds them together is loose, and often scarcely percepti-

---

* Diod. Bibliothec. Histor. lib. iii. c. 6.   † Ibid.

ble. In Ethiopia this band was of a twofold nature; first, religion or a certain worship resting upon oracles, and secondly, commerce,—unquestionably the strongest chains by which barbarians could be bound; for the one gratified the superstitious, and the other the covetous and sensual. Eratosthenes relates, that in his time the island comprised a variety of people; of whom some followed agriculture, others a nomadic or pastoral life, and a third class the more active pursuits of hunting. All chose what seemed best adapted to the particular district in which they lived.*

As the line of road through the desert which connects Atbara with Abyssinia has not been trodden in modern times by any native of Europe, we cannot trace the architectural features of the two countries to any distinct point of resemblance. The habits, too, of the people between the Nile and the Red Sea, who, living almost constantly in the field either as soldiers or as herdsmen, shunned the accommodation of large towns, afforded little encouragement to the arts of sculpture and design. It is not, accordingly, until we approach the shores

---

* Historical Researches, vol. i. p. 419. Strabo, p. 1177—1194. The account given by Pliny of the peninsular tract of Meroë corresponds remarkably with the indications which still remain of its ancient greatness. "Ipsum oppidum Meroën ab introitu insulæ (*i. e.* a loco ubi confluunt Nilus et Astaboras) abesse LXX millia passuum. Juxtaque aliam insulam Tadu dextro subeuntibus alveo quæ portum faceret. Ædificia oppidi pauca. Regnare fœminam Candacen, quod nomen multis jam annis ad reginas transiit. Delubrum Hammonis et ibi sacrum. Et toto tractu sacella." Lib. vi.

For some able remarks on the latitude of Meroë, as given by Pliny and Eratosthenes in Strabo, we refer to Dr Vincent's work on the Commerce and Navigation of the Ancients, vol. ii. p. 91, &c. This learned writer availed himself of the assistance of Bishop Horsley and Mr Wales, whose scientific deductions confirmed the statements of the Greek and Roman geographers.

of the Arabian Gulf that we find the traces of a civilized condition, and begin to discover the tokens of that refinement and command of the mechanical powers, which excite our surprise in Nubia and Egypt.

At Axum have been examined the remains of ancient works, which, though different from those of Dendera, Thebes, and Meroë, are sufficiently great to have called forth the admiration of the most competent judges; increasing, at the same time, the curiosity of the philosopher and the engineer in regard to the resources of artificers who could remove from the rock and raise to an upright position obelisks exceeding a hundred feet in length. That there was a large city on the ground which still displays so many interesting ruins, there is reason to conclude both from history and tradition, though it has now dwindled down to a few insignificant cottages. The native chroniclers carry back its origin to the days of the patriarch Abraham, while others are disposed to claim for it a still higher antiquity; but, as we have already remarked, it was unknown to Homer and Herodotus, and is not commemorated by any Grecian author before the time of Strabo. Nor is there the slightest cause to doubt that, whatever may have been the date of its foundation, it was greatly embellished by the successors of Alexander, who appear to have carried their arms southward along either shore of the Red Sea, and even to have established a temporary throne at Axum.

When Poncet was in Abyssinia this metropolis was known by the name of Heleni. "It has," says he, "a fair monastery and a magnificent church. It is the fairest and largest I have seen in Ethiopia.

It is dedicated to St Helena, and from that church in all likelihood the town has taken its name. In the middle of the spacious place before the church, are to be seen three pyramidical and triangular spires all filled with hieroglyphics. Amongst the figures of these pyramids I observed upon each face a lock, which is very singular, for the Ethiopians have no locks, and are even unacquainted with the use of them. Although you see no pedestals, yet these spires are no less high than the obelisk of the palace before St Peter's at Rome, placed upon its pedestal. It is believed that this was the country of the Queen of Saba; several villages depending upon this principality bear to this day the name of Sabaim. They get marble in the mountains which no way yields to that of Europe; but what is more considerable is, that they also find a great deal of gold even in tilling their ground. They brought me privately some pieces which I found to be very fine. The religious, or monks, of that church are habited in yellow skins, and wear a little cap of the same material and colour."*

Before Bruce paid his celebrated visit to these curiosities, two of the three great obelisks which the French physician found standing had fallen. In the square, which is imagined to have been the centre of the town, there were not fewer than forty in a prostrate condition, none of which, however, had any hieroglyphics upon them. Each consists of one piece of granite; and on the top of that which is still erect, there appeared to be a patera exceedingly well carved in the Grecian style. Below there is

* A Voyage to Ethiopia made in the years 1698, 1699, and 1700, p. 106.

the door-bolt and lock which Poncet speaks of, carved on the pillar, as if to represent an entrance through it to some building behind. The lock and bolt are precisely those which are used at this day in Egypt and Palestine, but were never seen in Ethiopia. This traveller holds the opinion that the monument now described, and the two larger ones which are fallen, are the work of Ptolemy Euergetes, the second of the Macedonian dynasty. There is, he assures his readers, a great deal of carving upon the face of the obelisk, in a Gothic taste, something like metopes, triglyphs, and guttæ, rudely disposed and without order, but, he adds, there are no characters or figures.

After passing the convent of Abba Pantaleon, and the small obelisk situated on the rock above, " we proceed south by a road cut in a mountain of red marble, having on the left a parapet wall above five feet high, solid, and of the same materials. At equal distances there are hewn in this wall solid pedestals, upon the tops of which we see the marks where stood the colossal statues of Sirius, the Latrator Anubis or dog-star. One hundred and thirty-three of these pedestals, with the marks of the statues I have just mentioned, are still in their places; but only two figures of the dog remained when I was there, much mutilated, but of a taste easily distinguished to be Egyptian. These are composed of granite; but some of them appear to have been of metal. Axum being the capital of Siris or Siré, from this we easily see what connexion this capital of the province had with the dog-star, and consequently the absurdity of supposing that the river derived its name from a Hebrew word, *shihor*, signifying black. There are likewise pedestals whereon the figures of the sphinx have been placed. Two magnificent flights of steps several hundred feet long, all of granite, exceedingly well fashioned and still in their places, are the only remains of a magnificent temple. In the angle of this platform, where that temple stood, is the present small church of Axum, in the place of a former one destroyed by Mohammed Gragné in the reign of King David III.; and which was probably the remains of a temple built by Ptolemy Euergetes, if not the work of times more remote."*

In reference to some of the points now stated, the accuracy of Bruce has been justly called in question, though in a spirit which does little honour to the critic and traveller to whom we owe the correction. During Mr Salt's first visit to Abyssinia, he was pleased to cast doubt on many parts of his predecessor's narrative, and even to charge him with downright fabrication, in matters of which a more minute inquiry afterwards completely established the truth. Of these hasty strictures we shall have occasion to produce some examples, when we come to review the manners and customs of the inhabitants; meantime we shall proceed to examine the details in which the former writer has manifestly failed in exactness of description.

He tells us, that " within the outer gate of the church, below the steps, are three small square enclosures all of granite, with small octagon pillars in the angles apparently Egyptian; on the top of which formerly were small images of the dog-star,

---

* Travels to discover the Source of the Nile, vol. iv. p. 321.

probably of metal. Upon a stone in the middle of one of these the king sits and is crowned, and always has been since the days of paganism; and below it, where he naturally places his feet, is a large oblong slab like a hearth, which is not of granite but of freestone. The inscription, though much defaced, may safely be restored.

ΠΤΟΛΕΜΑΙΟΥ ΕΥΕΡΓΕΤΟΥ
ΒΑΣΙΛΕΩΣ

"Poncet has mistaken this last word for Basilius; but he did not pretend to be a scholar, and was ignorant of the history of this country."*

Now it is proved beyond all reasonable scepticism, that there is no inscription whatever on the king's seat, and that the letters which Mr Bruce has given as Greek are in fact Ethiopic characters, and are found on a slab at the distance of thirty yards from the royal chair. Besides, Poncet makes not the slightest allusion to any such carving on the stones which compose that relic of antiquity; and it is now fully ascertained, that the reference to a tablet with the word "Basilius" on it, is in the work of another author who wrote at an earlier period. In a word, it must be acknowledged that the distinguished traveller whose statements we are now examining, could only have written his account of the ruins at Axum from an indistinct reminiscence, aided by the publications of the Jesuit missionaries; and that he has accordingly, in more than a single instance, confounded one monument with another.

Still, it may be suggested, that the errors com-

---

* Travels, vol. iv. p. 323. Second edition.

mitted by him are not of so atrocious a nature as to justify the severe remarks of Mr Salt, who, alluding to his description of the standing obelisk, not only undervalues his acquirements as an artist, but also impeaches his truth and honour as a man. " I am now perfectly satisfied," says he, " that all Bruce's pretended knowledge of drawing is not to be depended upon; the present instance affording a striking example both of his want of veracity and of his uncommon assurance, in giving, with a view to correct others, as a geometrical elevation, so very false a sketch of this monument." This intense vituperation, too, is the more misapplied, inasmuch as, in regard to the very same obelisk, Mr Salt found it necessary, when he examined it five years afterwards, to make two very material alterations; and hence there is an essential discrepancy between his report of it in Lord Valentia's Travels, and that contained in his own volume, the Travels in Abyssinia. In the former he assigns to it a height of eighty feet, whereas in the latter it is reduced to sixty; and while, in the beautiful plate with which he adorned his lordship's book, he represents the patera on the top as terminating in rather a sharp point, he admits in his own pages that " it ought to have been round." Two such blunders by so complete a master of the pencil were hardly to be expected, and more especially in one who was so ready to condemn the " pretended knowledge of drawing" in others! To Bruce, on the other hand, he will not allow the benefit of that very modified candour which regards a mistake in numbers and position as involuntary, or the mere effect of an imperfect recollection. He asserts, on the contrary, " It appears to me, that nothing but the fallacious presumption that no one, after the difficulties he had described with so much exaggeration, would dare to follow his steps, could have induced him to venture on such unsupported assertions, which the very next European who should travel that way would so certainly refute."*

But it must not be concealed that Bruce was more unfortunate in his omissions than his misstatements; for he left Axum without seeing a monument to which former travellers had in fact alluded, and which is now regarded as the most valuable relic in that ancient capital. About half a mile from the church, though somewhat concealed by rising ground, is an upright slab eight feet in length, three and a half broad, and one foot in thickness, which contains an inscription in the Greek language illustrative of the ancient history of the country. The characters, which are fairly and deeply cut, are nearly two inches long. For the preservation of the engraving in so perfect a state it is greatly indebted to a fortunate inclination towards the north, which the nature of the ground has given to the stone, by which that side of it is entirely sheltered from the rain. The translation in Mr Salt's work is as follows:—

> " (We) Aeizanas, King of the Axomites and
> of the Homerites, and of Raeidan, and of the Ethiopians, and of the Sabeans, and of Zeyla,
> and of Tiamo, and the Boja, and of the Taquie, King of Kings, son of god,
> the invincible Mars—having rebelled
> on an occasion the nation of the Boja,
> We sent our brothers
> Saiazana and Adephos

---

* Valentia's Travels, vol. iii. p. 98.

to make war upon them; and upon
their surrender (our brothers), after subduing them,
brought them to us with their families;
of their oxen 112, and of their sheep
7424, and their beasts bearing burthens;
nourishing them with the flesh of oxen, and giving them a
supply of bread, and affording them to drink
beer (sowa) and wine (maize), and water in abundance.
Who (the prisoners) were in number six chiefs,
with their multitude in number ***
making them bread every day of wheat-
en cakes *2* and giving them wine for a month
until the time that they brought the whole body to us;
whom therefore supplying with all things
fit, and clothing, we compelled them to change their
abode, and sent them to a certain place of our
country called M——a, and we ordered them
again to be supplied with bread, furnishing
to these six chiefs oxen 4*.
In grateful acknowledgment to him who begat me,
the invincible Mars,
I have dedicated to him a golden statue, and one
of silver, and three of brass, for good."

This inscription, taken by itself, is of no great value, for it merely records the result of a successful attack upon a barbarous tribe; but it possesses no small importance when applied to the illustration of a dark period in Ethiopian history, as well as to determine the precise date at which the monument itself was erected. Aizana, as was formerly observed, was king of Abyssinia, or rather of the Axumites, in the reign of the Roman emperor Constantius; and there is still extant, in the works of Athanasius, a letter from that popular ruler to the African prince, at the time he was reigning conjointly with his brother Saizana, whose name is also mentioned on the slab. From comparing the date of the imperial communication with the circumstances to which it is known to have had a reference,—the disgrace of Frumentius and the orthodox clergy,—it is concluded that the inscription must have been engraved about the year 330 of the Christian epoch.*

Mr Salt remarks, that all the information which could be procured concerning the singular remains at Axum was obtained from the priests, who, on the authority of their sacred books, related, that their ancient monuments and obelisks, originally fifty-five in number, of which four were as large as the one now standing, were erected by Ethiopus, the father of Abyssinia, about one thousand five hundred and forty years ago. They add, that the great reservoir, from which every house in the town was formerly supplied with water, was constructed during the reign of King Isaac by the Abuna Samuel, who died at Axum three hundred and ninety-two years ago, and was buried under the daroo-tree, which still remains near the church. They moreover subjoin the interesting fact, that in the year 1070 a female named Jadit (or Judith), who had great au-

* Valentia's Travels, vol. iii. p. 186. Considering that monument has stood one thousand five hundred years, the circumstance of its being found in so very perfect a state is somewhat remarkable; and it strongly proves the want of research among the Fathers who visited this country in the fifteenth century, as the following account given of it by Tellez will sufficiently prove. " Non procul abhinc erectum est saxum, tribus cubitis latum, insculptum literis partim Græcis partim Latinis, sed temporis injuria ferè exesis. Hoc indicium est, omnes istas structuras esse artificum Europæorum a temporibus Justini et aliorum Imperatorum Orientalium, qui (teste Procopio) magnam cum regibus Ethiopiæ amicitiam coluerunt. Quamvis tunc temporis mixtura fuerit linguarum Græcæ et Latinæ, quia milites unius et alterius idiomatis in iisdem castris militabant—Verum imaginari mihi non possum mixtam scripturam in illis saxis reperiri, multo minus rationem istius rei valere puto. Oculatiores inspectores (aut nimium fallor) aliquando reperient scripturam mere Græcam, atque in ea literas A. B. E. T. I. K. M. N. O. P. T. X. quas Latini cum Græcis communes habent, quamvis non in omnibus æqualis sint pronuntiationis."

Hence it is manifest that, when this learned Father travelled in Abyssinia, not only were the contents of the Axum-inscription unknown, but it was still doubtful in what language it was expressed.

thority, came from Amhara, and, excited by a superstitious motive, destroyed as far as she was able these remains of ancient art; threw down the obelisks, broke the altars, and laid the whole place in ruins; an account by no means improbable, as it is admitted that there is every appearance of many of the largest altars having been shattered by great force, and removed from their place.*

The great obelisk has been universally admired even from the days of the Portuguese mission, when the knowledge of it was first conveyed to modern Europe. The more minutely it was examined by Mr Salt, who could compare it with others of Egyptian, Grecian, and Roman origin, the more deeply was he struck with the consummate skill and ingenuity displayed in its formation; and he thought himself justified in pronouncing it the most perfect monument of its kind.†

Most of our readers are aware that there was a similar inscription at Adulis, an ancient town near the Bay of Masuah, which was copied by Cosmas Indicopleustes, who, as has been already mentioned, visited that coast in the sixth century. The work into which this record has been transcribed is entitled "Topographia Christiana," and was intended by its author to prove that the earth is a plane, in opposition to the philosophical notion of its being a sphere, which he conceived to be an heretical opinion and contrary to divine revelation. He had himself travelled much, and in the parts he visited he still found they were all on the same level or flat surface with Greece, his native land. His deductions from

---

* Valentia's Travels, vol. iii. p. 98.
† Travels in Abyssinia, p. 405.

this hypothesis are rather extraordinary; but the facts he relates, and the countries he describes, are given with all the characters of truth that simplicity can afford.

Adulis, says he, " is a city of Ethiopia, and the port of communication with Axiomis and the whole nation, of which that city is the capital; in this port we carry on our trade from Alexandria and the Elanitic Gulf; the town itself is about two miles from the shore, and as you enter it on the western side by the road that leads from Axiomis, there is still remaining a chair or throne which appertained to one of the Ptolemys, who had subjected this country to his authority. This chair is of beautiful white marble; not so white indeed as the Proconnesian, but such as we employ for marble tables; it stands on a quadrangular base, and rests at the four corners on four slender and elegant pillars, with a fifth in the centre, which is channeled in a spiral form. On these pillars the seat is supported, as well as the back of the throne, and the two sides on the right and left. The whole chair, with its base, the five pillars, the seat, the back, and the two sides, is of one entire piece carved into this form; in height about two cubits and a half, and in shape like a patriarch's chair."

At the back of it is a tablet of basanite or Egyptian granite three cubits in height; it is now indeed fallen down, and the lower part of it broken and destroyed; but the whole slab, as well as the chair itself, is filled with Greek characters. " Now it so happened when I was in this part of the country about five and twenty years ago, in the beginning of the reign of Justin the Roman emperor, that

Elesbaan the king of the Axiomites, when he was preparing for an expedition against the Homerites on the other side of the Red Sea, wrote to the governor of Adulis, directing him to take a copy of the inscription which was both on the chair of Ptolemy and on the tablet, and to send it to him. The governor, whose name was Asbas, applied to me, and to a merchant of the name of Menas, to copy the inscription. Menas was a Greek of my acquaintance, who afterwards became a monk at Raithû, and died there not long ago. We undertook the business together, and having completed it, delivered one copy to the governor and kept another for ourselves. It is from this copy that I now state the particulars of the inscription, and I ought to add, that in putting them together and drawing my own conclusions from them, I have found them very useful for forming a judgment of the country, the inhabitants, and the distances of the respective places. I ought to mention, that we found the figures of Hercules and Mercury among the carvings at the back of the seat."

Cosmas supplies his readers with a drawing, which was copied from his manuscript by Montfaucon, and is given by Dr Vincent in the second volume of his work on the Commerce and Navigation of the Ancients. The inscription on the tablet or slab, found lying behind the chair, is as follows :—

" Ptolemy the Great, king, son of Ptolemy, king, and Arsinoe, queen, gods, brother and sister; grandson of the two sovereigns, Ptolemy, king, and Berenice, queen, gods-preservers; descended on the father's side from Hercules son of Jupiter, receiving from his father the kingdom of Egypt, Africa, Syria, Phenicia, Cyprus, Lycia, Caria, and the Cyclades, invaded Asia with his land and sea forces, and with elephants from the country of the Troglodytes and Ethiopians. This body of elephants was first collected out of these countries by his father and himself, and brought into Egypt and tamed for the service of war. With these forces Ptolemy, advancing into Asia, reduced all the country on this side the Euphrates, as well as Cilicia, the Hellespont, Thrace, and all the armies in those provinces. In this expedition, having captured also many Indian elephants, and subjected all the princes to his obedience, he crossed the Euphrates, entered Mesopotamia, Babylonia, Susiana, Persis, Media, and the whole country as far as Bactria, and brought it all under his dominion. In Persis and Susiana he collected all the spoils of the temples which had been carried out of Egypt by Cambyses and the Persians, and carried them back again to that country, with all the treasures he had accumulated in his conquests and all the forces which had attended him on the expedition; all these he embarked upon the canals."

This, says Cosmas, was the inscription on the tablet, "so far as we could read it; and it was nearly the whole, for only a small part was broken off. After that we copied what was written on the chair, which was connected with the inscription already given, and ran thus:"

Our limits will not permit us to insert this commemoration of a series of conquests over the barbarian tribes of Eastern Africa and Arabia, from the borders of Egypt to the shores of the Indian Ocean. There is no doubt, however, that the monarch carried his arms into the hilly parts of Abyssinia, and perhaps into Sennaar and Kordofan. "I reduced," says he, "Ava, and Tiamo or Tziamo, Gambêla and the country around it, Zingabênè, Tiama, and the Agathai, Kalaa, and Semênè, among mountains difficult of access and covered with snow. In all this region there is hail and frost, and snow so deep that the troops sunk up to their knees. I passed the Nile to attack these nations, and subdued them." In conclusion his majesty says, "Thus having reduced the whole world to peace under my own authority, I came down to Adulis, and sacrificed to Jupiter, to Mars, and to Neptune, imploring his protection for all that navigate these seas. Here also I reunited all my forces (which had been employed on both sides of the Red Sea), and sitting on this throne, in this place, I consecrated it to Mars in the twenty-seventh year of my reign."*

In the learned work of Dr Vincent the reader will find much amusing commentary on these inscriptions, and an account of all the places in Asia and Africa mentioned by the boastful conqueror. Mr Salt thinks that the two records, on the chair and on the tablet, apply to different sovereigns at an earlier and a later period,—considering the first as a record of the victories of Ptolemy in Asia, and the second as a memorial of the exploits of an Abyssinian king. For the reasons on which these several opinions are supported, we refer to his learned dissertation inserted in the third volume of Lord Valentia's Travels.†

---

* See Vincent's Periplus of the Erythræan Sea, in his second volume, p. 530—542. Montfaucon's Nova Collectio Patrum, 2 vols. fol. Paris, 1706. Lord Valentia's Travels, vol. iii. p. 192.
† See p. 195.

We refrain from any farther details respecting the architectural monuments of ancient Ethiopia; but we cannot conclude this chapter without adding a few reflections on that magnificence and power of which they are now the only remaining tokens. While we find all our efforts fruitless in attempting to trace the rise of those political institutions, which conferred upon Egypt a glory at once so early and so permanent, we are rewarded with an unexpected success in marking the vestiges of religious architecture as we follow its progress more than four hundred leagues along the valley of the Nile. We detect the workings of the same mighty spirit, from the rock-cut temples of Nubia to those masterpieces of human skill and perseverance, the temples of Thebes and the pyramids of Djizeh.

The structures of Luxor and Karnac excite an astonishment that increases in proportion to the care with which they are examined. The hypostyle hall at the latter place, for example, is represented as the most stupendous and sublime of all the remains of Egyptian palaces or temples. Every thing connected with it is colossal; its area is nearly 58,000 square feet, and its roof is supported by a hundred and thirty-four pillars, some of which are little short of eleven feet in diameter. Each column of the two central rows, which are somewhat taller than the others, measures sixty-five feet in height and thirty-three feet in circumference. The whole from top to bottom is ornamented with sculpture relating to religious affairs. The procession of the boat, or holy ark, is often repeated on the walls. So great, however, is the number of these carvings that no one has been able to count them, much less to copy them. No description, says an eyewitness, can adequately express the sensations inspired by this astonishing sight, in which the magnificence and might of the ancient rulers of Egypt are made perceptible to the eye. Of what deeds, of what events, now lost to the history of the world; of what scenes have these columns been the witnesses! Can it be doubted that this was the spot where those rulers of the world, of the nations in the East and in the West, exhibited themselves in their glory and power, and in which they concentrated the fruits of their victories, the spoil or tribute of many vanquished kingdoms? Well might Champollion exclaim that the imagination, which in Europe rises far above our porticos, sinks abashed at the foot of the one hundred and forty columns of the hypostyle hall of Karnac!*

The great temple of Karnac too, which is one of the best preserved monuments in this part of Egypt, combines magnitude with splendour in a very high degree; being surrounded with colonnades, gigantic figures, and stately porticos. It is without doubt one of the most ancient structures in the country, and yet it offers a confirmation of the opinion to which, in the mind of certain travellers, the examination of the palace gave rise; namely, that both were partly built of the materials of more

---

* Heeren, vol. i. p. 248. "But we shall form a more exact idea of this enormous work, by comparing it with some standard of which we can judge. The church of St Martin's in the Fields, one of the finest and largest of modern religious edifices in London, is $137\frac{2}{3}$ feet long and 81 wide, measured along the outside basement, not including the steps and portico. This will give an area of nearly 11,150 square feet; which is not so much as one-fifth part of the great hall of Karnac."—*British Museum*, p. 89.

ancient edifices, ornamented with the same hieroglyphics, the same colours, and the same highly-finished sculptures. To what profound contemplations on the antiquity of the arts, and on the progress of civilisation so closely connected with their culture, do these observations lead !*

In describing the ruins which still remain on various points of the Nile, we have had frequent occasion to mention the sacred ship or boat sculptured on the walls. Sesostris is said to have dedicated one of cedar-wood to Ammon, the god of Thebes; it was 420 feet long, gilded all over on the outside and covered with silver within. The use of this emblem was supposed to denote the foreign extraction of their priesthood and religious rites, and to draw the attention of the worshippers to some distant land whence their ceremonies were originally derived. " Once a-year," as we are informed by Diodorus Siculus, " the sanctuary or shrine of Zeus is taken across the river to the Libyan side, and after a few days it is brought back, as if the deity were returning from Ethiopia." This procession, too, is represented in one of the reliefs on the temple of Karnac; the sacred ship of Ammon being on the Nile with its whole equipment, and towed along by another boat. This must therefore, says Heeren, have been one of the most celebrated festivals, since, according to the interpretation of antiquity, Homer alludes to it when he speaks of Jupiter's visit to the Ethiopians and his twelve days' absence. That such attendance, paid by the gods of a colony to those of the parent state,

---

* Heeren, vol. i. p. 252.

were common, and considered as proofs of national relationship, is well known from numerous instances in the ancient world. The forms only were different; in one case this affinity might be commemorated by such a procession as we have described, in another by sending a sacred embassy. When Alexander took Tyre, he found there a religious mission from Carthage, the most important of its colonies.*

The same principle applies to all the nations of the Eastern World; for a common religion was one of the strongest ties amongst men in ancient times, and tended more, perhaps, than any thing else to perpetuate among them those friendly feelings which had their origin in a kindred blood. The primitive seat of their faith was still held as the metropolis of all the tribes and people who sprang from the same root. Thus we find, that at the stated season devout men of Jewish extraction went from every nation under heaven to worship at Jerusalem, the holy city of their fathers; a practice well illustrated by the journey of the Ethiopian treasurer, who, in order to fulfil a pious duty, passed the frightful deserts which intervened between the country of Candace and the capital of Palestine.

Aided by this principle we can more easily trace the lineage of the divinities acknowledged by Greece and Rome. The Jupiter of Olympus was only a cadet, so to speak, of that ancient family of gods, who, through the medium of the branches established in Egypt, extended their authority and worship

---

* Diod. Sic. lib. i. c. 97. Κατ' ἐνιαυτὸν γὰρ παρὰ τοῖς Αἰγυπτίοις τον νεὼν τοῦ Διὸς περαιοῦσθαι τὸν ποταμὸν εἰς την Λυβυην, καὶ μεθ' ἡμέρας τινὰς παλιν ἐπιστρηφειν, ὡς ἐξ Αἰθιοπίας του θεου παρόντος. Heeren, vol. i. p. 301. British Museum, 96.

from the shores of the Indian Ocean to those of the Baltic. The homage, therefore, which was paid by the junior deities to the parent gods at the ancient seat of their power, was not only a mark of respect to antiquity but an acknowledgment of inferiority and dependence in the more recent people. It implied, besides, all the duties of a vassal state; for he who carried a gift to the shrine of a national divinity, confessed thereby that his allegiance was pledged, and his services bound to the land in which he presented his offering.

We have elsewhere mentioned the alarm which was excited among the Hebrew tribes, who under the command of Joshua had settled on the western side of the Jordan, when it was reported to them that their brethren of Gad and Reuben had erected an altar on the opposite bank in the pastoral district of Gilead. This act was considered as equivalent to a political schism, or a permanent separation of interests. And when they heard of it, " the whole children of Israel gathered themselves together at Shiloh, to go up to war against them." An appeal to arms was prevented, by an assurance on the part of the suspected herdsmen that they had no intention to offer sacrifices, but were ready to repair for all religious usages to the place where the ark of the covenant should be deposited.

In surveying the wonders which crowd the banks of the Nile from Meroë to Memphis, we are struck with the reflection that the wealth, power, and genius, whence they derived their origin, have entirely passed away. In some portions of that extensive tract a race little superior to savages pass a rude and precarious life, ignorant of the arts, and insensible equally to the beauty and the magnificence of the ruins which they tread under foot. They have ceased even to claim connexion with the people who raised the splendid monuments of Ebsamboul, Karnac, and Dendera; and, accordingly, they ascribe the anxiety which our countrymen display, in regard to those remains of antiquity, to the desire of visiting the tombs of a European nation, who are supposed by them to have built the temples and sculptured the obelisks.

The Nubians, especially, have relapsed into that low condition where even curiosity has become dormant, and in which the eye can be every day fixed on the noblest works of human ingenuity without suggesting any speculation as to their authors, their epoch, or their design. Throughout the whole world, in short, there is no greater contrast to be witnessed than between what now is, and what must once have been, in Ethiopia and Egypt. There is even great difficulty in passing, by an effort of thought, from the one condition to the other, through the various scenes of conquest and desolation which seem necessary to have produced the effects we contemplate. We might question history, but we should receive no answer, as to events and characters which the lapse of three thousand years has thrown into an impenetrable obscurity. Surrounded with darkness we grope our way amidst superb structures, dedicated to gods and heroes whose names make but a faint impression on our ears; and we satisfy ourselves with the conclusion, that a great people had existed there before the era of recorded time, whose literature and philosophy have been outlived by their architectural monuments.

CHAPTER V.

Religion and Literature of Ethiopia.

Abyssinia received Christianity at an early Period—Influence of Religion on its Political State and Civil History—Story of Frumentius—Jewish Ceremonies mixed with the Gospel—Arian Heresy—Constantius—Invasion of Arabia—Heresy of Eutyches—Conversion of Nubians—Justinian and Theodora—Zara Jacob—His Letter to the Monks of Jerusalem—Council of Florence—Pagans of Samen—Arrival of Paez—Dispute with Clergy—The King Za Denghel becomes Roman Catholic—His Letter to the Pope—Accession of Susneus—His Adherence to the Roman Form—Rebellion—Formal Declaration in favour of Popery—Death of Paez—Arrival of Mendez—His Proceedings as Patriarch—Encroachments and Tyranny—The King alarmed insists on Moderation—Rebellion—Basilides, or Facilidas, the Prince—Hopes of the People—Letter from the Pope—Additional Concessions—Popery abolished—Jesuits banished—Capuchins—Franciscan Friars—Attempt by Louis XIV.—Poncet and Brevedent—Massacre of Catholic Priests—Arrival of Abuna—His Proceedings—The Psalter—Doctrines of Abyssinians—Zaga Zaba, Ludolf, and Lobo—Mode of Worship—Form of Churches—Circumcision, Baptism, and Communion—Prayers for the Dead—Fixedness of Manners and Habits—Sabbath—Chronology—Last Attempt of Catholics—Literature—Resemblance to Jews—Books—Philosophy—Law—Medicine—Modern Translations.

WE have alluded to the singular fact, that Abyssinia, which received the Christian faith at an early period, has retained it, amidst a great variety of fortune, down to the present day. The arms and the policy of the Moslem, which prevailed in Egypt, Asia Minor, the northern shores of Africa, and even over a large portion of Greece, could not make any permanent impression among the Ethiopians. A furious war, it is true, raged between the Mohammedan chief, who took possession of the country near Adel, and the King of the Axumites; but it does not appear that, either by conquest or negotiation, the tenets of the Koran were ever admitted into any of the Abyssinian provinces.

This distinction will be found the more remarkable, when we consider the imperfect means which were used for establishing the gospel in that remote kingdom, and we may add, the rather defective form in which it was received by the new converts. The principles of Christianity were not expounded there by the apostles nor by their personal missionaries, as at Corinth, Ephesus, Galatia, and Thessalonica; and yet, while the Seven Churches of Asia have left nothing but a name in the page of ecclesiastical history, the believers in Ethiopia, who fifteen hundred years ago "stretched out their hands unto God," still glory in their ancient creed.

There is another peculiarity in regard to this people, so far at least as their connexion with this part of the world is considered, which is, that it is chiefly through the medium of their religious attachments their civil affairs have been made known among European nations. So soon as it was rumoured that a Christian state existed on the eastern coast of Africa, surrounded by bigoted Mussulmans and infidel pagans, a deep interest was excited among all classes of men. Kings, warriors, merchants, and navigators, were seized with a pious curiosity to know the actual condition of a people whose history, they concluded, must be strange, and who, if they should require it, were entitled as brethren in the faith to their aid and protection. The legend, too, respecting Prester John, had its full influence in animating their zeal in the search of a monarch, whose name was associated in their minds with every sentiment of veneration and wonder.

We have already had more than one occasion to allude to the story of Frumentius, who is usually supposed to have conveyed to Abyssinia the knowledge of the Christian faith. In company with a fellow-student he was under the care of Meropius, a philosopher, when the ship in which they sailed happened to be wrecked on the Ethiopian coast. The preceptor was murdered by the barbarians, but the lives of the two pupils were spared; after which occurrence the young men were conducted to Axum, where their accomplishments soon procured for them an honourable employment at court. It is even said that, through the influence of the queen, Frumentius was appointed tutor to the prince her son, during whose minority the seeds of the gospel were sown by the zealous stranger.

On his return to Egypt he communicated to Athanasius, who at that time filled the patriarch's chair, the success which had attended his first endeavours to disseminate the principles of the true religion. To enable him to complete the good work which he had so auspiciously begun, he was forthwith clothed with the episcopal character, and sent back as Bishop of Axum. But his progress was soon afterwards interrupted by the prevalence of the Arian heresy, which, being patronised by Constantius, was so extensively propagated throughout the empire, that at length it signalized its triumph by the degradation of the distinguished divine, who, as we have just noticed, occupied the patriarchal throne of Alexandria. We have repeatedly mentioned the letter which the emperor wrote to the brothers Aizana and Saizana, who exercised a joint power at Axum, denouncing their bishop, and requesting that he might be sent to the Egyptian capital, where, " by conversing familiarly with Venerable George and other learned men, he would reap great benefits, and return to his see well instructed in all ecclesiastical discipline." This invitation or command received no attention either from the prelate or his sovereigns; and hence the church of Ethiopia continued orthodox, while the majority of the oriental Christians were beguiled into error by the reasoning of Arius, or by the authority of the father of Constantine.*

It cannot be concealed, that with the doctrines of Christianity they either incorporated many ceremonies which they had borrowed from the Jews, or, it may be, they received the gospel mixed with many of their rites, which had not, in the early period of the Egyptian church, been entirely separated from it. It is equally certain, however, that the faith which they adopted with enthusiasm they maintained with great firmness; for they not only withstood the importunity employed by the imperial envoys to draw them aside from the truth, but even employed their arms to defend the believers in Arabia against the enemies of the Cross. So highly esteemed, indeed, were their zeal and influence, that the head of the Roman empire did not regard it as unsuitable to his dignity to solicit their co-operation in opposing the Persians, aided by the infidel Hebrews, who threatened the eastern shore of the Red Sea.

---

* Ludolfi Hist. Ethiop. lib. iii. c. 2. The names of the royal brothers in the language of the country were Abreha and Atzbeha.

The interval between the reign of Constantius and the government of Justinian presents to the historian little more than an absolute blank. We read, it is true, that from time to time many holy men went from Egypt, who were invariably received with reverence by the inhabitants; particularly nine of great sanctity, about the year 480, whose memory is still respected in the province of Tigré, where a corresponding number of churches were built and called after their names.*

But at length the disputes which tore asunder the great body of the Greek church reached the remote provinces of Abyssinia. The theological error, which is associated with the name of Eutyches, respecting the nature of Christ, found a favourable reception in Egypt, and was communicated by the Patriarch to the subordinate prelate of Axum. The opinion that the Redeemer consisted of only one nature, as the Divine Word, and partook not in any degree of the qualities of flesh and blood, is known among ecclesiastical writers as the *monophysite* heresy; and which, though it was variously modified by subsequent authors, at no time ceased to respect the essential point of faith now described. As it seems to be characteristic of the Abyssinians never to relinquish what they have once been taught on sufficient authority, they resisted every attempt made by the orthodox party to induce them to an abjuration of their heretical notions.

Nubia, more recently converted to our holy religion, was infected with the same errors and subjected

---

* Geddes's Church History of Ethiopia, p. 14. Ludolfi Hist. Ethiop. lib. iii. c. 3.

to the same controversies. It unfortunately happened that Justinian and his consort had adopted opposite conclusions on the great subject, the discussion of which so greatly divided the Christian world; and as the zeal of the latter was not less active than that of the emperor himself, she propagated her favourite views from the Danube to the borders of Sennaar. It was recommended to her to bring within the pale of the church all the black nations who dwell beyond the tropic of Cancer; a pious undertaking, in which she soon found herself emulated by her husband. Rival missionaries were accordingly despatched at the same time; but the empress, from a motive of love or of fear, was more effectually obeyed; and the orthodox priest was detained by the governor of the Thebaid, while the King of Nubia and his court were hastily baptized into the faith of Eutyches. The tardy envoy of Justinian was received and dismissed with honour; but when he denounced the heresy and treason which had been perpetrated in defiance of his master, the negro prince was taught to reply, that he would never abandon his brethren, the true believers, to the persecuting agents of the Synod of Chalcedon. During several ages the bishops were named and consecrated by the Patriarch of Alexandria: as late as the twelfth century the profession of the gospel was preserved; and at the present day we can still trace, along the banks of the Upper Nile, the ruins of Christian churches, or of temples which had occasionally been employed for that purpose, and even a lingering respect for ceremonies of which the real import has ceased to be understood. The Nubians, assailed by the Moslem and deriving no aid from their parents in the faith, gradually relapsed into the state of paganism; and at length some tribes of them, who maintained an intercourse with Egypt, exchanged the New Testament, which they had not been able to read, for the Koran, whose success they were taught to identify with the proof of a divine commission.

There is reason to believe that the same emulation which distinguished the imperial couple in behalf of the Nubians was not less efficient in regard to Abyssinia. The industry of the lady was again successful; and the pious Theodora had the satisfaction of establishing in that kingdom the tenets and discipline of the Jacobites, a sect who held the doctrine of the one nature. But we find from the history of John Malala, that the zeal of the emperor, so far from being deemed intrusive, was invited by the ruler of Ethiopia. This annalist informs us that the King of the Axumites, when he had obtained the victory over the Arabians, despatched two of his relations with two hundred followers to Alexandria, for the purpose of soliciting from Justinian that a bishop and some holy men might be sent to instruct his subjects in the mysteries of the Christian faith. The emperor being informed of these things by Licinius, his viceroy at Alexandria, gave an order that the ambassadors should be allowed to make choice of whomsoever they pleased; and they accordingly chose John, the almsgiver of St John in Alexandria, a good and pious man about sixty-two years of age, and took him, then a bishop, together with several holy men, to their country to Anda, or Ameda, their king.*

---

* Joan. Malal. Chronographia, p. 168, quoted by Mr Salt in his Travels in Abyssinia, p. 467.

But the army of Elesbaan, the same who is called Anda by the chronographer just quoted, could not support the cause of the believers on the opposite side of the gulf, and hence a path was left open for the introduction of a new religion. If a Christian power, says a great writer, had been maintained in Arabia, Mohammed must have been crushed in his cradle, and Abyssinia would have prevented a revolution which has changed the civil and religious state of the world.*

In following the current of events, as they respect the ecclesiastical affairs of Ethiopia, we have to lament the total absence of historical facts from the sixth to the middle of the fifteenth century. Coming down to the reign of Zara Jacob, who ascended the throne about 1434, we find that a convent for Abyssinians had already been founded at Jerusalem, of which this pious monarch greatly increased the endowments. A similar privilege was also obtained at Rome; a fact which of itself gives some probability to the assertion of certain Dominican authors, who record that an intercourse had been occasionally maintained between the Pope and the sovereign of Axum. We present to our readers a single specimen of the correspondence which the negash negashi, or king of kings, thought proper to carry on with the monks in the holy city:—

"I, Zara Jacob, whose name, since God was pleased to place me on the throne of the empire, is Constantine, in the eighth year of my reign, do bequeath unto you the land of Zebla, and half of all tributes arising from it for two years, which amounts

---

* Gibbon's Decline and Fall of the Roman Empire, vol. ix. p. 309, &c.

to a hundred ounces of gold, toward your food and raiment; and do give it to the monastery of Jerusalem, that it may be a memorial of myself and of our Lady Mary, and for the celebration of her feasts; to wit, that of her Nativity on the 1st May, that of her Death on the 22d January, and that of her Translation on the 15th August; as also of the feasts of her Son, our Lord Jesus, on the 29th December, when he was born, to be celebrated by you at Bethlehem, together with the festivities of his Passion and lively Resurrection from death. You shall likewise celebrate all the festivities of our Lady Mary, which in the Book of her Miracles are thirty-two in number. And you shall furthermore keep a lamp burning for me in the sepulchre of our Lord, and another in the entry thereof; and so on the right side, one, and on the left, another; also at the place of his burial, three; three at the monument of our Lady Mary in Gethsemane; and at the place where Mary Magdalene saw him, one; and in our chapel, three; one also at Bethlehem, where our Lord was born; and another at the place on the Mount of Olives where our Lord ascended. Let them be all maintained at my charge, and take care not to suffer them to go out at any time, nor to give way to any person contributing towards them. And since I do rely on the bond of your love, so let your prayers and benedictions be with me through all ages. Amen."

His majesty adds the following postscript, which seems to import more than meets the eye:—

" My beloved, do not you offer to say, Light descendeth only upon us, that your glorying in yourselves be not in vain; since you know that evil attends glorying, and blessing humility."

The reign of Zara Jacob is farther remarkable for the part which his clerical representatives acted in the Council of Florence. At his desire a number of priests were sent by the Abba Nicodemus, not only to protect the interests of the church of Abyssinia, but also to make known to the sovereign pontiff the sound views on religion which were still entertained in the country celebrated for the pious docility of the Ethiopian treasurer. These missionaries, however, adhered to the opinion of the Greeks on the long-disputed topic of the procession of the Holy Ghost, which, as every one has heard, created a schism between the Christians of the East and of the West. This embassy was thought of sufficient consequence to be made the subject of a painting in the Vatican; to which work of art we are principally indebted for our knowledge of the fact, that such a deputation had been sent from Eastern Africa to the centre of Italy. We may add, that from this time forward the Roman communion possessed a certain influence in Abyssinia, and disputes on doctrinal points occasionally exercised the ingenuity of the court as well as of the professional orders.

Although the established religion was that of the church of Alexandria, a variety of superstitions prevailed in different parts of the country. On the coast of the Red Sea, and in the low provinces adjoining to the kingdom of Adel, the greatest part of the inhabitants were Mohammedans; and the convenience of trade had induced these enemies of the Christian creed to settle in many villages throughout the high country, especially in Wogara and the neighbourhood of Gondar. In Dembea, in the rugged district of Samen, and near the sources of the Nile, a species of sabaism still gave exercise to the devotional feelings of the people; while some, who had either failed to keep pace with the progress of their countrymen or had anticipated a more advanced stage of improvement, offered up their adoration to the cow and the serpent. The king, offended at a debasement so gross and irrational, ordered these rude worshippers to be seized and brought before him. Sitting in judgment, with the heads of his clergy and the principal officers of state around him, he had the satisfaction to hear all the culprits capitally convicted and ordered for execution. A proclamation from his majesty immediately followed, declaring that all persons who did not carry upon their right hands an amulet with these words, "I renounce the devil for Christ our Lord," should forfeit their personal estates and be liable to corporal punishment.*

This expedient of Zara Jacob—the adoption of a heathenish practice to effect a Christian object—might have been justified by the principle stated by St Paul, that the whole Jewish system of rites and ordinances was added to the patriarchal religion, "because of transgressions;" that is, it was imposed upon an idolatrous people to prevent them from rushing into the more flagrant usages of Gentile worship. But it is probable that the zealous monarch knew not the full bearing of the precedent to which we have now alluded.

The close of the fifteenth century was disturbed by the revival of opinions similar to those which had

---

* Bruce, vol. iii. p. 260.

been approved by the Council of Chalcedon. An assembly of the clergy was called, and those who denied the true faith were either put to instant death, or exposed without food or clothing to perish on the tops of the highest mountains.

The intercourse with Europe which marked the beginning of the following age led to a new series of events in the Abyssinian church. The Portuguese, who by their valour and superior arms defeated the designs of the Mohammedan states, claimed the right of giving counsel to their allies in the important article of religion. No progress, however, was made towards this object till the arrival of Paez at the close of the sixteenth century. This able Jesuit, repairing to the monastery at Fremona, made himself master of the Geez language in the first instance, after which he began to teach others; and so great was his success in this undertaking, that the fame of his acquirements reached the ears of the king, whose name was Za Denghel.

In the year 1604, accordingly, Peter, attended by only two of his young disciples, presented himself at court, which was then held at Dancaz. He was received by his majesty with great honours, to the deep mortification of the native monks, who could not fail to anticipate on his side a still more important triumph. In a dispute held next day before the sovereign, Paez thought it enough to produce the two boys as his only advocates for the Catholic faith, and as fully qualified to silence all the theologians in Abyssinia. The result corresponded to his expectation, and did not fail to establish his influence to a greater extent than ever in the eyes of the royal family. Mass was then said agreeably to the usage of the church of Rome, which was followed by a sermon,—among the first preached in that country,—so far surpassing in elegance and purity of diction any thing yet pronounced in the learned language, that all the hearers began to look upon this as the first miracle on the part of the missionary. Za Denghel was so delighted with it, that he not only determined to embrace the Roman Catholic religion, but instantly made known this resolution to Paez himself, under an oath of secrecy that he should conceal it for some time. Proceeding to realize his views he prohibited the observance of Saturday, which, as the Jewish sabbath, had till that period been kept holy, and directed letters to be addressed to the Pope and the kings of Spain and Portugal, announcing his conversion and soliciting their friendship.[*]

But the Abyssinian monarch soon discovered that his subjects were not yet prepared to accompany him in such sweeping innovations. The Abuna, stimulated by Za Selassé a brave commander, absolved the people from their allegiance, and sanctioned an open rebellion. The issue of the war was favourable to the insurgents; the emperor was slain, his troops were dispersed, and the most devoted of his friends shared his fate on the field of battle.

As the letter addressed by Za Denghel to Clement VIII. is not unworthy of notice, we lay before the reader the following extract:—" After we had ascended the throne, a certain friar whose name is Peter Paez, of the society of Jesus, and who hath the yoke of the law of Christ upon his neck, did

---

[*] Bruce, vol. iii. p. 264.

visit us; and has given us a very particular account how your holiness labours even to the shedding of your blood to destroy sin. May the eternal God who hath begun this work bring it to a happy issue! He hath likewise told us that you are always ready to assist Christians who are in necessity, and to afford them strength and comfort; having learned the lesson of St Paul, who, in his Epistle to the Galatians saith, While we have time let us do good to all men, but chiefly to those who are of the household of faith; for which reason your holiness assists Christian kings chiefly. Wherefore, since God hath been pleased to bestow upon us the empire of our fathers, we are desirous of entering into a strict friendship with you and with our brother Philip king of Spain; and, in order to make it the closer and more lasting, we do wish that he would send his daughter hither to be married to our son, and with her some soldiers to help us: For we have infidel enemies called Galls, who when we go against them flee before us; but, so soon as our back is turned, are making inroads upon us again. For the destruction of this enemy it is that we desire to have some troops from you, with artificers of all trades, and fathers to instruct us, that we may be of one heart and one body; and that the faith of Christ which is destroyed by the hands of infidels may be established, and that there may be peace and love among us."*

After the short reign of Jacob the throne was occupied by Socinios or Susneus, or, as he is more frequently denominated, the Sultan Segued. Induced by reasons similar to those which led Za Denghel to

---

* Geddes, p. 251.

relinquish the communion of Alexandria, he also declared his adherence to the Roman Catholic form. He determined at all events to attach the Portuguese to his interests, whose leaders, he was aware, could not be influenced by any other consideration so readily as by that of religion. For this reason he made advances to their priests, and sent for Paez to court; where, after the usual disputes about the Pope's supremacy and the two natures in Christ, mass was said and a sermon preached,—the common method of acknowledging submission to Rome. To crown their triumph, the Jesuits procured from the king a grant of land near the Lake Dembea, on which they erected a stately convent.

But this important point was not carried without much opposition. The Abuna complained to the king that unusual and irregular things had been permitted without his knowledge; and that conferences upon articles of faith had been held without asking him to be present, or even allowing him to afford to his clergy the advantage of his assistance in the controversies which ensued. Socinios, who did not believe that the eloquence or learning of the bishop would materially affect the issue of the question, ordered that the disputations should be renewed. The king, after a patient hearing, declared that the Abyssinian orators were vanquished, and signified it as his sovereign pleasure, that for the future no one should deny that there are two natures in Christ, distinct in themselves, but divinely united in one person; declaring, at the same time, that should any person thereafter deny or call in doubt this solemn doctrine, he would chastise him for seven years. On the other hand the Abuna, supported by Emana Christos the half-brother of his majesty, published a sentence of excommunication, and affixed it to the door of one of the churches belonging to the palace, in which they denounced all persons as accursed who should maintain two natures in Christ, or vindicate any of the errors of the Roman See.

A conspiracy was immediately formed under the auspices of the Abuna, Emana Christos, Kefla Wahad the master of the household, and Julius the governor of Tigré. Their intention was to murder the king in his own house; but this plan being defeated they had recourse to arms, and led their troops into the field. Julius and the primate were killed in the first battle, and the insurrection was for the time suppressed. Emana, whom the royal party attempted to assail with the weapons of argument, replied, that he stood forward in defence of the ancient faith of his country, which was now without reason trodden under foot in favour of a creed which he described as a false one, if they understood it, and a useless one if they did not. He admitted that he was aware of his danger; but neither his connexion with the king, nor his being related to Sela Christos, could weigh with him against his duty to God and his native land. The emperor and his brother, he added, might be right in embracing the Romish belief, because they were convinced of its truth; he had used however the same means, had heard the same arguments urged by the same fathers, which, unluckily for him, had only more fully satisfied his mind that their tenets were erroneous.*

Socinios, a conqueror both in the field and in the theological chair, became more decided in his ad-

---
* Bruce, vol. iii. p. 346.

herence to the new faith. To his proclamation, establishing the creed of Chalcedon as to the two natures of the Redeemer, he added an injunction that "all out-door work, such as plowing and sowing, should be publicly followed by the husbandman on Saturday, under penalty of paying a web of cotton cloth for the first omission; and the second offence was to be punished by a confiscation of moveables, and the crime not to be pardoned for seven years,"—the greatest punishment for misdemeanours in Abyssinia. In order to show that he was in earnest, he ordered the tongue of a monk to be cut out for supporting the monophysite doctrine; and Buco Damo, one of his principal generals, was beaten with rods and degraded for observing the rest of the Jewish Sabbath. Nay, it is said he was urged by the Jesuits to pronounce a curse on the soul of Zara Jacob his great-grandfather, for not having, at the early period when he possessed the throne, strictly conformed to the ritual recommended by the Portuguese.*

It was not, however, until he had triumphed over several rebellious chiefs in the different provinces that the sultan, as he was pleased to be addressed, formally avowed himself a member of the Roman church. Having come to this resolution he sent for Paez, who had already acted as his confessor, and communicated it to him; stating also as a proof of his sincerity, that he had put away all his wives except the first, the mother of his eldest son, who was destined to succeed him in the empire. The Jesuit having accomplished this great object, the

---

* Bruce, vol. iii. p. 350. Geddes, p. 24.

main purpose of his mission, returned to his convent with the words of pious exultation in his mouth, "Lord, now lettest thou thy servant depart in peace!" No sooner did he arrive at the establishment on which he had bestowed so much labour than he was seized with a putrid fever, the effect of fatigue at an unfavourable season, which put an end to his life on the 3d of May 1623. He had been seven years a captive in Arabia, and nineteen a missionary in Abyssinia during the worst of times, and had always extricated himself from the most perilous situations with honour to his fraternity and advantage to his religion.*

The open renunciation of the Alexandrian faith on the part of Socinios, accompanied, as it was, with a furious attack on the clergy of the whole kingdom, was followed by another war, in which some brave officers and a great number of soldiers were sacrificed to the demon of bigotry. The royal arms were once more victorious; and the joy which arose from such continued success was soon afterwards greatly increased by the arrival of Alphonso Mendez, who had been consecrated at Lisbon as head of the Ethiopian church. On his appearance at Gongora, the monastery founded by Paez, he was graciously received by the king, who placed him on his right hand on a throne equal in height to his own, and fixed the day for taking the oath of submission to the See of Rome.

On the 11th of February 1626, this ceremony was completed with great ostentation and parade. The

---

* Bruce, iii. p. 355. "In person he was very tall and strong, but lean from continual labour and abstinence. He was red-faced, which Tellez ays proceeded from the religious warmth of his heart."

new patriarch, as a mark of his superiority to the
Abuna, preached a sermon in the Portuguese language on the supremacy of the chair of St Peter over
all Christian communities. He took pains, at the
same time, to adorn his harangue with many Latin
quotations; a display of scholarship which is said to
have had a wonderful effect on the minds of the
king and his courtiers, not one of whom understood
a word either of Latin or Portuguese. After a suitable declaration of his faith and adherence to the
religion of the West, Socinios, with the New Testament spread open before him, proceeded to take
the following oath:—" We, Sultan Segued, emperor of Ethiopia, do believe and confess that St Peter, prince of the Apostles, was constituted by Christ
our Lord head of the whole Christian church; and
that he gave him the principality and dominion over
the whole world by saying to him, *Thou art Peter,
and upon this rock will I build my church; and
I will give unto thee the keys of the kingdom of
heaven:* and again, when he said, *Keep my sheep.*
Also we believe and confess that the Pope of Rome,
lawfully elected, is the true successor of St Peter, the
apostle, in government; that he holdeth the same
power, dignity, and primacy, in the whole Christian
church: And to the holy father Urban, the eighth
of that name, by the mercy of God, pope, and our
lord, and to his successors in the government of
the church, we do promise, offer, and swear true
obedience, and with humility subject at his feet
our person and empire. So help us God, and these
holy gospels before us!"*

---

* Geddes's Church History of Ethiopia, p. 342. Ludolfi Hist.
Ethiop. lib. iii. c. 12. The Patriarch in his sermon introduced the

This act of submission on the part of the king was followed by a similar ceremony, as applied to the princes, governors, officers, ministers, and monks, who did " promise, offer, and swear the same obedience." The duties of the day were concluded with an excommunication pronounced by Mendez against those who should at any time violate their oaths. He likewise issued two proclamations, the one prohibiting all Abyssinian priests from performing any ecclesiastical office before they had presented themselves officially to him; and the other commanding all the subjects of the empire, upon pain of death, to embrace popery, and to discover all such as adhered to their ancient religion; enjoining also the observance of Lent and Easter according to the Roman manner and time.

Having the royal power transferred to his hands for all ecclesiastical purposes, the Patriarch did not fail to employ it for the accomplishment of his own views. He directed that all the clergy should be re-ordained, and their churches consecrated anew; that all persons, children and adults, should be rebaptized; that the moveable feasts and fasts should be reduced to the calendar of Rome; and finally, that circumcision, polygamy, and divorce, should be abrogated for ever. It was moreover announced that all questions arising from the discussion of such

---

following statement :—" There are four principal chairs in the world, which are as the four rivers that flow out of Paradise, or as the four universal winds, or as the four elements; but above all the chair of St Peter has the dignity and primacy; and in the second place that of St Mark at Alexandria; in the third place that of St John; in the fourth that of Antioch, which was also St Peter's, from which four all the other bishops are derived." This he described as a canon of the Council of Nice.

matters, and which were formerly understood to belong to the jurisdiction of civil courts, should thereafter be decided at his tribunal exclusively.

Emboldened by success, the Patriarch attempted to secure a permanent revenue for the catholic priesthood, arising from a territorial domain. It is however a fundamental law of the Abyssinian monarchy that all the land belongs to the king, and that no property of this nature shall be permanently vested in the church; such portions as are set apart for the maintenance of the national religion being resumable at pleasure, and always under the management of lay commissioners appointed by the crown. It happened that a nobleman at court, much respected for his rank and services, had been put in possession of some fields which were formerly occupied by a Romish monk, who, instead of appealing to the civil authority, carried his cause before the ecclesiastical tribunal of Mendez. This prelate summoned the grandee to appear at his judgment-seat, and to answer to the charge brought against him by the complainer; and upon the other refusing to comply, he condemned him in his absence, and gave sentence that he should forthwith restore the disputed grounds.

Failing in obedience to this unwonted decision, the chief heard himself excommunicated in church one day while attending the king, and without ceremony or reserve given over, soul and body, to the devil. The nobleman, though otherwise brave, was so much affected with the terms in which his doom was pronounced, that he instantly fell into a swoon; and it was not until the Patriarch, at the intercession of his majesty, consented to withdraw or modify the curse, that he completely recovered. The fierce zeal of the bishop, and his systematic encroachment on the royal prerogative and common rights of the subject, contributed not a little to alienate the affections of the people, the great mass of whom were still attached to the ancient form of worship. But their indignation was still more excited by another instance of intemperate bigotry, as applied to the body of a deceased monk, the superior of the convent at Devra Libanos. One of the priests of the new order, finding that the corpse of the abbot now mentioned was interred under the altar at which he officiated, represented the case to Mendez; who instantly declared that the church was defiled by the burial of that heretical schismatic, and suspended the celebration of divine worship till the remains were actually dug up and thrown out of the sacred edifice in a most indecent manner. A profound discontent spread throughout the whole country; and from that moment the friends of the old religion began to recover strength, while the catholics were very generally regarded with hatred as well as with terror.

The king, though a sincere convert, could no longer refuse to sympathize with the just fears and resentment of his people. He desired the Patriarch to permit the use of the ancient liturgies of Ethiopia, which had been altered by Mendez himself in every thing where they did not agree with the Roman ritual. With this requisition he was obliged to comply, because it seemed reasonable that men should pray to God in a language which they understood, rather than in a foreign tongue, the precise import of which they could not comprehend.

But this concession to the wishes of the natives weakened the power of the European priests; for no sooner were the former allowed to use their own books of devotion than they rejected the emendations of the stranger, and adhered exclusively to their wonted method.

This cause, however, which at first engaged the attention only of churchmen and a few of the more zealous members of the court, was finally decided in the field of battle. The governors of provinces, whose allegiance was bound to the throne by very weak ties, seized the occasion for breaking out into rebellion against Socinios; regarding, perhaps, the breach that had been made on their ancient faith and constitution by a privileged body of foreigners as an attack on their national independence. Tecla Georgis, a son-in-law of the king, raised the standard of rebellion in Tigré, declaring his determination no longer to endure the Roman religion, but to defend the church of Alexandria to the utmost of his power. With the view at once of convincing his countrymen of his sincerity, and of precluding all possibility of reconciliation with his sovereign, he tore down the crucifixes from the walls of churches, defaced all the ornaments which had a reference to the late innovations, and removed the figures of popish saints. He then called before him Abba Jacob his catholic chaplain, and having stripped him of his sacerdotal vestments slew him with his own hand.

This act of violence was soon afterwards severely punished by the death of Tecla Georgis, who was taken prisoner in battle, and who with his sister fell under the hand of the executioner. But the suppression of one rebellion only led to another more determined, until the finest parts of the empire were soaked with blood. At length the hopes of the people were directed to Basilides or Facilidas, the king's eldest son, who to great military talent added much prudence and moderation. He was thought unfriendly to the Catholic party, because he did not espouse their cause; yet he lived with the Jesuits on such a footing that they themselves knew not whether to calculate on his support or his enmity. He kept one of them, Father Angelis, constantly in his household, and treated him not only with respect, but also with confidence. He was besides submissive to his parent in all things, and never opposed any of his measures for the ecclesiastical government of the state. But it was observed that, when he received a flattering message from Urban VIII., he did not think proper to return any answer; while those who attempted to penetrate his motives saw reason to conclude that he would not submit to the restraint imposed on the sovereign by the Portuguese missionaries, under the semblance of filial reverence for the head of the universal church.

The expectation that Facilidas would put an end to the foreign influence which enthralled his father, induced some of the subordinate officers to practise an undue severity towards the Romanists. When, for example, Serca Christos was appointed to the government of Gojam, a priest whose name was Za Selassé was heard to say, "There is an end of the Catholic faith in this province." Being called before the military ruler, he was forbidden to perform mass according to the form employed in Europe.

To this order he dutifully submitted; but when he was desired to renounce the doctrine of the two natures in our Saviour, he declared that this was a point of faith which he could not surrender, being convinced that Christ was perfect God and perfect man. Upon this the governor commanded that he should be put to death, and he was accordingly thrust through the body with numerous lances; exclaiming, as long as he had strength to utter a word, "God and man! God and man!"

As we have mentioned the letter addressed by the Pope to the Prince Facilidas, we shall, as it is not very long, submit it to the consideration of the reader, who will observe that it recommends the use of strong measures for the support of orthodoxy.

"OUR MOST BELOVED SON IN CHRIST, HEALTH AND APOSTOLICAL BENEDICTION.

"The wealth of Nile floweth to the glory of your name; and you, the son of the Ethiopic empire, do grow up in the hopes of a most powerful principality. You do nevertheless understand, God having taught you, how miserable you had been had you not drunk of the streams of the gospel out of the fountain of the Catholic church, and if you had not, by adoring St Peter in the Roman pontificate, been made the son of God, whose possession and workmanship, the whole frame of heaven and earth, is in the Roman church. The holy choir of reigning priests and of obedient natives do applaud the heir that is to rule in Ethiopia with Christian virtue; rejoicing that a kingdom is prepared for you, out of which your triumphant father, the sceptre of whose empire is the rod of direction, does through the divine assistance extirpate the synagogue of Satan. You having been educated in the domestic imitation of such splendid virtues, and being in a part that draws the eyes of heaven and earth upon you, such counsels are expected from your wisdom as are to be like the lights of the holy spirit and the thunderbolts of the divine vengeance. And since it is thus, beloved son, you must not think of living at ease in your father's palace, before you have made all Ethiopia throw itself at the feet of St Peter, that so they may find heaven in the Vatican: For the doctrines of the Pope will not be only the hope of salvation to you, but they will be also the author of quietness and the safety of your dominions. We do embrace you, most dear son, with the arms of apostolical charity, and do wish you an obedient people, and favourable angels amidst the trophies of your arms and the joys of your prosperity; and we do from the bottom of our heart impart our fatherly benediction to you.

" Dated at Rome at St Peter's, under the ring of the Fisherman, the twenty-eighth of December 1630, in the seventh year of our pontificate."*

Socinios, alarmed by the growing disaffection in his army, issued a proclamation, the object of which was to relax some part of the severity imposed by the Patriarch, and granting among other indulgences permission to fast on Wednesday instead of Saturday, the latter being one of the ancient festivals of the native church. Mendez, in a letter, the tone

---

* Geddes's Church History of Ethiopia, p. 367. Ludolfi Hist. Ethiop. lib. iii. c. 10, 11, 12. Bruce, vol. iii. p. 400.

of which was neither mild nor prudent, remonstrated with his majesty on this exercise of power,—warned him that God would call him to the strictest account for this presumption,—and reminded him of the words of Azarias the chief priest to King Uzziah, and of the punishment of leprosy which followed the royal encroachment on the ecclesiastical function. The emperor found it necessary to modify the terms of his edict, and to limit it to three articles: first, that no liturgy unless amended or revised by the patriarch should be used in divine service; secondly, that all feasts, excepting Easter and those which depend upon it, should be kept according to the ancient computation; and thirdly, that whosoever chose might fast on Wednesday instead of the last day of the week. But while making this concession he did not conceal from the prelate his displeasure at the application to him of the historical fact respecting Azarias and Uzziah; and suggested to his reverence, that as the Roman religion was introduced into Abyssinia by the king, it might be altered from time to time by the same authority which at first established it.

After this compromise Socinios engaged in war with the Agows of Lasta, a fierce people who occupied the strongest country in Abyssinia. Some idea may be formed from the accompanying plate of the steep mountains on which they encamped, and from which they were wont to hurl stones on their invaders when attempting to make their way through the passes.

At first the emperor sustained severe losses, and his men, finding their arms constantly employed against their fellow-citizens, became disheartened

Mountains between Lasta and Samen.

and did not conceal their aversion to such hostilities. Victory indeed at length declared in their favour, and thousands of the warlike Agows were left dead on the field; the sight of which suggested to the prince the following remarks addressed by him to his father. " These men whom you see slaughtered on the ground were neither Pagans nor Mohammedans, at whose death we should rejoice; they were Christians, lately your subjects and your countrymen, some of them your relations. This is not victory which is gained òver ourselves. In killing these you drive the sword into your own entrails. How many have you put to an untimely death, and how many have you yet to destroy! We are become a proverb even among the infidels and Moors for carrying on this war, and for apostatizing, as they assert, from the faith of our ancestors."

His majesty made no reply, but went back disconsolate to Dancaz, where the victory appeared to be turned into mourning. The Patriarch, who was displeased with his late proceedings, upbraided him with his indifference to the true faith, alleging that he had ceased to support it at the very moment Providence had put all his enemies under his feet. In his own defence the king recapitulated the bloody wars in which he had engaged for the Catholics, the myriads who had been slain, and the chiefs who had been sacrificed, and ended by making known his resolution to permit his people to choose their own religion. Mendez now saw it expedient to relinquish his pretensions so far as to concede to the inhabitants of Lasta the privilege which they demanded, because they had never professed themselves members of the Roman church; but in regard to such as had acknowledged the supremacy of the Pope and received the communion from the hands of the Jesuits, he would not consent to grant the freedom of renouncing their engagements.

It was no longer time to deliberate on minute points with a functionary who, it was manifest, would have been content with nothing short of absolute power in all matters spiritual and ecclesiastical. Socinios did not conceal from him, that the authority of government had greatly diminished in his hands, and that he must now act a decided part, or consent to be deprived even of the semblance of royalty. He therefore issued the following proclamation, which at once threw down the fabric of the Roman ritual and hierarchy in Abyssinia, and removed the hope of ever again establishing it in that kingdom.

"Hear us! hear us! hear us! First of all we gave you the Roman Catholic faith, as thinking it a good one; but many people have died fighting against it, as Julius, Gabriel, Tecla Georgis, Serca Christos, and finally these rude peasants of Lasta. Now therefore we restore to you the faith of your ancestors: let your own priests say their mass in their own churches; let the people have their own altars for the sacrament and their own liturgy, and let them be happy. As for myself, I am now old and worn out with war and infirmities, and no longer capable of governing: I name my son Facilidas to reign in my place."

This document was published on the fourteenth of June 1632, and in the month of September the king died. He was buried with great pomp in the church of Ganeta Jesus, which he himself had built; professing to the last his preference of the Roman creed, and his attachment to the forms of that communion. But the Jesuits, considering only the catastrophe and unmindful of the strenuous efforts made by him during his whole reign to establish their religion, have denounced him as an apostate, for giving way to the demand of his subjects to have their ancient ritual restored. This judgment on their part is equally unjust and ungrateful. It ought to have been remembered that, in the last years of his life, when left without a soldier to fight for their cause, he resigned his crown but retained his belief; and it was not until he had quenched the fire of numerous insurrections in the best blood of his land, that he resolved to sheath his sword and confer liberty of conscience.

The young monarch, who had acted with so much discretion during his father's reign, lost no time in giving notice to the Patriarch that he and his followers must forthwith quit Abyssinia. To accelerate this movement he at the same time informed Mendez that an Abuna, consecrated at Alexandria, was already on his way to assume the ecclesiastical government of the kingdom; and commanded that the Jesuits should immediately repair from their convents in Gojam and Dembea to the establishment at Fremona, whence they might more conveniently embark for India or Europe. The Catholics endeavoured to postpone their fate by offering new concessions and indulgencies; but Facilidas informed them that it was now too late for negotiation, and recommended a speedy departure, lest they should be visited with evils which he might not have it in his power to avert.

Finding all his arts unavailing, the Patriarch began his march towards the coast, accompanied by a large body of sacerdotal dependants, and guarded by a detachment of the royal troops. Still, hoping that some accident might turn the tide of affairs to their advantage, or that a reinforcement of Portuguese might arrive from the Eastern colonies to their relief, the monks made various attempts to retain a footing in the country, though in direct opposition to the orders of the king. As a last resource they threw themselves on the protection of the Baharnagash, who at that period was in a state of rebellion, and therefore not in any degree disinclined to thwart the views of his sovereign. But they did not long enjoy the asylum provided for them by the barbarian governor of the coast. Facilidas opened a correspondence with him, giving assurance not only of pardon but of favour, if he would deliver into his hands the refractory priests who had so far abused his indulgence. The latter, however, having pledged his word to his guests, would not consent to give them up to the angry prince; but, by a special refinement in the politics of humanity, he agreed to sell them all as slaves to the Turks. In return, accordingly, for a certain sum paid by the pasha of the neighbouring ports, Mendez, his priests, and his monks of all degrees, were consigned to captivity as the property of infidels. Two individuals only were left behind, who longed to terminate a weary life by the honours of martyrdom; an expectation which was very soon realized. To prevent the recurrence of an evil from which so many sufferings and so much disquietude had arisen, the young emperor concluded a treaty with the Moslem commanders at Suakin and Masuah, the object of which was to prevent any Portuguese from passing into Abyssinia. In short, both parties, the Mohammedans and Christians, for their mutual safety, peace, and advantage, had resolved to exclude the missionaries from both shores of the Red Sea.*

After a considerable detention at Suakin, and the payment of a heavy ransom, the Patriarch found his way to Goa, where he died; having in vain attempted to rouse the military officers in that settle-

---

* See Geddes's Church History, p. 380—433. Ludolfi Hist. Ethiop. lib. iii. c. 12, &c. Bruce, iii. p. 434.

ment, the Pope, and the powers of Europe, to make a great effort for the recovery of Ethiopia. The letters and memorials which passed between him and Facilidas, in relation to the interests of the church and the reasons for restoring the ancient forms in Abyssinia, are very entertaining, and, at the same time, throw a valuable light on the views of both parties in reference to that most interesting of all subjects, the maintenance of a national faith. In one of his epistles, the emperor, after complaining that the Jesuits denied the cup in the holy communion, rebaptized the people, treated the priests and deacons as if they were not in sacred orders, and even tore down their altars to be replaced by others of their own consecration, proceeds as follows:—

"Your lordship, in being acquainted with this, will know the reason why you are turned out of your place which God and the emperor had bestowed on you; and that the very same emperor who sent for your lordship, and gave you your authority, was the person that deprived you of it. Wherefore, since an Alexandrian Abuna is on his way hither, and has sent us word that he cannot be in the same country with a Roman Patriarch and fathers, we have ordered you to repair to Fremona, and there to remain. As to what your lordship now offers, which is, that if the people of Ethiopia will but continue in the obedience of the Roman church, you will dispense with them as to all matters which are not contrary to the faith: that comes too late now; for how is it possible for them to return to that which they have not only forsaken but do abominate, now that they have a taste of their old religion again? Your lordship farther desires that we would assemble our learned men to dispute with you, before you depart, about matters of faith. This also ought to have been done in the beginning. Besides, is that cause likely to be supported by arguments which has been maintained hitherto only by force and violence, by taking estates from some, and throwing others into prison, and punishing a third class still more severely, and that for no other reason than because they would not embrace your faith? And as if that had not been sufficient, you have dragged great multitudes out of the deserts, who would have been contented to live there upon herbs, and confined them to prisons; nay, the poor people that would have been glad to bury themselves in caves did not escape your persecution. Now what a barbarity would it be to go and tease poor people with arguments who have suffered so much already! It would surely be a very unjust thing both in the sight of God and man."

This revolution in the church of Abyssinia occasioned great regret at Rome, although there were many who consoled themselves with the reflection that the disappointment had arisen, not from any aversion to the doctrine and rules of the West, but solely from the pride, violence, and obstinacy of the Jesuit missionaries. It was therefore imagined, that if men more conciliatory in their manners and less bigoted to external rites were sent out under proper auspices, there would be no doubt of ultimate success. With this view six capuchins, all natives of France and members of the reformed order of their founder, were despatched from Italy by the College *De Propaganda Fide*, armed with protections from the Grand Seignior. Of these, two attempted to enter Ethiopia by landing at Magadoxo, on the shore of the Indian Ocean, who, after advancing a very short way into the country, were slain by the Galla. Two penetrated directly into Abyssinia, and were stoned to death; but the remaining couple, informed at Masuah of the fate of their companions, instead of exposing themselves to similar destruction, returned home with an account of their bad success. Even after this, three other capuchins were sent from Europe, who, on their arrival at Suakin, forwarded notice to Facilidas of their intention to visit his kingdom as ministers of the Roman church. He recommended to the pasha to treat them according to their deserts; who instantly ordered their heads to be struck off, and stripped of the skin, which was sent to the capital for inspection,—the colour denoting that they were Franks, and the tonsure affording the certainty of their being priests. No farther attempt was made during many years to introduce European missionaries into the Abyssinian monarchy.*

---

* See Ludolf, Geddes, and Bruce, at the places already indicated; the narratives of all the three being drawn from the same source, the works of the missionaries. The reader will peruse with pleasure the following abridgment of the occurrences mentioned in the text:— "The Jesuits themselves deplore the fatal indiscretion of their chief, who forgot the mildness of the gospel and the policy of his order, to introduce with hasty violence the liturgy of Rome and the inquisition of Portugal. A new baptism, a new ordination was inflicted on the natives; and they trembled with horror when the most holy of the dead were torn from their graves, when the most illustrious of the living were excommunicated by a foreign priest. In the defence of their religion and liberty the Abyssinians rose in arms with desperate but unsuccessful zeal. Five rebellions were extinguished in the blood of the insurgents, two Abunas were slain in battle, whole legions were slaughtered in the field or suffocated in their caverns, and neither merit, nor rank, nor sex, could save from an ignominious death the enemies of Rome. But the victorious monarch was finally subdued by the constancy of the nation, of his mother, of his son, and of his most faithful friends. Segued

But the seeds of discord, which were sown in that country by the foreigners now expelled, soon grew up and greatly annoyed the government. In the days of Yasous, the grandson of Facilidas, some turbulent monks, for example, attempted to embroil the kingdom by theological disputes; but a little wholesome restraint, accompanied with an unbending firmness on the part of the sovereign, prevented the rise of many evils which there was just ground to apprehend from that quarter.

At the time Bruce travelled in Abyssinia there was a convent of Franciscan friars in Upper Egypt, established about the end of the seventeenth century, for the protection of such Catholic Christians as were supposed to have fled into Nubia and Sennaar when the Patriarch was driven out by the heir of Socinios. Every one interested himself in behalf of these fugitives, who were imagined to preserve the relics of a pure faith among the savage tribes on the banks of the Nile, far beyond the Cataracts. Pope Innocent XII. was so convinced of the truth of this story as to raise a considerable fund to support the expense of an Ethiopic mission; a convent was erected at Achmin, the ancient Panopolis, where the monks were to afford refreshment to those of their brethren who should return weary and exhausted from preaching among the barbarians. They

---

listened to the voice of pity, of reason, perhaps of fear; and his edict of liberty of conscience instantly revealed the tyranny and weakness of the Jesuits. On the death of his father, Basilides expelled the Latin Patriarch, and restored to the wishes of the nation the faith and the discipline of Egypt. The monophysite churches resounded with a song of triumph, that the sheep of Ethiopia were now delivered from the hyenas of the West; and the gates of that solitary realm were for ever shut against the arts, the science, and the fanaticism of Europe."—*Decline and Fall*, vol. viii. p. 373.

were entrusted, besides, should an opportunity present itself, with the care of penetrating into Abyssinia, in order to keep alive the embers of orthodox belief and discipline, until a proper season should come for converting the whole realm. But, on inquiry, it was discovered that no Christians had taken refuge in any part of the country between Syené and Dongola, nor even on the higher parts of the river nearest the scene of persecution; and it is admitted that all endeavours to convert the natives in the contiguous districts proved fruitless and unavailing.

In the reign of Louis XIV. an effort was made by the Jesuits to repair the mischief which Alphonso Mendez had done, and to introduce once more into Ethiopia the principles of their institution. Father Fleurian was authorized by the celebrated De la Chaise, the king's confessor, to instruct the consul-general at Cairo, to send into Abyssinia a proper person to negotiate with the emperor, and to pave the way for an embassy to Paris. The Grand Monarque at the same time took upon himself the protection of the intended mission, and solicited, through Cardinal Jansen, the concurrence and advice of the Pope. Verseau, who was employed as his envoy on this occasion, informed his holiness that his majesty, who took a great interest in the success of this pious undertaking, had fixed his eyes on the Jesuits as the best qualified for discharging a duty at once so delicate and arduous. Innocent dissembled: he extolled in the most magnificent terms the king's great zeal for the advancement of religion, approved of the choice he had made, and praised the resolution of the preachers. But it soon appeared that, notwithstanding this flattering language, he had no intention either to gratify the disciples of Loyola or to comply with the wishes of the French sovereign; for without communicating his views to the one or the other, he appointed the superior of the Franciscans to be his legate *a latere* to the Emperor of Abyssinia, providing him with presents to that prince and the chief noblemen of his court.

At this period Maillet was in Egypt, the representative of the French government, and eagerly employed in endeavouring to accomplish the purposes of his royal master. Various intrigues ensued which we shall not take time to describe; it being sufficient to mention that the dark and laboured policy of the two rival orders terminated at length in the selection of Poncet, a medical practitioner, and of Brevedent, a Jesuit friar, who consented to attend him as his servant. Yasous, at the epoch in question, was threatened with a mortal disease, and had sent a special messenger to Cairo to obtain the aid of a European physician; and hence an opportunity was created for introducing a disguised priest into the very centre of the Abyssinian provinces. But Brevedent died before the journey was completed; while Poncet, after having administered successfully to the distempered ruler, returned in due time, without attempting any thing in favour of the Catholic creed or the monachism of Spain.

It would appear from several instances of persecution, which are recorded in the more recent annals of Ethiopia, that certain individuals, animated with zeal for the interests of religion, had from time to time made their way into the country, and were even favourably received at court. In the reign of Oustas, for instance, who mounted the throne in the year 1709, three priests were concealed in the province of Walkayt, to whom his majesty frequently repaired to hear mass and receive the communion. Under the government, however, of his successor, David IV., who was an ardent supporter of the Alexandrian rites of worship, information was lodged against the heretical friars, and they were immediately brought to trial. The interrogation proceeded as follows: Do you or do you not receive the decisions of the Council of Chalcedon as a rule of faith? And do you believe that Leo the Pope lawfully presided at it and regularly conducted it? To this the prisoners answered without reserve, that they looked upon the Council of Chalcedon as the fourth general council, received it as such, and held its decisions as a rule of faith; and were moreover satisfied that Leo lawfully and regularly presided at it, as being head of the Catholic church, successor to Saint Peter, and Christ's vicar upon earth. Upon this a general shout was heard from the whole assembly, mixed with cries to stone them,—" Whoever throws not three stones is accursed, and an enemy to Mary!" Ropes were instantly fastened round the necks of the monks, and they were dragged to a place behind the church of Abbo, where they were, according to their sentence, stoned to death, suffering with meekness and resignation after the example of the first martyrs.*

When Pearce was in Abyssinia, about twelve years ago, a certain latitudinarianism seems to have prevailed; for, besides an open schism among the

---

* Bruce, vol. iv. p. 60.

members of the Greek church themselves, there was a Roman party, whose voice commanded some respect in the public deliberations. It is true that the English seaman is not the best authority in matters of religion, so far as we regard nice distinction in points of faith; but from his narrative of facts, which appears honest and unbiassed, it becomes perfectly manifest that the theological school of Alexandria no longer enjoyed an undisputed pre-eminence.

Fifteen years had passed amidst insurrections and civil broils, during which no Abuna or metropolitan was consecrated for Ethiopia; and at length, when Mohammed Ali did listen to the entreaties of his Christian neighbours to supply them with a spiritual head, he and the Patriarch seem to have consulted their own views rather than the cause of the gospel in the selection of a priest to fill that high office. Nor was this favour obtained altogether gratuitously; on the contrary, the Ras proclaimed by beat of drum that every governor of a village throughout his dominions should collect from his tenants two dollars each, in hard money, cloth, or salt, and the larger towns from ten to twenty each, as a subscription to pay the expenses of bringing his Reverence from Egypt. In this manner ten thousand dollars were soon collected, and a party of priests despatched with some Mohammedans, bearing a present of fourteen slaves and several pieces of the finest Abyssinian cloth to Ali Pasha. We give an account of the holy man's reception in the words of Mr Pearce.

On the 23d January 1816, "the Ras with his army and all the priests of the country went to meet the

Abuna at Dola; in the afternoon, as they again entered Chelicut, every thing appeared in an uproar. I never before beheld such a multitude of people assembled. The mountains around Chelicut were covered with them. Gangs of priests and monks, some in white and some in yellow dresses, were seen in the different quarters, while thousands of other orders, dressed in their sheep-skins, kept moving along the sides of the mountains, apparently like large flocks of sheep. Numerous chiefs with their armies held different situations on the heights, all moving in confusion, their lances glittering in the air; and the manner in which they strove by shoving against each other to advance as near as they could to the Patriarch, appeared like a close battle; numbers were trodden to death. The Ras rode on a mule with his horsemen in the rear of the Abuna. The multitude of priests, with all the ornaments of their respective churches, were at some distance in front; and in their rear before the Abuna, a number of people with large ploughmen's whips were continually whipping to keep the road clear."*

If the character given of this prelate has not been darkly coloured by malice or fear, we must conclude that he was very little qualified either for the arduous duties of his station, or to extend the reign of meekness and charity among the turbulent people whose spiritual interests were committed to his superintendence. His insolence on some occasions proceeded beyond all bounds, not exempting even the head of the government from his wrath and contumelies. He kept the Ras at his door more than a quarter of

---

* Pearce's Life and Adventures, vol. ii. p. 61.

an hour waiting for an audience; and when at length he was admitted, the communication made by him was so disagreeable that the old priest struck the interpreter on the mouth, and commanded him never to exercise his office again. The warlike chief was grieved and incensed to a high degree. " The tongue of that Abuna," said he, "has speared me to the heart; I cannot resent; I am bound by my religion to bear it; still I think we are rather a weak-minded people."*

As a long interval had elapsed without the ministrations of a metropolitan, a multitude of clergy and of all other classes assembled at the dwelling of the bishop; but, before he would consecrate new altars, ordain priests and deacons, or admit any one to the privileges of the Christian church, he commanded a proclamation to be issued, declaring that, according to the practice established by former Abunas, every man who wished to be retained in his office must pay four pieces of salt. A similar return was expected for admission to the lowest order of clerical functionaries; and all the people, with their young children who had not been confirmed by the late Patriarch, were required to pay one piece. More than a thousand priests and deacons were ordained the first day; many of whom entered upon a profession for which they were very ill prepared, with the sole view of securing an exemption from military service.

The Abuna next proclaimed throughout all Abyssinia, that no man should be considered a priest who did not bind himself by a formal oath to receive all

---

* Pearce, vol. ii. p. 64.

the articles of the Coptic creed, and to submit to the discipline of the Alexandrian communion; and, farther, that none of the sacraments should be administered in any of their churches until the clergy had renounced, in a manner equally solemn, all the errors of the Greek and Roman faith. This measure threw the whole country into commotion. The adherents of the Egyptian ritual had already united to enforce the commands of their superior; the members of the Greek church likewise arrayed themselves in a formidable body to oppose the injunction; while those of the Roman Catholic persuasion, whose number was small, were content to act on the defensive. After a vain attempt at an accommodation, rage burst out on all sides; and every priest held up his cross, about to lead his people to protect their own altars, or to overthrow those of their opponents. Before the actual effusion of blood, however, it was agreed among the leaders, that such as held the established belief should be permitted to follow their own mode of worship; but that they should not be entitled to share in the blessing or protection of the Abuna, and should be considered as an inferior caste. To this humiliating arrangement the multitude, as might have been expected, showed the utmost aversion, and became more furious than ever against their ecclesiastical ruler. In the end he found himself obliged to grant a general toleration, without any infringement of the rank and privileges which were secured to the people by their civil constitution.

Pearce obtained through the exertions of Mr Salt some Ethiopic psalters, to be distributed among the Abyssinians, and if possible to get in exchange for them some copies of their scriptures. The superstitious people, he tells us, not only found fault with the print being too small, and with the sacred names because they were not done in red ink; but the perfect similarity of the books made them suppose that they had been completed by some supernatural agent. Those, however, who possessed any degree of knowledge, readily admitted that they far excelled their own manuscripts. The Englishman does not conceal that, although many were disposed to accept his volumes as a present, he could not obtain any thing in exchange. Having procured a mule, he went, somewhat in the character of a pedlar, to the different monasteries, hoping to dispose of his psalters to some advantage; but the monks, who were not inclined to become merchants, found many faults with the workmanship, and it was not until they discovered the sheets might be had for nothing, that their eyes opened to their merits and to the expediency of receiving them as a gift. He acknowledges that he was occasionally remunerated by the presentation of a sheep, a goat, or a little honey; but adds that such things are customary even on a common visit.*

There is no small difficulty in ascertaining the dogmas of the Abyssinian church, in regard to those points of theology which occupy the first station in the articles of all other Christian communions. In the works on ecclesiastical history to which we have occasionally made reference, there are several symbols or compends of faith, whence the curious reader may derive the requisite information. The volume

---

* Pearce, vol. ii. p. 128.

of Dr Geddes, in particular, contains an "Account of the Habassin Religion and Customs, composed by Zaga Zaba the King of Ethiopia's ambassador, and written with his own hand at Lisbon." Perhaps the envoy's notions were in some degree influenced by the position which he occupied in Europe; it being manifest that there is a striking coincidence between his tenets and those of the court to which his master had sent him. But the document, notwithstanding, possesses great value as a memorial of the progress made by the Jesuit missionaries in the arduous task of inducing a semi-barbarous people to relinquish, even for a time, the doctrines which they had received from their fathers.[*]

In Ludolf's Commentary there is a confession of faith attributed to the Emperor Claudius, who reigned about the middle of the sixteenth century, and which he describes as the belief of his ancestors and of the flock within the precincts of his kingdom. " We believe in one God, and in his only Son, Jesus Christ, who is his Word and his Power, his Counsel and his Wisdom; who was with him before the world was created. But in the last days he came to us,—not, however, that he might leave the throne of his divinity,—and was made man of the Holy Ghost and of the holy Virgin Mary, and was baptized in Jordan in his thirtieth year; and was perfect man; and was hanged on the wood of the Cross in the days of Pontius Pilate; suffered, died, and was buried, and rose again the third day; and afterwards on the fortieth day he ascended with glory into heaven, and sitteth on the right hand of his

---

[*] Page 81.

Father. And he shall come again with glory to judge the quick and the dead, and of his kingdom there shall be no end. And we believe in the Holy Ghost, the Lord and Giver of life, who proceedeth from the Father. And we believe in one baptism for the remission of sins. And we look for the resurrection of the dead, for eternal life to come."*

We must content ourselves with referring to a modern work, for a view of the latest creed or confession issued for the use of the Ethiopian Christians. This document is entitled, " Instructions of Mark, Patriarch of Alexandria, addressed to the Abyssinian churches, on points of religion at present controverted in Abyssinia." It was written in Arabic, but immediately translated into the ecclesiastical language of the country by command of the Ras. The manuscript was obtained by Mr Salt from Welled Selassé the governor of Tigré, and was rendered into English by the late Professor Murray, for the British and Foreign Bible Society, the committee of which granted to Mr Jowett permission to insert it in his Christian Researches.†

These " Instructions" of the Patriarch are much too replete with controversy, and subtile distinctions in the mere use of words, to prove of any value as a guide to faith. They are occupied almost entirely with those unprofitable discussions respecting the nature of Christ, on which the Abyssinians have long wasted their boundless zeal and their small portion of learning; and which, when conveyed through the medium of a version, are equally unintelligible and incapable of abridgment.

---

* Ludolfi Com. p. 237. Jowett's Christian Researches, p. 176.
† Page 180.

In the work of Father Lobo, who made a voyage to Abyssinia in the year 1622, and served in that country under the celebrated Mendez, we have a brief account of the pious usages of the people. Incensed by their bigoted attachment to the customs of their ancestors, he denounces their religion as a mixture of Christianity with Jewish and Mohammedan superstitions. He admits, however, that they retain the belief of the principal mysteries of our faith; that they celebrate with a great deal of piety the sufferings and death of our Lord; reverence the cross; pay a profound devotion to the blessed Virgin, the angels, and the saints; observe the festivals, and pay a strict regard to Sunday. Every month they commemorate the Assumption of the Virgin Mary; and are of opinion that no Christians besides themselves have a true sense of the greatness of the mother of God, or render the honours which are due to her name. There are some tribes among them by whom the crime of swearing by her is punished with the forfeiture of goods, and even with the loss of life. Every week they keep a feast in honour of the apostles and angels; they come to mass with great devotion, and love to hear the word of God; they receive the sacrament often, but do not always prepare themselves for it by confession. The severity of their fasts is equal to that of the primitive church; in Lent they never eat till after sunset; and their abstinence is the more rigid, because milk and butter are forbidden to them. No reason or plea of necessity can procure for them permission to eat flesh; and as their country produces hardly any fish they are compelled to exist on roots and pulse only.

There is no nation, he adds, where excommunication carries greater terrors than among the Abyssinians; a circumstance which gives the priests great power over them, as they frequently exert their spiritual authority for personal purposes not quite consistent with the utmost purity of motive. They have certain opinions peculiar to themselves about purgatory, the creation of souls, and some other mysteries. They repeat baptism, or the semblance of it, every year; retain the practice of circumcision; observe the Jewish Sabbath; abstain from eating all those animals which are forbidden by the Mosaical law; and brothers espouse the widows of their brothers, according to the precept of the same ancient institute.

The churches, at the period under consideration, were extremely numerous in the larger towns and even in villages. So close to each other were the religious houses, that the monks chanting the service in one could hear their brethren similarly employed in some adjoining edifice. They sing the Psalms of David, of which, as well as the other parts of Holy Scripture, they have an exact translation in their own language; rejecting none which Roman Catholics esteem canonical except the Books of the Maccabees.

There is something fantastic in their mode of conducting Divine service. Their musical instruments are little drums, which they hang about their necks and beat with both their hands; and this exercise is performed even by the chief men as well as by the gravest of their ecclesiastics. They have sticks likewise with which they strike the ground, accompanying the blow with a motion of their whole bodies.

They begin their devotions by stamping with their feet on the floor, and playing gently on the drums; but when they become warm and animated they leave off beating, and proceed to leap, dance, and clap their hands, straining their voices at the same time to the highest pitch, till at length they have a greater resemblance to an infuriated crowd than to a religious assembly. For this manner of worshipping they quote the psalm of David, "*O clap your hands, all ye nations.*"

The statement of Lobo, as to the great number of churches in Abyssinia, is fully confirmed by the narrative of Bruce, who remarks that in the most confined landscape the traveller may see at one view five or six of those structures. Every great man who dies thinks that he atones for all his wickedness if he leaves a fund for the erection of a place of worship. The king builds many; it being customary to commemorate any success in the field of battle by rearing a temple to the service of God. The situation is always chosen near a running water, for the convenience of the priests, who, in respect to the periodical purifications and ablutions, strictly observe the Levitical law. It is usual also to surround these buildings with beautiful trees and flowering shrubs; so that the country owes much of its picturesque appearance to the taste displayed by the ecclesiastical architects.

All the churches we are told are of a round form with thatched roofs; their summits are perfect cones; the outside is encircled by a number of wooden pillars, being trunks of the cedar-tree, placed so as to support the edifice; and as the roof projects about eight feet beyond the walls, an agreeable walk or colonnade is thereby formed, which proves of great use in hot or rainy weather. The inside is divided into several apartments, nearly according to the directions which are given in the Law of Moses. The first is a circle somewhat wider than the inner one: here the congregation say their prayers. Within this is a square which is divided by a vail or curtain, corresponding to the Holy Place and the Holy of Holies in the Jewish Tabernacle. The latter is so narrow that none but the priests are admitted into it.

It has been already observed that the Abyssinians practise circumcision; a rite which they maintain was not borrowed from the Jews, but derived from their own neighbours the descendants of Ishmael. Much controversy has existed as to the reason and authority of this usage, for the details of which we refer to the volumes of Bruce and the dissertations of Le Grand.*

In regard to the precise object of the annual ceremony of bathing in remembrance of our Saviour's baptism, much doubt continues to prevail. The Jesuits insist that it is a regular and formal repetition of the sacrament; and if the description given of it by Alvarez were to be literally received, we should find it necessary to admit their conclusion. But the Roman missionaries laboured under a deep prejudice against the native clergy, and are suspected to have failed in their wonted accuracy in their notices of the Abyssinian ritual. The account supplied by Bruce is not liable to the same objection. It is as follows: " The small river running between the town of Adowa and the church had been dam-

---

* Lobo's Voyage to Abyssinia with Le Grand's Dissertations.

med up for several days; the stream was scanty, so that it scarcely overflowed. It was in some places three feet deep, in some perhaps four, or a little more. Three large tents were pitched the morning before the Feast of the Epiphany; one on the north for the priests to repose in during the intervals of the service, and, beside this, one to communicate in: on the south there was a third tent, for the monks and priests of another church to rest themselves in their turn. About twelve o'clock at night the monks and priests met together, and began their prayers and psalms at the waterside, one party relieving the other. At dawn of day the governor, Welled Michael, came hither with some soldiers to raise men for Ras Michael, then on his march against Waragna Fasil, and sat down on a small hill near the river; the troops all skirmishing on foot and on horseback around them. As soon as the sun began to appear three large crosses of wood were carried by three priests dressed in their sacerdotal vestments, and who coming to the side of the river dipped the cross into the water; and all this time the firing, skirmishing, and praying, went on together. The priests with the crosses returned, one of their number carrying before them something less than an English quart of water in a silver cup or chalice. When they were about fifty yards from Welled Michael, that general stood up, and the priest took as much water as he could hold in his hand and sprinkled it upon his head, holding the cup at the same time to his mouth to taste; after which the priest received it back again, saying, 'May God bless you!' Each of the three crosses was then brought forward to Welled Michael, and he kissed them. The ceremony of sprinkling the water was then renewed to all the great men in the tent, all cleanly dressed. Some of them, not contented with aspersion, received the water in the palms of their joined hands and drank it; more water was brought for those who had not partaken of the first; and after the whole of the governor's company was sprinkled, the crosses returned to the river, their bearers singing hallelujahs, and the skirmishing and firing continuing."*

The same ceremony was performed on the traveller himself, who, however, declined to drink from the sacred cup. The people meanwhile crowded to the bank of the stream, where two or three hundred boys, of the order of deacons, threw water upon them. Afterwards horses, mules, asses, armour, pots, and platters, were brought for purification, and the scene ended in a mixture of holy joy and unbridled riot. Bruce positively denies that the baptismal form of words was used in any instance on the occasion now described.

The Abyssinians receive the holy sacrament in both kinds. The loaf is unleavened, and instead of wine they use dried grapes bruised, with the husk and stones as they grow, and so thick as to resemble marmalade. It is put into the mouth with a spoon. The pieces of bread given to the communicants are large in proportion to their rank, and are literally stuffed into the mouths of the recipients by the priest, sometimes at the risk of suffocation. After receiving, a pitcher of water is brought forward, of which the worshippers in their turn take a large draught; then

---

* Travels, vol. v. p. 12.

engage some time in silent prayer with their faces turned to the wall.

Le Grand labours assiduously to prove that the clergy of Abyssinia believe in transubstantiation, although he considers their form of words, and perhaps even their official authority, as radically defective. Ludolf, on the contrary, maintains that in their notions of the Eucharist they coincide with the Protestants; admitting, however, that their language is extremely ambiguous.

There is no unanimity among the Abyssinians on the subject of a middle state, or the condition of the soul between death and the resurrection. Owing to the ignorance in theological matters of those persons to whom we are indebted for the most recent information respecting that country, it is extremely difficult to determine the opinions which are actually held by the clergy. But if we form a judgment on this point from the liturgies used in public worship, we shall find all doubt removed as to their complete coincidence with the doctrines of Christian antiquity, relative to paradise or the place of safe-keeping, where the spirits of men await their final doom at the last day. When any person dies, alms are given and prayers are offered for the souls of the departed; a practice which would have no meaning did they believe that the individuals for whom they make entreaty are already in the presence of God, and in the full possession of eternal happiness. In their daily service they say, " Remember, O Lord, the souls of thy servants, our father Abba Matthias, and the rest of our saints, Abba Salama, and Abba Jacob." In another place they use these words, " Remember, O Lord, the kings of Ethiopia, Abreha and Atzbeha, Caleb, and Guebra Mascal." And again, " Release, O Lord, our father Antonius and Abba Macarius."*

The following prayer is more general, and contributes to place the question in a clearer point of view:—" Remember likewise, O Lord, the priests and laymen; grant, Lord, that their souls may repose in the bosom of the saints Abraham, Isaac, and Jacob; send them into that happy place where refreshing waters may be found; into that paradise of delights from whence are banished all sighs, sadness, and sorrow of heart, and where they may rejoice in the light of thy saints. Remember, O Lord, our fathers and our brethren who have died in the true faith; give them rest with thy saints, and with those whom we have now commemorated; give rest to sinners, and remember those who have made these offerings, and those for whom they are made. Remember, O Lord, those who have died in the true faith of our fathers and our brethren; grant that their souls may rest with the saints and the just; conduct them and assemble them in a pleasant place near cool and living water, in a paradise of delight, and with those whose names we have now repeated."†

We shall not enter into the topics controverted by Le Grand, who maintains that the Abyssinians practise auricular confession, invocation of saints, and extreme unction. Their usages perhaps justify the inferences of the Frenchman, while the abstract opinions collected by Ludolf would unquestionably lead to an opposite conclusion. But in our eyes the facts with which we are supplied, through the me-

---

* Bruce, vol. v. p. 25. † Le Grand's Dissertation in Lobo.

dium of their several works, possess their principal value from the circumstance that they show the state of Christianity at the time it was first introduced into Ethiopia; such being the unchangeable nature of habits, manners, and customs, in the East, that the lapse of a thousand years produces hardly any alteration. For example, the traveller in Arabia at the present day witnesses, in the employments and mode of living which characterize the people, a scene little different from that which might have been seen in the age of the patriarchs Abraham and Isaac. There are the same pastoral pursuits, the same hospitality, the same dwelling in tents, and the same predatory alarms which oftener than once called the father of the faithful into the field of battle, and rendered the quiver and the bow necessary implements in the house of every shepherd. Even the powerful influence of European commerce and enterprise has not reached the bosom of their deserts, nor produced any material innovation on their wonted manners. The camel, loaded with the spices and balm of the "far country," still makes his periodical journey over the sandy waste, and thereby connects, in the links of a commercial intercourse, the beginning of which cannot now be traced, the banks of the Indus with the shores of the Red Sea.

The same perpetuity exists in their opinions and belief, wherever they have been exempted from the direct operation of conquest. Their tenets and worship are those which they received from their fathers; and in this respect the Abyssinians appear to manifest the same tenacity of established usages, whether of thought or of action, and the same re-

LITERATURE OF ETHIOPIA. 317

luctance to change, which distinguish their neighbours on the eastern side of the Gulf. From the date at which Frumentius carried to them the seeds of the gospel down to the arrival of the Portuguese, there is an interval of nearly twelve hundred years; but during that period they were not exposed to any such disturbance from the arrival of strangers as would unsettle their creed, or interfere with the forms of their religious service. Hence, we repeat, there is good ground for believing that the Christianity which the European missionaries found in Abyssinia, in the sixteenth century, preserved the general features of the doctrine and practice which they received from the disciple of Athanasius.

In confirmation of the opinion now stated we shall mention a few particulars which, the more minutely they are considered, will contract a greater degree of interest in the view of a theological antiquary. The first is the use of circumcision, which, it is well known, was continued among Jewish converts long after the complete establishment of the gospel in the various cities of the Roman empire. The example of the apostles did not discountenance this usage as applied to the descendants of Abraham; on the contrary, these holy men confined their reprehension to an undue confidence in its efficacy, and to the attempt made by some of their followers to extend its obligation beyond the limits of the ancient covenant. It is extremely probable, therefore, that in the days of Frumentius the ritual of Moses retained its authority so far as to justify certain practices which were afterwards laid aside in the churches of the East and West. The case of Timothy, recorded by St Paul himself, might, in the estimation of a rude people disposed to outward ceremonies, seem to warrant more than a simple connivance.

The purifications of their priests, as we have already stated, may perhaps be traced to the same source, and be found also to rest on the usage of apostolical times. The laws, too, imposed upon women after childbirth, which bear so close a resemblance to the Mosaical institution, were, it is probable, derived from the habits of the early Christians; who, we may presume, could not be induced to regard such salutary practices as holding a place among the things which were to be abolished.

But we discover a still more remarkable circumstance in the observance of the Sabbath as well as of the Lord's Day, which no reader of ecclesiastical history requires to be informed was continued many generations among the followers of Christ. The intimate mixture of the primitive disciples with the Jews, who were, generally speaking, of the same extraction, almost necessarily led to this union of sacred rites, in things of which both equally admitted the divine origin. It is not easy to determine when this reverential regard for the seventh day of the week was entirely laid aside by the Christians; but from the conduct of the Abyssinians we may venture to conclude that, at the period they received our holy faith, the Sabbath was still sanctified as the rest of Jehovah, and held as preparatory to the more solemn duties of the succeeding day. The partial remission from toil and study, which is still enjoyed on Saturday in our public offices and schools, is the only relic of the ancient usage which so long combined the institutions of the law and the gospel, and taught the worshipper to venerate the same great Being through the only two channels of revelation vouchsafed by Him to the human race.

It has usually been supposed that, admitting the accuracy of the Abyssinian legend which derives their religion and royal house from the visit paid to Solomon by the Queen of Sheba, the customs now described may be traced to a direct and positive intercourse with the Jewish people. But the story on which so weighty a structure is reared appears too slight to bear it; and, after a due consideration of the question, we think it more probable that, when the gospel was carried into Ethiopia, it continued to retain some of the external forms and practices with which it is known to have been invested during the first and second centuries. This conclusion derives no small support from the fact, that the principles of chronology which the Abyssinians retain are those which were held by the whole Christian church in those primitive ages; reckoning five thousand five hundred years from the creation to the birth of Christ, instead of four thousand and four, according to the calculation of the modern Jews. This peculiarity is mentioned by Bruce, who remarks that, "in the quantity of this period they do not agree with the Greeks, nor with other eastern nations, who reckon 5508. The Abyssinians adopt the even number 5500, casting away the odd eight years; but whether this was done for ease of calculation or for some better reason, there is neither book nor tradition that now can teach us."* This system of dates it is manifest could not

---

* In another work I have attempted to explain the intricacies of oriental chronology, with a reference to the opinions of the Jews

have been obtained from Menilec, the fabled son of Solomon by the queen of the South; it could not have been introduced by the Jews during their short ascendancy in a part of Ethiopia, because, being disappointed as to the coming of the Messiah, they had already relinquished it and adopted a more limited scheme of chronology; hence, we are necessarily brought to the conclusion, that together with the principles of the gospel they received the calculations as to the age of the world which were then held and taught by all Christian divines. Their remote situation protected them afterwards from the innovations, as well as excluded them from the improvements, which marked the progress of a thousand years in Europe and Western Asia.

Before we conclude this brief sketch of the religious history and opinions of the Abyssinians, we shall mention the last attempt that has come to our knowledge to revive amongst them the authority of the Roman church. In the year 1751, a mission was sent into their country consisting of three Franciscan friars, named Remedio and Martino of Bohemia, and Antonio of Aleppo, who succeeded in penetrating as far as Gondar, where they rose into great favour with Yasous the Second, as well as with the queen-mother and many of the principal nobility about court. An account of this enterprise is contained in a manuscript journal written in Italian, and now in the possession of Lord Valentia, who permitted Mr Salt to publish a translation of it at the end of his Travels in Abyssinia.

---

and early Christians; both of whom held the epoch mentioned in the text, and counted about 5500 from the Creation to the birth of the Redeemer.—See *Connection of Sacred and Profane History*, vol. i. p. 49—168.

On first meeting with this narrative the latter was inclined to doubt its authenticity, from not having seen any notice of such a mission in Mr Bruce's volumes; but he subsequently ascertained several circumstances which seemed to place its credit beyond dispute, especially the correct mention of the names which the two emperors, Bacuffa and Yasous, assumed on their accession to the throne. There is besides, in Bruce's original memoranda, an observation which proves that his great friend Ayto Aylo had actually been won over to the Roman faith by one of these very monks. It is incidentally noticed, " that he had been converted by Father Antonio, a Franciscan, in 1755."*

The memoir of Remedio is extremely interesting. After detailing the perils of their journey from Girgeh in Upper Egypt, and their correspondence with the Abyssinian government, he relates, that on the 19th March 1752 they arrived at Gondar, where they were received with great joy, and pleasantly lodged in the royal palace. On the following day the emperor, who at that time resided at Kahha, sent for them to an audience; and after they had made a profound reverence he addressed them in the following words:—" I embrace you with all my heart,—I welcome you with gladness, and congratulate you on your happy arrival. While yet a child I wished ardently to have men like you in my kingdom; on this account I exceedingly rejoice at your coming, and I promise you as long as I live my favour, protection, and assistance."

---

* Appendix to vol. vii. p. 65, third edition; and Salt's Travels, p. 484.

He then began to interrogate them with respect to the following points: 1st, Where are the tables of Moses? 2dly, Concerning the Queen of Sheba? 3d, In what language Christ will judge the world? 4th, In what language did he speak when conversing with men; and what was the first spoken language? He asked many other questions respecting Europeans, their customs, and manner of living; which they answered to the content and satisfaction of the emperor; " who, gratified by our discourse, rose from his throne, which was fashioned like a bed, and spoke thus,—' This house shall be your habitation.' "

The favour shown to the Italian monks produced as usual a furious rebellion, and rendered their departure from the kingdom a matter of necessity. But the friars did not yield a willing submission; on the contrary, they addressed the sovereign and his mother with evangelical license on the Catholic faith, and threatened them with eternal damnation if they did not show obedience to the truths of the Gospel. At length, however, they were driven out of the palace by main force; " in leaving which we shook the dust off from our feet, and publicly upbraided the emperor and his people with their infidelity, exclaiming with a loud voice, ' We are driven away by false Christians; let us fly then and seek refuge among the Gentiles.' "*

The literature of the Ethiopians, like that of the ancient Jews, appears to have been confined to their religious service and the chronicles of their nation. Their history, which Mr Bruce had the merit of

---

* Salt, Appendix, p. xxxi., &c.

making known to Europe, bears a striking resemblance to the narratives of the Hebrew priests, whose duty it was, under divine superintendence, to record the acts of their kings as well as to transmit their characters to succeeding generations. The poetry of Abyssinia, too, like the pious effusions of the Israelites, is confined to sacred subjects,—the praises of God, or the celebration of the triumphs and deliverances achieved by the fathers of their people guided by the hand of Providence. For lighter compositions, such as amused the leisure or gratified the taste of the Greeks and Romans, they entertain the most sovereign contempt; regarding it as rather an unholy exercise to employ the fascinating powers of music and poetical numbers for any purpose less exalted than religion. Their only pastime which partakes at all of a literary nature are riddles and enigmas; reminding the traveller of the entertainments which enlivened the marriage of Samson, and of the simple state of society in which that champion flourished.

The Abyssinians have the entire Scriptures as we have, and reckon the same number of books; but these are very seldom found in the habitation of any one individual; as few of them, from extreme poverty, are able to purchase the whole, either of the historical or prophetical portion of the Old Testament. The same remark applies to the New Testament, complete copies of which are extremely scarce. Nowhere indeed except in churches is there to be seen more than the Gospels and the Acts of the Apostles; and the possession of even these implies no ordinary degree of wealth. The Revelation of St John is a piece of favourite reading among the priests, and so is the Song of Solomon, although the latter is forbidden to deacons, laymen, and women. They make no distinction between canonical and apocryphal books. Bel and the Dragon is perused with equal reverence as the Acts, and it is suspected with equal edification; a spirit of impartiality which extends even to the history of St George and other legends having no better foundation in ecclesiastical history.

Next to the New Testament they place the Constitutions of the Apostles, which as far as a certain class of questions is considered may be called the written law of the country. They have also a general Liturgy or Book of Common Prayer, besides a variety of manuals appropriated to particular festivals. Selections from the volumes of the Greek Fathers occasionally occur, as also versions of the more practical and devotional tracts of Anathasius, Basil, Chrysostom, and Cyril. But the most popular work is the Flower of the Saints, in which are recorded the lives and miracles of their holy men, mixed with fables of the most incredible and even ridiculous nature. The book of Enoch, which though quoted by St Jude, has been universally held as apocryphal, likewise finds a place in their sacred library. It deserves the same reception as has been bestowed on the Organon Denghel or Musical Instrument of the Virgin Mary; a treatise which is said to compensate by the beauty of its style for the manifold absurdities it every where contains.

Among the works mentioned by Ludolf, there is one entitled the Book of Philosophy, which he acknowledges it was not his good fortune to see. The notions on general physics entertained by the Abyssinians are extremely limited, and carry us back to the first efforts made by the human mind to connect effects with causes. They maintain that man was formed out of the four elements, the moist, the dry, the cold, and the warm; that the soul proceeds from the inspiration of the Almighty and never dies; but that the spirit of life, which consists in the blood, is mortal and perishes with the body. They hold that the corpse of a Christian is not unclean; because, though it has ceased to retain either the intellectual or the sensitive soul, it has not been deprived of the grace conferred on it by baptism.

In regard to the system of the world and the structure of our globe, they hold that the latter is a plain, and that the sun and stars find their way, from the west where they set to the east where they rise, by a secret path under the earth.

Among such a people we must not expect that law should be found elevated to the rank of a science. Custom and a certain analogy grafted upon it constitute the only guide to the magistrate and judge, who decide most cases on a general principle of equity applied according to circumstances.

The art of healing is likewise in a very low state; for the use of the burning iron continues to supersede all other surgical instruments. A few herbs, recommended by experience, are found beneficial in attacks of the viscera. The tertian fever is cured by means of the torpedo or electrical eel, which is said to cause indescribable torture. When the plague or any contagious epidemic appears, the people flee from their villages with their cattle and goods, seeking in the mountains an escape from so formidable an evil.

The attempts which have been lately made by the Protestant societies in this country will, it is hoped, soon render the literature of Abyssinia more familiar to the European scholar. The Scriptures, or at least a portion of them, have been translated into the principal dialects of the Ethiopic tongue, especially those of Amhara and Tigré. The Jesuits in former days distinguished themselves by their zealous application to the study of the native languages, and even brought home some trophies of their success in conquering difficulties, though placed in circumstances so unfavourable to literary pursuits. To them we are indebted for the New Testament in the Ethiopic, which is inserted in Walton's Polyglott. In the Christian Researches of Mr Jowett will be found an account of certain efforts, made by him during his residence in the East, to procure for the Bible Society versions of the Sacred Writings in the forms of speech most commonly used in the several provinces of Abyssinia. His labours, though not altogether fruitless, were not attended with such results as might inspire universal confidence; but the acquisitions already attained will assist materially in facilitating the progress of more accomplished workmen than he had it in his power to employ.*

It cannot be denied, that the condition of Abyssinia at the present moment presents strong claims to the aid and sympathy of the Christian world. Nearly thirty years ago, Lord Valentia pointed out the importance of opening a direct communication between that country and Britain; stating his con-

---

* Page 196, &c.

viction that our holy religion in its better forms, if offered to their acceptance with caution and moderation, would meet with a favourable reception. At any rate, the improvements in art and science, which always follow commerce, would meliorate the national character, and assist in bringing back their belief and worship to a purity which they have long lost. The restoration of tranquillity to the provinces, and a legal trade to the empire, would also have the very important effect of putting an end to the exportation of slaves; which here is not only liable to the same objections as on the western coast of Africa, but to the still greater one that the individuals thus sold and expatriated are Christians, and are moreover carried into Arabia, where they inevitably lose at once their liberty and their religion.

Mr Salt announced that the nation with its religion was fast verging to ruin. The Galla and Mussulman tribes around are daily becoming more powerful; and " there is reason to fear that the very name of Christ may be lost among them."*

---

* Lord Valentia's Travels, vol. iii. pp. 247, 256.

CHAPTER VI.

Manners and Customs of Ethiopia.

Present State of Abyssinia—Weakness of the Monarch—Nature of Succession—Court of Justice—Modes of Punishment—Similarity to the Persians—Humane Maxims—Aversion to eat with Strangers—Complexion and Features—Marriage Ceremonies—Manner of Christening—Whimsical Practice to preserve the Life of Children—Superstitions—Buda—Singular Anecdotes—The Zackary—Strange Delusion of *Tigré-ter*—Mode of Cure—Example witnessed by Mr Pearce—Case of his own Wife—Trembling Picture—The Crying Cross—Delusion by a Dofter—Opinion of Welled Selassé—Chastisement of the Dofter—Astonishing Mimic—Diseases and Death ascribed to Demons—Fevers—Small-pox—Inoculation—Practice of Galla—Scrofula—Tapeworm—Customs at Funerals—Criers—Lawyers—Practice in regard to Punishment of Murderers—Agriculture—Cookery—Usages at the Table—Cutting of the *Shulada*—Narrative of Bruce—Disbelieved in Europe—Questioned by Mr Salt—Description of a Feast—Mode of Feeding at Table—Attempt to reconcile Bruce and Salt—Change of Manners in the Interval—Character of the Nobility and Higher Classes—Rigid Fasts—Disorderly Conduct of the Clergy—Extract from Purchas' Pilgrims—Conclusion.

ABYSSINIA in our days presents the singular spectacle of an absolute monarchy divested of all regal power, and stripped of the advantages which arise from hereditary succession. By the principles of the ancient constitution, the sovereign was clothed with a degree of authority and an extent of prerogative, which, if exercised, must have soon proved incompatible with all personal rights and individual property. Not only was the whole land in the empire held as fiefs from the crown revocable at pleasure, but the life and liberty of every subject could be taken away at the will of the prince without remonstrance or appeal.

To guard against these manifest evils, the nobility, and more especially the governors of provinces, have contrived to disarm the prerogative by retaining in their hands the power of the sword. The Ras appointed to each large section of the kingdom became in fact the ruler of it; limiting his obedience according to circumstances, and marching his troops against his master more frequently than against the public enemy. Hence the Emperor of Abyssinia during the last hundred years has possessed nothing of sovereignty but the name; and as the succession to the throne is not determined by fixed laws, it is usually filled by the most active partisan or the most daring rebel. In short, as the crown is hereditary in one family but elective in the person, the presumptive heirs, under a system of polygamy, must have multiplied so much as to create constant disputes; so that it was found necessary to provide a remedy for the anarchy as well as the effusion of royal blood which was likely to follow, by confining the junior members of the king's house to a high mountain, where they were maintained with at least some regard to their rank and prospects.*

---

* A similar custom appears to have prevailed among the ancient Hebrews, for in the threatening denounced by God against Jeroboam and Ahab, namely, the extinction of their male progeny, it is said, "I will cut off him that is shut up and left in Israel." In Palestine as well as in Abyssinia the practice seems to have undergone a change, for we are told that the seventy sons of Ahab, who were in Samaria, lived with the great men of the city who brought them up. This is now the usage in the latter country also; the establishment at Wechné having been discontinued, and the inmates

When Bruce was in Abyssinia, it was perfectly understood that the choice of a sovereign rested with the principal officers in the army and the strongest party at court. There was no preference given to birthright or legitimacy. It was only necessary that the candidate should have sprung from royal lineage and be unmutilated in his person. When a king dies and the succession is not disputed, he is usually put into his coffin before the proclamation of the next. The body is then brought into a large hall of the palace; the queen and royal family, with the chief courtiers, make the most frantic exclamations and show of grief; the whole city is in mourning; the people cut their hair and cover themselves with mean apparel. The young king is then brought into the banqueting room; the priests, judges, and nobles, who happen to be near the capital, attend; they spread carpets on the floor and place him on the throne; the Kees Hatze or royal almoner, who represents the priest that officiated at the Jewish coronation, pours olive oil from a horn on his head; and the Serach Maseri, or chamberlain, crowns him with these words: "David, king of kings, is dead; Yasous our king liveth: his we were who is dead; his we are who is alive. Mourn ye for the dead, and rejoice for the living." At this the female mourners, appointed for the special service, raise a shriek of lamentation; while the nobles shout for joy, exclaiming, Long live King Yasous! and, prostrating themselves at his feet, kiss his hand.*

---

intrusted to the charge of the nobility throughout the empire.—Commentators, neglecting the habits of oriental nations, have not been successful in explaining the portions of Scripture now alluded to; 1 Kings, xiv. 10, xxi. 21.

* We have inserted names at discretion.

When this burst of joy is ended, the funeral obsequies of the deceased monarch are performed. The body being embalmed in a particular manner, by persons who follow this profession, is conveyed with great ceremony to the vault of some favourite church. When they approach the sacred edifice, the priests read a burial service from the Psalms of David; after which the coffin is placed in the sepulchre of the kings in presence of the imperial family and nobles.

It is well known that the royal standard of Abyssinia displays the lion of the tribe of Judah, to indicate the descent of its kings from Solomon; a fiction, it may be presumed, by which the clergy flattered the vanity of the monarch and preserved the relic of a custom older than Christianity. In the fair season of the year his majesty was always in the field. The form of the camp was so established by ancient usage, that in every place it assumed the same appearance and regular order. It is said that even their palaces and towns were modelled according to the plan which was followed in the distribution of the tents. The household was very numerous, and the members of it were distinguished by badges which indicated their respective stations.

A little removed from the royal pavilion or station was a large square tent, with six seats on either side, and one at the end higher than the others, which indicated the presence of the king. This was the hall of justice where causes were heard, and whence the opinion of the judges was conveyed to his majesty, who from a concealed recess or alcove expressed his concurrence or dissent. Before proceeding to business in that court, or Saccala as it was termed, the official persons pronounced a prayer, and then chanted the following sentences:—

" From the day of vengeance; from the day of doom,
How shall the soul escape?
When the mother cannot save her child, and the earth shall surrender her prisoners,
How shall the soul escape?
When the assembly shall accuse us with terrors; when our deeds shall be opened and spread out, and all that we have done shall be read,
How shall the soul escape?
When our Lord shall sit on the Mount of Olives, on the day of the Sabbath, and all his disciples beside him,
How shall the soul escape?"

With such holy exercise the assessors of the Abyssinian monarch were wont to prepare themselves for the solemn duty of awarding justice between man and man; and in all cases, where the immediate interests of the crown were not concerned, the path of equity is said to have been followed with no small degree of self-denial and steadiness.

The troubles, indeed, which followed the successes of the Galla rendered property extremely insecure, and in fact suspended the authority of law. While Pearce was in the country the only protection to which the lower classes had recourse was the appearance of extreme indigence. The people of Tigré, he informs us, were treated by their governors better than the natives of Amhara; a poor man among the former could get some justice done to him when wronged, whereas in the latter province he dared not even wear a good cloth on his back, for fear of being stripped by the soldiers of Guxo, the victorious leader of the barbarians. An old man, who had been three years a faithful servant to Mr Coffin, requested leave to repair to Gondar, where he had two sons and a daughter, whom he had not seen for nine years. His master gave him permission to go, but wished him to buy a new dress previously, that he might appear respectable when he should arrive in his native place. The other replied that the rags would suit him best; for, says he, "If I have a new cloth on, some of Guxo's Galla will strip me, but if I have a ragged one they will leave it to me, and that will be at least more decent than to go naked."

When on the subject of justice we may remark, that in Abyssinia when a prisoner is condemned to death he is not remitted to prison, which is thought cruel, but is immediately carried forth to execution. The capital punishments are various, and among others the cross. Socinios, we find in the annals quoted by Bruce, commanded that Arzo his competitor, who had fled for assistance and refuge to Phineas king of the Falasha, should be crucified without the camp. Nor is it uncommon for great malefactors to be flayed alive; an instance of which occurred when Woosheka was made prisoner in the campaign of 1769. He had taken away the life of Ozoro Esther's husband; and she, kind and humane in all other respects, declared that she would not be satisfied with a less severe atonement. Lapidation, or stoning to death, is likewise practised in the same country. This is chiefly inflicted upon strangers for religious causes, and more especially on the Catholic priests who have been detected there since the days of Facilidas. In the streets of Gondar are still seen heaps of stones, which cover the bodies of those unfortunate missionaries whose labours in the cause of the gospel were thus requited. The plucking out of the eyes is a torture commonly reserved for such as are taken in actual rebellion. After the battle of Fagitta, according to the narrative of the British traveller, twelve chiefs of the Pagan Galla underwent this fate, and were afterwards turned out to starve in the valleys below the town. Several prisoners of another rank were subjected to the same operation; and, what is wonderful, not one of them died in consequence, though it was performed in the coarsest manner with an iron forceps or pincers. It is added, that the dead bodies of criminals executed for high treason, murder, or violence on the highway, are seldom buried, but are left to be devoured by the dogs, hyenas, and other wild beasts.

In all these respects there is a similarity so striking between the usages of the Abyssinians and those of the Persians, that some writers have attempted to establish on this ground alone the proof of one origin for the two nations. Such a resemblance, however, may be easily explained on the basis of the historical fact, that the latter people were long in possession of Arabia, between which and the opposite coast of the Red Sea there was a very ancient intercourse. In truth, the customs mentioned in several authors as peculiar to Persia, were at a certain period common to all the East, and were only lost in other countries when they were overrun and subdued by more barbarous tribes. As the laws, manners, and habits of Susa and Ecbatana were committed to writing, and stamped with the character of perpetuity, they survived for a time the conquests which changed the face of society in a large portion of Western Asia, and thereby acquired for their authors the reputation of universal legislators. The accident of having been many ages excluded from the ingress of foreigners has secured for Abyssinia a corresponding originality; or, in other words, has enabled her to preserve, in a state more entire than they are now found any where else, a set of usages both national and domestic, which we may presume formerly prevailed from the Nile to the remotest shores of the Asiatic continent.

The Abyssinian monarchs, like those of Persia, were seldom seen by their subjects; a seclusion which was intended to increase the reverence of the multitude for the person and office of a sovereign. This expedient, however wise in some respects, was found to give rise to serious abuses. In the court of Persepolis it produced two officers, one of whom was called the king's eye and the other the king's ear; and their employment was to see and hear for his majesty. In Abyssinia it led to a similar appointment, the chief who held it being denominated the king's mouth or voice; for the latter being seen by nobody, his deputy spoke of course in the third person. The usual form of royal mandates is, "Hear what the king says to you;" and what follows has always the validity and obligation of law. The Assyrians, the Medes, the Persians, and even the Hebrews, adopted the same method and style in their communications to the people.

It is not unworthy of notice, that no man is condemned by the emperor in person to die for the first fault, unless the crime be of a very atrocious nature, such as parricide or sacrilege. In general, too, the earlier life and merits of the prisoner are weighed against his immediate guilt; and if his former good conduct is thought to have conferred on the state a benefit greater than the injury for which he is now called to account, he is usually absolved by the monarch.

The Abyssinians retain the ancient aversion to eat and drink with strangers, although they seem not to understand the reason upon which the prohibition was originally founded. They break or purify every vessel that has been used by one who is not of their own blood. The history of religion can alone explain such usages, which, in fact, had a reference to the sacred nature of certain animals, worshipped by one tribe and killed for food by another, and therefore viewed alternately as gods and as abominations.

In attempting to delineate the physical character of the inhabitants of this part of Ethiopia, Bruce informs us that their complexion resembles the colour of pale ink. He has selected, as specimens of the features which distinguish the higher class, the portraits of two ladies who figured at court; the wife of Ras Michael, and Tecla Mariam the daughter of an able statesman. The latter of these females was esteemed very beautiful by the natives, and is pronounced by the traveller just named as deserving of all the praise which was bestowed upon her fine appearance. The reader is here supplied with an opportunity of forming a judgment.

Pearce assures us that the Abyssinians vary much in their colour; some being very black with hair nearly straight, others copper coloured, some much fairer with the hair almost woolly, and a

Tecla Mariam.

fourth description having the same complexion with long hair. This mixture arises from the unsettled nature of family relations, which partake of the constant changes in local government and property. A woman may be the mother of six or seven children, whose fathers have migrated from as many different provinces; for, as soon as one chief expels another, the followers of the vanquished leader accompany him into some new district, leaving wives and children to the protection of their more fortunate successors.

Nothing in truth appears to be more insecure than the marriage tie in Abyssinia. Perhaps it might be asserted, that there are no other obligations than such as are contracted by mutual consent, and which subsist only as long as both parties are inclined to respect them. After separation these engagements may be again renewed, again violated, and a third time repeated. Bruce met at Koscam, in the presence of the queen-mother, a lady of great rank with seven men who had all been her husbands, and no one of whom could claim her for wife at that particular juncture. When married individuals agree to part they divide the children according to certain rules. The eldest son falls to the mother, and the eldest daughter to the father. If there is but one girl, and all the rest boys, she is assigned to the male parent; and if there is but one son, and all the others girls, he is the right of the mother. If the numbers are unequal after the first selection, the remainder are distributed by lot. From the king to the beggar there is no distinction between legitimate and illegitimate offspring; there being in fact no principle on which the preference could be made to rest, except in the case of the royal family, where the mother of the heir is previously selected and usually crowned.

In his ordinary marriages the king uses no other ceremony than the following: He sends an officer to the house where the lady lives, who announces to her that it is the king's pleasure that she should remove instantly to the palace. She then dresses herself in her best manner and immediately obeys. Thenceforward he assigns her an apartment in the royal dwelling, and gives her a house elsewhere in any place she may choose. There is an approach to a regular marriage when he makes one of his wives Iteghé; for on that occasion he orders a judge to pronounce in his presence that " the king has chosen his handmaid for his queen." The crown is then applied to her brows, but she is not anointed. The beautiful story of Ahasuerus and Esther will occur to the recollection of every reader; for it was when she " had found grace in his sight more than the other virgins that he placed a golden crown upon her head." This coronation in Abyssinia conveys a great political privilege, constituting her majesty regent during the nonage of her son; a point of correspondence which history does not enable us to trace in any of the mighty kingdoms that covered the banks of the Euphrates.

The ordinary method of contracting the matrimonial union among people of condition and " such as fear God" is the following: A man, when he resolves to marry a girl, sends some person to her father to ask his consent. When this is granted the future husband is invited to the house, and an oath is mutually taken by the parties that they will maintain due fidelity to each other. Then the parent of the bride presents to the young suitor the fortune that he intends to give; consisting usually of a particular sum of gold, some oxen, sheep, or horses, according to their circumstances in society. The bridegroom, however, is obliged to find surety to the amount of the goods, in case he should wish to dismiss his wife, and prove unable to restore all that he has gotten. He is also obliged to secure an additional sum of money, or its equivalent in effects, to the lady, lest he should choose to separate from her without any valid reason.

A certain period, twenty or thirty days, is also determined by a reciprocal oath, before the expiry of which they vow to go to church together and receive the sacrament. When the time appointed for the marriage arrives the intended spouse appears again at the bride's residence, examines in her company the moveables and clothes which she is to carry with her, and swears again that he will respect her property, use her well, never leave her without food and raiment, keep her in a good house, and discharge faithfully all the duties incumbent upon him as the head of a domestic establishment. His surety or sponsor likewise binds himself to see all these obligations punctually fulfilled. Matters being suitably adjusted, the bridegroom takes his wife on his shoulders, and carries her to his own house if in the neighbourhood; but if not, he limits the procession to a complete circuit of her father's dwelling; after which he sets her down, and conducts her into it. No sooner is this ceremony performed than a solemn banquet takes place, consisting of raw beef and bread, honey-wine, and another beverage called bouza, extracted from fermented grain. The feast being ended, the parties mount on mules and ride to the gentleman's abode, where are concluded all the rites necessary to marriage before they live together. When they have completed the specified term, they appear in church, and declare before the priest that they are husband and wife, and that they are come to receive the sacrament. The clergyman, satisfied with these assurances, performs mass; the young couple communicate and return home.

This, we are told, is the established form of those marriages which are celebrated canonically, or according to ecclesiastical rules. But it is clear that the peasants and soldiers do not encumber themselves with so much ceremony. No settlement, surety, or oath, being necessary, they kill an ox or some sheep, which they eat raw, drink a great deal of bouza, dance, shout, and practise various kinds of fooleries; and if a priest be at hand he sprinkles them with holy water, and repeats a hallelujah. The company join in the benediction; and, as we might suppose in such circumstances, this slight formality is distinguished by a greater degree of mirth than delicacy of manners.

The usage at the marriage of a prince or princess is described in these terms: The match having been previously settled according to the views of the court, preparations are made for the festival, which is generally held during the rainy season, while the country is secure and abandoned to pleasure. The king being seated on his throne in the large hall of audience, the parties are introduced into his presence with their respective attendants. After kissing his hand they are all magnificently clothed in dresses of brocade or other rich stuffs. The crown is sometimes set on their heads; they receive the benediction of the Kees Hatze, or royal almoner; after which they retire clothed with the caftan. Having mounted horses given them by his majesty, they ride in great state, in the midst of loud acclamations, to the house of the husband. A dinner is prepared, in the course of which many oxen are slaughtered at the door in order to furnish *brind*, which is served up reeking and quivering from the body of the animal. Deep drinking then commences, in which the ladies and gentlemen indulge to a degree which to a European appears altogether incredible. These marriages, it is added, are by no means permanent; many of the Ozoros entering into new engagements as often as they please, and dissolving the preceding contract at the suggestion of convenience or fancy.*

The manner of christening, too, is somewhat singular. A man does not stand godfather for a girl, nor does a woman stand godmother for a boy; the parents usually look out for persons who are able to make a present to the child. During the whole ceremony the priest swings to and fro a brass vase suspended by four chains of the same metal, with small bells attached to it, in which there is frankincense burning, the fumes of which fill the chamber with an agreeable odour. Before he places the child in the new cloth held by the godfather, he dips it in a large basin of water, and then takes a small wooden cross, and beginning on the forehead says, "I baptize thee in the name of the Father, the Son, and the Holy Ghost." After repeating this he makes the sign of the cross upon every joint of the body behind and before; he then takes a feather dipped in a certain oil, which is obtained from Egypt and is called *meiron*, repeating this formula, "In the name of the Father, the Son, and the Holy Ghost, I anoint thee with the holy oil, as a token that thou hast entered into Christ's flock." All this having been performed in the churchyard near the entrance gate, the mother takes the infant into the church, and there waits till the sacrament is administered to the people and also to her child.

Pearce mentions a singular practice, which he remarks might appear fabulous to any one who had

---

* Balugani, in Bruce, vol. vii. p. 69.

not witnessed it. When a woman has lost two or three children by death, she is induced, in the hope of saving the life of another just born, to cut a piece from the tip of the left ear, roll it up in a piece of bread and swallow it. "For some time," says he, "I was at a loss to conjecture the reason why a number of grown people of my acquaintance had one ear cut; and when told the truth I could scarcely believe it, till I went into the house of a neighbour, though contrary to custom, purposely to see the operation. An old woman cut off the tip of the ear, and put it into a bit of cold cooked victuals called *sherro*, when the mother of the infant opened her mouth to receive it, and swallowed it, pronouncing the words, 'In the name of the Father, Son, and Holy Ghost!'" They have recourse to many other superstitious and whimsical practices to prevent children from dying.*

The superstitions of such a people indeed occupy a prominent place in their statistics; and of these none is more remarkable than the prejudice which expels from society, and even from the holy sacrament, all men who work in iron or pottery. One reason for this strange aversion is, that such artisans are considered even by their nearest neighbours as possessing the supernatural power of changing themselves into hyenas and other ravenous beasts. All convulsions or hysterical disorders, which are as common in Abyssinia as in other parts of the world, are attributed to the evil eye of these unfortunate workmen. They are known by the name of *Buda;* and many marvellous exploits are attributed to them,

---

* Life and Adventures, vol. i. p. 307.

not only by the vulgar, but even by individuals of superior intelligence. Though excluded from the more sacred rites of Christianity, they still profess great respect for religion, and are not surpassed by any of their countrymen in the strictness with which they keep Lent and the other stated fasts.

Pearce readily acknowledges his inability to trace this whimsical notion to any plausible source. Mr Coffin, who was in the country at the same time, and who appears to have enjoyed the gift of deeper reflection than his comrade, is equally puzzled, and regards some of the facts which came immediately under his own knowledge as almost inexplicable. The Budas are distinguished, it seems, from other classes, by a peculiarly-formed gold ring, worn by the whole race, and which kind of ring he declares he has frequently seen in the ears of hyenas that have been shot, caught in traps, or speared by himself; but in what way these ornaments came to be so strangely applied, he declares that, after taking considerable pains to investigate the subject, he had been utterly unable to discover. Besides the power that these persons are supposed to have of transforming themselves into wild animals, they are imagined, as we have already stated, to possess the still more dangerous attribute of inflicting disease by directing a malign look towards their victim. So fully convinced, too, are the Abyssinians that these unhappy blacksmiths are in the habit of rifling the graves in their character of hyenas, that no one will venture to eat what is called *quanter*, or dried meat, in their houses, though they have not the smallest repugnance to sit down with them to a repast of *raw flesh*, where the killing of the cow or sheep before their eyes dissipates at once the horrible illusion.

Mr Coffin relates a story respecting one of these Budas, the circumstances of which fell under his own observation. It happened that among his servants he had hired an individual of this gifted class, who, one evening when it was still perfectly light, came to request leave of absence till the next morning. His petition was immediately granted, and the young man withdrew; but scarcely had the master turned round to his other servants, when some of them called out, pointing in the direction the Buda had taken, "Look! look! he is turning himself into a hyena!" Mr Coffin instantly looked round, and though he certainly did not witness the transformation, the youth had vanished, and he saw a large hyena running off at the distance of about a hundred paces. This happened in an open plain, where there was not a bush or tree to intercept the view. The absentee returned in the morning, and was attacked by his companions on the subject of his metamorphosis, which, according to the usual practice of his brethren, he rather affected to countenance than to deny.*

---

* Perhaps few readers are aware that a very similar superstition existed among the Greeks as well as the Romans, with respect to men turning themselves into wolves. Pliny calls the persons possessing this power of transformation, *versipelles ;* remarking that "it is a fabulous opinion not worthy of credit." He afterwards explains more particularly the popular belief on this head, and makes mention, from a Greek author, " of a man who lived nine years in the form of a wolf;" adding, " but it is astonishing how far the Greeks carried their credulity, for there is no falsehood, however impudent, that wants its testimony among them."—*Hist. Nat.* lib. viii. c. 22.

The following extracts from Petronius give a complete view of this singular imagination :—" Deinde ut respexi comitem, ille exuit se ; omnia vestimenta secundum viam posuit. Stabam tanquam

From the latter circumstance it has been inferred that the belief in this most extravagant superstition is, owing to some motive or other, encouraged by the Budas themselves. The trades they follow are the most lucrative in the country; and as these are exclusively in the hands of particular families, in whom the right of exercising them descends from father to son, it is not improbable that, in order to prevent all competition, they may choose to envelop their persons and their craft in a certain degree of mystery. With this view, it may be presumed, they place the ornaments described above in the ears either of such young hyenas as they may happen to catch, or of old ones, which are frequently entrapped, and then dismiss them to the wilderness with their newly-acquired embellishments. This idea was stated to Mr Coffin, who thought the conjecture more than probable, and promised on his return to the country to do all in his power to ascertain the fact. He remarked at the same time, that he had never seen a very young hyena with the gold ring in its ear.*

The Zackary, we are told, are another extraordinary set of beings; who, though esteemed good

---

mortuus—at ille circumminxit vestimenta sua, et subito lupus factus est. Postquam lupus factus est ululare cœpit et in sylvas fugit. Ego primitus nesciebam ubi essem—deinde accessi ut vestimenta ejus tollerem; illa autem lapidea facta sunt. Lupus villam intravit et omnia pecora tanquam lanius sanguinem illis misit, nec tamen destitit, etiamsi fugit, servus enim noster lancea collum ejus trajecit—postquam veni in illum locum in quo lapidea vestimenta erant facta, nihil inveni nisi sanguinem. Ut verum domum veni, jacebat comes meus in lecto, et collum illius medicus curabat. Intellexi illum *versipellem* esse, nec postea cum illo panem gustare potui, non si me occidisses."

* See a note by the Editor of Pearce's Life and Adventures, vol. i. p. 287.

Christians, go roaring about the towns, making a dreadful noise, torturing themselves with whips, and even cutting their flesh with knives. They are most numerous in the province of Tigré, where they have a church, which is frequented by no other class of men. They style themselves the descendants of St George. In their place of worship there is a light, which they assert burns continually without the aid of any human means. To put their miracle to the test of experiment, Pearce confesses that he oftener than once watched for an opportunity to blow it out; but those who had the charge of it were too attentive to their duty to allow him to succeed.

One of the most annoying of their superstitions is the belief or affectation of being possessed with a certain kind of evil spirit, which cannot be expelled in any other way than by music and dancing. This complaint is called *tigré-ter*, and is more common among women than among men. It seizes the body as if with a violent fever, then turns to a lingering sickness, which, unless the proper remedy can be procured, often reduces the patient to the greatest extremity. During the paroxysm the speech is changed to a kind of stammering, which no one can understand but those who have been afflicted with the same disorder. When the relatives find the malady established, they join together to defray the expenses of curing it; the first step towards which is to procure the assistance of a learned dofter or priest, who reads the gospel of St John, and drenches the sufferer with cold water for the space of seven days—an application that very often proves fatal. A more effectual remedy is found to consist in a band of trumpeters, drummers, and fifers, a full supply of liquor, and an assemblage of juvenile personages to enjoy these means of hilarity.

Pearce once saw a young woman who had the misfortune to be afflicted with this disorder, and as she was the wife of an intimate friend he visited her very frequently. Her voice was so much affected, that she could not be understood by her nearest relations; and it was observed that the sight of a book or a priest threw her into great agony, during which a torrent of tears, like blood mingled with water, flowed from her eyes. After allowing her to linger three months in this miserable condition, the husband resolved to employ the wonted remedy, however expensive and inconvenient to him. For this purpose he collected a band of music, and likewise borrowed from all his neighbours their silver ornaments, with which to load her arms, legs, and neck.

The evening this singular experiment was tried, our countryman attended to give his assistance. About two minutes after the trumpets commenced, he observed her shoulders begin to move, and soon afterwards her head and breast, and in less than a quarter of an hour she sat up on the couch. The wild look she had, though she occasionally smiled, made him withdraw to a greater distance, being alarmed to see a person reduced almost to a skeleton exert such strength; her head, neck, shoulders, hands, and feet, all moved to the sound of the instruments, and in this manner she proceeded for some time, till at length she started up and stood on the floor. Afterwards she began to dance and to jump about, and at last as the music and noise of the singers increased she often sprang three feet from the ground. When the band slackened she appeared quite out of temper, but when it became louder she smiled and was delighted. During this violent exercise she never showed the least symptom of being tired, though the musicians were thoroughly exhausted; and whenever they stopped to take a little rest she manifested signs of the utmost discontent and impatience.

Next day, according to the prescribed method in the cure of this disorder, she was taken to the market-place, where several jars of maize were provided for the respective performers. When the crowd had assembled and the music was ready, she advanced into the centre, where she began to dance and throw herself into the maddest postures imaginable, and continued to exert herself in the same manner throughout the whole day. Towards evening she was seen to drop the silver ornaments from her neck, arms, and legs, one at a time, so that in the course of three hours she had stripped herself of every article. As the sun went down she made a start with such swiftness that the fastest runner could not keep pace with her; and when at the distance of about two hundred yards, she fell to the ground on a sudden as if she had been shot. Soon afterwards a young man fired a matchlock over her body, struck her on the back with the side of his large knife, and asked her name, to which she answered as when in possession of her senses; a sure proof that the cure was accomplished, for during this malady those afflicted with it never answer to their Christian name. She was now taken up in a very weak condition and carried home; and a priest came and baptized her again, as if she had just come into the world or assumed a new nature.

Mr Pearce had soon afterwards a less agreeable opportunity of becoming acquainted with the characteristics of this strange disease. His own wife was seized with some of the most alarming symptoms; but having a strong suspicion that this ailment sprang from the weak minds of women, who were gratified with the display, the rich dresses, and music, which accompany the cure, he determined not to yield to her fancy. He thought the application of a whip might be attended with a good effect, and actually had recourse to a few strokes when there was no one present to witness the proceeding. But what was his surprise when, instead of profiting by his skill, she appeared like a corpse, her joints stiffened, and life seemed to become extinct. Alarmed and grieved at the want of success, he immediately consented to pay for the band, the drink, and the other apparatus used in similar cases; and the result proved a complete reward for his connubial affection. " One day," says he, " I went privately with a companion to see my wife dance, and kept at a short distance, as I was ashamed to go near the crowd. On looking stedfastly upon her, while dancing and jumping, more like a deer than a human being, I said that it was certainly not my wife; at which my companion burst into a fit of laughter, from which he could scarcely refrain all the way home."*

There is little doubt that on some occasions there was fraud mixed up with Abyssinian superstition.

---

* Life and Adventures, vol. i. p. 291.

Pearce, whose mind was possessed with all the incredulity of a Protestant, was constantly endeavouring to obtain a peep behind the scenes; and, in one instance at least, he was completely successful. At an excavated church near Adowa there is a picture of the Virgin suckling her Child, painted probably in the time of the Portuguese, as the workmanship differs materially from that of the native artists. It is placed in a window, adjoining which is a dark recess; and the priests told the Ras and the chiefs who were with him, that when any sinful person looked at it the figures trembled violently. As Pearce himself witnessed the agitation of the picture when some individual, not remarkable for purity, happened to fix his eyes on it, he looked about to discover whether there were any secret entrance by which one might get to the back of it, and soon observed a monk crawling out of a very small opening in an obscure place. Accordingly, when the attention of the bystanders was otherwise employed, the sceptical sailor crept in, and after turning round a dark corner he saw a priest behind the canvass shaking it every now and then with a piece of string. He did not presume to interrupt him, but being satisfied with his discovery retired from the scene of imposture. He did not forget, however, to tell Welled Selassé at a convenient season, who said he believed it; but added, " It will not do to quarrel with these rascals, for if I were to set them against me I should not long be Ras."*

At another place there is an exhibition of a mira-

---

* Life and Adventures, vol. i. p. 176.

culous nature, which bears some resemblance to the annual prodigy achieved at Naples, when the blood of St Januarius becomes liquid in the hands of a holy man. It is, we believe, on one of the festivals of the blessed Virgin that the wonder now alluded to is performed, known by the designation of the *crying cross* of Axum. On a day appointed, the king, the Ras, and a number of chiefs met at the church-gate, where a large body of priests were ready to receive them. The latter were all arrayed in their most splendid vestments, and about ten o'clock, as the sun was coming to his strength, they formed in a line in front of the sacred edifice; upon which the cross was brought out and uncovered. The king first ascended the steps and kissed it; the Ras followed his example, which again was imitated by the noblemen and others who were entitled to take part in the ceremony. It was the ratification of a solemn treaty between persons of great power, and intended to secure the peace of an extensive province. The people believe that the cross, when used on such momentous occasions, never fails to shed tears, or at least to exude a liquid matter, which, at a little distance, appears very similar. Many individuals, we are assured, come from remote districts, and pay large sums to be allowed to kiss it; imagining that their sins are thereby washed away. Indeed there is so much anxiety to behold this sacred relic, that those at a distance call out to the priests, " For God's sake hold it higher, that our eyes may see it!" Pearce had no doubt that the crafty wretches anointed it with some thick oily substance, which, when held in the sun, melted and shone like drops of water; but no one being allowed to touch it except a priest or a monk, it was impossible that the cheat could be discovered.

We learn also that there was a great dofter, who used to travel about the country, and had become rich by deluding the poor and ignorant. He was wont to attend the sick, and was also employed to purify places supposed to have been haunted by the devil or evil spirits. It was remarked of him that he always commenced his operations in the heat of the sun, when he ordered all fires to be removed; and having taken his seat on a sheltered place near the door, he desired the people to withdraw to a little distance while he prayed. Taking advantage of this opportunity, he contrived, by using the bottom of a broken bottle, to set fire to some dry horse-dung with the rays of the sun; he then threw on some frankincense, which caused a great smoke; and rising up with his face towards heaven, he called upon his illiterate audience, telling them in a solemn tone of voice that God had heard him, and sent down fire from above to destroy all their enemies visible and invisible. Pearce repeated the experiment in the presence of the Ras, who had no difficulty in penetrating the deception; but, notwithstanding, it was deemed imprudent to enlighten the multitude and expose the learned dofter.

The few of the Abyssinians who can write usually devote their acquirement to the manufacture of charms, by means of which they undertake to prevent hail from destroying the corn, and the locusts from approaching the cultivated districts, as well as to cure all manner of diseases. Welled Selassé, in conversations with his English visiters, had frequently alluded to the influence of these persons, and hinted how dangerous they were to those who had given them any offence. Nor did he seem at all displeased when he was assured that it was all owing to the foolish superstitions of the lower classes; that they had no more power than other men; and that, instead of being encouraged or protected, they ought to be punished as impostors. A dofter from Gojam came one day to ask the Ras to put him at the head of the clergy in some rural district, assuring him that he could prevent the ravages of the small-pox, of the locusts, and of the hail. Selassé, smiling, recommended him to Pearce and Mr Coffin, who were sitting with him at dinner; upon which the applicant with much respect and earnestness addressed himself to them. On their return home he followed them, and they desired their gatekeeper to allow him to enter the yard, that he might be more within the reach of the discipline with which they meant to try his constancy. The two gentlemen soon issued from their mansion, each with an English cart-whip in his hand, a part of the equipment sent by Mr Salt when he forwarded the artillery, harness, and carriages. The dofter asked what might be the use of such long weapons? "We are going to show you," said Mr Coffin; "and if you can save others from the wrath of God, save yourself from the whipping you are about to receive." Upon this they commenced a furious flagellation, which they continued till the pious enchanter fell at their feet, imploring their mercy, and declaring that he possessed no supernatural gifts, nor was in any respect wiser than his brethren. After this acknowledgment they gave him abundance of raw meat and maize, on which he gorged himself without restraint; but, not satisfied with a good dinner, he demanded money, and at length became very troublesome and abusive. Mr Coffin was so much provoked that he charged his blunderbuss, and putting the blood of a fowl which he had just killed on the top of the powder, went to the gate and discharged it at him. No sooner did the priest see his person covered with gore, than, imagining himself to be seriously wounded, he ran to the top of a neighbouring hill, where he remained till the evening; and then descending to the gate of the palace, he demanded justice against the white men, who, he declared, had shot him. Upon learning the particulars the Ras was much amused, while the Gojam graduate was so greatly annoyed at the jest, that he was never again seen in the same part of the country.*

The Abyssinians have not yet passed that low stage of mental improvement at which the licenses of a professional buffoon are tolerated or enjoyed. At the court of Welled Selassé there was a remarkable person of this description, who supplied to the chiefs in attendance upon the Ras the want of a circus, an opera, and a theatre. Mr Salt assures us that he was one of the cleverest mimics he had ever seen, the command which he possessed over his features almost equalling that which was displayed in London by Suet, an actor to whom in other respects he bore a considerable resemblance. One of his main acquirements consisted in the singular art of making other people,—pàrticularly strangers who had not been apprized of his intention,—

---

* Life and Adventures, vol. i. p. 332.

imitate the contortions of his features; a power which Mr Salt repeatedly saw him exercise with success, and which, on one occasion, drew himself into the same kind of ridiculous situation without his being conscious of the changes in his countenance, till he was roused by a friendly hint from the Ras.

At the desire of his master, he afterwards performed some finished pieces of acting, which evinced very extraordinary native talent. One of these was the imitation of a chief in the field of battle, who had not been remarkable for his courage. At first he came in very pompously; calling out in an overbearing manner to his soldiers, and vaunting what he would do when the enemy approached. He then mimicked the sound of horns heard from a distance, and the low beating of a drum. At hearing this he represented his hero as beginning to be a little cautious, and to ask questions of those around him whether they thought the enemy strong. This alarm he continued to heighten in proportion as the adverse party advanced, until at length he depicted the unfortunate leader as nearly overcome by his fears; the musket trembling in his hand, his heart panting, and his eyes completely fixed, while, without being sensible of the movement, his legs began to make a very prudent retreat. This part of his acting excited among the spectators the share of contempt due to the original character; when, dexterously laying hold of the circumstance, he affected to be ashamed of his cowardice, mustered up his whole stock of courage, and advanced, firing his matchlock at the same moment in a direction exactly contrary to that in which the enemy was supposed to stand, when, apparently frightened at the noise of his own gun, he sank down on his knees and begged for mercy. During this time the expression of his countenance was inimitable; and at the conclusion the whole of the spectators burst into a shout of admiration.*

Totte Mazé, for this was the name of the performer, had one day so much offended the Ras by certain liberties, that he commanded him never again to set foot on his carpet, which it may be remarked extends in Abyssinia only half way down the room. On the morrow, however, to the great surprise of the company, the jester made his appearance mounted on the shoulders of one of his attendants, in which ludicrous position he advanced close up to his master, and with a very whimsical expression of features cried out, " You cannot say that I am on your carpet now!" Welled Selassé, who like most of his countrymen delighted in humour, could not refrain from smiling, which ensured the forgiveness of the mirth-maker and his return to office.

The diseases of such a people are so closely connected with their superstitions, that the treatment of the one always indicates the character and extent of the other. The notion that most of the disorders which afflict mankind are produced by the agency of evil spirits, leads to some very absurd practices considered under the head of remedies or palliatives. For instance, when Mr Pearce on one occasion returned from a journey, he had the misfortune to find that his gatekeeper and gardener had been dead four days; and the neighbours insisted that they had been killed by devils, as they were both

---

* Salt's Travels in Abyssinia, p. 372.

found corpses in the morning, having gone to bed in perfect health, and their bodies being free from external wounds. The priests, who interposed their services and advice, obliged him to discharge all his fire-arms before any one should venture into the house, and then to sprinkle the blood of a newly-killed sheep on the ground floor. A jar or two of maize were likewise to be expended on the occasion, which, with the flesh of the victim, were meant to console the survivors, as well as to render effectual all the other means that were employed against their invisible enemies.

In all parts of Abyssinia it is customary, when a building has been left uninhabited for some time, to kill a cow or a sheep, and distribute the carcass within the walls; an offering which it is presumed satisfies the ghost of the place, who immediately leaves it in peace. But when such houses are abandoned or neglected, the offended demon haunts the mouldering remains, and kills those whom it finds taking up even a temporary residence amongst them, without appeasing its wrath by the customary oblations.

To the same prejudice in regard to the influence of evil spirits in creating distempers, especially such as affect the nervous system, may be ascribed the practice, already mentioned, of beating drums, sounding trumpets, and in short of using the most noisy instruments, in order to dislodge the malignant agent whose delight it is to occasion torture and alarm. When a man is seized with the species of fever called *tigré-ter*, which leads to such fooleries among the women, his relations show him all the gold and silver ornaments they can collect, making at the same time a deafening noise with drums, to drive the devil out; "For," says the historian, "they believe that all diseases come from the devil."*

The common distempers, with the exception of the small-pox and measles, are not usually dangerous. Fevers, too, are very rare, except in the low country at the commencement of the rains; which, occasioning an unhealthy vapour, give rise to the opinion that this class of ailments are produced by the blow of a bad spirit. The only remedy employed is the juice of some cooling leaves rubbed over the temples of the patient. They also fasten different roots and herbs about the head and body, as well as a variety of written charms; which last, however, are not employed for the cure of this disorder in particular, but worn by every person in sickness and in health. Colds and sore eyes are general, and are usually caught through personal neglect; for the Abyssinians sleep much in the sun by day, and expose their persons to the heavy dews of night with scarcely a rag to cover them. The leprosy prevails greatly among the lower class, especially in the southern provinces, where thousands may be seen who have lost their fingers and toes, and have their bodies covered all over with large white spots.

But the small-pox, as has just been intimated, is the most destructive complaint known in Abyssinia. As soon as its approach towards any district is ascertained, the inhabitants collect their children and others who have not had the disease, for the

---

* Pearce, vol. i. p. 282.

purpose of inoculation. Every one carries a piece of salt or a measure of corn, with which they proceed together to the nearest town in search of an operator. Having selected a person covered with healthy tubercles, they procure a dofter well skilled in his art, who takes a quantity of matter from him into an egg-shell, and then cutting a small cross with a razor in the arm of his patients, he introduces a little of the virus, and finishes by binding it with a piece of rag. After this process they all return home, singing and shouting praises to God in a joyful manner, and beseeching him to preserve them from death during the approaching disease. So far all is very well, but the subsequent treatment is most injudicious. From the moment the fever begins they are put into a close hut, where not a breath of air, and if possible not a beam of light, can enter. Here they are laid naked upon river-sand or wood-ashes, the latter being generally preferred when the eruption is copious. No male animal, dog, cat, or cock, is allowed to remain near the house; there being certain superstitions which connect the presence of that sex with the anger of wicked spirits who seek the life of the sufferers.

In all the Galla districts, except those converted to the Mohammedan or Christian religion, the inhabitants on the appearance of the small-pox burn their villages and retire to a distance. As the diseased are consumed along with the houses in which they dwell, fathers, mothers, and the nearest relations, if unable to remove, fall indiscriminately a sacrifice to this barbarous practice. Horrid as it may appear, the natives esteem it a prudent, as well as a humane method of stopping the progress of a frightful malady, and reproach the Christians for not following their example, and, by devoting a few, preserve the lives of the community.

A species of scrofula, which they call *meshero*, is of frequent occurrence in Ethiopia. The more common remedies are attempted through the medium of purgatives and sudorifics, although some practitioners have recourse to the hazardous method of excision. With a razor they make two deep cuts in the shape of a cross on the swelling, and then putting in the little finger, they bring to the surface a kernel about the size of a common nut. Having disengaged this from the flesh with the sharp instrument, they bind up the wound with some pounded herbs prepared for the purpose, and boast of a permanent cure.

No disease is more painful and disgusting, both to natives and foreigners, than the tape-worm, which appears to be universal throughout Abyssinia. It was at one time attributed by Europeans to the practice, so common in that country, of eating raw flesh; but as Pearce and Coffin, who did not in this respect comply with the custom of the inhabitants, were afflicted with it to a great extent, it is more probable that it arises from the climate and the qualities of the water. There is a plant called *cusho*, which proves a certain cure for this dreadful disorder; and the application of it every two months is so absolutely necessary to the enjoyment of the most ordinary health, that without this active medicine the principle of population would be materially impaired.

In regard to the mode of conducting the burial of the dead, some particulars fell under the notice of

Pearce on the loss of his son, which are too interesting to be omitted. The funeral follows the demise of the sick person without any delay. The moment the breath departs, the cries and shouts, which have been kept up for hours before, are recommenced with fury; the priests read prayers of forgiveness while the body is washed, the hands fastened across the lower part of the trunk, and the two great toes tied together. The corpse is then wrapped in a clean cloth and sewed up; after which the skin called *neet*, the only bed that an Abyssinian has to lie upon, is bound over all, and the procession forthwith commences towards the church. According to the distance the whole route is divided into seven equal parts, at every one of which the bier is laid down and prayers for the welfare of the deceased are addressed to heaven. Every neighbour assists in digging the grave, and they all carry implements for the purpose, trying to outwork one another.

It is customary, too, on such occasions to bring gifts to the relatives of the departed, or what are called *devves* in the language of the country. Pearce relates that in his case, before the cry was over, the people stood in crowds about his house, striving who should get in first, till the door was completely blockaded. Some brought twenty or thirty cakes of bread, some a jar of maize, some cooked victuals, fowls, and even sheep; and in this manner his dwelling was so fully stuffed that he was obliged to remove into the yard. The head priest came with a jar of maize and a cow. But whatever is collected in this way is understood to be common property, and every individual who contributes expects to be invited to the feast. Then " they talk and tell stories to divert your thoughts from the sorrowful subject; they force you to drink a great deal: but I have remarked that at these cries, when the relations become a little tranquil in their minds, some old woman will make a sudden dismal cry, saying, ' Oh! what a fine child; and is he already forgotten?' This puts the company into confusion, and all join in the cry, which will perhaps last half an hour; during which the servants and common people drink out all the maize, and, when well drunk, form themselves into a gang at the door and begin their cry."*

There are numbers of men and women who get a living by making rhymes and attending at cries. They are often called to a great distance to grace the funeral of persons of distinction; and if they are also celebrated as poets they receive a high pay in corn, cattle, or cloth. Mr Pearce knew a very handsome middle-aged female who, though she had a large estate, had studied poetry from her youth, and attended gratuitously at all cries of a public nature, for no other purpose than to display her benevolence and her uncommon powers. She was esteemed the best maker of verses either in Amhara or Tigré. Many great men had offered to marry her, but she could never be prevailed on to listen to their proposals; not that she had any predilection for a single life,—a very rare choice indeed among the sex in Ethiopia.

---

* Such practices appear to have introduced themselves among the Hebrews in their latter days; for the Gospel mentions at the death of the Ruler's daughter, " the minstrels and the people making a noise."—*Matthew*, ix. 23.

In courts of law, whether held by the governor of a province or by a subordinate magistrate, the plaintiff and the defendant stand up with their dress tied round their middle, leaving the upper part of the body naked; a custom which is observed even in the severest weather. The *tuvverkas*, or lawyers, stand on either side of them pleading in a loud tone of voice their several causes; during which process wagers of mules, cows, sheep, and gold, are continually laid by these orators that they will prove such and such charges contained in the libel; and in all cases the forfeit becomes the perquisite of the presiding judge. They also bind themselves in a similar way not to speak until their antagonist shall have finished his address; but, as often happens, the falsehoods related by the one incense the other to such a degree that, although he holds his mouth with his hand, he forgets himself, and exclaims, " A lie !" He is instantly addressed by the governor's servant, whose office it is to watch for such slips, and is obliged either to give bond for the payment of his bet or to submit to personal restraint.

In cases of murder the law in Abyssinia is administered as follows: After the fact has been proved to the satisfaction of the chief, he passes sentence of death, when the nearest relation to the person slain proceeds to put it in execution. Should the deceased party have no other relative but a female, though she may have a husband, friend, or other connexions, yet she, being next of kin, must either with a spear or knife strike the first blow, upon which her acquaintances despatch him immediately. Unless this ceremony were observed, the family of the criminal would have reason to complain that his blood had been shed unjustly. The principal prosecutor is in all cases bound to execute the sentence; his hand must be the first raised against the offender to put him to death, even should he happen to be his own brother, the son of his mother.*

Though a capital sentence is pronounced against a homicide, the family of the defunct may, if they see proper, take cattle in place of the murderer's life; one hundred of these animals being the customary price of redemption. But when the assassin is put to death, the relations are permitted to bury him in the church, a privilege formally granted by the laws; though in case of self-destruction, no one can be interred even within the walls of the churchyard. We may remark, in conclusion, that the Ras, or other provincial chief, has the power of compelling the aggrieved party, even in the case of murder, to accept the wonted equivalent for the life which has been taken away.

Agriculture, as might be expected in a state of society where there are so few rewards for industry, is still in a very rude condition; the occupiers of land trusting much more to the natural fertility of the soil than to any system of management. The ploughs are so extremely inartificial that they sometimes consist of nothing more than the crooked branch of a tree pointed with a small piece of iron. Two varieties of wheat are cultivated, of which bread is made for the tables of the great. Teff, which is the more usual food, graduates in its colour from white to black. The same remark applies to

---

* See Deuteronomy, xiii. v. 6—9.

barley, of which also two kinds are raised. They first sow this grain about the end of April or beginning of May; that is, a little before the commencement of the rains. It comes to maturity in June, and is immediately carried off the fields that it may not be destroyed by the excessive moisture. Then they sow vetches, which likewise ripen during the rainy season. In September they sow wheat or teff, either of which is ready to be cut down in December; and if they have water they repeat barley or tares in January. In Wogara, where there are constant means of irrigation, seedtime and harvest follow each other every month of the year. The rent paid to the king is one-tenth of the crop; but as the produce is small the peasants never become affluent. Their five harvests combined are not equal to one in Egypt, while the labour is still greater even in proportion.*

At the beginning of the rains, the fields at a distance from the villages are very much injured by hogs and monkeys, which last sometimes drive the keepers from the grounds. The soil is much overrun with weeds, which, if not plucked up before the ear is formed, are exceedingly destructive. The Abyssinians usually assist one another in this important labour, which is done with a due regard to ceremony. A chief, for example, musters every soldier in his service, and marches at their head to a corn-field, where they lay down their arms, fall into line, join in a song suitable to the occasion, and, placing themselves under the command of a female, advance in regular order along

---

* Bruce, vol. vii. p. 63.

the ridges. When the work is done the military labourers receive an entertainment from their leader, consisting generally of the blood-warm steaks of a cow, and a hornful of maize.*

In their cooking, with some slight exceptions, the people of Abyssinia are entitled to the praise of cleanliness. Fowls, after being cut into pieces, are washed in a dozen waters at least, and the same is practised in regard to fish. Both dishes are prepared with curry, a mixture of hot pepper, onions, and salt, with the addition of some butter and spices, which altogether form a compound too hot for most European throats to swallow. Partridges, guineafowl, and other game are always dressed in the manner now described, while the flesh of the sheep and the goat is only a little broiled. A favourite dish, are the paunch and liver of these quadrupeds minced, to which are added a little of the substance from the entrails that has not been digested and a few drops from the gall, mixed all together with a second compound of red pepper and salt, called *horzy*. Another sauce consists of the thin substance from a cow's entrails boiled with mustard, and the mixture termed horzy and butter, which they generally eat with the raw beef. A third dish, which is seldom seen except at the tables of the higher ranks, is made from a part of the cow called *chickkiner*. This portion of the animal, which is thought very tender, is cut down raw into small mince-meat, then mixed with black pepper, and a great quantity of the oil that runs from the joints of the knees and other limbs during the process of dissection. Pearce ob-

---

* Pearce, vol. i. p. 345.

serves, that the man may consider himself a great favourite who gets his mouth crammed full of this rare dainty!

Every one knows, that it is the custom in Abyssinia for those who entertain friends at a meal to feed them by actually stuffing the meat into their mouths. When a man invites a neighbour to dine with him, it is thought extremely uncivil if the lady does not cram the guest with her own hands; and the more voraciously the visiter eats the more is his good-breeding esteemed. In fact the picture exhibited by Bruce, of the grossness and sensuality of even the highest class in this respect, was one of the main causes of the incredulity with which his work was received in Europe; and as this is a subject which is not yet divested of all importance, we may be excused for entering into a few details, relative to the several statements now before the public.

The traveller relates, that in the neighbourhood of Axum he overtook three persons, apparently soldiers, who were driving a cow before them. When arrived at a certain point they threw the animal down; and one of them sat across her neck, holding down her head by the horns, while another who had a knife in his hand made a very deep wound on the upper part of her body. Upon Bruce proposing to his servants to bargain for part of the carcass, he learned that it was not the intention of the men to kill the beast; that in fact she did not belong wholly to them, and that they could not sell her. "This," says he, "awakened my curiosity; I let my people go forward, and stayed myself, till I saw with the utmost astonishment two pieces thicker and longer than our ordinary beef-steaks cut out of the higher part of the buttock. How it was done I cannot positively say; because, judging the cow was to be killed from the moment I saw the knife drawn, I was not anxious to view that catastrophe, which was by no means an object of curiosity; but whatever way it was done, it surely was adroitly, and the two pieces were spread on the outside of one of their shields. One of them still continued to hold the head while the two others were busied in curing the wound. This, too, was done not in an ordinary manner: the skin that had covered the flesh was left entire, and flapped over the wound, and was fastened to the corresponding part by two or more small skewers or pins. Whether they had put any thing under the skin between that and the wounded flesh I know not; but at the river side where they were, they had prepared a cataplasm of clay, with which they covered the wound. They then forced the animal to rise, and drove it on before them, to furnish them with a fuller meal when they should meet their companions in the evening."

It is observed by the latest biographer of Bruce, that it was upon the recital of this fact that his " reputation split, and sunk like a vessel which had suddenly struck upon a rock." He was attacked on all hands with satire, ridicule, and even with grave argument; and because he would neither suppress nor modify the description, he was denounced to the world as a fabulist, or a dreamer of dreams. Even so late as 1805, when Lord Valentia touched on the coast, Mr Salt was pleased to state that he repeatedly inquired as to the truth of cutting flesh out of live animals, and "all to whom we spoke denied its ever being done." But Pearce and Coffin, who remained in Abyssinia, and became intimately acquainted with the manners of the people, afterwards fully confirmed in the most literal acceptation of his words the whole narrative of Bruce on this disputed point. The former, in the journal published by Salt himself, relates that, when on a march, a soldier attached to the party proposed to cut out the *shulada* from one of the cows they were driving, to satisfy the cravings of their hunger. This term Mr Pearce did not at first understand, but he was not long left in doubt upon the subject; for the others having assented, they laid hold of the animal by the horns, threw it down, and proceeded without further ceremony to the operation. This consisted in cutting out two pieces of flesh from the buttock near the tail, which together he supposed might weigh about a pound. As soon as they had taken these away, they sewed up the wounds, plastered them over with cow-dung, and drove the animal forward, while they divided among their party the still reeking steaks. Mr Coffin also declared to Major Head, that he had not only seen the excision performed, but that he himself has repeated it, and that he did so at Cairo in presence of an English nobleman of high character, to whose name he publicly referred.*

A similar degree of scepticism has been entertained in regard to the mode of supplying *brinde*, or raw meat, to the guests in the fashionable parties at Gondar, the capital of Abyssinia. When the company have taken their seats at table, a cow or bull

---

* Bruce, vol. iv. p. 332. Salt's Travels, p. 295. Head's Life of Bruce, p. 253.

is brought to the door, and his feet strongly tied; after which the cooks proceed to select the most delicate morsels, nearly in the manner described by the travellers. Before killing the animal, all the flesh on the buttocks is cut off in solid square pieces, without bones or much effusion of blood. Two or three servants are then employed, who, as fast as they can procure the *brinde,* lay it upon cakes of teff placed like dishes down the table, without cloth or any thing else beneath them. By this time all the guests have knives in their hands, and the men prefer the large crooked ones, which in the time of war they put to all sorts of uses. The company are so ranged that one gentleman sits between two ladies; and the former with his long knife begins by cutting a thin piece, which would be thought a good steak in England, while the motion of the fibres is yet perfectly distinct.

In Abyssinia no man of any fashion feeds himself or touches his own meat. The women take the flesh and cut it lengthwise like strings, about the thickness of one's little finger, then crosswise into square pieces somewhat smaller than dice. This they lay upon a portion of the teff bread, strongly powdered with black pepper, or cayenne, and fossil salt, and then wrap it up like a cartridge. In the mean time the gentleman, having put up his knife, with each hand resting upon his neighbour's knee, his body stooping, his head low and forward, and mouth open, very like an idiot, turns to the one whose cartridge is first ready, who stuffs the whole of it between his jaws, at the imminent risk of choking him. This is a mark of grandeur. The greater the man would seem to be, the larger is the piece which he takes into his mouth; and the more noise he makes in chewing it, the more polite does he prove himself. None but beggars and thieves, say they, eat small pieces and in silence. Having despatched this morsel, which he does very expeditiously, his neighbour on the other hand holds forth a second pellet, which he devours in the same way, and so on till he is satisfied. He never drinks till he has finished eating; and before he begins, in gratitude to the fair ones who have fed him, he makes up two small rolls of the same kind and form. Each of the ladies opens her mouth at once, while with his own hand he supplies a portion to both at the same moment. Then commence the potations, which, we are assured, are not regulated with much regard to sobriety or decorum.

All this time the unfortunate victim at the door is bleeding, but bleeding little; for so skilful are the butchers, that while they strip the bones of the flesh, they avoid the parts which are traversed by the great arteries. At last they fall upon the thighs likewise; and soon after, the animal, perishing from loss of blood, becomes so tough that the unfeeling wretches who feed on the remainder can scarcely separate the muscles with their teeth.*

In the description now given, we have purposely omitted some features which, it is not improbable, have been a little too highly coloured, if not even somewhat inaccurately drawn. But there is no reason to doubt the general correctness of the delineation, not excepting the grossest and most repulsive particulars. It is true that the statement has

---

* Bruce, iv. 485.

been called in question by Abyssinian travellers, especially by Mr Salt, who seems to have derived peculiar gratification from exposing the slips of his predecessor; but it is no less true that the cutting of the *shulada* was denied on a similar authority, and yet no fact has been more fully established by the most unimpeachable evidence.

Besides, neither Salt nor Pearce ever penetrated to Gondar, the metropolis of the empire, and the scene of its greatest luxury, sensuality, and pleasure. The latter of these gentlemen, too, in describing the marriage feast of the more respectable class of people, informs us that cattle are brought to the door to be slaughtered, and that the raw meat is handed about while it still reeks and shivers under the large two-edged knife with which every man is furnished. Nor does he conceal that, at a certain stage of the entertainment, it is customary for all the party to become quite intoxicated; a concession which might perhaps be regarded as implying all that Mr Bruce has alleged against the morals of the Abyssinians. Mr Salt himself confirms the account given of the irregular conduct of the ladies, but not those open indecencies described by the older traveller. It deserves notice, however, that Ras Welled Selassé entertained views on this subject quite uncommon in his country, and exacted a degree of outward decorum to which the court had never before been accustomed. Bruce, on the contrary, saw it in a state of peculiar license; so that an actual variation in the manners at these different periods is extremely probable.*

---

* See Leyden's Discoveries and Travels in Africa, by Hugh Murray, Esq. vol. ii. p. 92.

The nobility, and all those of a certain rank, it is admitted, live in a state of great licentiousness and debauchery even when married. They are seldom jealous of each other, says Pearce, at least never show their suspicions, knowing well each other's character. But notwithstanding the freedom of their conduct they strictly keep all the fasts, which are very numerous; and on those occasions they never eat or drink till about three o'clock in the afternoon, contriving to calculate the hour by measuring the shadow of their bodies on the ground. The days of abstinence amount to no fewer than a hundred and sixty-five in the year. It is to be lamented that the clergy fail to check by their example the immoral practices of the people; being themselves " more like drunken beasts than civilized beings," while the quantity of raw meat they consume, and " the ravenous manner in which they devour it, exceed all belief." Pearce, however, knew one at Chelicut who always conducted himself like a true father of the faith, and strove earnestly to bring all classes to a right sense of their duty. He even delivered a discourse in the church against the abomination and disgrace of eating raw meat; but before he could finish his address he was interrupted by the clerical portion of his hearers, who threatened him with deposition should he persevere in his heretical notions. The pious reformer forthwith relinquished his situation; but the Ras, hearing of the occurrence, entreated him to resume his office, and permit the people to do as their fathers had done before them.

We are unwilling to conclude this chapter without adding an extract from " Purchas his Pilgrimes" on the condition of the Abyssinians nearly three hundred years ago. "Antonius Fernandez," says he, "thus writeth of their apparel. The richer sort buy garments of the Saracens, and clothe themselves in their fashions. The rest, both men and women, cover their bodies either with a skinne or pelt, or with a coarse hempen cloth without other arte than the weaver's. When they doe reverence to any, they put off this cloth from the shoulders to the middle, remayning half naked. They let their haire grow, and that serves them for a hat and head-tyre. For finer braverie they curle and anoint their haire with butter, which shewes in the sun like grasse in the morning dew. Lest their locks and curles should be disordered when they goe to bed, each one pitcheth a forke or crutch a foot high in the ground, betwixt the hornes whereof hee reposeth his necke, and sleepeth with his head hanging. They use to brande markes on their bodies, especially in the face. And on the little fingers they suffer the nailes to grow as long as they will, like cocke's spurres, which also they sometimes cut from cockes and fit to their fingers. They colour their hands and feet (which are bare) with the juice of a reddish barke. They usually are artlesse and lazie, neglecting hunting and fishing; and whereas wooll, hempe, and cotton, might easily be had, yet the vulgar are clothed with undressed pelts, each wearing a ramme's skinne tyed to his hands and feet. They lie on oxe-hides without quilts or mattresses; for tables they use great bowles of wood rudely hollowed, without any naperie. Vessels they have of blacke chalke. Few but Saracens use merchandise, and in few places; most exercise husbandrie; the gentry follow armes and the court. They have no great cities, but villages unwalled and unfortified. Their greatest towne hath scarcely one thousand six hundred houses. Their houses are small, without elegance, without storie, almost without arte, round, and covered with earth and straw. They write no letters, nor use records in judgments or other writings, but in their holy things and offices of accompts for the king. They use no dirges or devotions for the dead. They use pictures, but not carved nor graven images. They paint Christ, the Blessed Virgin, and other saints in blacke forme, as devils and wicked men in white. So they paint Christ and his apostles at the Maundie black, and Judas white; Christ in his Passion blacke, and Annas, Caiaphas, Pilate, Herod, and the Jewes white; Michael blacke, and the devil white."*

We shall not fatigue the attention of the reader with minute details on the music, the dancing, and other pastimes of the Abyssinians, which differ not much from those of mere barbarians. The same reason has induced us to abstain from a recital of the amusements and domestic manners of the Nubians, who live in a state still more artless than their eastern neighbours, and retain a larger share of that simplicity which characterizes the pursuits of the savage, or at least of the human being in the very lowest condition of civilized existence.

---

* Vol. ii. pp. 1183, 1184.

GEOLOGY.

CHAPTER VII.

Exhibiting the more remarkable Features in Nubia and Abyssinia.

Want of attention to this subject on the part of Travellers—Primitive Rocks—Granite, Gneiss, Porphyry, Quartz, and Serpentine—Similar Structure towards the Eastern Frontier—Mountains of Cosseir—Marble—Emerald Mountains—Batn-el-Hadjar—Dar Mahass—Primary Rocks—Secondary Formation at Berber—Primitive Strata re-appear—El Querebyn—Fazoglo—Singueh—Mountains of Abyssinia—Taranta—Lamalmon—Ganza—Singular Shapes—Occasioned by Periodical Rains—Theory of the Earth—Reflections.

No one has written on the geological structure of Ethiopia without expressing regret, that the enterprising travellers, to whom we are indebted for so much valuable information in other respects, should not have found it convenient to devote more attention to the character and distribution of mineral substances. Above the first cataract the banks of the river, or rather the channel of the stream itself, may be considered as constituting the great highway which connects Egypt with Sennaar and Abyssinia; a line from which tourists have hitherto deviated so little, that whatever is situated a few hundred yards on either side of it may be pronounced utterly unknown to Europeans. The rocks that project into the current, or form the partial obstacles over which it precipitates its waters, may have been hastily inspected by the passing stranger, who describes them as sandstone or granite according to the extent of his knowledge, and gives them a place in a system agreeably to the principles of the school in which he has happened to be initiated. Hence nothing is less satisfactorily determined than the nature and succession of those stony bodies which compose the basin of the Upper Nile, except perhaps the magnificent ranges of mountains which stretch from the Nubian frontier to the shores of the Arabian Gulf.

We have elsewhere observed that the hills of secondary formation, which bound Egypt on the east and west, graduate into primitive masses as they approach the neighbourhood of Syené. At this point, where the calcareous strata of the north give place to the granitic ridge which has been traced far into the south, the rocks, from a certain intermixture of hornblende, assume a peculiar aspect, and are described by a specific term. The granite itself appears to be occasionally diversified by alternations of gneiss, porphyry, clay-slate, quartz, and serpentine, which contain as embedded minerals a great variety of carnelians and jaspers. There has also been discovered in the vicinity a true marble, or granular foliated limestone, exhibiting the various hues of white, gray, yellow, blue, and red; and which, when combined with the green tint of the serpentine, forms the well-known *verde antico*.

In an eastern direction we can trace indications of a similar structure across the whole extent of the desert; the specimens presenting in some places a splintery or conchoidal fracture, a gray or variegated colour, and numerous petrifactions of shells, corals, and fishes. The mountainous country near Cosseir contains many calcareous eminences in which gypsum predominates; while, in the valleys which intersect the elevated ground, the sand is partly calcareous and partly siliceous, denoting the quality of the strata from the waste of which it is formed. It is even said that the ridge in question consists of three kinds of rock; the first of which is a small-grained granite; the second is a breccia or puddingstone of a particular sort, known by the name of *breccia de verde;* and to this succeeds, for the space of thirty miles, a schistose deposite which seems to be of a contemporaneous formation with the breccias, since they are connected by gradual transitions, and contain rounded masses of the same substance.

The mountains observed by Bruce on his way to Cosseir are described by him as being composed of green and red marble; and after a journey of two hours he found hills of porphyry, out of which the Egyptian monuments appear to have been hewed. The stone in this case was perfectly purple, though rather soft and brittle when newly separated from the quarry. This formation was succeeded by a lofty ridge, the greatest part of which was marble, *verde antico*, and by far the most beautiful that he had ever seen. Proceeding still towards the south, he examined a range of mountains, the prevailing rock in which was a kind of granite, with reddish veins throughout, and black spots of a square or triangular form. Nearer the shore of the gulf the green marble once more appeared, which was succeeded by a very high mountain composed of serpentine; and " through about one-third of the thickness ran a large vein of jasper, green, spotted with red. Its exceeding hardness was such as not to yield to the blows of a hammer."*

The descriptions of the traveller, while they leave no doubt that the country through which he made his journey consists of primary rocks, afford but a faint light as to their order and distribution; and our regret on this head is not diminished by the reflection, that subsequent writers have not removed the darkness in which he left one of the most important branches of natural history.

Near the coast, on the eastern boundaries of Nubia, there occurs a singular chain of slaty hills, presenting in their composition rock-crystal and steatite; though, at a little distance, they suddenly change their character, the greater part of them appearing in the form of limestone or alabaster, in strata lying nearly north and south. Here are the remains of the *astrea diluviana;* and among the rocks considered by geologists as of later formation, are observed specimens of a schistose structure, together with porphyries not distinctly characterized. Here also the bottoms of the valleys are covered with immense fragments; among which are clay-slate, gneiss, porphyry, granite, and certain other compound rocks, exhibiting in their structure actynolite, steatite, and nodules of a species of lamellated spar.

In the same neighbourhood are situated the famous Emerald Mountains, of which mention is made by several ancient writers. The highest of the group, which is called Zubara, was visited both by Bruce and Belzoni, whose descriptions of it verify the details of the Greek and Roman authors, although the treasures of which the latter were wont to boast have entirely disappeared. The old excavations were found to consist of low galleries much obstructed with rubbish, and rendered dangerous by the looseness of the roof. The passages went very far into

---

* Travels, vol. ii. p. 89.

the body of the hill, along beds of mica and marble; and the emeralds appear to have been procured at a great distance from the surface, and chiefly at the place where two calcareous strata, enclosing the mica between them, met one another.

In tracing the progress of Cailliaud, Waddington and Hanbury, Richardson, English, and other travellers up the Nile, we are supplied with such incidental notices as remove all doubt in regard to the prevailing character of the rocks which constitute its banks. In the neighbourhood of the second cataract, and indeed throughout the Batn el Hadjar, the formation is obviously primitive; for we find granite, slate, and a very compact sandstone, about which last, however, there is some variety of opinion. At the beginning of the Falls the felspar is of a dark colour, and lends to the cliffs a very sombre appearance; but at Wady Ambigo it assumes a red tint, and becomes much more lively and agreeable to the eye.

A similar formation, it would appear, extends into Dar Mahass, where rocks of the oldest class appear on every hand, and which is distinguished by a large mountain, called Fogo, containing " a great deal of agate and fine quartz, and every variety of granite." Cailliaud discovered, besides those just mentioned, a number of fragments composed almost entirely of a beautiful green felspar; but these relics rather served to indicate the nature of the mountains which had once covered the edge of the desert, than to afford any key to the actual condition of the mineral kingdom in circumstances so materially changed. When the Egyptian army under Ishmael approached the island of Kandy, they observed some granitic rocks, composed in general of white felspar and a considerable proportion of mica of the same colour, and remarkable for its pearly aspect. The prince sent a portion of it to the Frenchman to ascertain whether or not it was silver. The miners attached to the suite of the pasha did not hesitate to affirm that the resemblance of this substance to one of the metals which exercise so much power over the minds of men, could not fail to conduct them to the discovery of veins immensely rich. The mica, according to these learned mineralogists, was nothing else than silver which had not yet attained to maturity.

According to the author just quoted, the primitive rocks cease to appear when the traveller approaches the country of Berber. The granite, gneiss, and slate, give way to sandstone, which, says he, forms the basis of the whole plain. But we cannot refrain from remarking that, as his description of the latter strata is very brief and imperfect, there is room for doubt whether there is any actual change of formation, and whether the sandstone may not, in the character of a quartz rock, also belong to the same order as the gneiss and granite. Our suspicions on this head are confirmed by the fact, that the primary rocks soon afterwards appear on the banks of the river, and continue as far as the tenth degree of latitude, the remotest point to which the researches of the moderns have extended under that meridian.*

The appearance of the mountains near Gerri denotes that they are primitive; but it must be admitted that they were not examined. There is no doubt, however, in regard to the range in the neighbourhood of El Querebyn, the principal ingredient of which is a foliated syenite, having the felspar of a pale rose-colour, and being much charged with hornblende. The round blocks into which it is divided exhibit in their superposition the same appearance as the rocks of Es Souan and Philæ; an arrangement so closely resembling a work of art that the natives imagine they must have been piled up by the hands of man.

The high hill in the vicinity of Fazoglo is composed chiefly of granite. There are found in it, at the same time, rocks of hornblende and felspar, with veins of the latter nearly as white and as much crystallized as loaf sugar. On the banks of the Toumat, also, the mountains exhibited the same composition,—granite and felspar; a geological aspect, says M. Cailliaud, which satisfied them that they were approaching the district celebrated for its treasures of gold.†

At Singueh, in like manner, granite rocks with white felspar were observed on all hands, affording a clear proof that the travellers had not yet left a primitive country. Darfûr and Kordofan present similar formations; whence we may conclude that the greater part of Eastern Africa, between the parallels of 10° and 24°, belongs to the oldest class of deposites with which geologists are acquainted.

---

* "Ici finit le sol primitif et commence le grès, qui constitue celui de la plaine." Vol. ii. p. 92. † Vol. ii. p. 415.

In a region where so little examination has taken place on the great scale, we must not expect that mineralogy, or the knowledge of simple bodies, has been accurately studied. But from the prevailing features of the landscape, viewed in relation to geology, we may infer that the precious stones which are found elsewhere in similar circumstances are not denied to the Nubians.

Abyssinia is remarkable for the lofty ranges of mountains by which it is traversed. One of these, named Taranta, is on the east of the kingdom, and extends in a direction nearly parallel to the Red Sea. Another occupies the centre; and, besides a third situated towards the southern border, there are numerous detached groups in the intermediate plains. The second of these is known by the name of its highest summit, Lamalmon; the last is usually denominated the chain of Ganza. The former contains the mountains of Amhara and Samen, which are reputed to be the most elevated in the kingdom; the other, from the circumstance of its exhibiting a semicircular form, was imagined by Mr Bruce to constitute part of the range celebrated as the Mountains of the Moon,—an absurd appellation given to an immense chain, supposed, on very inadequate grounds, to stretch across the African continent. The geology of Abyssinia is indeed very imperfectly known; but from the magnitude of the hills, the mode of arrangement, and the sharp peaks which rise into the sky, there is every reason to conclude that they belong to the primitive formation.

The province of Tigré is all mountainous, and some of the groups are of great height. Indeed the older travellers maintained that the Alps and Pyrenees were not to be compared to them in respect to elevation; an assertion which has been found inconsistent with a more exact measurement. It is not, however, the extreme altitude of the Abyssinian mountains that occasions surprise, but their number, and the uncommon forms which they present to the eye. " Some of them are flat, thin, and square, in shape of a hearth-stone or slab, that scarce would seem to have base sufficient to resist the winds. Some are like pyramids, others like obelisks or prisms, and some, the most extraordinary of all, pyramids pitched upon their points with their base uppermost, which, if it was possible, as it is not, they could have been so formed in the beginning, would be strong objections to our received ideas of gravity."*

In this delineation there are, no doubt, some traces of that vivid fancy which was so apt to carry the author beyond the precise boundaries of fact, and occasionally disposed him to touch his canvass with the most striking colours. But, making the proper allowance for this constitutional exaggeration, it must still be granted that the mountains of Tigré and Adowa are distinguished by features of a very peculiar character, and, at the same time, most interesting as connected with the principles of geology. Even Mr Salt, whose more sober judgment and chastened eye were constantly employed in noting any little deviations from the exact line of reality, acknowledges that " a thousand different-shaped hills were presented to the view, which bore the appearance of having been dropped on an irregular plain."

The singular forms now mentioned are the result of those periodical rains which carry the soil of Ethiopia to the shores of the Mediterranean, and which, after fertilizing Egypt, are continually adding to its extent at the various mouths of the Nile. The mountains, composed of various strata and rocky deposites, yield unequally to the torrents which rush upon them from the clouds; the softer parts melting down and disappearing, while the granite with its kindred masses resists, during a longer period at least, the operation of a cause which in the end will certainly prove irresistible. The seacoast occasionally presents similar phenomena on a small scale. The waves acting on the barrier of rocks perforate some, undermine others, and give rise to those angular forms and projections which at a distance assume the most grotesque appearances. It is not easy to calculate the power of a principle which, though constantly in action, proceeds with great irregularity, within any given space of time; but the effects of the rain on the hilly surface is known to be very great, while the skeleton aspect of the highest mountains confirms in this point of view the evidence of experience. When, for example, Bruce was ascending Taranta, a sudden noise was heard on the heights louder than the loudest thunder; and almost immediately a river, the channel of which had been dry, came down in

---

* Bruce, vol. iv. p. 317.

a stream about the height of a man, and the breadth of the whole bed it used to occupy. "The water was thick tinged with red earth." Hence, it is not surprising that the sides of the hills should in many parts be washed away, and that the rocks should project on high like steeples and obelisks, and be broken into a thousand different forms.*

There is a celebrated theory of the earth, which rests on the assumption, that all the land now above water will in the course of ages be swept into the sea, to be re-formed into new continents, and in due time raised above the surface, as the abode of future generations, both of men and of the inferior species. Whatever degree of truth there may be in the geological speculations connected with this hypothesis, it will be admitted that no part of the world supplies a better illustration of its leading principles than Abyssinia, or diminishes to a greater extent the feeling of improbability which appears inseparable from its first announcement. The actual condition of the mountains, resembling in some places an animal body stripped of the flesh, affords an ample proof that no element but time is wanting to complete the disintegration of the whole surface of Eastern Africa, and thereby to reduce it to the level of the ocean.

These facts would lead to reflections quite unsuitable to the limits of this chapter. Following such a train of thought, the geologist would see himself in the midst of a vast ruin, where the precipices which rise on all sides, the sharp peaks of the granite mountains, and the huge fragments that surround their bases, seem to mark so many epochs in the progress of decay, and to point out the energy of those destructive causes which even the magnitude and solidity of such great bodies have been unable to resist. Perhaps he would see reason to infer that the northern deserts of Africa occupy the place of extensive hills which have been crumbled down by the hand of time; while the dry channels of ancient rivers might be held as indications of the line in which the waters rushing from them were conveyed to the Mediterranean.†

---

* Travels, vol. iv. pp. 261 and 307.　　† Playfair, vol. i. p. 122.

ZOOLOGY.

CHAPTER VIII.

Notices regarding some of the principal Features in the Zoology of the Countries described in the preceding Chapters.

Peculiarity in the Physical Structure of the Inhabitants of Upper Egypt—Animals numerous in Abyssinia—Monkeys—Bats—Canine Animals—Fennec—Hyenas—Lynxes—Feline Animals—Supposed Origin of our Domestic Cat—Jerboa—Different Kinds of Wild Hog—Hippopotamus—Rhinoceros—Equine Animals—Giraffe—Antelopes—Birds of Prey—Lammergeyer—Vulture—Owls—Pigeons—Hornbills—Parrots—Bustard—Storks—Water Fowl—Reptiles—Crocodile—Cerastes—Fishes—Shells—Pearl Muscles—Insects—Tsaltsalya Fly—Locusts.

It has been the practice of several natural historians to commence their systematic expositions with a " Nosce teipsum," followed by a brief description of the human race,—thus, with more modesty than truth, affecting to classify themselves with the beasts that perish. That many of us are very " brutish persons," is a fact which cannot be gainsaid; but still there is something sufficiently preposterous in the grave and formal enunciation of those characters by which mankind in general are allied to, or distinguished from, the brute creation. The human race possesses indeed the attributes of animal life in common with the inferior orders; but we should never cease to retain a firm conviction that these are " the accidents not the essentials of our nature;"* and that, however proper it may be to mention them as the technical statements of physiology, they are yet totally inadequate to the description of a being who bears within him the germ of an immortal life, and knows that he was created " but a little lower than the angels." " Those persons," says Buffon, " who see, hear, or smell imperfectly, are of no less intellectual capacity than others;

---

* Grinfield's Letters to Laurence.

an evident proof that in man there is something more
than an internal sense. This is the soul of man, which
is an independent and superior sense,—a lofty and spiritual
existence,—entirely different in its essence and action from
the nature of the external senses."*

In conformity with these impressions we have hitherto,
in the zoological disquisitions of the Edinburgh Cabinet
Library, assigned the most prominent place to the quadrumanous order, which we regard as the most highly or-
ganized of the brute creation, and have altogether avoided
what we consider as the degradation of the human race.
We shall not here depart from the observance of an accustomed rule, farther than to notice very briefly a peculiarity in the physical structure of some of those tribes,
with the general history of which the reader has already
been made acquainted.

It is long since Winkelman observed that the ear was invariably placed much higher in the Egyptian statues than in
the Greek; but he attributed this peculiarity to a systematic practice in Egyptian art, of elevating the ears of their
kings in like manner as the Greek artists are known to
have exaggerated the perpendicularity of the facial angle
in the heads of their gods and heroes. M. Dureau de la
Malle, in his recent visit to the museum at Turin, so rich
in Egyptian monuments, was particularly struck with
this feature in all the statues of Phta, Mœris, Osymandias, Ramesses, and Sesostris. Six mummies recently
arrived from Upper Egypt were at that time under examination, and afforded him the means of ascertaining
whether this special character of the higher situation of
the orifice of the ear really existed in the skulls of the
natives of the country. He was surprised to find in them,
as well as in many other skulls from the same place, of
which the facial angle did not differ from that of the European race, that the orifice of the ear, instead of being,
as with us, on a line with the lower part of the nose, was
placed on a line with the centre part of the eye. The
head, in the region of the temple, was also much depressed, and the top of the skull elevated, as compared with
those of Europe, from one and a half to two inches. It
is somewhat singular that this character should have
hitherto eluded the observation of so many professional ana-

---

* Encyclopædia Britannica, 7th Edition, vol. iii. p. 159.

tomists, and of all the travellers who have traversed Egypt. As a striking corroboration of so singular a structure, which may not inaptly be regarded as the Egyptian type, and a newly-observed variety of the Caucasian race, M. Dureau cites as an example M. Elias Boctor, a Copt, native of Upper Egypt, who has been twenty years in Paris as a professor of Arabic. He was well known to M. Dureau, who had constantly remarked the great elevation of his ears, which indeed had rather the appearance of two little horns than of the ordinary human appendages. The Hebrew race are moreover said to resemble the Egyptians in several particulars. The same author examined and found that the ears of M. Carmeli, a Jew, professor of Hebrew, although not placed so high as in the mummies or Copts of Upper Egypt, were still very remarkable as compared with those of the natives of Europe.*

Before proceeding to notice a few of the more remarkable of the wild species, we may observe that the domesticated animals of Abyssinia consist, as is usual in most countries, of oxen, sheep (chiefly a small black variety), goats, horses, mules, asses, and a few camels. Two kinds of dogs are frequent, one of which, like the Pariah dog of India, owns no master, but lives in packs attached to the different villages; while the other is a fleet and powerful animal, of general use for the purposes of the chase. From its earliest days the latter is taught to run down game, especially guinea-fowls, and Mr Salt informs us that its expertness in catching them is astonishing. It never loses sight of the birds for an instant, after it has once started them from their haunts. Tame cats are to be seen in every house in Abyssinia.†

According to Bruce, no country in the world produces a greater number and variety of animals, whether wild or tame. The mountains, where free from wood, are covered to their summits with a rich and luxuriant verdure. The long and refreshing rains of summer are not too suddenly absorbed by the solar rays, and the warmth is sufficient to promote vegetation without producing those withering effects which usually result from heat without moisture. The horned cattle, some of which are furnished with humps, are of various kinds and colours. Certain

---

* Revue Encyclopédique, and Literary Gazette, June 23, 1832.
† Salt's Voyage, Appendix, p. 38.

breeds are without horns, while others are remarkable for the gigantic size of these organs. " But the reader may with confidence assure himself, that there are no such animals as carnivorous bulls in Africa, and that this story has been invented for no other purpose but a desire to exhibit an animal worthy of wearing these prodigious horns. I have always wished that this article, and some others of early date, were blotted out of our Philosophical Transactions; they are absurdities to be forgiven to infant physic and to early travels, but they are unworthy of standing among the cautious well-supported narrations of our present philosophers. Though we may say of the buffalo that it is of this kind, yet we cannot call it a tame animal here; so far from that, it is the most ferocious in the country where it resides; this, however, is not in the high temperate part of Abyssinia, but in the sultry kolla, or valleys below, where, without hiding himself as wild beasts generally do, as if conscious of superiority of strength, he lies at his ease among large spreading shady trees near the clearest and deepest rivers, or the largest stagnant pools of the purest water. Notwithstanding this, he is in his person as dirty and slovenly as he is fierce, brutal, and indocile; he seems to maintain among his own kind the same character for manners that the wolf does among the carnivorous tribe."*

We possess a very imperfect knowledge of the quadrumanous tribes of this portion of Africa, although we know that several species of monkeys abound throughout the wilder districts, the largest of which Mr Salt says is called *Gingero*, and is nearly allied to those found in Arabia. Another smaller species, with a black face, is named *Alestoo* in the Tigré, and *Tota* in the Amharic language. The fields of millet in Abyssinia are frequently destroyed by flocks of them, aided by baboons.

The family called *Cheiroptera* includes those remarkable flying quadrupeds generally known by the name of bats. The genus *Molossus* of Geoffroy is distinguished by the fierceness of its aspect, and by a large head and blunted muzzle, from which have no doubt been derived the generic name, which signifies mastiff. Their limbs

---

* Bruce's Travels, vol. v. p. 82.

are strong and muscular, their bodies heavy, and their organs of flight rather disproportioned to their general size. They dwell in caverns and other subterranean excavations, and it is probable that they live chiefly by escalading precipices and trunks of trees, as in some species, such for example, as *M. alecto* and *abrasus*, the wings are narrow, and so cut up by the arching of the posterior margin of the flying membrane as to serve rather the purpose of a parachute than for regular or sustained flight. It was long thought that all the species of the genus were peculiar to the New World, but this idea is now discovered to be erroneous. The travels of M. Rüppel in Arabia, Egypt, and Nubia, have made us acquainted with many new species which are truly referable to the genus in question. It will also no doubt prove interesting to the student of the classics as well as to the natural historian to learn that many of the animals indicated by Aristotle and Pliny have been discovered by that enterprising traveller. His investigations prove that these classical species differ in many important points from those with which they have hitherto been vaguely regarded as identical, and that modern naturalists have erred in asserting their existence in the countries of *Southern* Africa.

The species described by M. Temminck, and named *Dysopes Rüppelii* in honour of the traveller, is nearly related to that mentioned by Geoffroy under the name of *Nyctinomus Egyptiacus*. Its size is the same as that of the *Vespertilio murinus* of Europe. The ears are excessively large, shell-shaped, overshadowing the face; their internal margin is not reunited, but projects in front from a common base; a large internal fold covers the eyes. The tail is thick and depressed, and does not exceed the length of the body, while rather less than the half is enveloped in the interfemoral membrane. The great toe of the posterior limbs is somewhat more free than the others. The fur is fine, close set, and abundant, and there is a border of it on both sides of the membranous wings, along the flanks, close to the body. The muzzle is thinly covered with black divergent hairs. The lips are large, plaited, and somewhat pendulous. The upper surface is throughout of a uniform mouse-colour; the inferior parts are very similar in colour, but of a paler hue. The hair upon the toes is long, rather arched, and whitish.

The wings are very narrow, but of considerable extent. The male measures from tip to tip about 15 inches, the female not much above 13. The total length of the body and tail is about six inches. This species inhabits the vaults of the ancient Egyptian buildings, and other subterranean places in the north of Africa. Specimens exist in the museums of Leyden and Frankfort.

Among the canine animals we shall specify the *Aboukossein* of Nubia, described by Rüppel (pl. xi.) under the name of *Canis pallidus*. This species is suspected by Baron Cuvier (Règne Animal, vol. i. p. 152) to be identical with the *Adive* or *Canis corsac* of Gmelin, so common over the vast deserts of Central Asia, from the Volga to India. It is said never to drink, and its general habits are those of a fox.

The jackal (*Canis anthus*) is well known in these parts of Africa. It stands higher on its legs, has a sharper muzzle and shorter tail than those of India, being identical with such as occur in Senegal.

As a sub-genus of the dogs we may rank the painted hyena of Temminck, described by Mr Burchel under the name of *Hyæna venatica*. Mr B. kept a living specimen of this animal chained up in a stable-yard for 13 months, during which time it retained its natural ferocity of disposition. It hunts in packs both during the night and day. The fur is irregularly blotched or mottled with white and fawn colour, gray and black. Its ears are large with black tips. Its size is that of a wolf. This species though classed with the hyenas, which in some respects it greatly resembles, possesses however the dental system of a dog. We notice it in this place, in consequence of its having been recently ascertained by M. Rüppel to inhabit Kordofan.*

Great contrariety of opinion has existed among naturalists as to the nature and relationship of the animal described by Bruce under the name of fennec, and in addition to merely scientific discussion, some not very amiable inferences have been deduced by that spirit of rivalry, which, though useful in as far as emulation is inconsistent with lethargy, is sometimes apt, especially in acrimonious minds, to overflow its bounds. The discovery

---

* Atlas zu der Reise im Nördlichen Afrika, Taf. xii.

of the animal in question, though usually assigned to our Abyssinian traveller, is likewise claimed by a Swedish gentleman, Mr Shioldebrand, who is asserted by the former to have got the start of him in this matter by some petty artifice. Neither the one nor the other, however, has described the species with such a degree of scientific accuracy as to be of any avail in determining its place in the system; and the consequence of this has been, that each compiler has referred it to a different genus. Some have classed it with the most carnivorous species, others have looked upon it as a canine animal. Illiger made it the type of a new genus, under the name of *Megalotis*, while it has also been placed with the squirrels in the order *Glires*, and has even been regarded as a quadrumanous species belonging to the genus *Galago*. Although known by various appellations, such as zerdo, zerda, fennec, &c., it is, nevertheless, more commonly called the " anonymous animal," as if it had no name at all. One writer describes it as inhabiting the desert wastes of the Sahara, where it digs itself a subterranean dwelling; and he adds, that there is no auditory passage in its ears, lest it should be incommoded by the loose and arid sand; while another assures us that it dwells habitually amid the summits of the loftiest palm-trees, and in fact owes its name to that circumstance, the term *fennec* being asserted to signify a palm. In consequence of these contradictory accounts, some recent authors deny its existence as a species altogether, while others allege that the so-called anonymous animal constitutes in fact a distinct genus, consisting of two easily-distinguished species.

Buffon published a figure of the fennec from a drawing transmitted to him by Bruce. As his views of systematic arrangement were extremely fanciful, we need not be surprised that he should have placed it between the squirrel and the hare. Blumenbach, from Bruce's description, refers it to the civets, and Sparrman maintains its identity with a South African species called zerda,—in consequence of which it continues to bear that name in many systematic works. Illiger, as we have already mentioned, makes it the type of a genus under the title of *Megalotis*, and M. Desmarest also elevates it to the rank of a genus under the appellation of *Fennecus*. A feeble light was thrown upon its actual station by these transpositions.

At a more recent period, however, the museum of Frankfort was visited by two intelligent zoologists, almost at the same time,—we mean M. Temminck and Dr Sigismond Leuckart, of Heidelberg, both of whom recognised the fennec in an animal sent from Dongola by the traveller Rüppel. It appears in fact to be a canine animal nearly allied to the subdivision which contains the foxes, and approaching particularly to the *Canis corsac*. The teeth, the feet, the number of toes, and the form of the tail, are precisely those of a fox; but the limbs are higher and more slender in proportion. The head is rendered of a peculiar aspect by the prodigious size of the ears. The upper parts of the body are of a straw-yellow, the under of a yellowish-white. The latter colour also characterizes the fore-legs, and the greater portion of the hinder ones. The woolly portions of the coat are long, soft, and white; the silky are also very soft, and are annulated with white and straw-colour,—with, here and there, a few black points. The general colour of the tail, especially of its superior portion, is brownish-yellow, but blackish towards the point and root. Our information is still defective regarding the manners of this species; but it appears to be the opinion of those who have studied its characters and history, that the fact reported by Bruce of its living on trees is erroneous, and that it is more probably a ground, or even subterranean animal, supporting itself, in the state of nature, on small quadrupeds, birds, and insects.

" Though his favourite food," says Mr Bruce, speaking of this animal, " seemed to be dates, or any sweet fruit, yet I observed he was very fond of eggs, and small birds' eggs were first brought him, which he devoured with great avidity; but he did not seem to know how to manage that of a hen, but when broke for him he ate it with the same avidity as the others. When he was hungry, he would eat bread, especially with honey or sugar. It was very observable that a bird, whether confined in a cage near him, or flying across the room, engrossed his whole attention. He followed it with his eyes wherever it went, nor was he, at this time, to be diverted by placing biscuit before him; and it was obvious, by the great interest he seemed to take in its motions, that he was accustomed to watch for victories over it, either for his pleasure or his food. He seemed very much alarmed at the approach of a cat, and endeavoured to hide himself, but

Ethiopian Hog.   Addax.   Fennec.

showed no symptom of preparing for any defence. I never heard he had any voice; he suffered himself, not without some difficulty, to be handled in the day, when he seemed rather inclined to sleep, but was exceedingly unquiet and restless so soon as night came, and always endeavouring his escape, and though he did not attempt the wire, yet with his sharp teeth he very soon mastered the wood of any common bird-cage. From the snout to the tail he was about ten inches long, his tail five and a quarter,— near an inch on the tip of it was black." The ears are described as being above three inches long, covered on the borders with soft white hair, but bare in the middle, and of a rose-colour. They were about an inch and a half broad, and the cavities within were very large. It was very difficult however to measure them, for he was extremely impatient of having his ears touched, and always kept them erect except when terrified by a cat. The pupil of the eye was large and black, and surrounded by a deep blue iris. He had a sly and wily appearance; but as his habits are not gregarious, and for other reasons, Bruce doubts the propriety of this animal being regarded as the *Saphan* of the Scriptures, an opinion advocated both by Jewish and Arabian writers. The right-hand figure of the annexed wood-cut represents the fennec. In Bruce's figure the ears are too large.

The hyena tribe in general are characterized by possessing three false molars above and four below, all conical, blunt, and singularly large; their superior carnivorous tooth has a small tubercle within and in front, but the inferior has none, and presents only a couple of strong cutting points; with these powerful weapons they can crush the bones of the largest and most obdurate prey. The tongue is rough, each foot has four toes, and there is a glandular pouch beneath the tail. The muscles of the neck and jaws are so powerful that it is impossible to wrest any thing from between their teeth when once they have firmly seized it,—on which account, among the Arabians, the name is the symbol of obstinacy.

The common hyena, that is to say, the striped species (*H. vulgaris*), is an animal fully better known and more abundant in Abyssinia than elsewhere. "I do not think," says Mr Bruce, "there is any one that hath hitherto written of this animal who ever saw the thousandth part of them that I have. They were a plague in Abyssinia in every situation both in the city and in the field, and I think surpassed the sheep in number. Gondar was full of them from the time it turned dark till the dawn of day, seeking the different pieces of slaughtered carcasses which this cruel and unclean people expose in the streets without burial, and who firmly believe that these animals are Falasha from the neighbouring mountains, transformed by magic, and come down to eat human flesh in the dark in safety. Many a time in the night, when the king had kept me late in the palace, and it was not my duty to lie there, in going across the square from the king's house, not many hundred yards distant, I have been apprehensive they would bite me in the leg. They grunted in great numbers around me, though I was surrounded with several armed men, who seldom passed a night without wounding or slaughtering some of them. One night in Maitsha, being very intent on observation, I heard something pass behind me towards the bed, but upon looking round could perceive nothing. Having finished what I was then about, I went out of my tent, resolving directly to return, which I immediately did, when I perceived large blue eyes glaring at me in the dark. I called upon my servant with a light, and there was the hyena standing nigh the head of the bed, with two or three large bunches of candles in his mouth. To have fired at him I was in danger of breaking my quadrant or other furniture, and he seemed, by keeping the candles steadily in his mouth, to wish for no other prey at that time. As his mouth was full, and he had no claws to tear with, I was not afraid of him, but with a pike struck him as near the heart as I could judge. It was not till then he showed any sign of fierceness; but, upon feeling his wound, he let drop the candles, and endeavoured to run up the shaft of the spear to arrive at me, so that, in self-defence, I was obliged to draw a pistol from my girdle and shoot him, and nearly at the same time my servant cleft his skull with a battle-axe. In a word the hyena was the plague of our lives, the terror of our night-walks, the destruction of our mules and asses, which above all others are his favourite food."

Hyenas generally inhabit caverns and other rocky places, from whence they issue under cover of the night to prowl for food. They are gregarious, not so much from any social principle, as from a greediness of dispo-

sition, and a gluttonous instinct, which induce many to
assemble even over a scanty and insufficient prey. They
are said to devour the bodies which they find in ceme-
teries, and to disinter such as are hastily or imperfectly
inhumed. There seems, indeed, to be a peculiar gloomi-
ness and malignity of disposition in the aspect of the
hyena, and its manners in a state of captivity are savage
and untractable. Like every other animal however it is
perfectly capable of being tamed. A contradictory feature has been observed in its natural instincts. About
Mount Libanus, Syria, the north of Asia, and the vicinity
of Algiers, the hyenas, according to Bruce, live mostly
upon large succulent bulbous roots, especially those of the
fritillaria, &c., and he informs us that he has known
large patches of the fields turned up by them in their
search for onions and other plants. He adds that these
were chosen with such care, that after having been peeled,
if any small decayed spot became perceptible, they were
left upon the ground. In Abyssinia, however, and many
other countries, their habits are certainly decidedly carnivorous,—yet the same courage, or at least fierceness,
which an animal diet usually produces does not so obviously
manifest itself in this species. In Barbary, according to
Bruce, the Moors in the daytime seize the hyena by
the ears and drag him along, without his resenting that
ignominious treatment otherwise than by attempting to
draw himself back; and the hunters, when his cave is
large enough to give them entrance, take a torch in their
hands, and advance straight towards him, pretending
at the same time to fascinate him by a senseless jar-
gon. The creature is astounded by the noise and glare,
and allowing a blanket to be thrown over him, is thus
dragged out. Bruce locked up a goat, a kid, and a lamb,
all day with a Barbary hyena which had fasted, and he
found the intended victims in the evening alive and
uninjured. He repeated the experiment, however, on
another occasion, during the night, with a young ass, a
goat, and a fox, and next morning he was astonished to
find the whole of them not only killed, but actually devoured, with the exception of some of the ass's bones!

The general size of the striped hyena is that of a large
dog. Bruce regarded the Abyssinian species as distinct
from those described as natives of other parts of Africa,
but recent observation has failed to confirm that impres-

sion of the Scottish traveller. This species was known to the ancients, and was exhibited at Rome for the first time in the reign of Gordian. One which died a few years ago in Paris was of an irritable and dissatisfied disposition, and had eaten away in its impatience all the toes of its hind-legs.

Of species more nearly allied to the feline tribes our present portion of Africa presents us with several beautiful examples. We shall speak in the first place of the lynx tribe. These animals are chiefly distinguished from the cats by the length of their fur, the comparative shortness of their tails, and by the possession of a pencil or tuft of hair at the tips of their ears.

The caracal (*Felis caracal*), commonly called the Barbary lynx, is about the height of a fox, but much stronger and more ferocious. It has been known to attack a hound and instantly tear it to pieces. Though naturally a wild and savage animal, it has been trained when young to the chase of various small quadrupeds, and the larger kinds of birds. The colour of its body is of a uniform wine-red, without spots; the ears are black externally,* and white within; a spot above and below the eye, the circumference of the mouth, a stripe all along the lower part of the body, and the inside of the thighs, are white; a black line passes from the eye to the nostril, and there is a black spot at the origin of the whiskers. This species occupies a considerable extent of country throughout the warmer latitudes of the Old World. It is found in almost all the regions inhabited by the lion, and has been said to follow that noble creature for the purpose of feeding on the remains of its prey. It varies considerably in its appearance, like most animals which range over a wide territory. It is to the caracal that the ancients probably applied the name of lynx, as the species now distinguished by that name has never been found in those countries of which the lynx of the ancients was said to be a native. Pliny assigns Ethiopia as the native country of the lynx, and according to Ovid (Metam. lib. xv.),

"Victa racemifero lyncas dedit India Baccho."

---

* The namé of caracal is said to be derived from the Turkish *kara*, black, and *kalach*. ear. The Persian name of *siagoush* is believed to have the same signification.

The caracal is evidently the animal described by Dr Parsons from a live specimen in the Tower in 1762 (Phil. Trans.). It was sent from India by General Clive to the Duke of Cumberland.

The species described by Bruce under the name of booted lynx, and which was for some time regarded as a mere variety of the preceding, is now considered as a distinct species, under the name of *Felis caligata* (Temminck.*) It is intermediate in size between the lynx and the wild cat, and is said to prey much on guinea-fowl. Its tail is long and slender; its ears long, pointed, and externally of a lively *red* colour, with short brown tufts. It is to this species that M. Geoffroy has erroneously applied the title of *Felis chaus*, as if it were identical with the species so named by Guldenstaedt.† It inhabits both the north and south of Africa, and occurs likewise in the southern parts of India. It is abundant both in Barbary and at the Cape of Good Hope. The specimen killed by Bruce in Abyssinia appears to have been a young one. M. Geoffroy procured it in the adult state from an island in the Nile. In its general manners it rather resembles the wild cat of Europe than a lynx. It climbs trees, and conceals itself among crags and thickets.

Another species of lynx, which inhabits the banks of the Nile as far as Nubia, is the chaus (*Felis chaus* of Guldenstaedt and Temminck), called *Kir-myschak* by the Tartar nations. It is about the size of the European lynx. The legs are long, the muzzle very blunt, the tail one-third of the length of the head and body, the ears terminated by very short pencils, and a black band runs from the anterior margin of the eye towards the muzzle. The prevailing colour is a yellowish-gray. The name of chaus was originally applied by Pliny to the common lynx, and was used by Guldenstaedt in reference to the species just noted. M. Geoffroy, however, transposed the title by mistake to the booted lynx (*F. caligata*, Temm.), which has occasioned some confusion in the synonymy of the species. The true chaus, in addition to the localities above named, inhabits swampy and wooded districts along the shores of the Caspian Sea, and the banks of the streams which flow into that great receptacle. It does not, however, occur on the Volga, although common in

---

* Monographies de Mammalogie, p. 123.
† Nov. Comm. Petrop. vol. xx.

many parts of the Persian dominions. It hunts during the night, preys on birds and small quadrupeds, sometimes also on fish, and is extremely impatient of captivity, and consequently difficult to tame. This species rarely climbs trees. Its skin, even in a mutilated condition, is extremely rare in collections of peltry; and the only perfect specimen which has come to our knowledge is that in the museum of Frankfort.

Of the larger feline animals, the hunting-leopard or chittah (*Felis jubata*), a species of great beauty of aspect, and well known in many eastern countries as a useful accessory in the chace, has been recently ascertained to inhabit Nubia. Its head is smaller, and its general proportions more slender and lengthened than those of most feline species; and its claws, though strong, are less powerful, in consequence of their not being retractile as in the rest of the cat tribe. But the most remarkable fact in the history of this animal is the vast extent of its geographical distribution. According to Thunberg, it is common in the south of Africa,—a fact confirmed by Lichtenstein, who saw the chief of a horde of Caffres clothed in its beautiful and sumptuous skins; and Temminck has ascertained its existence along the western shores of that division of the world. It is widely spread over India and other continental countries of the East, and the forests of Sumatra abound with hunting-tigers. Lastly, —which is our reason for its introduction here,—several specimens have been lately transmitted from Nubia by Rüppel to the Frankfort museum. The species is remarkable for its mildness and docility in the domestic state.

Another feline animal lately ascertained to inhabit Nubia is the *Felis maniculata* of Temminck, which that naturalist regards as the origin of our domestic species. Its proportions agree with those of the wild cat of Britain and the continent of Europe, but it is smaller by about one-third. Its tail, also, is in comparison rather longer and more slender. The soles of the feet and the posterior portion of the metatarsus and metacarpus are quite black. The nature of its coat and the distribution of its colours resemble those of the female wild cat; but the general hue is still that yellowish ash-colour which prevails in the natural tinting of so many of the quadrupeds of Northern Africa. We may here record a curious observation, that almost all the animals of Egypt, without excepting even the birds and reptiles, are characterized by what may be called a *local tint*. The dogs, so abundant in that country, the antelopes, the jerboas, the meriones, and many more of the glires or gnawers, are remarkable for their general uniformity of colouring. If this does not arise from (which it can scarcely do), it is at least in *keeping* with the vast deserts so characteristic of African countries.*

The opinion generally received, and adopted even by the greater number of naturalists, in regard to the origin of the domestic species, which we find a half-reclaimed captive wherever man is in any measure civilized and gregarious, is that it is derived from the wild cat (*Felis catus*). Yet we know by the experience of many other cases, that the effect of domestication, and of the superabundant nourishment which usually accompanies that state of bondage, is to increase the dimensions of whatever animals have been for an almost immemorial period subjected to such influences. All our other domestic creatures are larger than their original races; but the domestic cat, supposing it to have sprung from the indigenous woodland species, appears to have reversed the rule; for never, even in its most pampered and overgrown condition, does it in any way equal the powerful dimensions of its supposed original. The tail of the domestic variety (or species) is also longer, and terminates in a sharpened point; while that of the wild cat, besides being comparatively shorter, is nearly of equal thickness throughout its entire length, and appears as if truncated at the extremity.

When we seek to ascertain the origin of any anciently domesticated species, the mind naturally reverts to periods of antiquity, and to the history of such nations as are characterized by remote records. It was from within the sacred precincts of the temples of Isis, and under the reign of the Pharaohs or Egyptian kings, that the earliest rays of science dawned upon the nations; and there the heroic Greeks " drew golden light," and from thence were distributed, by more or less direct gradations, the knowledge and civilisation which, long waning with a feeble and uncertain gleam from their parent source, have burned with a steady and unconsuming fire in those " barbarian lands" to which they were conveyed. Egypt, so remarkable in

---

* See Temminck's " Monographies," p. 129, *note*.

the early civilisation of the human race, might be reasonably supposed, even *a priori*, to have furnished the primitive families of mankind with one or more of its domesticated animals; and, in relation more particularly to the present subject, we know that of all the ancient nations of whom we possess records, the Egyptians were the most noted for their appreciation of the useful qualities of the cat. We also know that it was even embalmed in their temples, in common with the mystical body of the ibis, and we doubt not it must have become familiar to them from its beneficial qualities as a domestic species. That they derived it from an indigenous source is more than probable, especially as a wild Egyptian species, of all others, bears the closest resemblance to the domestic breeds. At all events, it could scarcely be drawn from the European wild cat; for although that species is most extensively disseminated over all the wooded countries of Europe, and spreads through Russia into Siberia, and over a great range of Asiatic territory, it is unknown on the banks of the Nile, and seems to hold its centre of dominion rather in the temperate than the warmer regions of the earth. Another argument against the derivation of our domestic cats from the indigenous woodland species may be drawn from the extreme scarcity of the former in the early ages of our history. It is known that in the time of Hoel the Good, king of Wales, who died in the year 948, laws were enacted to preserve and establish the price of cats and other animals remarkable for being alike rare and useful. The price of a kitten before it could see was fixed at one penny; till proof could be given of its having caught a mouse, twopence; after which it was rated at fourpence,—a great sum in those days when the value of specie was extremely high. It was further declared, that if any one stole or slew the cat that guarded the prince's granary, he was either to forfeit a milk ewe, her fleece and lamb, or as much wheat as when poured on the cat suspended by the tail (its head touching the floor) would form a heap high enough to cover it to the tip. Now all these precautionary regulations would seem to indicate that our domestic cats were not originally natives of our island, but were introduced from some of the warmer countries of the East, and required for a time considerable care and attention to preserve the breed. This would scarcely have been necessary had the original stock been found prowling in every thicket and *corrie* of the country, which the wild cat undoubtedly was in those distant days.

M. Temminck is decidedly in favour of the claims of a species already mentioned, called the gloved cat (*Felis maniculata*), which inhabits Northern Africa, and was first found in Nubia by the traveller Rüppel, in the neighbourhood of Ambakol. Skins of a species which seems identical are sometimes observed in supplies of these articles from the Levant, and the same animal occurs in Egypt. It would be highly interesting to compare the osteology of a recent example with the structure of the skeleton of an embalmed specimen from the catacombs of Memphis.

Several other feline animals inhabit Abyssinia, of which we shall merely mention the lion, as an occasional dweller in the sandy districts bordering on the Tacazze. The killing of one of these animals, according to Mr Salt, confers high honour upon a chief, and gives him the privilege of wearing its paw upon his shield. Some analogous custom, no doubt, gave rise, among the European nations to the idea of quartering heraldic arms. Its skin is afterwards formed into a dress resembling that worn by the Caffre chiefs in the vicinity of the Cape, but more richly ornamented.

The ancients represented in their sculptures a lion without a mane, which some modern writers regard as an extinct, while others view it as a fictitious species. We have mentioned on a former occasion its occurrence on the hieroglyphical monuments of Upper Egypt; and a singular confirmation of its existence has been received of late years from Nubia, where it is alleged a very large and maneless lion has been recently discovered.

Among the Rodentia, the foremost place in our systematic arrangements is usually assigned to the squirrels, of which genus we may notice, as an Abyssinian representative, the *Sciurus rutilus* of Rüppel (Atlas, Taf. 24). Including the tail, it measures above a foot in length. The colour of the upper parts is of a shining red, of the under, white. The tail is distichous, the ears are short and rounded.

Several murine species occur both in Nubia and Abyssinia. We shall pass over these diminutive creatures for the sake of the beautiful jerboa, which occurs in a con-

siderable portion of the African continent. The genus
Jerboa (*Dipus*, or two-legged, so called from the erroneous notion that these animals, in walking, made use of their hinder extremities only) is composed of several species, one of which is abundant in Barbary, in Upper and Lower Egypt, and Syria, and likewise makes its appearance again in more northern countries situated between the Tanais and the Volga. The tail of the jerboa usually exceeds in length that of the body. It is covered with smooth short hair, except at the extremity, where there is a long silky tuft. Though this organ appears, from the experiments of M. Lepechin, to be of great use in locomotion, it is not by any means thick and muscular, as among the kangaroos. The jerboa usually walks on all fours, but when alarmed, it seeks its safety by prodigious bounds, which it executes with great force and rapidity. When about to leap, it raises its body by means of the hinder extremities, and supports itself at the same time upon its tail. Meanwhile the fore feet are so closely pressed to the breast, as to be scarcely visible. Hence probably its ancient name of two-footed mouse. It then springs into the air, and alights upon its four feet; but erecting itself again almost instantaneously, it makes another spring, and so on in succession, and with such rapidity as to appear constantly either in an erect or a flying position. The cruel experiments above alluded to, consisted in maiming or cutting off the tails of these poor creatures. In proportion as that organ was reduced in length, their power of leaping diminished, and when it was entirely lopped off, they not only could not run at all, but fell backwards whenever they attempted to raise themselves with a view to their accustomed spring.

" The jerboa," says Bruce, " is a small harmless animal of the desert, nearly the size of a common rat; the skin very smooth, and the ends of the hairs tipt with black. It lives in the smoothest plains or places of the desert, especially where the soil is fixed gravel, for in that chiefly it burrows, dividing its hole below into many mansions. It seems to be apprehensive of the falling in of the ground; it therefore generally digs its hole under the root of some spurge, thyme, or absinthium, upon whose root it seems to depend for its roof not falling in and burying it in the ruins of its subterraneous habitation. It seems to delight most in those places that are haunted by the cerastes, or horned viper. Nature has certainly imposed this dangerous neighbourhood upon the one, for the good and advantage of the other, and that of mankind in general. Of the many trials I made, I never found a jerboa in the body of a viper, excepting once, in that of a female big with young, and the jerboa itself was then nearly consumed."* This animal may be used as food. In taste it is scarcely distinguishable from a young rabbit. The ancients described it at an early period, and it is represented in some of the first medals of the Cyrenaicum, sitting under an umbellated plant, supposed to be the silphium, the figure of which is likewise preserved on the silver medals of Cyrene. Bruce informs us that he never saw a rabbit in Abyssinia, but that there is an abundance of hares.

Abyssinia produces several remarkable animals of the pachydermatous order, among which we rank the Ethiopian hog (*Phascochærus* of F. Cuvier). This extraordinary genus contains at least two species frequently confounded together, under the names of *Sus Africanus* and *Sus Æthiopicus*, specific titles by no means happily chosen, in as far as both are natives of the African continent, and that called Ethiopian, *par excellence*, inhabits more particularly the Cape of Good Hope. The imperfection of this nomenclature, it has been remarked, is certainly the chief cause of the confusion which has long reigned in the history of these animals. The most remarkable distinction between the two species just named, consists in the former being provided with incisive teeth, which are wanting in the latter. For this reason the one is named *Ph. incisivus*, the other *Ph. edentatus*, by M. F. Cuvier.† These animals, though gentle, lively, and easily tamed when taken young, are of a peculiarly ferocious disposition after attaining to the adult condition in the state of nature. Yet their mode of dentition shows that they are naturally much less omnivorous than the wild boar, and we know in fact that their food consists entirely of roots and other vegetable produce. Their sight is said to be defective, owing to the peculiar position of

---

* Travels, vol. v. p. 121.

† The hindmost or left-hand figure of the wood-cut at p. 394 of this volume represents the head and fore quarters of the species figured by Rüppel, under the name of *Ph. Æliani*. Atlas, Taf. 26. It was observed in Kordofan.

their eyes, but their hearing is good, and their sense of smell exquisitely delicate.

The wild boar in these parts of Africa is smaller and smoother than that of Europe or of Barbary. It inhabits swamps and the wooded banks of rivers. This animal is accounted unclean in Abyssinia, both by Mohammedans and Christians, and that it has not multiplied greatly, in consequence of being neglected by the hunters, is probably owing to its young being devoured by hyenas.

That huge animal the hippopotamus is well known in Abyssinia. Mr Salt had no sooner reached the banks of the Tacazze, a tributary to the Nile, than his attention was excited by the cry of his attendants, of " Gomari! gomari!" the Abyssinian title for the hippopotamus. At that time, however, he only obtained a momentary glance, during which he could merely observe that its action resembled the rolling of a grampus in the sea. Between the different fords of the river which, at the place alluded to, might be about fifty yards across, there are pools of almost immeasurable depth, resembling the mountain tarns of the north of England, and it is in these pools that the amphibious giant loves to dwell. Being desirous to attack it, Mr Salt and his party stationed themselves on a high overhanging rock which commanded one of the favourite pools, and they had not remained long before a hippopotamus rose to the surface, at a distance of not more than twenty yards. He came up at first very confidently, raising his enormous head out of the water, and snorting violently. At the same instant their guns were discharged, the contents of which appeared to strike directly on its forehead; on which it turned round its head with an angry scowl, and making a sudden plunge, sunk to the bottom, with a peculiar noise, between a grunt and a roar. They for some minutes entertained a sanguine hope that he was killed, and momentarily expected to see his body ascend to the surface. But it soon appeared that a hippopotamus is not so easily slain; for he rose again, ere long, close to the same spot, and apparently not much concerned at what had happened, though somewhat more cautious than before. They again discharged their pieces, but with as little effect as formerly; and although some of the party continued firing at every one that made his appearance, they were by no means certain that they produced the slightest impression upon any of them.

This they attributed to their having used *leaden* balls, which are too soft to enter his almost impenetrable skull.

It appears from what they witnessed, that the hippopotamus cannot remain more than five or six minutes at a time under water. One of the most interesting parts of the amusement was to witness the perfect ease with which these animals quietly dropped down to the bottom; for the water being exceedingly clear, they could distinctly see them so low as twenty feet beneath the surface.*

The elephant, rhinoceros, and giraffe, or camelopard, all distinguished for their great dimensions and imposing aspect, likewise inhabit the low hot countries of Abyssinia. It has been noted as remarkable, that such common animals as the former two should have escaped the description of the sacred writers. Moses and the children of Israel, when sojourning either in Egypt or Arabia, were long in the vicinity of countries which produced them; and when we take into consideration the close connexion maintained by Solomon with the south-east coast of the Red Sea, it seems almost impossible that he should not have been acquainted with them, especially as both his father David and himself used abundance of ivory. Some, however, take the *behemoth* of the Scriptures to be the elephant, while the *reem* is regarded as identical with the species now designated under the name of rhinoceros.

The Abyssinian hunters of the last-named animal are called *agageer*, from agaro, to kill, by cutting the hams or the tendon of Achilles with a sword. The eyes of the rhinoceros are extremely small, and as his neck is stiff, and his head cumbrous, he seldom turns round so as to see any thing that is not directly before him. To this, according to Bruce, he owes his death, as he never escapes if there is as much plain ground as to enable a horse to get in advance. His pride and fury then induce him to lay aside all thoughts of escaping but by victory. He stands for a moment at bay, then starting forward, he suddenly charges the horse, after the manner of the wild boar, which animal he greatly resembles in his mode of action. But the horse easily avoids his ponderous onset, by turning short aside, and this is the fatal instant,— for a naked man armed with a sharp sword drops from behind the principal hunter, and, unperceived by the

---

* Salt's Voyage to Abyssinia, p. 354.

rhinoceros, who is seeking to wreak his vengeance on his enemy, he inflicts a tremendous blow across the tendon of the heel, which renders him incapable of either flight or resistance. In speaking of the large allowance of vegetable matter necessary to support this enormous living mass, we should likewise take into consideration the vast quantity of water which it consumes. No country, according to Bruce, but such as that of the Shangalla, deluged with six months' rain, full of large and deep basins hewn by nature in the living rock, which are shaded by dark woods from evaporation, or one watered by extensive rivers which never fall low or to a state of dryness, can supply the vast draughts of its enormous maw. As an article of food he is himself much esteemed by the Shangalla, and the soles of his feet, which are soft like those of a camel, and of a grizzly substance, are peculiarly delicate. The rest of his body resembles that of the hog, but is coarser, and is pervaded by a smell of musk.*

Of equine animals, the zebra or zecora occurs chiefly in the southern provinces of Abyssinia. Its mane is much used for making a particular kind of collar, which on state-days is fixed as an ornament round the necks of the war-horses belonging to the chiefs. This privilege, however, seems to be confined to a few of the principal men. The wild ass (probably the quagga) is said to occur in the same districts as the zebra. In regard to the giraffe of Nubia and Abyssinia, we shall mention, in the first place, that, from some difference in the spots, and in the curvature of the cranium of the few individuals hitherto brought to Europe, M. Geoffroy St Hilaire is of opinion that it is not of the same species as that from the southern portions of the African continent. It is an animal of a shy nature, and rarely to be met with in consequence of its frequenting chiefly the interior districts uninhabited by the human race. Its skin forms an article of barter in some of the provinces; and an ornament made of the hair plucked from the tail is commonly fastened to the butt-end of the whips used by the inha-

* Mr Salt is of opinion that the figure of the African rhinoceros given by Bruce must have been copied from the one-horned species of Buffon, with the addition of the second horn, as the two-horned rhinoceros wants the folds in the skin, which are nevertheless given by the Abyssinian traveller.

bitants for the purpose of brushing away flies, which are exceedingly troublesome during the hot season. These whips, Mr Salt informs us, are themselves formed from the skin of the hippopotamus, and are called " hallinga."

Of the antelope tribe, which is numerously represented in these parts of Africa, the only example we shall here name is the Nubian species called *Addax* by M. Lichtenstein (*Act. Acad. Berlin*, 1824, pl. xi.) Its horns are long and slender, and form three curves. It is represented on several of the ancient monuments of Egypt.*

We shall terminate these brief notices of mammalia by giving in a note below a list of the species described and figured by M. Rüppel in the atlas to his *Reise im Nördlichen Afrika*.†

The feathered race, especially birds of prey, are very numerous in Abyssinia. In the gigantic carcasses of slaughtered elephants and other large quadrupeds, of which only small portions are consumed by the hunters, they find a frequent supply of food. Vast quantities of field-rats and mice make their appearance after harvest, and swarm in every crack and fissure, and are greedily

---

* See the central figure of the wood-cut at page 394.

† Felis maniculata.
Canis zerda.
Antilope montana.
Felis chaus.
Canis famelicus.
Vespertilio Temminckii.
Antilope Addax.
Camelopardalis giraffa.
Canis variegatus.
C. pallidus.
C. pictus.
Mus dimidiatus.
M. Cahirinus.
Antilope dama.
Canis Niloticus.
C. anthus.
Rhinolophus divosus.
Antilope Sæmmerhingii.
Lepus Isabellinus.
Antilope Saltiana.
Psamnomys obesus.
Sciurus rutilans.
Phascochærus Æliani.
Dysopes pumilus.
Taphozous nudiventris.
Nyctecejus leucogaster.
Vespertilio leucomelas.
V. marginatus.
Meriones robustus.
Mus Orientalis.
Meriones Gerbillus.

It is briefly reported in the foreign journals, that M. Rüppel has discovered, during the second journey in which he is still engaged, a species of Dugong, which is found in the Red Sea, and differs in a remarkable degree from the only species hitherto known, which is an inhabitant of the Indian Ocean. It was with the skin of this species that the Jews of old were by the Mosaic law compelled to veil the tabernacle. On this account M. Rüppel has bestowed upon it the name of *Halicore tabernaculus*.—*Athenæum*, No. 261, p. 700.

devoured by hawks and kites. These and other causes, combined with "the number of men that perish by disease and by the sword, whose carcasses are never buried by this barbarous and unclean people, compose such a quantity and variety of carrion that it brings together at one time a multitude of birds of prey: it would seem there was not such a number in the whole earth."*

The Abyssinians entertain a singular superstition regarding a species of hawk designated by Mr Salt under the name of white-breasted lanner. When they set out on a journey and meet with one of these birds, they watch it very carefully, for the purpose of drawing good or bad omens from its motions. If it sit still with its breast towards them until they have passed, this is regarded as a peculiarly good sign, and every thing is expected to go on well during the course of the journey. If its back be turned towards them, it is considered an unpropitious sign, but not sufficiently so to create any very great or immediate alarm; but if it should fly hastily away on their approach, some of the most superstitious among them immediately return back to their homes, and wait till a more favourable opportunity for commencing their expedition occurs. From this circumstance, as well as from the resemblance of its form to the sculptured hieroglyphics of Egypt, Mr Salt was led to the belief that this species was probably the sacred hawk once held in such veneration by the ancient inhabitants of that country.

The bird described by Bruce under the name of Abou Duck'n, or Father Long Beard, appears to be identical with the *Vultur barbatus,* or lammergeyer of the Swiss Alps. On the highest summit of the mountain Lamalmon, while the traveller's servants were refreshing themselves after the fatigue of a toilsome ascent, and enjoying the pleasures of a delightful climate and a good dinner of boiled goat's flesh, a lammergeyer suddenly made his appearance among them. A great shout or rather cry of distress attracted Bruce's attention, who, while walking towards the bird, saw it deliberately put its foot into the pan, which contained a huge piece of meat prepared for boiling. Finding the temperature somewhat higher than it was accustomed to among the pure gushing springs of

---

* Bruce, vol. v. p. 150.

that romantic region, it suddenly withdrew its foot, but immediately afterwards settled upon two large pieces which lay upon a wooden platter, into which it trussed its claws and carried them off. It disappeared over the edge of a "steep Tarpeian rock," down which criminals were thrown, and whose mangled remains had probably first induced the bird to select that spot as a place of sojourn. The traveller, in expectation of another visit, immediately loaded his rifle, and it was not long before the gigantic bird reappeared.

> As when a vulture on Imaus bred,
> Whose snowy ridge the roving Tartar bounds,
> Dislodging from a region scarce of prey,
> To gorge the flesh of lambs or yeanling kids
> On hills where flocks are fed, flies towards the springs
> Of Ganges or Hydaspes, Indian streams;
> But in his way lights on the barren plains
> Of Sericana, where Chineses drive
> With sails and wind their cany waggons light;—

so landed the lammergeyer within ten yards of the savoury mess, but also within an equal distance of Bruce's practised rifle. He instantly sent his ball through its body, and the ponderous bird sunk down upon the grass with scarcely a flutter of its outspread wings. We have elsewhere noticed the great geographical range of this species.*

The species described by Bruce under the name of rachamak is the *Vultur percnopterus* of Linnæus, known in Egypt by the title of Pharaoh's bird. It is well known as a scavenger in most Eastern countries, and is found sculptured on the monuments of Egyptian art. Even at the present day it is exempted from injury, and pious Mussulmans sometimes bequeath sums of money for its maintenance in a state of comfortable captivity. It is believed that the *Vultur Kolbii* of Rüppel, figured on the following page, is the yearling male of this species.

There are few owls in Abyssinia; but one or two of the species are of large size and great beauty. Bruce never saw either sparrow or magpie in the country, although we know that the natural distribution of both these species is elsewhere widely extended. Pigeons are numerous and of various kinds, all excellent as articles of food. They are chiefly birds of passage, except one which dwells in the eaves of houses and in the holes of walls. This species is not eaten, from an absurd notion

---

* Edinburgh Cabinet Library, No. viii. (India, vol. iii. p. 81.)

Vultur Kolbii.

that, because its claws are large, it partakes of the nature of a hawk, and is therefore unclean. This is a parallel to the Turkish idea, that because a turkey has a bunch of bristles on its breast it is allied to the hog.

The African hornbill (*Buceros Africanus*) is entirely black and nearly as large as a turkey. The Abyssinian species (*B. Abyssinicus*) appears to have been first distinctly described by Bruce, who informs us that, in the eastern parts of the country, it is known under the name of *abba gumba*. In Sennaar it is called *Teir el Naciba,* or the bird of destiny. Its prevailing colour is a sooty black, but the ten larger feathers of the wings are of a milk-white colour both without and within. The tip of the wings reach nearly to the tail. The beak and head measure together eleven inches and a half. The male has protuberances on his neck like those of a turkey; they are generally of a light-blue colour, but turn red when the bird is chafed, or when his hen is laying. He has very large eyelashes, especially the upper. From the point of the bill to the extremity of the tail this species measures three feet ten inches; and the wings, when stretched, extend six feet. Bruce observed it, followed by eighteen young ones. It runs along the ground more willingly than it flies; but, when once raised, it flies both strong and far. It has a rank smell, and is asserted in Abyssinia to live on dead carcasses. This, however, has been doubted. " I never," says Mr Bruce, " saw it approach any of these; and what convinces me this is untrue is, that I never saw one of them follow the army, where there was always a general assembly of all the birds of prey in Abyssinia. It was very easy to see what was its food by its place of rendezvous, which was in the fields of teff, upon the tops of which are always a number of green beetles: these he strips off by drawing the stalk through his beak, so that it appears to be serrated; and, often as I had occasion to open this bird, I never found any thing in him but the green scarabæus or beetle. He has a putrid or stinking smell, which, I suppose, is the reason he has been imagined to feed on carrion. He builds in large thick trees, always, if he can, near churches; has a covered nest, like that of a magpie, but four times as large as an eagle's: it places its nest firm upon the trunk, without endeavouring to make it high from the ground; the entry is always from the east side."

Although parrots are by no means numerous, they are not altogether unknown in Abyssinia. A small species is described in the Appendix to Lord Valentia's Travels under the name of *Psittacus Taranta*. It was found to be not uncommon near the pass from which it derives its specific name. Another species is figured in Rüppel's Atlas, with the title of *Psittacus Meyeri*. It is found in Kordofan.

The ostrich is known in the low districts north of Abyssinia, but we believe its occurrence is very rare within the actual limits of the country.

Of gallinaceous birds we shall name only the Guineafowl, now well known in Britain as a domesticated species. It occurs in the wild state in these parts of Africa; and so expert are the natives in the use of the matchlock, that they constantly kill it with a single ball. Quails and redlegged partridges also occur in Abyssinia.

Arabian Bustard.

Many fine species of the order Grallatores inhabit these countries. The Arabian bustard (*Otis Arabs*), is nearly as large as the common bustard of Europe. It is found both in Asia and Africa. Its flesh is excellent; its manners are but slightly known. Rüppel found it in Kordofan. We are indebted to him for the figure from which the wood-cut here given was engraved.

The tribe of storks were regarded by Linnæus as congeners with the herons and cranes. They are birds of lofty stature and great power of wing, and are met with in most countries where reptile food abounds. As the creatures on which they prey are impatient of cold and disappear beneath the waters or in the holes of the earth on the approach of winter, so the storks themselves migrate from one country to another to avoid a low temperature and the consequent deficiency of their favourite food. In addition to their frequent destruction of noxious or unseemly creatures, the habits of certain species are familiar

Saddle-billed Stork.

and domestic, and they have for many ages been regarded with respect, or even veneration, by nations in no way habitually influenced by enthusiastic or romantic feeling. Though the affection of these birds for their parents may be regarded as a doubtful characteristic, their extreme attachment to their young must be considered as certain, since, at the burning of Delft, a stork was observed to perish in the flames rather than desert its newly-hatched offspring. A notable species, which the accuracy of our wood-cut saves us the trouble of describing in detail, is the saddle-billed stork (*Ciconia ephippiorhyncha*). We shall only mention that it measures between four and five feet in height.

Water birds are by no means numerous. There are few geese either wild or tame, except the species called the golden goose, or goose of the Nile, and a duck allied to the *Anas Lybica.* A species of gull with a black head, white eyelids, and cinereous back, takes its flight occasionally into Abyssinia from the shores of the Red Sea. The same bird occurs in the Caspian and the rivers of the East Indies. It is the *Larus ichthyœtus* of Pallas.*

---

* As the limits to which we are necessarily restricted in this article prevent our entering into a detailed history of the species, we shall here present two lists which will put the reader in possession of at least the names of the principal birds of Abyssinia, and those other portions of the north of Africa to which the present volume is devoted.

Our first list is extracted from that furnished by Dr Latham, and originally published in the Appendix to Salt's Travels.

Lanius poliocephalus.
L.   Cubla.
L.   ferrugineus.
L.   humeralis.
Psittacus Taranta.
Coracias afra ?
Bucco Saltii.
Cuculus, var. of Edolius, Le Vail.
C.   Senegalensis.
Picus Abyssinicus.
Alcedo Cheliculi.
Merops erythropterus.
M.   furcatus.
Upupa erythrorhynchos.
Certhia Tacazze.
Tanagra erythrorhyncha.
Fringilla Senegala.
F.   Benghalus.
Muscicapa Paradisi.
M.   mutata.

Alauda Africana.
Sylvia pammelaina.
Hirundo Capensis.
Turdus phœnicurus.
T.   musicus.
T.   Capensis.
T.   nitens.
Colius striatus.
Loxia leucotis.
Emberiza Capensis.
Columba Guinea.
C.   Abyssinica.
Numida mitrata.
Scolopax calidris.
Tringa Senegalla.
Erodia amphilensis.
Alauda desertorum.
Cursorius Europæus.
Rallus Capensis.
Parra Africana.

Our second list is from the Atlas to Rüppell's *Reise im Nördlichen Afrika*, and contains the names of the species (many of which are new) figured in that work, in the order of publication.

Otis nuba.
Malurus clamans.
M.   gracilis.
Ciconia ephippiorhyncha.
Turdoides leucocephala.
Alauda bifasciata.
Caprimulgus infurcatus.
Nectarinia metallica.
Ciconia Abdimii.
Perdix Clapertonii.
Emberiza striolata.
E.   cœsia.
Psittacus Meyeri.

Malurus squamiceps.
Sterna velox.
S.   affinis.
Ploceus superciliosus.
Otis Arabs.
Larus ichthyœtus.
Malurus acaciæ.
Sylvia Rüppelii.
Bucco margaritatus.
Pelecanus rufescens.
Vultur occipitalis.
Trox plebejus.
Rhynchops Orientalis.

The reptile tribe are the next in succession in our systematic arrangements. We shall mention in the first place the lizard, called *El adda,* one of the few which the Arabians in all ages have admitted to be free from poisonous qualities,—for, however singular it may now appear to those better informed upon the subject, the writers of that nation have described almost the whole of the lizard tribe as venomous. The species just named measures six and a half inches in length. Though its legs are long it does not make use of them in standing up, but creeps with its belly almost close to the ground, and is capable of running with great agility. It burrows in the sand, and performs the operation so rapidly as to get out of sight in a few seconds, appearing not so much to be making a hole, as to have found one. It is a native of Atbara, beyond the ruins where Bruce supposes the island and city of Meroe to have anciently stood.

There are not many serpents in Upper Abyssinia, and few remarkable animals of that class even in the lower countries, if we except a species of boa, commonly so called, which attains to the length of 20 feet. It feeds upon antelopes, and the deer kind, which it swallows entire. Its favourite places of resort are by the sides of grassy pools of stagnant rivers, where it lies in ambuscade, ready to encircle in its horrid folds whatever quadruped approaches.

A remarkable and noted serpent of these parts is the cerastes or horned viper. It hides itself all day in holes in the sand, where it lives in little chambers similar and contiguous to those of the jerboa. Bruce kept a pair of them in a glass jar for two years without any food; they did not appear to sleep even in winter, and cast their skins during the last days of April. The cerastes moves with great rapidity. This poisonous reptile is very fond of heat; for, however warm the weather might be during the day, whenever Bruce made a fire at night it

Emberiza flavigaster.	Sylvia crassirostris.
Ardea Goliath.	Motacilla melanocephala.
Falco rufinus.	Saxicola pallida.
Pogonias melanocephala.	S. Isabellina.
Dacelo pygmæa.	Malurus pulchellus.
Lanius erythrogaster.	Sylvia brevicaudata.
Perdix rubricollis.	Malurus ruficeps.
Charadrius melanopterus.	M. inquietus.
Vultur Kolbii.	

seldom happened that fewer than half-a-dozen were found burnt to death by approaching too closely to the embers.

While Mr Salt's party were engaged in shooting at hippopotami, as already noticed, they occasionally observed several crocodiles, called by the natives *agoos*, rising at a distance to the surface of the river: they appeared to be of an enormous size and of a greenish colour. The Abyssinians entertain a great dread of these animals; and when any one goes to the Tacazze even to wash his hands, he takes a companion with him to throw stones into the water for the purpose of keeping off the crocodiles; and in crossing a ford it is usual with the natives to carry their spears and to make as much noise as possible, though these animals are seldom known to frequent the shallower parts of the stream; while the very thought of bathing in the river seemed to strike them with horror. Yet the thermometer at this time in the neighbourhood of the Tacazze stood at 95° in the shade, so that a bath could not have been otherwise than refreshing. Mr Legh while ascending the Nile first observed crocodiles between Cafre Saide and Diospolis Parva, the modern How. He thinks Girgeh the limit below which they do not descend. They were numerous between that place and the Cataracts.*

Although, as Bruce has well observed, the fish of Eastern countries are generally more distinguished for their beauty and variety of colour and the singularity of their forms than for their excellence as articles of diet, yet a species of binny found in Nubia is noted for the goodness of its taste. It is a large species, varying in weight from 30 to 70 pounds. The largest are caught about Rosetta and the mouth of the river, but they are also very numerous higher up as far as Syené and the first cataract. Many rare and remarkable fishes will be found represented and described in the Atlas to the *Reise*

---

* Some singular and beautiful reptiles from Nubia and Abyssinia have been of late years figured and described by Rüppel. The following is the catalogue of those engraved in the Atlas of that author:—

Uromastyx ornatus.	Stenodactylus scaber.
Stellio vulgaris.	Hemidactylus granosus.
Agama sinaita.	Bufo Arabicus.
Ptyodactylus scaber.	Varanus ocellatus.

FISHES. 419

im Nördlichen Afrika, already so frequently referred to. We give their names in the subjoined note.*

In regard to testaceous productions, there are three kinds of shell-fish in the Red Sea, which are zealously sought for on account of the pearls which they contain. The first is a muscle of unfrequent occurrence, found chiefly towards the north end of the gulf, and on the Egyptian side. Bruce saw them at Cosseir, where there was an

---

* Ostracion argus.
O. cyanurus.
Scolopsis lineatus.
S. bimaculatus.
S. kurite.
Sillago sihama.
Smaris öyena.
Cirrhites maculosus.
Pharopterix nigricans.
Lutodeira chanos.
Percis cylindrica.
Cheilinus lunulatus.
Julis purpureus.
J. aggula.
Balystis aculeatus.
B. cœrulescens.
Glyphisodon sordidus.
Pomacentrus trimaculatus.
P. marginatus.
Chætodon flavus.
C. dorsalis.
C. triangularis.
Anampses cœruleopunctatus.
Xyrichthys bimaculatus.
Amphacanthus siganus.
A. punctatus.
Apogon lineolatus.
Haliophis guttatus.
Cantharus filamentosus.
Trygon Lymna.
T. Forskali.
Rhinabatus Djiddensis.
R. halavi.
Acanthurus rokal.
Aspisurus elegans.
Acanthurus rubopunctatus.
A. velifer.
Tetraodon calamara.
T. honkenji.
T. diadematus.
Lebias dispar.

Platax orbicularis.
P. albipunctatus.
Diacope argentimaculata.
D. fulviflamma.
D. lineolata.
Scarus psittacus.
S. gibbus.
Scaris harid.
S. mastax.
S. bicolor.
Holocentrus ruber.
H. diadema.
H. samara.
H. spinifer.
Mirypristis murdjan.
Cæsiomorus quadripunctatus.
Nomeus nigrofasciatus.
Cybium Commersonii.
Caranx petaurista.
C. djeddaba.
C. macrophthalma.
C. bajad.
C. ferdau.
C. fulvoguttatus.
Citula ciliaria.
Serranus rogaa.
S. louti.
S. miniatus.
S. miryaster.
S. fuscoguttatus.
S. hemistiktos.
Petroscirtes mitratus.
Salaris quadripennis.
S. cyclops.
Opistognathus nigromarginatus.
Conger cinereus.
Muræna ophis.
M. geometrica.
M. tigrina.
M. flavomarginata.

ancient port called Myos Hormos, erroneously called the Port of the Mouse; whereas it signifies Muscle Harbour. The pearls found in this shell are of great beauty as to form and lustre, but they are seldom of a clear colour. The second sort of pearl-shell is called pinna. It is rough and figured on the outside, of a beautiful red colour, extremely fragile, and sometimes measures three feet long. It is clothed in the inside with a beautiful and sumptuous lining of nacre or mother-of-pearl, of a white colour tinged with a delicate blush of red. The third kind of pearl-bearing shell is not unlike our oyster. Its produce is characterized by its extreme whiteness. The most excellent are those which resemble a solution of alum,—limpid, milky-like, yet with a certain almost imperceptible cast of a fiery colour, but not transparent, as supposed by Theophrastus. In the Red Sea, where it holds the highest rank among pearls, it is called *lulu single*, or *lulu el Berber*, that is, the pearl of Berber, Barabra, or Beja, the country of the Shepherds.[*]

Ancient writers appear to have endowed testaceous animals with a higher capacity than corresponds to the station assigned them in these degenerate days. Pliny and Solinus inform us, that the pearl-muscles have leaders and go in flocks, and that the captain of the band is gifted with peculiar cunning to protect himself and his flock from the rapacious fishermen. It is added, that when the leader is taken, the others, hesitating and inexperienced, fall an easy prey. It has been observed that pearls are always the most beautiful in those places where a quantity of fresh water falls into the sea. Bruce, however, observed none of the pearl-shells on either side southward of the parallel of Mocha in Arabia Felix. In that part of the traveller's narrative where he relates his return through the Desert of Nubia, he alludes to the muscles which occur in the salt springs of these arid regions. They are said to travel far from home, and are sometimes surprised by the ceasing of the rains at a greater distance from their beds than they have strength or moisture to travel over. In many of these shells coarse excrescences occur which may be called pearls, but they are ill formed and of a bad colour. The value of these articles, it may be observed, depends upon their size, co-

---

[*] Bruce, vol. v. p. 221.

lour, smoothness, lustre, and regularity of form. In proportion to their size, they may be considered as the most valuable of all animal products, or next to the diamond of all the productions of nature. It is known that Cæsar gave to Servilia, the mother of Marcus Brutus, a pearl which was worth £50,000 of our money; and the famous vaunt of Cleopatra to her lover, that she would provide him with a supper which should cost two hundred and fifty thousand pounds, was accomplished by dissolving in a draught one of the precious pearls from her ear-rings. Its counterpart was afterwards carried to Rome by Augustus Cæsar, and, being cut in two, was affixed to the ears of the statue of Venus Genetrix.

We shall conclude our notice of this subject by observing, that an elegant and ingenious method of veneering or inlaying with nacre or mother-of-pearl is brought to great perfection, especially at Jerusalem. The substance used is chiefly taken from the *lulu el Berber*, commonly called the Abyssinian oyster. Great quantities are brought from the Red Sea to Jerusalem, and are formed into boxes, beads, and crucifixes, much sought after by Spaniards both in the Old World and the New.*

A sketch of the history of two of the most remarkable insects of these countries must bring our zoological chapter to a close. The fly called *Tsaltsalya* presents a singular example of the pervading influence of a creature which, were we to judge from its apparent or external characteristics, we should deem alike insignificant and powerless. In size it is little larger than a bee, and has pure gauzy wings without spot or colour. The head is large, and the mouth is furnished with three strong projecting hairs or bristles. Providence appears to have fixed the habitation of this insect to a soil composed of a black fattish earth of extraordinary fruitfulness; and there it reigns for a season as lord and master. According to Bruce, it absolutely prohibited the former inhabitants of the land, called Mazaga, and who were domiciled in caves and mountains, from deriving any advantage from beasts of burden. It deprived them of flesh and milk, and gave origin to another nation whose manners were exactly the reverse of the first. These were shepherds, who lead a

---

* Bruce, vol. v. p. 230.

wandering life, and preserve immense herds of cattle by conducting them into sandy regions beyond the limits of the black earth, and bring them back again when all danger from the fly has ceased. "We cannot read the history of the plagues which God brought upon Pharaoh by the hands of Moses without stopping a moment to consider a singularity, a very principal one, which attended this plague of the fly. It was not till this time, and by means of this insect, that God said he would separate his people from the Egyptians. And it would seem that then a law was given to them that fixed the limits of their habitation. It is well known, as I have repeatedly said, that the land of Goshen or Geshen, the possession of the Israelites, was a land of pasture, which was not overflowed by the Nile. But the land overflowed by the Nile was the black earth of the valley of Egypt, and it was here that God confined the flies; for he says, it shall be a sign of this separation of the people, which he had then made, that not one fly should be seen in the sand or pasture-ground, the land of Goshen; and this kind of soil has ever since been the refuge of all cattle emigrating from the black earth to the lower part of Atbara. Isaiah, indeed, says that the fly shall be in all the desert places, and consequently the sands; yet this was a particular dispensation of Providence to answer a special end, the desolation of Egypt, and was not a repeal of the general law but a confirmation of it; it was an exception for a particular purpose and a limited time."*

In the Chaldee version this insect is called simply *zebub*, which signifies the fly in general, as it is expressed in English. By the Arabs it is translated *zimb*, which has the same signification. Tsaltsalya is the word used in the Ethiopic translation, and that term is the true name of the fly in Geez. As soon as this plague appears, and its dreaded buzzing is heard, the cattle forsake their food and run wildly about the plain till they die, worn out with fear, fatigue, and famine; and no remedy remains for the inhabitants but to leave the region of the black earth and hasten down to the sands of Atbara. Even the sunburnt camel, emphatically called the *ship of the desert*, is soon destroyed by this destructive creature. The gigantic elephant and case-hardened rhinoceros, both of which are

---

* Bruce, vol. v. p. 190.

prevented by their enormous bulk, and the vast quantity of food and water which they consume daily, from removing to dry and desert places, are obliged to roll themselves in the mud, which soon dries and hardens on their obdurate coats, and enables them in some measure to withstand the attack of their winged and almost viewless assassin. The whole inhabitants of the seacoast of Melinda, down to Cape Guardafui, to Saba, and the south of the Red Sea, are obliged to remove to the next sands on the commencement of the rainy season, for the salvation of their flocks. " This," says Bruce, " is not a partial emigration; the inhabitants of all the countries from the mountains of Abyssinia, northward to the confluence of the Nile and Astaboras, are once a-year obliged to change their abode, and seek protection in the sands of Beja; nor is there any alternative, or means of avoiding this, though a hostile band was in their way, capable of spoiling them of half their substance." Hear the words of the inspired prophet :—" And it shall come to pass in that day, that the Lord shall hiss for the fly that is in the uttermost part of the rivers of Egypt."—" And they shall come, and shall rest all of them in the desolate valleys, and in the holes of the rocks, and upon all thorns, and upon all bushes."[*]

The only other insect which we shall notice is the Abyssinian locust, which Mr Salt informs us commits dreadful ravages in that country. During his stay in the Bay of Amphila a large flight of these insects came over to one of the islands, and in a few days destroyed nearly half the vegetation upon it, not sparing even the bitter leaves of the rack-tree. These locusts are named Terād in Yemen, and Anne in Dancali, and are frequently used as food by the wandering tribes of both these nations, who, after broiling them, separate the heads from the bodies, and devour the latter in the same manner as Europeans eat shrimps and prawns.[†]

---

[*] Isaiah, chap. vii. v. 18, 19.   [†] Voyage to Abyssinia, p. 172.

BOTANY.

CHAPTER IX.

General Description of the Vegetation as far as it is known—Brief Account of the most Remarkable and Useful Plants.

Vegetation of the Country—The Baobab—Acacia vera—Tamarind — Kantuffa — Kuara — True Sycomore—Kolquall—Cusso—Balsam of Mecca—Wooginoos—Coffee-tree—Wansey—Ensete—Doum-tree—Dhourra—Teff—Papyrus.

Few materials have been contributed by travellers towards a flora of Nubia and Abyssinia. Since the time of Bruce we know of two individuals only, Mr Salt and M. Cailliaud, who have made any considerable additions to our knowledge of the plants of those countries. Mr Salt has published a catalogue of the species collected by him; but it is, after all, merely a list of names.* M. Cailliaud preserved a smaller number; but the hundred species he obtained have been carefully described by M. Raffeneau Delile,† and thirty-five of them are new. Without entering into minute observations on the respective collections of these travellers, we may remark that on comparing them together, 20 species, or one-fifth of the whole of M. Cailliaud's collection are *leguminosæ;* while of Mr Salt's collection, which amounts to 140 species, only 11 are *leguminosæ*. And that it is equally remarkable that there should be 11 *labiatæ* in Mr Salt's list, and only a solitary representative of the order in that of M. Cailliaud.

A great sameness prevails in the vegetation of the deserts; the trees are mostly acacias, tamarix, date and doum palms. Plants, however, abound in the more cultivated regions, the banks of rivers, and the elevated

---

* Salt's Voyage to Abyssinia, App. p. 62.
† Voyage à Méroé, &c., par M. Frédéric Cailliaud, 1827, vol. iv. p. 293.

mountain-ranges; but of the peculiar features presented by the vegetation in different parts of the country we have few and very meagre descriptions. The most instructive one is contained in the notes of Bruce's Journey from Arkeeko to Dixan, over the mountain Taranta. The high range of which this mountain forms a part is described by him as constituting the boundary between the opposite seasons; the rains on the eastern side, or that looking towards the Red Sea, prevailing from October to April, and on the western side from May to October. At the same time a sensible difference is perceived in the character of the vegetation. Soon after leaving Laberhey the grass which covered the plain disappeared, and as the traveller and his party imperceptibly ascended, gave place to woods of acacias. The bed of a torrent soon became their only road, the banks of which were adorned with rack-trees (*Racka ovata*), capers, and tamarinds (*Tamarindus Indica*). The second grow to the size of an " English elm." These trees then became intermixed with abundance of the sycomore (*Ficus Sycomorus*), often measuring twenty feet or more in the circumference of their trunks. The forest, which here became so dense and luxuriant as to form natural arbours, and cast a gloomy shade, grew more open as the party ascended the eminences, which constituted the actual base of the mountain, through the midst of sycomore and jujeb trees of great beauty. This side of the mountain was thickly set with kolquall (*Euphorbia antiquorum*), a plant that Bruce afterwards saw in different parts of Abyssinia, but never in the same degree of perfection. The middle region of the ascent produced fewer plants, and was characterized by the prevalence of wild olives destitute of fruit. Towards the upper part, and on the summit itself, thick groves occurred of the arze, or berry-bearing cedar (*Juniperus Oxycedrus?*), the trees of which were, according to Bruce, tall and beautiful; while on the western side they became small shrubs and scraggy bushes. Mr Salt ascended the same mountain, and speaks of the kolquall being nearly forty feet in height. He observed the sweet-brier (probably the *Rosa Abyssinica*), as well as several highly aromatic shrubs, and a number of flowers some of which had bulbous roots. In the above description we have distinct traces of several zones of vegetation; but the absence of barometrical measurements, or even any estimate of elevation, deprives the account of much interest and usefulness.

Of the vegetation of the interior we can collect only scattered notices. The bases of the mountains are described as sometimes covered with brushwood, " aloes," thorny acacias, intermixed with canes and bamboos (probably *Bambusa arundinacea*). Some portions of the province of Siré are very beautiful. " Poncet," observes Bruce, " was right when he compared it to the most beauteous part of Provence. We crossed the plain (Selechlecka) through hedge-rows of flowering shrubs, among which the honeysuckle now made a principal figure, which is of one species only, the same known in England; but the flower is larger and perfectly white.* Fine trees of all sizes were every where interspersed; and the vine, with small black grapes of very good flavour, hung in many places in festoons, joining tree to tree as if they had been artificially twined and intended for arbours." Coffee-trees are scattered in many places; but in Narea, the southernmost province of the Abyssinian empire, they grow in great profusion. Acacias of several species are common, especially in some districts. For example, the whole territory of Aroose is shaded with the *Acacia vera*, the tree which, in the sultry parts of Africa, produces the gum-arabic. " These trees," says Bruce, " grow seldom above fifteen or sixteen feet high, then flatten and spread wide at the top, and touch each other, while the trunks are far asunder, and under a vertical sun leave you many miles together a free space to walk in a cool delicious shade. There is scarcely any tree but this in Maitsha; all Guanguera and Wainadega are full of them." Bruce adds that throughout Aroose the ground beneath these trees is covered with lupines, almost to the exclusion of every other flower.

Near Addergey, the same traveller encamped by the side of a rivulet called Mai-Lumi,—the river of limes or lemons,—the woods on its banks being full of " lemons and wild citrons." He also describes a species of *Polymnia*, which he calls *frondosa*, but which is *P. Abyssinica* of botanists, that yields an oil employed for domestic purposes throughout the country. The castor-oil

---

* This honeysuckle is probably quite distinct from the two common British species.

plant (*Ricinus communis*) is frequent in Nubia, according to Burckhardt, the product of which is called Oil of Kheroa by the natives.

We shall now proceed to notice in a more particular manner some of the vegetable productions of these countries.

The baobab or monkey-bread (*Adansonia digitata*),* is the most gigantic tree hitherto discovered. The trunk though frequently eighty feet in circumference, rarely exceeds twelve or fifteen feet in height; but on the summit of this huge pillar is placed a majestic head of innumerable branches fifty or sixty feet long, each resembling an enormous tree, densely clothed with beautifully green leaves. While the central branches are erect the lowest series extend in a horizontal direction, often touching the ground at their extremity; so that the whole forms a splendid arch of foliage, more like the fragment of a forest than a single tree. The grateful shade of this superb canopy is a favourite retreat of birds and monkeys; the natives resort to it for repose, and the weary traveller in a burning climate gladly flies to it for shelter. The roots of the baobab are admirably adapted for affording stability to the trunk, and for enabling the prodigious head to resist the force of the tempest, being of singular strength and upwards of a hundred feet in length. The bark of the trunk is thick, and very smooth. The leaves are quinate, smooth, resembling in general form those of the horse-chesnut. The flowers are white and very beautiful, eighteen inches in circumference. The fruit, which hangs in a pendant manner, is a woody gourd-like capsule with a downy surface, about nine inches in length and four in thickness, containing numerous cells in which brown kidney-shaped seeds are embedded in a pulpy acid substance. The timber is soft and spongy, and we are not aware that it is used for any economical purpose. It is very easily perforated, so that, according to Bruce, the bees in Abyssinia construct their nests within it, and the honey thus obtained, being supposed to have acquired a superior flavour, is esteemed in preference to any other. A more remarkable excavation is however made by the natives; diseased portions of the trunk are hollowed out and converted into tombs for the reception of the bodies

---

* Bot. Mag. vol. lv. Pl. 2791 and 2792.

of such individuals as, by the laws or customs of the country, are denied the usual rites of interment. The bodies thus suspended within the cavity, and without any preparation or embalmment, dry into well-preserved mummies. The juicy acid pulp of the fruit is eaten by the natives, and is considered beneficial in fevers and other diseases on account of its cooling properties. It was analyzed by Vauquelin, and found to consist chiefly of a gum, a saccharine matter, an amylaceous fecula, and malic acid. A kind of condiment is prepared from the bark and leaves, which, being dried and reduced to a fine powder, is used in cookery as we do pepper and salt. The negroes call this powder *lillo* or *lalo*, and believe that it tends to restrain inordinate perspiration. An excellent soap is obtained by boiling the leys of the ashes of the bark and injured fruit with rancid palm-oil. The duration of the baobab is not the least extraordinary part of its history, and has given rise to much speculation. In it we unquestionably see the most ancient living specimens of vegetation. " It is," says the illustrious Humboldt, " the oldest organic monument of our planet;" and Adanson calculates that trees now alive have weathered the storms of five thousand years. If this be true the surface of the African continent can have undergone but trifling geological changes during that space of time. The leaves of this great tree are deciduous, a fact mentioned by Bruce, who observes that the dry fruit hangs long after the leaves have disappeared, and confirmed by Bowdich, who says they fall before the rainy season.[*]

In the family of *Leguminosæ*, several plants occur of considerable interest. We have alluded to the abundance of acacia-trees: of these there are various species besides the *Acacia vera*. One is mentioned by Burckhardt under the name of Sellam-trees, the wood of which is valued for its great hardness. The Arabs " use it for the shafts of their lances, and cut the thin branches into sticks of about the thickness of the thumb, and three feet in length, the top of which they bend in the fire while the wood is yet green, and, rubbing it frequently with grease, it acquires greater weight and strength. Every man carries in his hand such a stick, which is called Sellamé." From the *Acacia vera* (*A. Nilotica* of De-

---

[*] Bowdich's Account of Banjole.

lile) is obtained the well known gum-arabic of commerce, and its pods, as well as those of *Cassia Sabak*, are employed in Nubia in the process of tanning. It is related by Burckhardt, that he found stunted trees of a kind of acacia growing on a saline plain, in his route from Taka to Suakin, all of which bore a parasitic species of cactus, that completely covered some of them like a net. Here we also find the tamarind (*Tamarindus Indica*), the name of which is derived from the Arab Tamar-hendi, signifying fruit of India. The tamarind is a large tree with an erect cylindrical trunk, widely-spreading branches, and pinnated, bright, nearly evergreen foliage. The fruit is a pendulous pod like a bean, three to five inches in length, the coat of which is double; the outer one dry and brittle, the inner one membranous. Between these coats is the thick acid pulp which, after being boiled with sugar, is imported from the East and West Indies. The very leaves and flowers are reported by Delile to be acid. Mr Salt and his party found this fruit a great refreshment while in Abyssinia. M. Delile informs us, that large quantities of tamarind-fruit are brought by caravans of negroes from Darfûr to Cairo, in the form of small round cakes, pierced with a hole through their centre, and weighing from one to four pounds. This preparation is hard, black, and very acid; it is composed of the pulp of the fruit, with portions of the pod itself, and occasionally some of the seeds. A finer kind is also brought to Cairo from the East Indies, more esteemed as a preserve, but supposed to possess inferior medicinal properties.[*] About forty tons of tamarind fruit are said to be annually imported into Great Britain. Another beautiful leguminose plant is thus introduced to our notice by Bruce:—" This thorn, like many men we meet daily in society, has got itself into a degree of reputation and respect from the noxious qualities and power of doing ill which it possesses, and the constant exertion of these powers." Such is the character of the kantuffa (*Pterolobium lacerans*, Br.). It is a bushy shrub, six or eight feet high, well furnished with thorns, and clothed with elegantly twice-pinnated leaves. In some parts of Abyssinia it is very abundant, and where it grows thickly is a sufficient impediment to

---

[*] Delile, in Cailliaud, Voy. à Méroé, &c. vol. iv. p. 323.

the march of a royal army. The common soldier, who is protected by the skins of animals, is alone indifferent to the thorns of this plant. The ordinary cotton cloths of the country, though some of them are as thick as a blanket, are no defence; for the thorns bury themselves in its substance, and are with the greatest difficulty disengaged. When the king, therefore, commences any warlike expedition, the clearing of the ground from this shrub becomes of primary importance; and one of the first proclamations runs, according to the traveller above mentioned, in the following pithy style:—" Cut down the kantuffa in the four quarters of the world, for I do not know where I am going." A very handsome tree in the southern and south-western parts of Abyssinia, called Kuara (*Erythrina Indica*), is highly interesting from a circumstance connected with it, recorded by Bruce. He observes, that it is abundant in the province of Kuara, of which it bears the name, in all Fazoglo, Nuba, and Guba, and the countries where there is gold. The flower is of the colour of fine red coral. The fruit is a pod, and the seeds small red beans, marked with a black spot. These beans are affirmed by Bruce to have been used in the earliest ages by the Shangalla as a weight for gold; and as the native name for the bean is *Carat*, he concludes that the modern expression in regard to gold and precious stones, of so many carats fine, or weight, originated in the gold-country of Africa.* A remarkable coincidence occurs in another derivation of the word carat. Some have supposed it to come from κεράτιον, in Latin *siliqua*, the carob-bean, because the carat used in weighing diamonds and other gems is four grains, and the carob-bean, or seed of the carob-tree (*Ceratonia siliqua*), is about the weight of four grains of wheat.

In the family *Artocarpeæ* we observe the sycomore-tree (*Ficus Sycomorus*). This is the true sycomore, a large evergreen tree, with a trunk several feet in diameter, producing a fruit which resembles the common fig. It grows, according to Norden, to the size of the beech. In some parts of the mountains, especially on Taranta, the Hazorta feed their flocks on the foliage, the succulent nature of the wood enabling them to cut down

---

* Bruce's Travels, App. p. 80. 8vo ed.

the branches with great ease. By this custom both Mr Bruce and Mr Salt found the forests deprived of much of their shade and beauty. The figs are produced in clusters on the main stem and branches; they are smaller than the common kind, sweet and delicate according to some authors, but too insipidly luscious in the opinion of others. In Egypt, " the people for the greater part live upon its fruit; and think themselves well regaled when they have a piece of bread, a couple of sycomore-figs, and a pitcher filled with water from the Nile."* Bruce mentions the singular fact, that, according to tradition, all the mummy-chests which have been found from former ages were made of sycomore, and that all those now found are constructed of the same material. The name of this tree has been applied very erroneously to the greater British maple (*Acer pseudo-Platanus*).

The kolquall belongs to the family of the *Euphorbiaceæ*; it is also manifestly a species of *Euphorbia*, and is referred, by botanists, to *E. antiquorum*. When young the whole plant consists of a succulent green column resembling a *cactus*, five or six inches in diameter, and of the same thickness from the bottom to the top, fluted and angled, the angles beautifully scalloped. From the summit of this column, which is at first like an aloe in substance, but afterwards hard and woody, the branches arise, succulent and angular like the young plant, and like it never producing leaves. In this manner an extraordinary tree is formed, which attains the height of nearly forty feet. Flowers of a golden colour are put forth at the ends of the branches, and are succeeded by a deep crimson triangular fruit. In such prodigious abundance was this tree observed on Taranta, when that mountain was visited by Bruce, and so thickly did the individuals stand together, that the coloured fruit made them appear to be covered with a veil of the most vivid crimson. Like other Euphorbias, the kolquall possesses very acrid properties, and exudes a copious milky fluid when wounded. Two of the finest branches of a flourishing tree, divided by Bruce, poured out a quantity that he estimated at the least to be four English gallons, and which was so caustic as to excoriate the fingers as if scalded with boiling water, and to leave an indelible stain on the sabre with which they

---

* Norden's Travels, vol. i. p. 50, pl. 38.

were cut. In decay, the branches wither and become filled with a pungent powder. Bruce again met with this plant at the source of the Nile, but much degenerated in size and appearance. The Abyssinians prepare hides for tanning by means of its acrid juice, which is effectual in removing the hair.*

A very beautiful tree of Abyssinia, called cusso (*Hagenia Abyssinica*), and belonging to the family *Meliaceæ?* is considered a specific in cases of worms,—a malady to which, it seems, the natives of that country are peculiarly subject. The tree is about twenty feet high, with a crooked trunk, and clothed with pinnated leaves of a pleasant opaque green colour. " It is planted always near churches, among the cedars which surround them, for the use of the town or village."† It is indigenous to the high country; and Bruce, in remarking that he never saw it in the Kolla, nor in Arabia, nor in any other part of Asia or Africa, considers it " an instance of the wisdom of Providence, that it does not extend beyond the limits of the disease of which it was intended to be the medicine or cure!"‡ The same author, in the fourth page from the quotation we have given, has favoured us with a most amusing specimen of logical deduction; he is speaking of the representation of the cusso in his work:—" As the figure of this plant is true and exact beyond all manner of exception, I cannot but think it may be found in latitudes 11° or 12° north, in the West Indies or America;"—thus not only making the existence of the plant in those countries depend upon the fidelity of his drawing, but demolishing in anticipation his example of the wisdom of Providence as exhibited in confining the plant to Abyssinia.

The next vegetable production which falls under particular notice is the balessan, balm, or balsam of Mecca (*Balsamodendron Opobalsamum*), belonging to the family *Burseraceæ*. It is a native of the eastern coast of Abyssinia, especially at Azab, and as far as the strait of Bab el Mandeb. Bruce says, it is a small tree above fourteen feet high, with scraggy branches and flattened top, like those which are exposed to the seaside blasts; the appearance is consequently stunted, and the leaves are

---

* Bruce's Travels, App. 8vo ed. p. 51.   † Ibid. App. p. 90.
‡ Ibid. App. p. 89.

besides small and few. He supposes that it was transplanted to Arabia, and there cultivated at a very early period. This was the *Balsamum Judaicum*, or Balm of Gilead of antiquity and of the Sacred Writings, it being supposed at one time to be produced only in Judæa. It seems, however, to have disappeared from that country, and the supply to have proceeded from Arabia. Many fables are connected with it. Tacitus says, that the tree was so averse from iron that it trembled when a knife was laid near it, and it was thought the incision should be made with an instrument of ivory, glass, or stone.*
Bruce was told by Sidi Ali Taraboloussi that " the plant was no part of the creation of God in the six days, but that in the last of three very bloody battles which Mahomet fought with the noble Arabs of Harb, and his kinsmen the Beni Koreish, then pagans, at Beder Hunein, Mahomet prayed to God, and a grove of balsam-trees grew up from the blood of the slain upon the field of battle; and that with the balsam which flowed from them he touched the wounds even of those that were dead, and all those predestinated to be good Mussulmans afterwards immediately came to life." An equally marvellous legend is the Arabic fable respecting El Wah, a shrub or tree not unlike our hawthorn in form and flower. From the wood of this tree they believe that Moses' rod was made when he sweetened the waters of Marah; and they say also, that by means of a rod of the same wood, Kaleb Ibn el Waalid, the great destroyer of Christians, sweetened the waters at El Wah,—the Oasis Parva of the ancients,—which were once bitter, and that he bestowed upon the place the name borne by the wonder-working plant. To return to the balsam-tree: the mode of obtaining it remains to be described. This, according to Bruce, is done by making incisions in the trunk at a particular season of the year, and receiving the fluid that issues from the wounds into small earthen bottles, the produce of every day being collected and poured into a larger bottle, which is kept closely corked. When first obtained, it is, says Bruce, " of a light yellow colour, apparently turbid, in which there is a whitish cast, which I apprehend arises from the globules of air that pervade the whole of it in its first state of fermentation;

---

* Bruce's Travels, App. p. 26.

it then appears very light upon shaking. As it settles and cools it turns clear and loses that milkiness which it first had. It has then the colour of honey, and appears more fixed and heavy. The smell at first is violent and strongly pungent, giving a sensation to the brain like to that of volatile salts when rashly drawn up by an incautious person. This lasts in proportion to its freshness; for being neglected, and the bottle uncorked, it quickly loses this quality, as it probably will at last by age, whatever care is taken of it."* The natives of the East use it medicinally in complaints of the stomach and bowels, as well as a preservative against the plague; but its chief value in the eyes of Oriental ladies lies in its virtue as a cosmetic,—although, as in the case of most other cosmetics, its effects are purely imaginary. Lady Mary Wortley Montague ascertained that it was in request by the ladies of the seraglio at Constantinople; but having tried it on her own person found it exceedingly irritating to the skin. Much of the virtue attributed to it depends on the costliness of the material.

Among the *Xanthoxyleæ* we observe an Abyssinian shrub dedicated to the traveller we have so often referred to. It is the *Brucea antidysenterica* of botanists, the Wooginoos of the aborigines. Bruce describes it as growing in the greater part of Abyssinia, especially in the valleys of the low country. In Ras el Feel it is found abundantly, and is regarded as a specific in cases of dysentery, a disease which prevails there continually. The root is the part employed, and Bruce himself was restored to health by its use. The plant has recently been found to contain a poisonous principle less powerful, but similar in its effects to strychnia, which has received the name of Brucia.†

The coffee-tree (*Coffea Arabica*), belonging to the family called *Cinchonaceæ*, is one of the indigenous plants of Abyssinia, as well as of Arabia. It is an evergreen tree or rather shrub, fifteen or twenty feet in height, with an erect slender trunk and long flexible branches. The white flower resembles that of the common jasmine, and the fruit is like a small red cherry, enclosing within a soft pulp the two oval seeds familiar to every one as the coffee of commerce. At what period the use of cof-

---

* Bruce's Travels, App. p. 29. † Turner's Chemistry, ed. 4. p. 776.

fee was adopted as an article of diet we have no information. On the authority of an Arabian manuscript, formerly in the library of the King of France, and now deposited in the Bibliotheque Nationale, Megaleddin, mufti of Aden in Arabia, had met with it in Persia, and on his return having continued to use the infusion, induced many others to follow his example. The beverage soon became popular in Aden, and rapidly extended to Mecca, Medina, and the other cities of Arabia Felix.* Coffee was introduced at Grand Cairo by dervises from Yemen resident in that city;† when it was however opposed on religious grounds, from the persuasion that it had an inebriating quality; and in 1523, Abdallah Ibrahim having denounced it in a sermon, a violent commotion was produced, and the parties came to blows. Upon this, says a writer in Rees' Cyclopædia, the Sheik Elbelet, commander of the city, assembled the doctors, and, after giving a patient hearing to their tedious harangues, treated them all with coffee, first setting the example by drinking it himself, and then dismissed the assembly without uttering another word. By this prudent conduct the public peace was restored; and coffee continued to be drunk at Grand Cairo without further molestation. At Constantinople it had also to encounter religious opposition. The dervises had the sagacity to discover, that coffee, when roasted, becomes a kind of coal; they therefore declaimed against it with fury, coal being one of the substances which their prophet declared not intended by God for human food. The mufti was of their party, and the coffee-houses were soon shut up. A more sensible mufti succeeded, who assured the faithful, that roasted coffee is not coal, and they were again opened.‡ Coffee experienced political persecution likewise in Constantinople, from the jealousy of the government, which looked upon the coffee-houses as little better than nurseries of sedition. It soon however triumphed over every obstacle, and being taxed, produced a considerable revenue. Public officers are appointed to inspect it and prepare it; and it is said, that a refusal to supply a wife with coffee is one of the legal grounds of divorce in Turkey. Coffee was brought into notice in the

---

* Rees' Cyclopædia, article Coffee.   † D'Herbelot, p. 234.
‡ Rees' Cyclopædia, article Coffee.

west of Europe in the seventeenth century. The first coffee-house in London was opened in George Yard, Lombard Street, in 1652, by Pasqua, a Greek servant of Daniel Edwards a Turkish merchant, and the number soon increased. In 1675, Charles II. attempted to suppress them as places of resort dangerous to government, but without effect; and in 1688 it was supposed that there were as many of these houses of entertainment in London as in Grand Cairo, besides those to be met with in the principal towns throughout the country. The coffee-tree begins to produce fruit in its second year, and yields, according to its age and size, from one to four or five pounds. It is cultivated in the East and West Indies, and has become of vast importance in the commercial world. The quantity annually consumed in Europe alone is now probably not far short of two hundred millions of pounds. In Abyssinia its value is said to have been known from time immemorial. The Galla, who have frequently to cross uncultivated deserts, carry with them small balls, made up of pounded coffee and butter, and upon this food, in preference to bread or flesh, they perform long journeys.

The next plant we have selected for a brief notice in this place is the wansey (*Cordia Abyssinica*), belonging to the *Cordiaceæ*. The wansey is an ornamental tree about twenty feet in height, and for some unknown reason has divine honours paid to it by the seven nations of the Galla. It is common in Abyssinia, and planted in all the towns. The flowering season is immediately after the periodical rains, when the pretty white blossoms expand so suddenly as to change the aspect of the country. Bruce indeed says that it blossoms the first day the rains cease; and that exactly on the first of September, for three years together, in a night's time it was covered with such a multitude of flowers that Gondar and the neighbouring towns appeared as if overspread with new-fallen snow. When called upon to choose a king, the representatives of the Galla nations meet under the shade of this tree, and the individual on whom the choice falls is crowned with a chaplet of wansey, and has a sceptre of the wood put into his hand, which is called *Buco;* this sceptre is carried before him like a mace wherever he goes, and is inseparable from royalty in the general meetings of the nations.

A very remarkable plant is both described and figured

by Bruce under the name of ensete, but in such a vague and unsatisfactory manner, that it is impossible to make out its botanical relations. It has been conjectured to be a kind of banana (*Musa*); but this is exceedingly doubtful, and we are rather inclined to think that it will prove to be a new genus, and the type of a new natural family of plants. The ensete is of frequent occurrence in Abyssinia, especially in the moist and warm parts of the country, but abounds " in that part of Maitsha and Goutto west of the Nile, where there are large plantations of it, and it there, almost exclusive of any thing else, forms the food of the Galla inhabiting that province." Bruce in his description gives us no data for judging of the size of the ensete; but he speaks of the stem being esculent for several feet in height. The whole plant is herbaceous; the leaves are sessile, numerous, somewhat resembling those of the banana, or some large species of *Arum*, and commencing at the very base, where they are the largest, become smaller by degrees till they reach the inflorescence. The fruit is borne on the upper part of the stem, of a conical form, an inch and a half in length, and about an inch in diameter, " in colour and consistence resembling a rotten apricot," containing a " stone half an inch long, of the shape of a bean." Above the part that produces the fructification, the stalk begins to be curved downwards, and is thickly set with small leaves (*bracteæ?*) " in the midst of which it terminates the flower in the form of the artichoke." No one can have a correct idea of the plant from such a description. The fruit is not eatable, but the body of the plant, according to Bruce, is to be preferred to all vegetables, and when boiled has the taste of the best new wheat-bread not perfectly baked. The individual plant represented in the Appendix to his Travels was ten years old. " When you make use of the ensete for eating, you cut it," says Bruce, " immediately above the small detached roots, and perhaps a foot or two higher, as the plant is of age. You strip the green from the upper part till it becomes white; when soft, like a turnip well boiled, if eaten with milk or butter, it is the best of all food, wholesome, nourishing, and easily digested."*

The doum-tree (*Cucifera Thebaica*), one of the *Pal-*

---

* Bruce, App. p. 49.

mæ, is a remarkable tree, between thirty and forty feet in height, the trunk of which exhibits a deviation rarely met with among palms, in being repeatedly branched in a dichotomous manner. A tuft of numerous leaves crowns the summit of each division of the trunk, six feet long and three feet broad, supported on footstalks, plaited, spreading like a fan, and split into radiating segments. The flowers are produced on a branched receptacle, called in botanical language a spadix, the whole being enclosed in a sheath or spatha, through the side of which it bursts when the flowers are about to expand. The fruit is oval, and suspended in grape-like clusters. The doum-tree is of great value to the inhabitants of the countries where it grows, as it often takes the place of the date-palm, and supplies them with food and various useful articles; besides, wherever it establishes itself in the desert, various shrubs and plants gradually rear their heads under its shade, and in process of time render the burning sand fit for cultivation. The fruit is about the size of a large walnut, and contains a pulp, the flavour of which is compared both by Poiret and Captain Lyon to gingerbread. A sherbet is prepared from it resembling that made with the pods of the carob-tree. Of the hard kernels beads are turned susceptible of a beautiful polish. The natives manufacture baskets from the leaves, of surprising neatness and beauty, as well as vessels for containing water. Burckhardt also mentions that he saw an encampment at Atbara, consisting of tents formed of mats made of the leaves of the doum-tree.

Several *Gramineæ*, natives of Nubia and Abyssinia, are cultivated for food. One of these is the dhourra (*Sorghum vulgare*), the stalks of which, according to Burckhardt, often rise to the height of sixteen or even twenty feet. In Upper Egypt it is much inferior in size. The grain is much esteemed. That grown in Taka is of so fine a quality as to be nearly equal to wheat. It is difficult to say whether dhourra is a name confined to a particular kind of grain in Africa. It is certainly applied to the *Sorghum vulgare*, which is the *Holcus Durra* of Forskahl, the *H. Sorghum*, L. and *H. rubens*, Willd. The maize is called dhourra-kyzan. Another grain in common use throughout Abyssinia is the teff (*Poa Abyssinica*), a kind of grass possessing little beauty, the seeds of which produce excellent flour. Wheaten-flour is used by individuals of rank, but the common bread of the country is made from the teff. From this bread, when fermented with water till the mixture acquires an acid taste, is prepared a kind of beer in general request by the Abyssinians. In addition to the above, Bruce mentions a gigantic wild oat, of frequent occurrence, having stalks at least eight feet long. It is sometimes so tall as to conceal both a horse and his rider. In cases of emergency, the people make huts of them like bee-hives. The soldiers, who carry no tents, make them very speedily for themselves of these oats, the straw of which is as thick as the little finger. The grain is not valued, but the taste is good, and Bruce often made the meal into cakes in remembrance of Scotland. He is of opinion that this is the common oat in its original state, and that it has degenerated in a European climate.

The plant to which we mean to devote the remainder of our limited space, is not the least interesting one in the Egyptian and Abyssinian floras,—the papyrus of the ancients. This celebrated vegetable, the *Cyperus Papyrus* of botanists, is a graceful marsh plant twelve or fifteen feet in height. The roots creep extensively and throw up numerous stems, sheathed at the base by a few sword-shaped leaves, and terminated with large and elegant umbels of flowers. Bruce obtained specimens from the lakes Tzana and Gooderoo in Abyssinia. The paper of antiquity was prepared from the inner portion of the stem; and, on the authority of Pliny, the best and most beautiful paper was made out of the very heart of the substance of the stem, and was composed of three layers, arranged in parallel and transverse rows and submitted to heavy pressure. A kind of size seems also to have been used, which glued the parts together and rendered the spongy texture fitter for the reception of writing. To be of good quality this paper was required to be fine, compact, white, and smooth. Several coarser kinds were made. It would appear from the same author, that the Egyptians formerly applied the plant to many purposes. "The inhabitants of Egypt do use the root instead of wood, not for fuel only, but also to make thereof sundry vessels and utensils in an house. The very bodie and pole of the papyr itselfe serveth very well to twist and weave therewith little boats, and the rinds thereof be good to make saile-clothes, curtains, mats, and coverlets, clothes also for hangings, and ropes. Nay, they use to chew and eat it both raw and sodden: but they swallow the juice only down the throat and spit out the grosse substance."* As for the flower it served no other purpose than for " chaplets to adorn the images of the gods." At one time the papyrus was in general request not only in Egypt but in other countries. Under the Ptolemies the books of the great Alexandrian library were copied on this paper; but when Eumenes, king of Pergamus, began to establish a rival library, a mean jealousy controlled the dissemination of knowledge and forbade the exportation of papyrus. Parchment came into more general use soon afterwards, and is said to have derived its Latin name *pergamenea* from the city of Pergamus, where it was substituted for the papyrus, which was no longer to be obtained.†

---

* Pliny, book 13, ch. 11. Holland's Translation.
† Vid. Vossii Etymologicon in voce Pergamenea.

THE END.